Building Embedded Linux Systems

SECOND EDITION

Building Embedded Linux Systems

Karim Yaghmour, Jon Masters, Gilad Ben-Yossef, and Philippe Gerum

O'REILLY®

Beijing · Cambridge · Farnham · Köln · Sebastopol · Tokyo

Building Embedded Linux Systems, Second Edition

by Karim Yaghmour, Jon Masters, Gilad Ben-Yossef, and Philippe Gerum

Copyright © 2008 Karim Yaghmour and Jon Masters. All rights reserved.
Printed in the United States of America.

Published by O'Reilly Media, Inc., 1005 Gravenstein Highway North, Sebastopol, CA 95472.

O'Reilly books may be purchased for educational, business, or sales promotional use. Online editions
are also available for most titles (*http://safari.oreilly.com*). For more information, contact our corporate/
institutional sales department: (800) 998-9938 or *corporate@oreilly.com*.

Editor: Andy Oram	**Indexer:** Joe Wizda
Production Editor: Loranah Dimant	**Cover Designer:** Karen Montgomery
Copyeditor: Genevieve d'Entremont	**Interior Designer:** David Futato
Proofreader: Loranah Dimant	**Illustrator:** Jessamyn Read

Printing History:

April 2003:	First Edition.
August 2008:	Second Edition.

ISBN: 978-0-596-52968-0

[LSI]   [2011-02-04]

1296521653

Table of Contents

Preface

When the author of this book's first edition, Karim Yaghmour, first suggested using Linux in an embedded system back in 1997 while working for a hardware manufacturer, his suggestion was met with a certain degree of skepticism and surprise. Today, Linux is either in use already or is being actively considered for most embedded systems. Indeed, many industry giants and government agencies are increasingly relying on Linux for their embedded software needs.

This book was very well received in its first edition, but a number of advances in the Linux kernel and accompanying tools since the book's appearance make Linux even more attractive. Foremost among these are a number of real-time extensions and companion environments, some of which are discussed in the last three chapters of this edition.

Also, since the first edition of this book, enthusiastic open source and free software programmers have simplified the building and installation of GNU/Linux components (we use "GNU" here to acknowledge the centrality of tools from this free software project in creating functional Linux systems). This second edition therefore introduces you to a world of wonderful high-level tools, including Eclipse and various tools that "build the build tools" for embedded Linux systems. But we preserve much of the low-level information for those who need it, and to help you understand what the helper tools are doing behind the scenes.

In keeping with the explosions of progress on various parts of Linux and accompanying tools, it's useful to get a variety of expert perspectives on topics in embedded and real-time Linux. Therefore, for the second edition of this book the authors are joined by a number of key participants in the GNU/Linux community, including those doing kernel development or creating related projects.

Focus on Self-Sufficiency

The widespread interest and enthusiasm generated by Linux's successful use in a number of embedded applications has led to the creation of a plethora of articles, websites, companies, and documents all pertaining to "embedded Linux." Yet, beyond the flashy announcements, the magazine articles, and the hundreds of projects and products that claim to ease Linux's use in embedded systems, professional developers seeking a useful guide are still looking for answers to fundamental questions regarding the basic methods and techniques required to build embedded systems based on the Linux kernel.

Much of the documentation currently available relies heavily on the use of a number of prepackaged, ready-to-use cross-platform development tools and target binaries. Yet other documents cover only one very precise aspect of running Linux on an embedded target.

The first edition of this book was a radical departure from the existing documentation in that, other than your desire to use Linux, it makes no assumptions as to the tools you have at hand or the scope of your project. All that is required for this book is an Internet connection to download the necessary packages, browse specific online documentation, and benefit from other developers' experiences, as well as share your own, through project mailing lists. You still need a development host and documentation regarding your target's hardware, but the explanations we outline do not require the purchasing of any product or service from any vendor.

Besides giving the greatest degree of freedom and control over your design, this approach is closest to that followed by the pioneers who have spearheaded the way for Linux's use in embedded systems. In essence, these pioneers have *pulled* on Linux to fit their applications by stripping it down and customizing it to their purposes. Linux's penetration of the embedded world contrasts, therefore, with the approach followed by many software vendors to *push* their products into new fields of applications. As an embedded system developer, you are likely to find Linux much easier to pull toward your design than to adapt the products being pushed by vendors to that same design.

This book's approach is to allow you to pull Linux toward your design by providing all the details and discussing many of the corner cases encountered when using Linux in embedded systems. Although it is not possible to claim that this book covers all embedded designs, the resources provided here allow you to easily obtain the rest of the information required for you to customize and use Linux in your embedded system.

In writing this book, our intent was to bring the embedded system developers who use open source and free software in their designs closer to the developers who create and maintain these open source and free software packages. Though a lot of mainstream embedded system developers—many of whom are high-caliber programmers—rely on third-party offerings for their embedded Linux needs, there is a clear opportunity for them to contribute to the open source and free software projects on which they rely.

Ultimately, this sort of dynamic will ensure that Linux continues to be the best operating system choice for embedded systems.

Audience for This Book

This book is intended first and foremost for the experienced embedded system designer who wishes to use Linux in a current or future project. Such a reader is expected to be familiar with all the techniques and technologies used in developing embedded systems, such as cross-compiling, BDM or JTAG debugging, and the implications of dealing with immature or incomplete hardware. If you are such a reader, you may want to skip some of the background material about embedded system development presented early in some sections. There are, however, many early sections (particularly in Chapter 2) that you will need to read, because they cover the special implications of using the Linux kernel in an embedded system.

This book is also intended for the beginning embedded system developer who would like to become familiar with the tools and techniques used in developing embedded systems based on Linux. This book is not an introduction to embedded systems, however, and you may need to research some of the issues discussed here in an introductory textbook.

If you are a power user or a system administrator already familiar with Linux, this book should help you produce highly customized Linux installations. If you find that distributions install too many packages for your liking, for example, and would like to build your own custom distribution from scratch, many parts of this book should come in handy, particularly Chapter 6.

Finally, this book should be helpful to a programmer or a Linux enthusiast who wants to understand how Linux systems are built and operated. Though the material in this book does not cover how general-purpose distributions are created, many of the techniques covered here apply, to a certain extent, as much to general purpose distributions as they do to creating customized embedded Linux installations.

Scope and Background Information

To make the best of Linux's capabilities in embedded systems, you need background in all of the following topics (which are treated distinctly in many books):

Embedded systems
> You need to be familiar with the development, programming, and debugging of embedded systems in general, from both the software and hardware perspectives.

Unix system administration
> You need to be able to tend to various system administration tasks such as hardware configuration, system setup, maintenance, and using shell scripts to automate tasks.

Linux device drivers
> You need to know how to develop and debug various kinds of Linux device drivers.

Linux kernel internals
> You need to understand as much as possible how the kernel operates.

GNU software development tools
> You need to be able to make efficient use of the GNU tools. This includes understanding many of the options and utilities often considered to be "arcane."

We assume that you are familiar with at least the basic concepts of each topic. On the other hand, you don't need to know how to create Linux device drivers to read this book, for example, or know everything about embedded system development. As you read through this book and progress in your use of Linux in embedded systems, you will likely feel the need to obtain more information regarding certain aspects of Linux's use.

Though this book discusses only the use of Linux in embedded systems, part of this discussion can certainly be useful to developers who intend to use one of the BSD variants in their embedded system. Many of the explanations included here will, however, need to be reinterpreted in light of the differences between BSD and Linux.

Organization of the Material

There are four major parts to this book. The first part is composed of Chapters 1 through 3. These chapters cover the preliminary background required for building any sort of embedded Linux system. Though they describe no hands-on procedures, they are essential to understand many aspects of building embedded Linux systems.

The second part spans Chapters 4 through 9. These important chapters lay out the essential steps involved in building any embedded Linux system. Regardless of your system's purpose or functionality, these chapters are required reading.

The third part of the book, which ended the first edition, is made up of Chapters 10 and 11 and covers material that, athough very important, is not essential to building embedded Linux systems.

The final part of the book, comprised of Chapters 12 through 14, is an in-depth discussion of real-time, including its different applications and when you should consider the various implementations and varieties available. We are lucky and honored to have chapters written by the implementors of the Xenomai cokernel and the RT patch to the Linux kernel.

Chapter 1, *Introduction*, gives an in-depth introduction to the world of embedded Linux. It lays out basic definitions and then introduces real-life issues about embedded Linux systems, including a discussion of open source and free software licenses from the embedded perspective. The chapter then introduces the example system used in other parts of this book and the implementation method used throughout the book.

Chapter 2, *Basic Concepts*, outlines the basic concepts that are common to building all embedded Linux systems.

Chapter 3, *Hardware Support*, provides a thorough review of the embedded hardware supported by Linux, and gives links to websites where the drivers and subsystems implementing this support can be found. This chapter discusses processor architectures, buses and interfaces, I/O, storage, general-purpose networking, industrial grade networking, and system monitoring.

Chapter 4, *Development Tools*, covers the installation and use of the various development tools used in building embedded Linux systems. This includes a discussion of Eclipse for embedded Linux development, and how to build and install the GNU toolchain components from scratch. It also includes sections discussing Java, Perl, Python, and other languages, along with a section about the various terminal emulators that can be used to interact with an embedded target.

Chapter 5, *Kernel Considerations*, discusses the selection, configuration, cross-compiling, installation, and use of the Linux kernel in an embedded system.

Chapter 6, *Root Filesystem Content*, updated for the second edition by Michael Opdenacker, explains how to build a root filesystem using the components introduced earlier in the book, including the installation of the C library and the creation of the appropriate */dev* entries. More importantly, this chapter covers the installation and use of BusyBox, embutils, and System V *init*.

Chapter 7, *Storage Device Manipulation*, updated for the second edition by kernel developer David Woodhouse, covers the intricacies of manipulating and setting up storage devices for embedded Linux systems. The chapter's emphasis is on solid-state storage devices, such as native flash and DiskOnChip devices, and the MTD subsystem.

Chapter 8, *Root Filesystem Setup*, explains how to set up the root filesystem created in Chapter 6 for the embedded system's storage device. This includes the creation of filesystem images (based on JFFS2, CRAMFS, or other specialized filesystems), and the use of disk-style filesystems over NFTL.

Chapter 9, *Setting Up the Bootloader*, discusses the various bootloaders available for use in each embedded Linux architecture. Special emphasis is put on the use of GRUB with DiskOnChip devices and U-Boot. Network booting using BOOTP/DHCP, TFTP, and NFS is also covered.

Chapter 10, *Setting Up Networking Services*, focuses on the configuration, installation, and use of software packages that offer networking services, such as SNMP, SSH, and HTTP.

Chapter 11, *Debugging Tools*, updated for the second edition by Michael Boerner, covers the main debugging issues encountered in developing software for embedded Linux systems. This includes the use of *gdb* in a cross-platform development environment, Eclipse, tracing, performance analysis, and memory debugging.

Chapter 12, *Introduction to Real-Time Linux*, explains the value of real-time and offers a candid discussion of when you need various real-time features, along with an introduction to the various ways you can achieve real-time behaviors using Linux. This chapter was written by the founder and maintainer of the Xenomai Real-Time System, Philippe Gerum.

Chapter 13, *The Xenomai Real-Time System*, also written by Philippe Gerum, offers a high-level view of how Xenomai achieves real-time goals and how it can be useful in conjunction with embedded Linux.

Chapter 14, *The RT Patch*, performs a similar function for the RT patch to the Linux kernel, explaining how to enable its features. The chapter was written by Steven Rostedt, a key developer on the patch.

Although Chapters 7 through 9 are independent, note that their content is highly interrelated. For example, setting up the target's storage device, as discussed in Chapter 7, requires a basic knowledge about the target filesystem organization as discussed in Chapter 8, and vice versa. So, too, does setting up storage devices require a basic knowledge of bootloader setup and operation as discussed in Chapter 9, and vice versa. We therefore recommend that you read Chapters 7 through 9 in one breath a first time before carrying out the instructions in any of them. When setting up your target thereafter, you will nevertheless follow the same sequence of operations outlined in these chapters.

Hardware Used in This Book

As you'll see in Chapter 3, Linux supports a very wide range of hardware. For this book, we've used a number of embedded systems to test the various procedures. Some of these systems, such as the OpenMoko-based NEO 1973, are commercial products available in the mainstream market. We included these intentionally, to demonstrate that any willing reader can find the materials to support learning how to build embedded Linux systems. You can, of course, still use an old x86 PC for experimenting, but you are likely to miss much of the fun, given the resemblance between such systems and most development hosts.

To illustrate the range of target architectures on which Linux can be used, we varied the target hardware we used in the examples between chapters. Though some chapters are based on different architectures, the commands given in each chapter apply readily to other architectures as well. If, for instance, an example in a chapter relies on the *arm-linux-gcc* command, which is the *gcc* compiler for ARM, the same example would work for a PPC target by using the *powerpc-linux-gcc* command instead. Whenever more than one architecture is listed for a chapter, the main architecture discussed is the first one listed. The example commands in Chapter 5, for instance, are mainly centered around PowerPC, but there are also a few references to ARM commands.

Unless specific instructions are given to the contrary, the host's architecture is always different from the target's. In Chapter 4, for example, we used a PPC host to build tools for an x86 target. The same instructions could, nevertheless, be carried out on a SPARC or an S/390 with little or no modification. Note that most of the content of the early chapters is architecture- independent, so there is no need to provide any architecture-specific commands.

Software Versions

The central software on which an embedded Linux system depends, of course, is the Linux kernel. This book concentrates on version 2.6 of the Linux kernel, and 2.6.22 in particular. Changes to the kernel will probably have only a benign effect on the information in the book. That is, new releases will probably support more hardware than Chapter 3 lists. But the essential tasks described in this book are unlikely to change.

In addition, this book discusses the configuration, installation, and use of over 40 different open source and free software packages. Each package is maintained independently and is developed at a different pace. Because these packages change over time, it is likely that the package versions covered in this book may be outdated by the time you read it. In an effort to minimize the effect of software updates on the text, we have kept the text as version-independent as possible. The overall structure of the book and the internal structure of each chapter, for example, are unlikely to vary regardless of the various software changes. Also, many packages covered in this book have been around for quite some time, so they are unlikely to change in any substantial way. For instance, the commands to install, set up, and use the different components of the GNU development toolchain, which is used throughout this book, have been relatively constant for a number of years and are unlikely to change in any substantial way in the future. This statement applies equally to most other software packages discussed.

Typographical Conventions

The following is a list of typographical conventions used in this book:

Constant width

> Used to show the contents of code files or the output from commands, and to indicate source code keywords that appear in code.

Constant width bold

> Used to indicate user input.

Italic

> Used for file and directory names, program and command names, command-line options, URLs, and for emphasizing new terms.

This icon indicates a tip, suggestion, or general note.

 This icon indicates a warning or caution.

Using Code Examples

This book is here to help you get your job done. In general, you may use the code in this book in your programs and documentation. You do not need to contact us for permission unless you're reproducing a significant portion of the code. For example, writing a program that uses several chunks of code from this book does not require permission. Selling or distributing a CD-ROM of examples from O'Reilly books does require permission. Answering a question by citing this book and quoting example code does not require permission. Incorporating a significant amount of example code from this book into your product's documentation does require permission.

We appreciate, but do not require, attribution. An attribution usually includes the title, author, publisher, and ISBN. For example: "*Building Embedded Linux Systems*, by Karim Yaghmour, Jon Masters, Gilad Ben-Yossef, and Philippe Gerum. Copyright 2008 Karim Yaghmour and Jon Masters, 978-0-596-52968-0."

Contact Information

Please address comments and questions concerning this book to the publisher:

O'Reilly Media.
1005 Gravenstein Highway North
Sebastopol, CA 95472
800-998-9938 (in the United States or Canada)
707-829-0515 (international or local)
707-829-0104 (fax)

We have a web page for this book, where we list errata, examples, or any additional information. You can access this page at:

http://www.oreilly.com/catalog/9780596529680

To comment or ask technical questions about this book, send email to:

bookquestions@oreilly.com

For more information about our books, conferences, Resource Centers, and the O'Reilly Network, see our website at:

http://www.oreilly.com

The authors also have a site for this book at:

http://www.embeddedlinuxbook.org/

Safari® Books Online

When you see a Safari® Books Online icon on the cover of your favorite technology book, that means the book is available online through the O'Reilly Network Safari Bookshelf.

Safari offers a solution that's better than e-books. It's a virtual library that lets you easily search thousands of top tech books, cut and paste code samples, download chapters, and find quick answers when you need the most accurate, current information. Try it for free at *http://safari.oreilly.com.*

Acknowledgments for the First Edition

E quindi uscimmo a riveder le stelle.[*] It is with these words that Dante ends *Inferno*, the first part of his *Divine Comedy*. Though it would be misleading to suggest that writing this book wasn't enjoyable, Dante's narrative clearly expresses the feeling of finishing a first iteration of the book you now hold in your hands. In particular, I have to admit that it has been a challenging task to pick up the bits and pieces of information available on the use of Linux in embedded systems, to complete this information in as much as possible, and put everything back together in a single, straightforward manuscript that provides a practical method for building embedded Linux systems. Fortunately, I was aided in this task by very competent and willing people.

First and foremost, I would like to thank Andy Oram, my editor. Much like Virgil assisted Dante in his venture, Andy shepherded me throughout the various stages of writing this book. Among many other things, he patiently corrected my nonidiomatic phrases, made sure that my text actually conveyed the meaning I meant for it to convey, and relentlessly pointed out the sections where I wasn't providing enough detail. The text you are about to read is all the much better, as it has profited from Andy's input. By the same token, I would like to thank Ellen Siever, with whom I initially started working on this book. Though our collaboration ended earlier than I wished it had, many of the ideas that have made their way into this final version of the book have profited from her constructive feedback.

I have been extremely fortunate to have an outstanding team of reviewers go over this book, and am very grateful for the many hours they poured into reading, correcting, and pointing out problems with various aspects of this book. The review team was

---

[*] "And from there we emerged to see the stars once more."

made up of Erik Andersen, Wolfgang Denk, Bill Gatliff, Russell King, Paul Kinzelman, Alessandro Rubini, David Schleef, and David Woodhouse. I'd like to especially thank Alessandro for his dogged pursuit of perfection. Any remaining errors you may find in the following pages are without a doubt all mine.

Writing about the use of Linux in embedded systems requires having access to a slew of different hardware. Given that embedded hardware is often expensive, I would like to thank all the companies and individuals who have stepped forward to provide me with the appropriate equipment. In particular, I would like to thank Stéphane Martin of Kontron for providing a Teknor VIPer 806 board, Wolfgang Denk of DENX Software Engineering for providing a TQ components TQM860L PPC board, and Steve Papacharalambous and Stuart Hughes of Zee2 for providing a uCdimm system.

I have found much of the incentive and thrust for writing this book from being a very satisfied open source and free software user and contributor who has profited time and again from the knowledge and the work produced by other members of this community. For this, I have many people to thank. Primarily, I'd like to thank Michel Dagenais for his trust, his guidance, and for giving me the chance to freely explore uncharted terrain. My work on developing the Linux Trace Toolkit, as part of my masters degree with Michel, got me more and more involved in the open source and free software community. As part of this involvement, I have met a lot of remarkable individuals whose insight and help I greatly appreciate. Lots of thanks to Jacques Gélinas, Richard Stallman, Jim Norton, Steve Papacharalambous, Stuart Hughes, Paolo Mantegazza, Pierre Cloutier, David Schleef, Wolfgang Denk, Philippe Gerum, Loic Dachary, Daniel Phillips, and Alessandro Rubini.

Last, but certainly not least, I owe a debt of gratitude to Sonia for her exceptional patience as I spent countless hours testing, writing, testing some more, and writing even more. Her support and care have made this endeavor all the more easy to carry out. *La main invisible qui a écrit les espaces entre les lignes est la sienne et je lui en suis profondément reconnaissant.*[†]

Acknowledgments for the Second Edition

When Karim first mentioned updating *Building Embedded Linux Systems*, I could not have imagined what a fun and wild ride it would be. I was in the final stages of moving from the U.K. to the U.S. at the time, and life was pretty hectic for quite a while. Along the way, some great friends and coauthors have helped to turn an idea into the reality of the book that you are now reading. And we collectively hope that we have served to increase the range of documentation available on embedded Linux.

[†] "The invisible hand that wrote the spaces between each line is hers, and I am profoundly grateful to her for this."

First and foremost, I would like to thank my friend Karim Yaghmour for letting me run amock with his original manuscript, Andy Oram for his patient advice and editorial wizardry, and Isabel Kunkle for assisting Andy in putting up with a bunch of authors with busy schedules. I would also like to thank Marlowe Shaeffer and the team at O'Reilly for their steadfast attention to detail, especially near the end of the project.

I would like to thank my coauthors for stepping up to the plate and helping to see this project through: Michael Boerner, Michael Opdenacker, Steven Rostedt, Gilad Ben-Yossef (CTO, Codefidence Ltd.), Phillipe Gerum, and David Woodhouse. I've known most of you for many years, even if we only get to meet once a year at the Linux Symposium, and I am grateful that you have helped to improve the overall quality of this book. In a similar vain, I am grateful to the review comments from Tim Rikers, Vince Skahan, and Mark VandenBrink, as well as the many others I have occasionally spoken with about this book. But all that said, any remaining mistakes and technical omissions are entirely my responsibility, though we hope there are few.

Embedded Linux would mean nothing without the hard work of many thousands of people all over the world. Some of those people have gotten involved in the first or second editions of this book, while there are many, many more people out there helping to make Linux the most valuable and viable choice for embedded developers. It would be tricky to even attempt to list these people by name, and so I would like to instead offer my most sincere thanks to everyone concerned—I'd also like to encourage readers to thank those who provide the upstream for their development projects. Please do also encourage your employers and customers to do the same through whatever means you feel is most appropriate.

I would like to thank my friends and family for their never-ending support of my many pursuits and random craziness. My mum and dad rarely see me these days (I live 3,000 miles away in another country, on an awkward time delay) but have always been the best parents you could wish for, in spite of their son turning out to be a "traitor's dog" (thanks, dad, for your whimsical historical insight right there!) who joined the Americans. My sister Hannah and brother-in-law Joe Wrigley (another Red Hatter!) have always been amazing, as has my youngest sister Holly. My grandmother keeps me informed of family goings on with her letters, which I always look forward to reading far away from a computer.

Many friends contributed to the overall success of this project without even realizing it. They include Deepak Saxena, Hussein Jodiyawalla, Bill Weinberg, Alison Cornish, Grace Mackell, Andrew Schliep, Ginger Diercks, Kristin Mattera and James Saunders, Karen Hopkins, Andrew Hutton, and Emilie Moreau (and also Denali and Nihao), Madeleine and Chris Ball, Tim Burke, Lon Hohberger, Chris Lumens, Jon Crowe, Rachel Cox, Catherine Nolan, Toby Jaffey (and Sara and Milly), David Brailsford, Jeff and Nicole Stern, Catherine Davis, Mary-Kay and Luke Jensen, Philippe De Swert, Matt Domsch, Grant Likely (of Secret Lab), Hetal Patel, Mark Lord, Chris Saul, Dan Scrase, and David Zeuthen. A special thanks to Sven-Thorsten Dietrich and Aaron Nielson for their like-minded craziness at just the right moments.

Finally, I am very grateful to my good friend David Brailsford of the University of Nottingham, and to Malcolm Buckingham and Jamie McKendry of Oxford Instruments for believing in me and letting me experiment with Linux and superconducting magnets, and to Ian Graham of MontaVista UK Ltd. for the opportunity to work on some great projects during my time there. I also owe Andrew Hutton and Craig Ross of Steamballoon (and organizers of Linux Symposium) thanks for their support of my embedded endeavors over the years. I would especially like to thank Gary Lamb (Global Engineering Services—our embedded team), Clark Williams, and Tim Burke of Red Hat, Inc. for their continued support, as well as all of my friends at Red Hat and at other great Linux companies.

—Jon Masters, Cambridge, Massachusetts

## CHAPTER 1

Introduction

Linux was first released into an unsuspecting world in the summer of 1991. Initially the spare-time hobby of a Finnish computer scientist by the name of Linus Torvalds, Linux was at first accessible only in software source code form to those with enough expertise to build and install it. Early enthusiasts (most also developers themselves by necessity) exploited the growth of the Internet in the early 1990s as a means to build online communities and drive development forward. These communities helped to build the first Linux software distributions, containing all the software components needed to install and use a Linux system without requiring users to be technical experts.

Over the next decade, Linux grew into the mature Unix-like operating system it is today. Linux now powers anything and everything from the smallest handheld gadget to the largest supercomputing cluster, and a nearly infinite range of different devices in between. Examples of the wide range of Linux use abound all around: digital TV receivers and recorders such as TiVo, cell phones from big names like Motorola, Hollywood's huge Linux "render farms" (used to generate many of the recent CGI movies we have seen), and household name websites such as Google. In addition, a growing number of multinational corporations have successfully built businesses selling Linux software.

In many ways, Linux came along at the right moment in time. But it owes a lot of its success to the work of projects that came before it. Without the hard work of Richard Stallman and the Free Software Foundation (FSF) over the decade prior to Linux arriving on the scene, many of the tools needed to actually build and use a Linux system would not exist. The FSF produced the GNU C Compiler (GCC) and many of the other tools and utilities necessary for building your own embedded Linux systems from scratch, or at least from pre-built collections of these tools that are supplied by third-party vendors. Software maintained by the Free Software Foundation comprises a collection known as GNU, for "GNU's Not UNIX," also known (to some) as the GNU system. This stemmed from the FSF's stated goal to produce a free Unix-like system.

Embedded systems running Linux are the focus of this book. In many ways, these are even more ubiquitous than their workstation and server counterparts—mostly due to the sheer volume of devices and consumer gadgets that rely upon Linux for their operation. The embedded space is constantly growing with time. It includes obvious examples, such as cellular telephones, MP3 players, and a host of digital home entertainment devices, but also less-obvious examples, such as bank ATMs, printers, cars, traffic signals, medical equipment, technical diagnostic equipment, and many, many more. Essentially, anything with a microprocessor that is not considered a "computer" but performs some kind of function using computing is a form of embedded system.

If you are reading this book, you probably have a basic idea why one would want to run an embedded system using Linux. Whether because of its flexibility, its robustness, its price tag, the community developing it, or the large number of vendors supporting it, there are many reasons for choosing to build an embedded system with Linux and many ways to carry out the task. This chapter provides the background for the material presented in the rest of the book by discussing definitions, real-life issues, generic embedded Linux systems architecture, and methodology. This chapter sets the stage for later chapters, which will build upon concepts introduced here.

Definitions

The words "Linux," "embedded Linux," and "real-time Linux" are often used with little reference to what is actually being designated with such terminology. Sometimes, the designations may mean something very precise, whereas other times, a broad range or a category of application is meant. In this section, you will learn what the use of these terms can mean in a variety of different situations—starting with the many meanings of "Linux."

What Is Linux?

Technically speaking, Linux refers only to an operating system kernel originally written by Linus Torvalds. The Linux kernel provides a variety of core system facilities required for any system based upon Linux to operate correctly. Application software relies upon specific features of the Linux kernel, such as its handling of hardware devices and its provision of a variety of fundamental abstractions, such as virtual memory, tasks (known to users as processes), sockets, files, and the like. The Linux kernel is typically started by a bootloader or system firmware, but once it is running, it is never shut down (although the device itself might temporarily enter a low-powered suspended state). You will learn more about the Linux kernel in Chapter 5.

These days, the term "Linux" has become somewhat overloaded in everyday communication. In large part, this is due to its growing popularity—people might not know what an operating system kernel is or does, but they will have perhaps heard of the term Linux. In fact, Linux is often used interchangeably in reference to the Linux kernel itself, a Linux system, or an entire prebuilt (or source) software distribution built upon the Linux kernel and related software. Such widely varying usage can lead to difficulties when providing technical explanations. For example, if you were to say, "Linux provides TCP/IP networking," do you mean the TCP/IP stack implementation in the Linux kernel itself, or the TCP/IP utilities provided by a Linux distribution using the Linux kernel, or all of the above?

The broadness of the usage of the term has led to calls for a greater distinction between uses of the term "Linux." For example, Richard Stallman and the Free Software Foundation often prefix "GNU/" (as in "GNU/Linux") in order to refer to a complete system running a Linux kernel and a wide variety of GNU software. But even terms such as these can be misleading—it's theoretically possible to build a complete Linux-based system without GNU software (albeit with great difficulty), and most practical Linux systems make use of a variety of both GNU and non-GNU software. Despite the confusion, as more people continue to hear of Linux, the trend is toward a generalization of the term as a reference to a complete system or distribution, running both GNU and non-GNU software on a Linux kernel. If a friend mentions that her development team is using Linux, she probably means a complete system, not a kernel.

A Linux system may be custom built, as you'll see later, or it can be based on an already available distribution. Despite a growth in both the availability of Linux distributions targeted at embedded use, and their use in embedded Linux devices, your friend's development team may well have custom built their own system from scratch (for reasons explained later in this book). Conversely, when an end user says she runs Linux on the desktop, she most likely means that she installed one of the various distributions, such as Red Hat Enterprise Linux (RHEL), SuSE Linux Enterprise Server (SLES), Ubuntu Linux, or Debian GNU/Linux. The end user's running Linux system is as much a Linux system as that of your friend's, but apart from the kernel, their systems most likely have very different purposes, are built from very different software packages, and run very different applications.

When people use the term Linux in everyday conversation, they usually are referring to a Linux distribution, such as those just mentioned. Linux distributions vary in purpose, size, and price, but they share a common goal: to provide the user with a prepackaged, shrinkwrapped set of files and an installation procedure to get the kernel and various overlaid software installed on a certain type of hardware for a certain purpose. In the embedded space, a variety of embedded Linux distributions are available, such as those from MontaVista, Wind River, Timesys, Denx, and other specialist vendors. These specialist embedded Linux distributions are generally not targeted at generic desktop, workstation, or server use like their "mainstream" counterparts. This means that they typically won't include software that is not suited for embedded use.

Beginning with the next chapter and throughout the remainder of this book, we will frequently avoid referring to the word "Linux" on its own. Instead, we will generally refer directly to the object of discussion, so rather than talking about the "Linux kernel," the "Linux system," and the "Linux distribution," we will generally refer only to the "kernel," the "system," and the "distribution," respectively. In each of these circumstances, "Linux" is obviously implied. We will use the term "Linux," where appropriate, to designate the broad range of software and resources surrounding the kernel.

What Is Embedded Linux?

Embedded Linux typically refers to a complete system, or in the context of an embedded Linux vendor, to a distribution targeted at embedded devices. Although the term "embedded" is often also used in kernel discussions (especially between developers who have "embedded concerns"—words often used in the community), there is no special form of the Linux kernel targeted at embedded applications. Instead, the same Linux kernel source code is intended to be built for the widest range of devices, workstations, and servers imaginable, although obviously it is possible to configure a variety of optional features according to the intended use of the kernel. For example, it is unlikely that your embedded device will feature 128 processors and terrabytes of memory, and so it is possible to configure out support for certain features typically found only on larger Linux systems. Chapter 5 covers the kernel in much greater detail, including where to get source code, embedded concerns, and how to build it yourself.

In the context of embedded development, you will typically encounter embedded Linux *systems*—devices that use the Linux kernel and a variety of other software—and embedded Linux *distributions*—a prepackaged set of applications tailored for embedded systems and development tools to build a complete system. It is the latter that you are paying for when you go to an embedded Linux vendor. They provide development tools such as cross-compilers, debuggers, project management software, boot image builders, and so on. A growing number of vendors have chosen to integrate much of this functionality into customized plug-ins for their own versions of the community-developed Eclipse graphical IDE framework, which you will learn more about later in this book.

Whether you use a vendor is entirely up to you—few of the examples mentioned in this book will make any assumption as to your reliance or otherwise on a Linux vendor. In fact, much of this book is intended to equip you to build your own tools and tailored Linux distributions. This helps both those who want to use vendor supplied tools and those who do not. Understanding is key in either case, since greater understanding will help you to get more done faster. The bottom line is, of course, about time and resources. Even though this book will help you, should you wish to go it alone, you may choose to buy into an embedded Linux vendor as a way to reduce your product time to market (and to have someone to yell at if things don't work out according to plan).

This book exclusively discusses embedded Linux systems, and therefore there is no need to keep repeating "embedded Linux" in every name. In general, we will refer to the host system used for developing the embedded Linux system as the "host system," or "host" for short. The target, which will be the embedded Linux system, will be referred to as the "target system," or "target." Distributions providing development frameworks will be referred to as "development distributions" or something similar. This kind of nomenclature should be familiar to anyone who has experience working with embedded systems.[*] Distributions that provide tailored software packages will be referred to as "target distributions."

What Is Real-Time Linux?

Initially, "Real-Time Linux" uniquely designated the RTLinux project released in 1996 by Michael Barabanov under Victor Yodaiken's supervision. The original goal of the project was to provide a mechanism for deterministic response times under a Linux environment. Later, the project was expanded to support much more than the originally intended applications, and today supports a variety of non-embedded uses, such as real-time stock market trading systems and other "enterprise" applications. RTLinux was sold to Wind River in early 2007.

Today, there are several other big name real-time projects for Linux, including one that is aiming to add real-time support to the official Linux kernel. You will learn much more about these projects in the latter chapters of this book (Chapter 12 onward), including coverage of some of the innovative concepts and development ideas being worked on. Of course, by the time you read this book much of this technology may be even more commonplace than it is now, especially once real-time capabilities are available in every kind of Linux system installed from here to Timbuktu.

Real Life and Embedded Linux Systems

What types of embedded systems are built with Linux? Why do people choose Linux? What issues are specific to the use of Linux in embedded systems? How many people actually use Linux in their embedded systems? How do they use it? All these questions and many more come to mind when pondering the use of Linux in an embedded system. Finding satisfactory answers to the fundamental questions is an important part of building the system. This isn't just a general statement. These answers will help you convince management, assist you in marketing your product, and most of all, enable you to evaluate whether your initial expectations have been met.

Types of Embedded Linux Systems

We could use the traditional segments of embedded systems such as aerospace, automotive systems, consumer electronics, telecom, and so on to outline the types of embedded Linux systems, but this would provide no additional information in regard to the systems being designated, because embedded Linux systems may be similarly structured regardless of the market segment. Rather, let us instead classify embedded

---

[*] It would be tempting to call these "host distributions," but as you'll see later, some developers choose to develop directly on their target, hence the preference for "development distributions."

systems by the criteria that will provide actual information about the structure of the system: size, time constraints, networkability, and degree of intended user interaction with the final system. The following sections cover each of these issues in more depth.

Size

The size of an embedded Linux system is determined by a number of different factors. First, there is physical size. Some systems can be fairly large, like the ones built out of clusters, whereas others are fairly small, like the Linux wristwatches that have been built in partnership with IBM. The physical size of an embedded system is often an important determination of the hardware capabilities of that system (the size of the physical components inside the finished device) and so secondly comes the size of the components with the machine. These are very significant to embedded Linux developers and include the speed of the CPU, the size of the RAM, and the size of the permanent storage (which might be a hard disk, but is often a flash device—currently either NOR or NAND, according to use).

In terms of size, we will use three broad categories of systems: small, medium, and large. Small systems are characterized by a low-powered CPU with a minimum of 4 MB of ROM (normally NOR or even NAND Flash rather than a real ROM) and between 8 and 16 MB of RAM. This isn't to say Linux won't run in smaller memory spaces, but it will take you some effort to do so for very little gain, given the current memory market. If you come from an embedded systems background, you may find that you could do much more using something other than Linux in such a small system, especially if you're looking at "deeply embedded" options. Remember to factor in the speed at which you could deploy Linux, though. You don't need to reinvent the wheel, like you might well end up doing for a "deeply embedded" design running without any kind of real operating system underneath.

Medium-size systems are characterized by a medium-powered CPU with 32 MB or more of ROM (almost always NOR flash, or even NAND Flash on some systems able to execute code from block-addressable NAND FLASH memory devices) and 64–128 MB of RAM. Most consumer-oriented devices built with Linux belong to this category, including various PDAs (for example, the Nokia Internet Tablets), MP3 players, entertainment systems, and network appliances. Some of these devices may include secondary storage in the form of NAND Flash (as much as 4 GB NAND Flash parts are available at the time of this writing; much larger size arrays are possible by combining more than one part, and we have seen systems using over 32 GB of NAND, even at the time that we are writing this), removable memory cards, or even conventional hard drives. These types of devices have sufficient horsepower and storage to handle a variety of small tasks, or they can serve a single purpose that requires a lot of resources.

Large systems are characterized by a powerful CPU or collection of CPUs combined with large amounts of RAM and permanent storage. Usually these systems are used in environments that require large amounts of calculations to carry out certain tasks. Large telecom switches and flight simulators are prime examples of such systems, as are *government* research systems, defense projects, and many other applications that you would be unlikely to read about. Typically, such systems are not bound by costs or resources. Their design requirements are primarily based on functionality, while cost, size, and complexity remain secondary issues.

In case you were wondering, Linux doesn't run on any processor with a memory architecture below 32 bits (certainly there's no 8-bit microcontroller support!). This rules out quite a number of processors traditionally used in embedded systems. Fortunately though, with the passage of time, increasing numbers of embedded designs are able to take advantage of Linux as processors become much more powerful (and integrate increasing functionality), RAM and Flash prices fall, and other costs diminish. These days, it often makes less economic sense to deploy a new 8051 microcontroller design where for a small (but not insignificant) additional cost one can have all the power of a full Linux system—especially true when using ucLinux-supported devices. The decreasing cost of System-On-Chip (SoC) parts combining CPU/peripheral functionality into a single device is rapidly changing the cost metrics for designers of new systems. Sure, you don't need a 32-bit microprocessor in that microwave oven, but if it's no more expensive to use one, and have a built-in web server that can remotely update itself with new features, why not?

16-Bit Linux?

Strictly speaking, the previous statement regarding Linux's inability to run on any processor below 32 bits is not entirely true. There have been Linux ports to a number of odd processors. The Embeddable Linux Kernel Subset (ELKS) project found at *http://elks.sourceforge.net/*, for example, was aimed at running Linux on 16-bit processors, such as the Intel 8086 and 286. It has seen several attempts at revival over the past few years, and even may well work for some users by the time you read this edition, but it is really strictly a research project at this point—you won't see a vendor offering support for Linux on an 80286. The point here is that if you choose to use Linux on a processor lower than 32 bits, it is absolutely certain that you will be on your own. Even if you get the kernel to boot, the range of applications is limited.

Time constraints

There are two types of time constraints for embedded systems: stringent and mild. Stringent time constraints require that the system react in a predefined time frame; otherwise, ca tastrophic events happen. Take for instance a factory where workers have to handle materials being cut by large equipment. As a safety precaution, optical detectors are placed around the blades to detect the presence of the specially colored gloves used by the workers. When the system is alerted that a worker's hand is in danger, it must stop the blades immediately. It can't wait for some disk I/O operation involving reading data in from a Linux swap device (for example, swapping back in the memory storing safety management task code) or for some running task to relinquish the CPU. This system has stringent time requirements; it is a *hard real-time* system. If it doesn't respond, somebody might lose an arm. Device failure modes don't get much more painful than that.

Streaming audio systems and consumer devices such as MP3 players and cell phones would also qualify as having stringent requirements, because any transient lagging in audio is usually perceived as bothersome by the users, and failure to contact a cellular tower within a certain time will result in an active call being dropped. Yet, these latter systems would mostly qualify as having *soft real-time* requirements, because the failure of the application to perform in a timely fashion all the time isn't catastrophic, as it would be for a hard real-time system. In other words, although infrequent failures will be tolerated—a call being dropped once in a while is an annoying frustration users already live with—the system should be designed to have stringent time requirements. Soft real-time requirements are often the target of embedded Linux vendors that don't want the (potential) liability of guaranteeing hard real-time but are confident in the abilities of their product to provide, for example, reliable cell phone base-band GSM call management capabilities.

Mild time constraints vary a lot in requirements, but they generally apply to systems where timely responsiveness isn't necessarily critical. If an automated teller takes 10 more seconds to complete a transaction, it's generally not problematic (of course, at some point, the user is going to give up on the system and assume it's never going to respond). The same is true for a PDA that takes a certain number of seconds to start an application. The extra time may make the system seem slow, but it won't affect the end result. Nonetheless, it's important that the system make the user aware that it is, in fact, doing something with this time and hasn't gone out for lunch. Nothing is more frustrating than not knowing whether a system is still working or has crashed.

Networkability

Networkability defines whether a system can be connected to a network. Nowadays, we can expect everything to be accessible through the network, even the refrigerator, toaster, and coffee machine (indeed, a disturbing number of coffee machines can now download new coffee-making recipes online). This, in turn, places special requirements on the systems being built. One factor pushing people to choose Linux as an embedded OS is its proven networking capabilities. Falling prices and standardization of networking components are accelerating this trend. Most Linux devices have one form or another of network capability, be it wired or wireless in nature. The Nokia N770, N800, and N810 Internet Tablets are great examples of embedded Linux devices, complete with 802.11g wireless networking and much more, while the One Laptop Per Child (OLPC) project uses Linux and builds self-assembling, self-managing WiFi mesh networks using 802.11n on the fly.

Networking issues are discussed in detail in Chapter 10.

User interaction

The degree of user interaction varies greatly from one system to another. Some systems, such as PDAs and the Nokia Internet Tablet devices mentioned earlier, are centered around user interaction, whereas others, such as industrial process control systems, might only have LEDs and buttons for interaction (or perhaps even no apparent I/O of any kind). Some other systems have no user interface whatsoever. For example, certain components of an autopilot system in a modern airplane may take care of controlling the wing ailerons but have no direct interaction with the human pilots (something you probably don't want to consider next time you're flying).

Reasons for Choosing Linux

There are a wide range of motivations for choosing Linux over a traditional embedded OS. Many of these are shared by those in the desktop, server, and enterprise spaces, while others are more unique to the use of Linux in embedded devices.

Quality and reliability of code

Quality and reliability are subjective measures of the level of confidence in the code that comprises software such as the kernel and the applications that are provided by distributions. Although an exact definition of "quality code" would be hard to agree upon, there are properties many programmers come to expect from such code:

Modularity and structure
> Each separate functionality should be found in a separate module, and the file layout of the project should reflect this. Within each module, complex functionality is subdivided in an adequate number of independent functions. These (simpler) functions are used in combination to achieve the same complex end result.

Readability
> The code should be readable and (more or less) easy to fix for those who understand its internals.

Extensibility
> Adding features to the code should be fairly straightforward. If structural or logical modifications are needed, they should be easy to identify.

Configurability
> It should be possible to select which features from the code should be part of the final application. This selection should be easy to carry out.

The properties expected from reliable code are the following:

Predictability
> Upon execution, the program's behavior is supposed to be within a defined framework and should not become erratic. Any internal state machine should be consistent in its function, including its error handling.

Error recovery

In case a problematic situation occurs, it is expected that the program will take steps to recover cleanly from the problem condition and then alert the proper authorities (perhaps a system administrator or the owner of the device running the software in question) with a meaningful diagnostic message.

Longevity

The program will run unassisted for long periods of time and will conserve its integrity, regardless of the situations it encounters. The program cannot fail simply because a system logfile became too big (something one of the authors of this book admits to having once learned the hard way).

Most programmers agree that the Linux kernel and other projects used in a Linux system fit this description of quality and reliability. The reason is the open source development model (see upcoming note), which invites many parties to contribute to projects, identify existing problems, debate possible solutions, and fix problems effectively. Poor design choices are made from time to time, but the nature of the development model and the involvement of "many eyeballs" serve to more quickly identify and correct such mistakes.

These days you can reasonably expect to run Linux for years unattended without problems, and people have effectively done so. You can also select which system components you want to install and which you would like to avoid. With the kernel, too, you can select which features you would like during build configuration. As a testament to the quality of the code that makes up the various Linux components, you can follow the various mailing lists and see how quickly problems are pointed out by the individuals maintaining the various components of the software or how quickly features are added. Few other OSes provide this level of quality and reliability.

> Strictly speaking, there is no such thing as the "Open Source" development model, or even "Free Software" development model. "Open source" and "Free Software" correspond to a set of licenses under which various software packages can be distributed. Nevertheless, it remains that software packages distributed under "Open Source" and "Free Software" licenses very often follow a similar development model. This development model has been explained by Eric Raymond in his seminal book, *The Cathedral and the Bazaar* (O'Reilly).

Availability of code

Code availability relates to the fact that Linux's source code and all build tools are available without any access restrictions. The most important Linux components, including the kernel itself, are distributed under the GNU General Public License (GPL). Access to these components' source code is therefore compulsory (at least to those users who have purchased any system running GPL-based software, and they have the right to redistribute once they obtain the source in any case). Other components are distributed under similar licenses. Some of these licenses, such as the BSD license, for instance, permit redistribution of binaries without the original source code or the redistribution of binaries based on modified sources without requiring publication of the modifications. Nonetheless, the code for the majority of projects that contribute to the makeup of Linux is readily available without restriction.

When source access problems arise, the open source and free software community seeks to replace the "faulty" software with an open source version that provides similar capabilities. This contrasts with traditional embedded OSes, where the source code isn't available or must be purchased for very large sums of money. The advantages of having the code available are the possibility of fixing the code without exterior help and the capability of digging into the code to understand its operation. Fixes for security weaknesses and performance bottlenecks, for example, are often very quickly available once the problem has been publicized. With traditional embedded OSes, you have to contact the vendor, alert it of the problem, and await a fix. Most of the time, people simply find workarounds instead of waiting for fixes. For sufficiently large projects, managers even resort to purchasing access to the code to alleviate outside dependencies. Again, this lack of dependence upon any one external entity adds to the value of Linux.

Code availability has implications for standardization and commoditization of components, too. Since it is possible to build Linux systems based entirely upon software for which source is available, there is a lot to be gained from adopting standardized embedded software platforms. As an example, consider the growing numbers of cell phone manufacturers who are working together on common reference software platforms, to avoid re-inventing the same for each new project that comes along (bear in mind that the cell phone market is incredibly volatile, and that a single design might last a year or two if it's very, very popular). The OpenMoko project is one such effort: a standard Linux-based cell phone platform that allows vendors to concentrate on their other value-adds rather than on the base platform.

Hardware support

Broad hardware support means that Linux supports different types of hardware platforms and devices. Although a number of vendors still do not provide Linux drivers, considerable progress has been made and more is expected. Because a large number of drivers are maintained by the Linux community itself, you can confidently use hardware components without fear that the vendor may one day discontinue driver support for that product line. Broad hardware support also means that, at the time of this writing, Linux runs on dozens of different hardware architectures. Again, no other OS provides this level of portability. Given a CPU and a hardware platform based/built upon it, you can reasonably expect that Linux runs on it or that someone else has gone through a similar porting process and can assist you in your efforts. You can also expect that the software you write on one Linux architecture can be easily ported to another architecture Linux runs on. There are even device drivers that run on different hardware architectures transparently.

Communication protocol and software standards

Linux also provides broad communication protocol and software standards support, as you'll see throughout this book. This makes it easy to integrate Linux within existing frameworks and port legacy software to Linux. As such, one can easily integrate a Linux system within an existing Windows network and expect it to serve clients through *Samba* (using Active Directory or NT-style Primary Domain Controller capabilities), while clients see little difference between it and an NT/Windows 2000 server. You can also use a Linux box to practice amateur radio by building this feature into the kernel, interface with a Bluetooth-enabled cell phone, or roam transparently between a variety of WiFi networks. The OLPC project uses a Linux-based device supporting the latest WiFi mesh networking (yet to be formally standardized at the time of this writing) to enable its laptop units to form self-assembling mesh networks on the fly.

Linux is also Unix-like, and as such, you can easily port traditional Unix programs to it. In fact, many applications currently bundled with the various distributions were first built and run on commercial Unixes and were later ported to Linux. This includes almost all of the fundamental software provided by the FSF. These days, a lot more software is written for Linux, but it's still designed with portability in mind—even portability to non-Unix systems, such as those from Microsoft, thanks to compatibility libraries such as Cygwin. Traditional embedded OSes are often very limited when it comes to application portability, providing support only for a limited subset of the protocols and software standards available that were considered relevant at the time the OS was conceived.

Available tools

The variety of tools existing for Linux make it very versatile. If you think of an application you need, chances are others already felt the need for it. It is also likely that someone took the time to write the tool and make it available on the Internet. This is what Linus Torvalds did, after all. You can visit the popular websites Freshmeat (*http://www.freshmeat.net*) and SourceForge (*http://www.sourceforge.net*) and browse around to see the variety of tools available. Failing that, there's always Google.

Community support

Community support is perhaps one of the biggest strengths of Linux. This is where the spirit of the free software and open source community can be felt most. As with application needs, it is likely that someone has encountered the same problems as you in similar circumstances. Often, this person will gladly share his solution with you, provided you ask. The development and support mailing lists are the best place to find this community support, and the level of expertise found there often surpasses what can be found through expensive support phone calls with proprietary OS vendors. Usually, when you call a technical support line, you never get to talk to the engineers who built the software you are using. With Linux, an email to the appropriate mailing list will often get you straight to the person who wrote the software. Pointing out a bug and obtaining a fix or suggestions is thereafter a rapid process. As many programmers experience, seldom is a justified plea for help ignored, provided the sender takes the care to search through the archives to ensure that her question hasn't already been answered.

Licensing

Licensing enables programmers to do with Linux what they could only dream of doing with proprietary software. In essence, you can use, modify, and redistribute the software with only the restriction of providing the same rights to your recipients. This, though, is a simplification of the various licenses used with Linux (GPL, LGPL, BSD, MPL, etc.) and does not imply that you lose control of the copyrights and patents embodied in the software you generate. These considerations will be discussed later in this chapter in "Copyright and Patent Issues." Nonetheless, the degree of liberty available is actually quite large.

Vendor independence

Vendor independence means that you do not need to rely on any sole vendor to get Linux or to use it. Furthermore, if you are displeased with a vendor, you can switch, because the licenses under which Linux is distributed provide you the same rights as the vendors. Some vendors, though, provide additional software in their distributions that isn't open source, and you might not be able to receive service for this type of software from other vendors. Such issues must be taken into account when choosing distribution. Mostly, though, you can do with Linux as you could do with a car. Since the hood isn't welded shut, as it is with proprietary software, you can decide to get service from a mechanic other than the one provided by the dealership where you purchased it.

Cost

The cost of Linux is a result of open source licensing and is different from what can be found with traditional embedded OSes. There are three components of software cost in building a traditional embedded system: initial development setup, additional tools, and runtime royalties. The initial development setup cost comprises the purchase of development licenses from the OS vendor. Often, these licenses are purchased for a given number of "seats," one for each developer. In addition, you may find the tools provided with this basic development package to be insufficient and may want to purchase additional tools from the vendor. This is another cost. Finally, when you deploy your system, the vendor will ask for a per-unit royalty. This may be minimal or large, depending on the type of device you produce and the quantities produced. Some mobile phone manufacturers, for instance, choose to implement their own OSes to avoid paying any royalties. This makes sense for them, given the number of units sold and the associated profit margins.

With Linux, this cost model is turned on its head. Most development tools and OS components are available free of charge, and the licenses under which they are typically distributed prevent the collection of any royalties on these core components. Most developers, though, may not want to go chasing down the various software tools and components and figure out which versions are compatible and which aren't. Most developers prefer to use a packaged distribution. This involves purchasing the distribution, or it may involve a simple download. In this scenario, vendors provide support for their distribution for a fee and offer services for porting their distributions to new architectures and developing new drivers, also for a fee. Vendors make their money through provision of these services, as well as through additional proprietary software packaged with their distributions. Some vendors do now have a variant of the per-unit royalty (usually termed a "shared risk," or similar approach), but it is not strictly the same as for those proprietary embedded OSes mentioned before—there's always a way to use Linux without paying a runtime fee.

Players in the Embedded Linux Scene

Unlike proprietary OSes, Linux is not controlled by a single authority who dictates its future, its philosophy, and its adoption of one technology or another. These issues and others are taken care of by a broad ensemble of players with different but complementary vocations and goals.

Free software and open source community

The free software and open source community is the basis of all Linux development and is the most important player in the embedded Linux arena. It is made up of all of the developers who enhance, maintain, and support the various software components that make up a Linux system. There is no central authority within this group (though there are obvious figureheads). Rather, there is a loosely tied group of independent individuals, each with his specialty. These folks can be found discussing technical issues on the mailing lists concerning them or at gatherings such as the [Ottawa] Linux Symposium. It would be hard to characterize these individuals as a homogeneous group, because they come from different backgrounds and have different affiliations. Mostly, though, they care a great deal about the technical quality of the software they produce. The *quality and reliability* of Linux, as discussed earlier, are a result of this level of care.

Note that, although many of these developers are affiliated with a given company, their involvement typically goes beyond company lines. They may move from one company to another, but the core developers will always maintain their involvement, no matter who is currently paying their salary. Throughout this book, we will describe quite a few components that are used in Linux systems. Each maintainer of or contributor to the components described herein is considered a player in the free software and open source community.

Industry

Having recognized the potential of Linux in the embedded market, many companies have moved to embrace and promote Linux in this area. Industry players are important because they are the ones pushing Linux as an end-user product. Often, they are the first to receive feedback from those end users. Although postings on the various mailing lists can tell the developer how the software is being used, not all users participate in those mailing lists. Vendors must therefore strike an equilibrium between assisting their users and helping in the development of the various projects making up Linux, without falling into the trap of wanting to divert development to their own ends. In this regard, many vendors have successfully positioned themselves in the embedded Linux market.

Here are some of the better known vendors.

 The vendors listed here are mentioned for discussion purposes only. Neither the authors nor the publisher have evaluated the services provided by any of these vendors for the purposes of this book, and therefore this list should *not* be interpreted as any form of endorsement.

MontaVista

Founded by Jim Ready, an embedded industry veteran, and named after a part of the town in which he lived at the time, MontaVista has positioned itself as a leader in the embedded Linux market through its products, services, and promotion of Linux in industrial applications. It produces a variety of products bearing the MontaVista name, including "Professional," "Carrier Grade," and "Mobile" variants. MontaVista has contributed to some open source projects, including scheduler enhancements and real-time extensions to the kernel, ViewML, Microwindows, and Linux Trace Toolkit (LTT). A little late converting from the 2.4 kernel over to the 2.6 kernel, MontaVista made up for this by being the first embedded vendor to ship a product featuring the real-time patches to the Linux kernel (this isn't RTLinux; see Chapter 14). It also makes various claims about capability, and have recently seen considerable success in the cell phone marketplace, especially with Motorola basing entire product families on their MontaVista MobiLinux product.

MontaVista has suffered a little from being the poster child of the embedded Linux revolution. It has seen a number of engineers splinter off and create smaller consultancies—Embedded Alley is one classic example, founded by a number of extremely knowledgeable ex-MontaVista folks—and changes in corporate direction as they decide where the market will take them. MontaVista does not maintain a public repository of its community code contributions (obviously it has developers who work on upstream projects), but it does have the *http://source.mvista.com/* website with some public-facing information about projects, such as its real-time initiatives. The primary MontaVista website lives at *http://www.mvista.com/*.

Wind River

A relatively latecomer to the embedded Linux scene, Wind River has a long history as author of the proprietary vxworks real-time OS. And this means it has a large customer base behind it, ranging from set top box vendors, to automotive companies, to "deeply embedded" applications (some very small-scale systems that Linux isn't suited for), to Mars rover robots launched by NASA. After a number of years testing the waters, Wind River finally decided to take the plunge and released an Eclipse-based development product supporting either vxworks or Linux as a target (a great migration tool for existing vxworks developers). The Wind River Linux Center includes various downloads and information, including more detail on its commitment to "Device Software Optimization" (DSO), a term it recently helped to coin. Generally, this is a reference to embedded operating systems such as Linux being more than just the sum of their (Free Software) components, and instead systems that need careful tuning and knowledge to make them useful in a given embedded product.

Wind recently acquired the technology of RTLinux from FSM Labs, and so it is expected to have a number of real-time Linux product offerings by the time you read this. You can find out more about Wind River at *http://www.windriver.com/*.

LynuxWorks

This used to be known as Lynx Real-Time Systems and is another one of the traditional embedded OS vendors. Contrary to other traditional embedded OS providers, Lynx decided to embrace Linux early and changed its name to reflect its decision. That, combined with the later acquisition of BSDi by Wind River[†] and QNX's decision to make its OS available for free download, indicated that open source in general, and Linux in particular, were making serious inroads in the embedded arena. That said, LynuxWorks still develops, distributes, and supports Lynx OS. In fact, LynuxWorks promotes a twofold solution. According to LynuxWorks, programmers needing hard real-time performance should continue to use Lynx, and those who want open source solutions should use BlueCat, its embedded Linux distribution (indeed, they have drawn some criticism for using anti-GPL-like tactics to advocate the use of Lynx OS over Linux in the past). LynuxWorks has even modified its Lynx OS to enable unmodified Linux binaries to run as-is. The fact that LynuxWorks was already a successful embedded OS vendor and that it adopted Linux early confirms the importance of the move toward open source OSes in the embedded market.

Timesys

Timesys has shifted away from producing a single one-size-fits-all embedded Linux distribution toward a software service model (DSO-like), specializing in custom-built, web-based, cross-compiled packages meeting a range of requirements. Its LinuxLink subscription service is aimed at providing a simple online experience

---

† Wind River has since changed its mind, and its relationship with BSD seems to be a thing of the past.

for customizing a selection of required software, having it build automatically for a wide range of targets, and providing a package that can be used on a target device. It claims that it can remove the uncertainty and the hassle of figuring out patches, versions, and dependencies by scripting and automating the process of building custom distributions on the fly. You can find out more at *http://www.timesys.com/*.

There are also a vast number of smaller players (and more all the time) who provide a variety of services around open source and free software for embedded device application. In fact, many open source and free software contributions are made by individuals who are either independent or work for small-size vendors. As such, the services provided by such small players are often on a par or sometimes surpass those provided by larger players. For example, Wolfgang Denk's DENX software is a small consultancy based outside of Munich, Germany, yet almost everyone in the embedded Linux space has heard of Wolfgang, his Das U-Boot firmware, or the extensive documentation provided as part of his company's free Embedded Linux Development Kit (ELDK). Thanks in part to the first edition of this book, vast numbers of embedded Linux developers also know of Karim Yaghmour and his Opersys consultancy.

Resources

Most developers connect to the embedded Linux world through various resource sites and publications. It is through these sites and publications that the Linux development community, industry, and organizations publicize their work and learn about the work of the other players. In essence, the resource sites and publications are the meeting place for all the people concerned with embedded Linux. Two resources stand out: LinuxDevices.com and magazines such as *Linux Journal*.

LinuxDevices.com was founded on Halloween day‡ 1999 by Rick Lehrbaum (related to one of the MontaVista founders). LinuxDevices.com features news items, articles, polls, forums, and many other links pertaining to embedded Linux. Many key announcements regarding embedded Linux are made on this site, and it contains an archive of actively maintained articles regarding embedded Linux. Though its vocation is clearly commercial, we definitely recommend taking a peek at the site once in a while to keep yourself up-to-date with the latest in embedded Linux (and with their weekly email newsletter, it's easy to do this). Among other things, LinuxDevices.com was instrumental in launching the Embedded Linux Consortium.

As part of the growing interest in the use of Linux in embedded systems, the *Embedded Linux Journal* (ELJ) was launched by Specialized System Consultants, owners of *Linux Journal* (LJ), in January 2001 with the aim of serving the embedded Linux community, but was later discontinued. Though ELJ is no longer published as a separate magazine, it was instrumental in encouraging other Linux magazines to get involved. Several

---

‡ The date was selected purposely in symbolic commemoration of the infamous Halloween Documents uncovered by Eric Raymond. If you are not familiar with these documents and their meaning, have a look at *http://www.opensource.org/halloween/*.

Linux magazines now run embedded features on a regular basis. Indeed, one of the authors of this book was responsible for such a column for a number of years and still writes articles on occasion.

Copyright and Patent Issues

You may ask: what about using Linux in my design? Isn't Linux distributed under some crazy license that may endanger the copyrights and patents of my company? What are all those licenses anyway? Is there more than one license to take care of? Are we allowed to distribute binary-only kernel modules to protect our IP? What about all these articles I read in the press, some even calling Linux's license a "virus"?

These questions and many more have probably crossed your mind. You have probably even discussed some of these issues with your coworkers. The issues can be confusing and can come back to haunt you if they aren't dealt with properly. We don't say this to scare you. The issues are real, but there are known ways to use Linux without any fear of any sort of licensing contamination. With all the explanations provided next, it is important to keep in mind that this isn't legal counsel and we are not qualified lawyers. If you have any doubts about your specific project, consult your company attorneys—that's what they're there for. Seriously, you want to figure this out now so that it's not a problem for you later; with a little understanding and forethought, it won't be.

Textbook GPL

For most components making up a Linux system, there are two licenses involved, the GPL and the LGPL, introduced earlier. Both licenses are available from the FSF's website at *http://www.gnu.org/licenses/* and should be included with any package distributed under the terms of these licenses.[§] The GPL is mainly used for applications, whereas the LGPL is mainly used for libraries. The kernel, the binary utilities, the gcc compiler, and the gdb debugger are all licensed under the GPL. The C library and the GTK widget toolkit, on the other hand, are licensed under the LGPL.

Some programs may be licensed under BSD, Mozilla, or another, but the GPL and LGPL are the main licenses used, but regardless of which one you use, common sense should prevail. Make sure you know the licenses under which the components you use fall and understand their implications. Also make sure you understand the "compatibility" of the licenses for different components that you may wish to use within the same project. Your attorney will be able to advise.

The GPL provides rights and imposes obligations very different from what may be found in typical software licenses. In essence, the GPL is meant to provide a higher degree of freedom to developers and users, enabling them to use, modify, and distribute

---

§ The licenses are often stored in a file called *COPYING*, for the GPL, and a file called *COPYING.LIB*, for the LGPL. Copies of these files are likely to have been installed somewhere on your disk by your distribution.

software with few restrictions. It also makes provisions to ensure that these rights are not abrogated or hijacked in any fashion. To do so, the GPL stipulates the following:

- You may make as many copies of the program as you like, as long as you keep the license and copyright intact.
- Software licensed under the GPL comes with *no warranty whatsoever*, unless it is offered by the distributor.
- You can charge for the act of copying and for warranty protection.
- You can distribute binary copies of the program, as long as you accompany them with the source code used to create the binaries, often referred to as the "original" source code.[||]
- You cannot place further restrictions on your recipients than what is specified by the GPL and the software's original authors.
- You can modify the program and redistribute your modifications as long as you provide to your recipients the same rights you received. In effect, any code that modifies or includes GPL *code*, or any portion of a GPL'd program, cannot be distributed outside your organization under any license other than the GPL. This is the clause some PR folks refer to as being "virus"-like. Keep in mind, though, that this restriction concerns source code only. Packaging the unmodified software for the purpose of *running* it, as you'll see, is not subject to this provision.

As you can see, the GPL protects authors' copyrights while providing freedom of use. This is fairly well accepted. The application of the modification and distribution clauses, on the other hand, generates a fair amount of confusion. To c, two issues must be explained: running GPL software and modifying GPL software. *Running* the software is usually the reason why the original authors wrote it. The authors of gcc, for example, wrote it for compiling software. As such, the software compiled by an unmodified gcc is not covered by the GPL, since the person compiling the program is only running gcc. In fact, you can compile proprietary software with gcc, and people have been doing this for years, without any fear of GPL "contamination." *Modifying* the software, in contrast, creates a *derived work* that is based on the original software, and is therefore subject to the licensing of that original software. If you take the gcc compiler and modify it to compile a new programming language of your vintage, for example, your new compiler is a derived work and all modifications you make cannot be distributed outside your organization under the terms of any license other than the GPL.

Most anti-GPL speeches or writings play on the confusion between running and modifying GPL software, to give the audience an impression that any software in contact with GPL software is under threat of GPL "contamination." This is not the case.

[||] The specific wording of the GPL to designate this code is the following: "The source code for a work means the preferred form of the work for making modifications to it." Delivering binaries of an obfuscated version of the original source code to try circumventing the GPL is a trick that has been tried before, and it doesn't work.

There is a clear difference between running and modifying software. As a developer, you can safeguard yourself from any trouble by asking yourself whether you are simply running the software as it is supposed to be run or modifying the software for your own ends. As a developer, you should be fairly capable of making out the difference.

Note that the copyright law makes no difference between static and dynamic linking. Even if your proprietary application is integrated to the GPL software during runtime through dynamic linking, that doesn't exclude it from falling under the GPL. A derived work combining GPL software and non-GPL software through any form of linking still cannot be distributed under any license other than the GPL. If you package gcc as a dynamic linking library and write your new compiler using this library, you will still be restricted from distributing your new compiler under any license other than the GPL. Some people have attempted to work around dynamic linking restrictions through cunning use of pipes, Unix IPC sockets, and other IPC/RPC protocols to integrate GPL software with their non-GPL product. Depending upon how it is done, such use might be acceptable, but it's probably not worth the trouble to try working around the GPL in this fashion within your own projects.

Whereas the GPL doesn't allow you to include parts of the program in your own program unless your program is distributed under the terms of the GPL, the LGPL allows you to use *unmodified* portions of the LGPL program in your program without any problem. If you modify the LGPL program, though, you fall under the same restrictions as the GPL and cannot distribute your modifications outside your organization under any license other than the LGPL. Linking a proprietary application, statically or dynamically, with the C library, which is distributed under the LGPL, is perfectly acceptable. If you modify the C library, on the other hand, you are prohibited from distributing all modifications (to the library itself) under any license other than the LGPL.

 When you distribute a proprietary application that is linked against LGPL software, you must allow for this LGPL software to be replaced. If you are dynamically linking against a library, for example, this is fairly simple, because the recipient of your software need only modify the library to which your application is linked at startup. If you are statically linking against LGPL software, however, you must also provide your recipient with the object code of your application before it was linked so that she can substitute the LGPL software.

Much like the running versus modifying GPL software discussion earlier, there is a clear difference between linking against LGPL software and modifying LGPL software. You are free to distribute your software under any license when it is linked against an LGPL library. You are not allowed to distribute any modifications to an LGPL library under any license other than LGPL.

Pending issues

Up to now, we have discussed only textbook application of the GPL and LGPL. Some areas of application are, unfortunately, less clearly defined. What about applications that run using the Linux kernel? Aren't they being linked, in a way, to the kernel's own code? And what about binary kernel modules, which are even more deeply integrated to the kernel? Do they fall under the GPL? What about including GPL software in my embedded system?

Let us start with the last question. Including a GPL application in your embedded system is actually a textbook case of the GPL. Remember that you are allowed to re-distribute binary copies of any GPL software as long as your recipients receive the original source code. Distributing GPL software in an embedded system is a form of binary distribution and is allowed, granted you respect the other provisions of the GPL regarding running and modifying GPL software.

Some proprietary software vendors have tried to cast doubts about the use of GPL software in embedded systems by claiming that the level of coupling found in embedded systems makes it hard to differentiate between applications and, hence, between what falls under GPL and what doesn't. This is untrue. As we shall see in Chapters 6 and 8, there are known ways to package embedded Linux systems that uphold modularity and the separation of software components.

To avoid any confusion regarding the use of user applications with the Linux kernel, Linus Torvalds has added a preamble to the GPL found with the kernel's source code. This preamble stipulates that user applications running on the kernel are not subject to the GPL. This means that you can run any sort of application on the Linux kernel without fear of GPL "contamination." A great number of vendors provide user applications that run on Linux and remain proprietary, including Oracle, IBM, and Adobe.

The area where things have been historically unclear is binary-only kernel modules. Modules are software components that can be dynamically loaded and unloaded to add functionality to the kernel. While they are mainly used for device drivers, they can and have been used for other purposes (for example, for new filesystems, crypto library support for cryptographic storage, and a whole multitude of other purposes). Many components of the kernel can actually be built as loadable modules to reduce the kernel image's size. When needed, the various modules can be loaded during runtime (as discussed in Chapter 5).

Although this was intended as a facilitating and customizing architecture, many vendors and projects have come to use modules to provide capabilities to the kernel while retaining control over the source code or distributing it under licenses different from the GPL. Some hardware manufacturers, for instance, provide closed-source binary-only module drivers to their users. This enables the use of the hardware with Linux without requiring the vendor to provide details regarding the operation of its device. This is especially true (in the consumer space) when it comes to graphics cards featuring high-end 3D capabilities. In the embedded space, binary modules can range from

NAND Flash drivers, to codec support modules, to almost anything else you can think of that someone might consider a valuable piece of intellectual property that they wish to prevent being distributed under the GPL. The authors of this book have seen it all —and so has the Linux community.

The problem is that once a module is loaded in the kernel, it effectively becomes part of the kernel's address space and is highly coupled to it because of the functions it invokes and the services it provides to the kernel. Because the kernel is itself under the GPL, many contend that modules cannot be distributed under any other license than the GPL because the resulting kernel is a derived work. Others contend that binary-only modules are allowed as long as they use the standard services exported to modules by the kernel. In fact, in response to this logic, the kernel community created wrapped macros EXPORT_SYMBOL, EXPORT_SYMBOL_GPL, and EXPORT_SYM-BOL_GPLFUTURE. The idea behind these is that over time, new symbols (kernel functions and data structures) will be exported to the rest of the kernel via one of the GPL macros and thus all symbols will ultimately transition toward being explicitly GPL-only.

For modules already under the GPL, this is obviously a non-issue, but for non-GPL modules, this is a serious issue. Linus has said more than once that he allows binary-only modules as long as it can be shown that the functionality implemented is not Linux-specific (for example, porting a pre-existing graphics driver from Windows to Linux just to make it available for use on Linux systems). Others, however, including Alan Cox and other leading members of the Linux kernel community, have come to question his ability to allow or disallow such modules, because not all the code in the kernel is copyrighted by him. Still others contend that because binary modules have been tolerated for so long, they are part of standard practice.

There is also the case of binary-only modules that use no kernel API whatsoever. The RTAI and RTLinux real-time tasks inserted in the kernel are prime examples. Although it could be argued that these modules are a class of their own and should be treated differently, they are still linked into kernel space and fall under the same rules as ordinary modules, whichever you think them to be.

At the time of this writing, the legal status of binary-only modules has not been tested in court, but there is a growing consensus amongst the Linux kernel community that they are illegal and should not be tolerated. More than one attempt has been made to ban them outright (through technological measures), but the developers involved pointed out that such a technological restriction would make the kernel community no better than those advocating other DRM solutions, which Linux users generally abhor. This issue won't go away any time soon. In fact, it generally comes up on a semi-annual basis when it appears for a brief moment that binary modules will finally be killed off, before the issue dies down once again. To save a great deal of headache, you are advised to consider strongly whether you really need to have binary kernel modules in the first place. Consult your legal counsel if you are in any way unsure of how to proceed; we can't tell you what the law says (only how the community will react to you).

One final issue of concern to many is the GPL version 3, which is in the early stages of adoption at the time of this writing. Version 3 updates the previous GPL version 2 from more than a decade ago and includes (ominous-sounding) provisions concerning patents and intellectual property. The goal is, apparently, squarely aimed at embedded developers in an effort to prevent GPL circumvention by means of patent or DRM. Indeed, the phrase "anti-TiVoization" has been applied (TiVo is a set-top box running a modified Linux kernel that uses cryptographic hashes in order to prevent users from replacing the software with their own customized versions). To Richard Stallman, the use of GPL software is undermined whenever an embedded developer introduces cryptographic or DRM measures that effectively prevent users from changing the system, even if the source code is available—a kind of loophole in version 2 that needs some closure. Of course, many are very unhappy at the prospect of making the GPL more militant in this fashion, and a large number of projects have already stated they have no intention of making the switch to version 3. This includes the Linux kernel (which, like many projects, could not convert anyway as it has too many contributors who would need to agree, some of whom have died in the interim). Other projects, such as BusyBox, have expressed discontentment.

We can't advise you on how version 3 of the GPL might affect your own efforts, but we do recommend, again, that you consult with your company attorney (or your vendor) if you are unsure about its impact.

RTLinux patent

Perhaps one of the most restrictive and controversial licenses you will encounter in deploying Linux in an embedded system is the license to the RTLinux patent held by Victor Yodaiken, the RTLinux project leader. The patent covers the addition of real-time support to general-purpose operating systems as implemented by RTLinux. This patent was recently acquired as part of the Wind River's purchase of RTLinux technology. At the time of this writing, its use and enforcement in the future is unclear.

Although many have questioned the patent's viability, given prior art, and Victor's handling of the issue, it remains that both the patent and the license are currently legally valid, at least in the United States, and have to be accounted for. The U.S. Patent Number for the RTLinux patent is 5,995,745, and you can obtain a copy of it through the appropriate channels. You can read more about the impact of the RTLinux patent on real-time Linux efforts and how they have changed direction in Chapter 12.

A Word on Distributions

Wouldn't it be simpler and faster to use a distribution instead of setting up your own development environment and building the whole target system from scratch? What's the best distribution? Unfortunately, there are no straightforward answers to these questions. There are, however, some aspects of distribution use that might help you find answers to these and similar questions.

To use or not to use

First and foremost, you should be aware that it isn't necessary to use any form of distribution to build an embedded Linux system. In fact, all the necessary software packages are readily available for download on the Internet, and it is these same packages that distribution providers download and package for you to use. This approach provides you with the highest level of control over and understanding of the packages you use and their interactions. Apart from this being the most thorough approach and the one used within this book, it is also the most time-consuming, as you have to take the time to find matching package versions and then set up each package one by one while ensuring that you meet package interaction requirements.

Therefore, if you need a high degree of control over the content of your system, the "do it yourself" method may be best. If, however, like most people, you need the project ready yesterday or if you do not want to have to maintain your own packages, you should seriously consider using both a development and a target distribution. In that case, you will need to choose the development and target distributions most appropriate for you.

How to choose a distribution

Every embedded Linux distribution has its own benefits, so it is difficult to make generalizations about the best one to use for your application. Depending on your project, you may also have other criteria not discussed in this book. In any case, if you choose commercial distributions, make sure you insist upon an evaluation and that you have clear answers to your questions from the distribution vendor before you make any subsequent purchasing decision. Know what kind of support is available to you, what the terms of use and the various licenses are, and how this will affect you. Several vendors (including MontaVista) have developed "shared risk" approaches where you can get discounts in return for subsequent payments. These are not termed royalties per se, but they have some similarities. Know what you are getting yourself into before you commit to anything.

As in any situation, if you ask broad questions, you will get broad answers. Use detailed questions and expect detailed answers. For example, don't ask whether the Linux kernel you are getting supports real-time applications; instead ask for precise figures, and understand what exactly is being guaranteed to you ahead of time. Make yourself a shopping list of features (and packages) that you would like to see from your chosen distribution and ask to know precisely what is being provided. Do you need to pay more to get additional packages and features? Unclear answers to precise questions are usually a sign that something is amiss. If the vendor (that is trying to do a sale) is unable to answer your questions before you buy the product, do you really expect it to be any different afterward?

Should you instead choose an open source distribution,[#] make sure you have as much information as possible about it. The difference between choosing an open source distribution and a commercial distribution is the way you obtain answers to your questions about the distribution. Whereas the commercial distribution vendor will provide you with answers to your questions about its product, you may have to look for the answers to those same questions about an open source distribution on your own.

An initial factor in the choice of a development or target distribution is the license or licenses involved. Some commercial distributions are partly open source and distribute *value-added* packages under conventional software licenses that prohibit copying and impose royalties (a form of targeted lock-in). Make sure the distribution clearly states the licenses governing the usage of the value-added software and their applicability. If unsure, ask. Don't leave licensing issues unclear. This will only serve to cause you undue pain should you ever decide to migrate away to a different embedded Linux distribution.

One thing that distinguishes commercial distributions from open source distributions is the support provided by the vendor. Whereas the vendor supplying a commercial distribution almost always provides support for its own distribution, the open source community supplying an open source distribution does not necessarily provide the same level of support that would be expected from a commercial vendor. This does not preclude some vendors from providing commercial support for open source distributions. Through serving different customers with different needs in the embedded field, the various vendors build a unique knowledge about the distributions they support and the problems clients might encounter during their use, and are therefore best placed to help you efficiently. Mainly, though, these vendors are the ones that keep up with the latest and greatest in Linux and are therefore the best source of information regarding possible bugs and interoperability problems that may show up.

Reputation can also come into play when choosing a distribution, but it has to be used wisely, as a lot of information circulating may be presented as fact but instead be mere interpretation. If you've heard something about one distribution or another, take the time to verify the validity of the information. In the case of a commercial distribution, contact the vendor. Chances are it knows where this information comes from and, most importantly, the rational explanation for it. This verification process, though, isn't specific to embedded Linux distributions, but what is specific is the reputation commercial distributions build when their vendors contribute to the open source community. A vendor that gives back by providing more open source software or by financing development shows that it is in contact with the open source community and therefore understands how the changes and developments of the various open source projects will affect its future products and, ultimately, its clients. In short, this is a critical link and a testament to the vendor's understanding of the dynamics involved

---

[#] An open source distribution is one that is maintained by the open source community, such as Debian. Inherently, such distributions do not contain any proprietary software.

in the development of the software it provides you. In the case of open source distributions, this criterion is already met, as the distribution itself is an open source contribution.

Another precious tool that commercial distributions might have to offer is documentation. In this day and age where everything is ever-changing, up-to-date and accurate documentation is a rare commodity. The documentation for the majority of open source projects is often out-of-date, if available at all. Linus Torvalds's words ring true here: "Use the source, Luke," meaning that if you need to understand the software you should read the source code. Yet not everyone can invest the amount of time necessary to achieve this level of mastery, hence the need for appropriate documentation. Because the open source developers prefer to invest more time in writing code than in writing documentation, it is up to the distribution vendors to provide appropriately packaged documentation with their distributions. When evaluating a distribution, make sure to know the type and extent of accompanying documentation. Although there is less documentation for open source distributions in comparison with commercial distributions, some open source distributions are remarkably well documented.

Given the complexity of some aspects of development and target setup, the installation of a development and/or target distribution can be difficult. In this regard, you may be looking for easy-to-install distributions. Although this is legitimate, keep in mind that once you've installed the distributions, you should not need to reinstall them afterward. Notice also that installation does not really apply for a target distribution as it was defined earlier, because target distributions are used to facilitate the generation of target setups and don't have what is conventionally known as an "installation" process. The three things you should look for in the installation process of a distribution are clear explanations (whether textually during the installation, in a manual, or both), configurability, and automation. Configurability is a measure of how much control you have over the packages being installed, whereas automation is the ability to automate the process using files containing the selected configuration options.

With some CPU models and boards being broadly adopted for embedded systems development, commercial distribution vendors have come to provide prepackaged development and/or target distributions specifically tailored for those popular CPU models and boards. If you intend to use a specific CPU model or board, you may want to look for a distribution that is already tested for your setup.

What to avoid doing with a distribution

There is one main course of action to avoid when using a distribution: using the distribution in a way that makes you dependent solely on this same distribution for all future development. Remember that one of the main reasons to use Linux is that you aren't subject to anyone's will or market decisions. If your development relies only on proprietary tools and methods of the distribution you chose, you risk being locked into continuous use of that same distribution for all future development. This does not mean, though, that you shouldn't use commercial distributions with value-added software that cannot be found on other distributions. It only means that you should have a backup plan to achieve the same results with different tools from different distributions, just in case. Many embedded vendors have already standardized on development tools such as Eclipse—with each vendor adding slightly different "value-add" plug-ins—and use of such tools should serve to minimize the disruption to your engineering efforts if you ever have to switch to a different Eclipse-based tool.

Design and Implementation Methodology

Designing and implementing an embedded Linux system can be carried out in a defined manner. The process includes many tasks, some of which may be carried out in parallel, thereby reducing overall development time. Some tasks can even be omitted if a distribution is being used. Regardless of the actual tools or methodology you use, Chapter 2 is required reading for all tasks involved in building an embedded Linux system.

Creating a Target Linux System

A target Linux system is created by configuring and bundling together the appropriate system components. Programming and development aspects are a separate subject, and they are discussed later in this chapter.

There are four main steps to creating a target Linux system:

1. Determine system components.
2. Configure and build the kernel.
3. Build the root filesystem.
4. Set up boot software and configuration.

Determining system components is like making a shopping list before you go to the grocery store. It is easy to go without a shopping list and wonder at all the choices you have, as many do with Linux. This may result in "featurism," whereby your system will have lots and lots of features but won't necessarily fulfill its primary purpose. Therefore, before you go looking at all the latest Linux gizmos, sit down and write a list of what you need. We find that this approach helps in focusing development and avoids distractions like "Look, honey, they actually have salami ice cream!" This doesn't mean that you shouldn't change your list if you see something pertinent; it is just a warning about the quantity of software available for Linux and the inherent abundance of choices.

Chapter 3 discusses the hardware components that can be found as part of an embedded Linux system. It should provide you with enough background and maybe even ideas of what hardware you can find in an embedded Linux system. As Linux and surrounding software are ever-evolving targets, use this and further research on the Net to find out which design requirements Linux meets. In turn, this will provide you with a list of items you need to develop in order to complete your system. This step of development is the only one that cannot be paralleled with other tasks. Determining system requirements and Linux's compliance to these requirements has to be completed before any other step.

Because of the evolving nature of Linux, you may feel the need to get the latest and greatest pieces of software for your design. Avoid doing this, as new software often needs testing and may require upgrades to other software because of the dependencies involved between packages. Hence, you may find yourself locked in a frantic race to keep up with the plethora of updates. Instead, fix the bugs with the current software you have and keep track of other advances so that the next generation projects you design can profit from these advances. If you have an important reason to upgrade a software component, carefully analyze the consequences of such an upgrade on the rest of your system before actually carrying it out. You may also want to try the upgrade on a test system before applying it to your main system.

Having determined which features are pertinent to your design, you can select a kernel version and relevant configuration. Chapter 5 covers the configuration and build process of the kernel. Unlike other pieces of software, you may want to keep updating your kernel to the latest stable version throughout your project's development, up until the beta stage. Though keeping the kernel version stable throughout the development cycle may seem simple, you might find yourself trying to fix bugs that have been fixed in more recent kernels. Keeping yourself up-to-date with recent kernel developments, as we discuss in Chapter 5, will help you decide whether updating to the most recent kernel is best for you. Also, you may want to try newer kernels and roll back to older ones if you encounter any serious problems. Note that using kernels that are too old may cut you off from community support, since contributors can rarely afford to keep answering questions about old bugs.

While we do encourage you to keep up-to-date, it is worth mentioning major changes to the kernel, the kind that happen every few years. Consider how the 2.4 series kernel remains in use in embedded designs even after the 2.6 kernel has long since proven itself. This isn't an accident; it happened because engineers became comfortable with the 2.4 kernel and felt no need to make the switch for their existing products and embedded designs. This doesn't mean you should use the 2.4 kernel in your new design, but it does mean that you should carefully consider the impact of major version changes of any software—including the Linux kernel. It's one thing to upgrade from kernel 2.6.20 to 2.6.21, but quite another to migrate from one major release to the next. Treat that kind of transition as you would any other major software component upgrade, especially if you have a series of product-specific modifications to forward port over to the newer kernel when you make the transition.

Regardless of whether you decide to follow kernel updates, we suggest you keep the kernel configuration constant throughout the project. This will avoid completed parts from breaking in the course of development. This involves studying the configuration options closely, though, in light of system requirements. Although this task can be conducted in parallel with other tasks, it is important that developers involved in the project be aware of the possible configuration options and agree with the options chosen.

Once configuration is determined, it is time to build the kernel. Building the kernel involves many steps and generates more than just a kernel image. Although the generated components are not necessary for some of the other development aspects of the project, the other project components tend to become more and more dependent on the availability of the kernel components as the project advances. It is therefore preferable to have the kernel components fully configured and built as early as possible, and kept up-to-date throughout the project.

In parallel to handling the kernel issues, you can start building the root filesystem of the embedded system, as explained in Chapter 6. The *root* filesystem of an embedded Linux system is similar to the one you find on a workstation or server running Linux, except that it contains only the minimal set of applications, libraries, and related files needed to run the system. Note that you should not have to remove any of the components you previously chose at this stage to obtain a properly sized root filesystem. In fact, if you have to do so, you probably did not determine system components adequately. Remember that this earlier stage should include an analysis of all system requirements, including the root filesystem size. You should therefore have as accurate an estimate as possible of the size of each component you selected during the first step of creating the target system.

If you are unable to predetermine the complete list of components you will need in your embedded system and would rather build your target root filesystem iteratively by adding the tools and libraries you need as you go along, then do so, but do not treat the result as your final root filesystem. Instead, use the iterative method to explore building root filesystems, and then apply your experience to building a clean root filesystem for your target system. The reason behind this is that the trial-and-error nature of the iterative method makes its completion time nondeterministic. The structured approach may require more forethought, but its results are known and can be the basis for additional planning.

Setting up and configuring the storage devices and the bootloader software are the remaining tasks in creating a target Linux system. Chapters 7, 8, and 9 discuss these issues in full. It is during these steps that the different components of the target system come together: the bootloader, the root filesystem, and the kernel. As booting is highly dependent on the architecture, different bootloaders are involved. Within a single architecture there are also variations in the degree of debugging and monitoring provided by the bootloaders. The methodology to package and boot a system is fairly similar among the different architectures, but varies according to the permanent storage device from which the system is booted and which bootloader is used. Booting a system from native flash, for instance, is different than booting a system from a SATA disk device or CompactFlash device, and is even more different than booting from a network server.

Setting Up and Using Development Tools

Software development for embedded systems is different from software development for the workstation or server environments. Mainly, the target environment is often dissimilar to the host on which the development is conducted. Hence the need for a host/target setup whereby the developer develops his software on the host and downloads it onto the target for testing. There are two aspects to this setup: development and debugging. Such a setup, however, does not preclude you from using Linux's multi-architecture advantage to test your target's applications on your host with little or no modification. Though not all applications can be tested in this way, testing target applications on the host will generally save you a lot of time.

Embedded development is discussed in Chapter 4. Prior to testing any code on the target system, it is necessary to establish a host/target connection. This will be the umbilical cord by which the developer will be able to interact with the target system to verify whether the applications he develops function as prescribed. As the applications cannot typically run on bare hardware, there will have to be a functional embedded Linux system on the target hardware. Since it is often impossible to wait for the final target setup to be completed to test target applications, you can use a development target setup. The latter will be packaged much more loosely and will not have to respect the size requirements imposed on the final package. Hence, the development root filesystem may include many more applications and libraries than will be found in the final *root* filesystem. This also allows different and larger types of permanent storage devices during development.

Obtaining such a setup necessitates compiling the target applications and libraries. This is achieved by configuring or building the various compiler and binary utilities for cross-development. Using these utilities, you can build applications for the target and therefore build the development target setup used for further development. With this done, you can use various integrated development environments (IDEs) to ease development of the project components, and use other tools such as CVS, Subversion, and GIT to coordinate work among developers.

Given the horsepower found on some embedded systems, some developers even choose to carry out all development directly on the target system. In this setup, the compiler and related tools all run on the target. This, in effect, combines host and target in a single machine and resembles a conventional workstation application development. The main advantage of such a configuration is that you avoid the hassle of setting up a host/target environment.

Whatever development setup you choose, you will need to debug and poke at your software in many ways. You can do this with the debugging tools covered in Chapter 11. For simple debugging operations, you may choose to use ad hoc methods such as printing values using `printf()`. Some problems require more insight into the runtime operations of the software being debugged; this may be provided by symbolic debugging. *gdb* is the most common general-purpose debugger for Linux, but symbolic debugging on embedded systems may be more elaborate. It could involve such things as remote serial debugging, kernel debugging, and BDM and JTAG debugging tools. But even symbolic debugging may be inadequate in some situations. When system calls made by an application are problematic or when synchronization problems need to be solved, it is better to use tracing tools such as *strace* and LTT. For performance problems, there are other tools more adapted to the task, such as *gprof* and *gcov*. When all else fails, you may even need to understand kernel crashes.

Developing for the Embedded

One of the main advantages of using Linux as an embedded OS is that the code developed for Linux should run identically on an embedded target and on a workstation, right? Well, not quite. Although it is true that you can expect your Linux workstation code to build and run the same on an embedded Linux system, embedded system operations and requirements differ greatly from workstation or server environments. Whereas you can expect errors to kill an application on a workstation, for instance, leaving the responsibility to the user to restart the application, you can't afford to have this sort of behavior in an embedded system. Neither can you allow applications to gobble up resources without end or behave in an untimely manner.* Therefore, even though the APIs and OS used may be identical, there are fundamental differences in programming philosophies.

Networking

Networking enables an embedded system to interact with and be accessible to the outside world. In an embedded Linux environment, you have to choose networking hardware, networking protocols, and the services to offer while accounting for network security. Chapter 10 covers the setup and use of networking services such as HTTP, Telnet, SSH, and/or SNMP. One interesting feature in a network-enabled embedded system is the possibility of remote updating, whereby it is possible to update the system via a network link without on-site intervention. (This is covered in Chapter 8.)

---

* Normal Linux workstation and server applications should not gobble up resources either. In fact, the most important applications used on Linux servers are noteworthy for their stability, which is one reason Linux is so successful as a server operating system.

Basic Concepts

As we saw in the previous chapter, there is a rich variety of embedded Linux systems. And as time moves forward, this diversity is increasing as new markets open up, be it for the millions of Linux-based cell phones sold every year, or for experimental amateur rockets with precise real-time requirements. In spite of such a variety, there are nevertheless a few key characteristics that apply uniformly to most embedded Linux systems. The purpose of this chapter is to present you with the basic concepts and issues that you are likely to encounter when developing any sort of embedded Linux system.

Many of the subjects introduced here will be discussed in far greater detail in other chapters. They are covered here briefly to give you an understanding of how the system forms a cohesive whole, and to avoid so-called undeclared forward references (a programming term for using something before it has been fully defined). The chapter starts with a discussion of the types of hosts most commonly used for developing embedded Linux systems, the types of host/target development setups, and the types of host/target debug setups. These sections are meant to help you select the best environment for developing embedded Linux systems or, if the environment is already specified, understand how your particular setup will influence the rest of your development effort. We will then present details of the structure commonly found in most embedded Linux systems, and the generic architecture of an embedded Linux system, explaining system startup, types of boot configuration, and the typical system memory layout, in addition to other related items.

If you are already broadly familiar with embedded systems concepts, you need only skim this chapter for Linux-specific issues. In such cases, you will want to pay particular attention to the latter parts of the chapter.

Types of Hosts

In the next chapter, we will cover the hardware most commonly found in modern embedded Linux targets. But although the target hardware is very important to your overall design, each possible target system can be developed using a wide variety of host systems. In the following section, we will discuss the types of hosts most commonly used, their particulars, and how easy it is to develop embedded Linux systems using them.

Linux Workstation

This is the most common type of development host for embedded Linux systems. It is also the one that we recommend you use if you are not already constrained by the use of a particular development environment. The reasoning behind this is simple: to gain experience with Linux, there really is no substitute for actually using a Linux system for your own development. Using Linux on a day-to-day basis, you will also become familiar with diagnosing and solving certain problems that may similarly affect your target embedded Linux system later on.[*]

A standard PC is your most likely Linux workstation. Do not forget, though, that Linux runs on a variety of hardware and you are not limited to using a PC-like system. Several of this book's authors, for example, regularly use PowerPC-based Linux systems for their embedded work.

You may use any of the standard Linux distributions on your host system. These include, but are by no means limited to, the following:

Debian GNU/Linux (http://www.debian.org)
> A popular community-supported and developed Linux distribution, maintained by an international team of developers and supported under the umbrella of the "Software In The Public Interest" registered charity organization. Debian prides itself on its high standards, but it is occasionally known to be a little more difficult to install and to use for the novice user. It is not released on any kind of predictable schedule.

Fedora (http://www.fedoraproject.org)
> A modern day continuation of the famous "Red Hat Linux," which no longer exists, despite many references to the now long since obsolete Red Hat Linux 9.0 that persist on the Internet. Fedora is developed internationally, but has traditionally had a strong affiliation with the company Red Hat, which uses Fedora as the base when creating its Red Hat Enterprise Linux distribution. Fedora is typically released on a 6–9 month semipredictable schedule. It has an unstable release, known as "rawhide," which is updated on a daily basis as individual components of the distribution undergo modification.

OpenSusE (http://www.opensuse.org)
> If Fedora is the modern day continuation of Red Hat Linux, OpenSuSE is the same for what was once simply known as SuSE. After Novell acquired SuSE and began

---

[*] One of the authors learned the hard way about system logfiles filling up system disks—first on a production server in a corporate environment, then on a target embedded Linux system. This was sufficient experience to eventually predesign future systems with limited space set aside for ever-expanding logfiles.

releasing SuSE Linux Enterprise Server (SLES), OpenSuSE became the new incubator for future technology. It is released on a similar schedule to Fedora, and it also has an unstable release, known as "Factory," that is updated on a daily basis.

Red Hat Enterprise Linux (RHEL) (http://www.redhat.com)
This is a commercial distribution from Red Hat and a direct descendant of the Red Hat Linux line. It is released on an 18-month schedule and is supported for many years following its release. Support is in the form of a subscription model, although several others have successfully repackaged RHEL into "free" Enterprise Linux distributions (which come with no support, but are virtually binary-identical to the official product) after removing all appropriate trademarks. Such practice is possible thanks to the open source licenses under which most software is distributed.

SuSE Linux Enterprise Server (SLES) (http://www.suse.com)
This is a commercial distribution from Novell, which also produces SLED (SuSE Linux Enterprise Desktop) and a variety of other products. One of these products is an enterprise real-time product that makes use of the RT patchset discussed in this book (in the case of Novell, this is intended for mission-critical trading and similar situations, rather than for embedded use—a testament to the generic usefulness and reusability of such technology). SLES is released on a basis similar to Red Hat Enterprise Linux and competes with it directly.

Ubuntu Linux (http://www.ubuntulinux.org)
This is a derivative of Debian GNU/Linux, but intended more for mass market use and released under a more predictable 6–12 month schedule. It is backed by Canonical, a company formed by billionaire Mark Shuttleworth, who became rich through a company he built that relied heavily upon Debian for its IT infrastructure. A number of popular PC makers are now considering supplying, or are already supplying, PCs with Ubuntu Linux preinstalled, in addition to the other aforementioned commercial Linux distributions.

Yellow Dog Linux (http://www.terrasoftsolutions.com)
This is a Red Hat Linux derivative for PowerPC systems, such as those from IBM (based on POWER/OpenPOWER/PowerPC processors) and formerly those from Apple Computer. Although not as common, it stands here as an example of a Linux distribution intended specifically for non-PC architectures in the first instance, and as an example of how you need not always choose one of the "big three" (Red Hat, Novell, Canonical) for your Linux needs.

There are numerous other Linux distributions available, for example, Slackware (famous for being one of the early Linux distributions still in widespread use), Gentoo (source-based, intended for optimized performance, but not for novice users—despite what you may hear to the contrary on this topic!), and even more obscure distributions, such as Rock Linux and Tom's Root Boot (a minimal Linux, with modern-day derivatives). The authors have used all of these, and many more, in the course of their Linux careers. And one thing is for sure: there will be many more, so don't get too fixated on one Linux distribution. Concern yourself more with understanding commonalities, such as the RPM package format (used extensively, though not universally).

The Linux marketplace continues to evolve over time. In the first edition of this book, the author made no reference to Ubuntu, or to Canonical, because neither existed.[†]

Today, it's hard to go anywhere without hearing about Canonical at the same time as the other two big players. And it is almost certain that there will be new players, new transitions, and new concerns that will arise following the publication of this edition. If you are really interested in keeping abreast of changes in the distribution space, you are encouraged to read distrowatch.com (*http://distrowatch.com*) on a semiregular basis. There you will find major announcements, popularity statistics, and a wide variety of other useful information. Throughout this book, we will assume you are running a common distribution, and although we are certainly not going to recommend any one distribution for your development efforts, we do nonetheless recommend that those inexperienced with Linux choose one of the aforementioned mainstream distributions over a more obscure and less easily supported one. At least for your first project!

 Although we've made an effort to keep this text independent of host distribution, the instructions in this book are slightly tilted toward Red Hat–type distributions—after all, those are what we use on a daily basis ourselves. You may therefore need to make minor modifications to a few commands, depending on the distribution installed on your host. Wherever possible, distribution-dependent commands are presented.

Of course, the latest and fastest hardware is every engineer's dream. Having the fastest machine around will certainly help you with your work, but you can still use a relatively mild-powered machine with appropriate RAM for this type of development. Remember that Linux is very good at making the best of the available hardware, and given a choice between a faster processor or more RAM, you will generally want to opt for more RAM. A fast processor is useless if your machine is spending its time constantly thrashing the disks as it attempts to swap programs and data into and out of main memory. It is, nonetheless, appropriate to set some minimum constraints upon what is a reasonable development platform, especially for those who must convince their management what to buy!

Generally speaking, you will want to ensure that any PC-based development platform has the following:

- At least 1 to 2 GB of RAM. More than 4 GB starts to become self-limiting, in that you can likely retain the entire Linux desktop, applications, and most of the Linux source code you are compiling in the host system's built-in kernel buffers (the "page

---

[†] For that matter, at the time of the first edition, none of the other Linux distributions in our list existed in the form that they now do. During that period, Red Hat still actively developed Red Hat Linux, whereas Novell and SuSE were distinct organizations (the former later purchased the latter).

cache") at this point. Opt for more RAM only if you frequently perform many kernel compilation sequences, build many applications in parallel, or will share one central development machine resource with other programmers.

- At least a 2 GHz CPU. More than two dual-core CPUs is currently considered to be on the high end.
- As much disk space as you can reasonably get away with.

A bit more about the last item: no matter what development work you are doing, one thing you can always use plenty of is disk space. Fortunately, storage is cheap. As of this writing, 500 GB (and even 1 TB) disks are not that uncommon (a far cry from the "2 to 3 GB" recommendation from the first edition of this book!), and larger capacities are likely to be available by the time you read this. 500 GB should be an order of magnitude more than enough for your needs, but with such a large amount of space available at such modest prices, you will be able to keep many redundant copies of your work, as you experiment with scratch builds or try out ideas. (Of course, you should additionally plan to back this up somewhere else, but that should be obvious.)

You are encouraged to consider RAID on any serious Linux development system. Linux has long since had great support for RAID1, RAID0+1, and RAID5 (using RAID0 is never advisable), and modern Linux distributions won't even require you to configure this for yourself. They'll take care of it during installation, just as long as you let them know you desire a RAID array configuration. Using RAID (especially RAID1—effectively doubling your disk use with a redundant copy of all data) can often result in much faster disk access, since many possible disks can be used for any given read and will usually increase reliability.

For further information about the different Linux distributions, as well as their requirements, and the kinds of hardware best suited to your environment, consult the individual distribution websites, *http://distrowatch.com*, this book's website (*http://www.embeddedlinuxbook.org/*), and a weekly dose of LinuxDevices.com articles.

Unix Workstation

Depending on your circumstances, you may be required to use a traditional Unix workstation, although you are strongly encouraged not to do this if Linux is available. Solaris workstations, for instance, are very common among telecommunication solutions developers. Although the use of such workstations is much less common than the use of Linux workstations for developing embedded Linux systems, it is still feasible. In fact, modern Solaris (and OpenSolaris) systems include a large amount of prebuilt GNU software, such as *gcc*, that can make your life easier.

Because Linux itself is very much like Unix, most of what applies to Linux also applies to Unix and other Unix-like systems, such as the various BSD flavors (OpenBSD, FreeBSD, and so on). This is especially true when it comes to the GNU development toolchain, since the main GNU tools—such as the compiler, the C library, and the binary utilities (more commonly known as *binutils*)—were developed and used on traditional Unix systems before Linux even existed. Although most of the recommendations given earlier for Linux systems will relate to traditional Unix systems, you are nonetheless strongly recommended to use a Linux system. The day has long since passed when you should encounter any significant resistance from your corporate IT/IS department about using a Linux system in place of a traditional Unix one.

Windows (Vista, XP, 2000, NT, 98, etc.) Workstation

In the early 1990s, embedded system development shifted toward Microsoft Windows workstations. This was largely due to the growth in graphical development tools available, which came just in time for a surge in demand for a shortened time-to-market on embedded projects. Many developers have since become used to working on this platform and many new developers have been initiated to embedded systems development on it. For these and other reasons, some developers would like to continue using Windows workstations to develop, ironically, embedded Linux systems.

Although we are encouraging you to use Linux for your development whenever possible, and in spite of the existence of cross-platform GUI development tools (such as Eclipse), we are nonetheless aware of the growing need for software tools that exist only for Windows. This includes a number of vendor-specific tools, such as debuggers, hardware FPGA/PROM/Flash programmers, and the like. We know that not all developers will want to retain two development systems—Linux for straightforward program development and Windows for the use of third-party Windows-only tools—and will opt to base themselves on Windows. But the beauty here is that you are free to use Windows on your host system if that is what you want to do. In fact, several of the authors have successfully developed shipping products using Windows host computers and embedded Linux targets.

At first glance, it would seem that the main problem in using Windows to develop programs for embedded Linux targets is the (seeming) lack of the GNU development toolchain. This is actually not a problem, because Red Hat provides the Cygwin environment, which is the Windows-compatible GNU toolchain. Many people have used it to build cross-platform tools for Linux, including a number of third parties. For example, Xilinx bases its development tools upon a modified Cygwin (formerly "Xygwin"), which allows it to produce tools for both Linux and Windows systems. You can find out more about Cygwin online at *http://www.cygwin.com*.

If you opt to use an embedded Linux development environment from one of the popular embedded Linux vendors, they will additionally be able to supply you with a version of their (invariably Eclipse-based) graphical tools and development environment running on Windows.

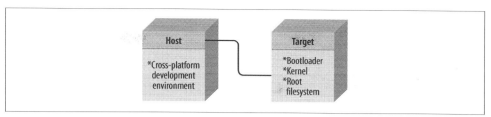

Figure 2-1. Host/target linked setup

Types of Host/Target Development Setups

Three different host/target architectures are available for the development of embedded Linux systems: the linked setup, the removable storage setup, and the standalone setup. Your actual setup may belong to more than one category or may even change categories over time, depending on your requirements and development methodology.

Linked Setup

In this setup, the target and the host are permanently linked together using a physical cable. This link is typically a serial cable or an Ethernet link. The main property of this setup is that no physical hardware storage device is being transferred between the target and the host. All transfers occur via the link. Figure 2-1 illustrates this setup.

As illustrated, the host contains the cross-platform development environment (discussed in Chapter 4), while the target contains an appropriate bootloader, a functional kernel, and a minimal root filesystem.

Alternatively, the target can use remote components to facilitate development. The kernel could, for instance, be available via trivial file transfer protocol (TFTP). The root filesystem could also be NFS-mounted instead of being on storage media in the target. Using an NFS-mounted root filesystem is actually perfect during development, because it avoids having to constantly copy program modifications between the host and the target, as we'll see later in "Types of Boot Configurations."

The linked setup is the most common. Obviously, the physical link can also be used for debugging purposes. It is, however, more common to have another link for debugging purposes, as we shall see later in "Types of Host/Target Debug Setups." Many embedded systems, for instance, provide both Ethernet and RS232 link capabilities. In such a setup, the Ethernet link is used for downloading the executable, the kernel, the root filesystem, and other large items that benefit from rapid data transfers between the host and the target, while the RS232 link is used for debugging.

Many modern "legacy free" PC systems, as well as PowerPC-based systems, lack an RS232 serial port. This is easily fixed by adding a USB serial dongle (a USB device that provides a serial port via a serial-like emulation). Note that you should never use these on the target if you plan to perform true serial console debugging.

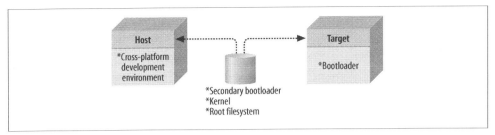

Figure 2-2. Host/target removable storage setup

Removable Storage Setup

In the removable setup, there are no direct physical links between the host and the target. Instead, a storage device is written by the host, is then transferred into the target, and is used to boot the device. Figure 2-2 illustrates this setup.

As with the previous setup, the host contains the cross-platform development environment. The target, however, contains only a minimal bootloader. The rest of the components are stored on a removable storage media, such as a CompactFlash IDE device, MMC Card, or any other type of removable storage device (even floppies and CD-ROM/DVDs have been used), which is programmed on the host and loaded by the target's minimal bootloader upon startup.

It is possible, in fact, for a target not to contain any form of persistent storage at all. Instead of a fixed flash chip, for instance, the target could contain a socket where a flash chip could be easily inserted and removed. The chip is then programmed by a flash programmer on the host and inserted into the socket in the target for normal operation.

This setup is mostly popular during the initial phases of embedded system development. You may find it more practical to move on to a linked setup once the initial development phase is over, so you can avoid the need to physically transfer a storage device between the target and the host every time a change has to be made to the kernel or the root filesystem.

Standalone Setup

Here, the target is a self-contained development system and includes all the required software to boot, operate, and develop additional software. In essence, this setup is similar to an actual workstation, except the underlying hardware is not a conventional workstation but rather the embedded system itself. Figure 2-3 illustrates this setup.

In contrast to the other setups, this one does not require any cross-platform development environment, since all development tools run in their native environments. Furthermore, it does not require any transfer between the target and the host, because all the required storage is local to the target.

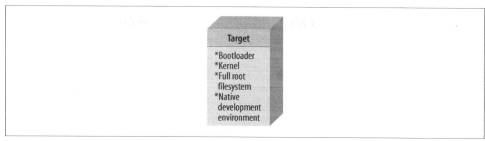

Figure 2-3. Host/target standalone setup

This type of setup is quite popular with developers building high-end PC-based embedded systems, such as high-availability systems, since they can use standard off-the-shelf Linux distributions on the embedded system. Once development is done, they then invest time in trimming down the distribution and customizing it for their purposes.

Although this gets developers around having to build their own root filesystems and configure the systems' startup, it requires that they know the particular distribution they are using inside out. Fortunately, this is made easier by various distributor efforts to create flexibility over the last few years. For example, the Fedora Project is actively working on allowing developers to create "custom spins" of Fedora, with only the packages they want installed. Nevertheless, if you are interested in this approach, you may want to take a look at Matthias Dalheimer and Matt Welsh's *Running Linux* (O'Reilly).

Note that a certain amount of flexibility exists in the definition of "standalone." For systems that will eventually need to function standalone, but nonetheless do include a network port, a serial port, or a similar device, there is value gained in a mixed standalone/linked setup. In such a setup, although the system is designed to function on a standalone basis, you might include an option to boot across a network, to mount a networked filesystem, or to use a serial connection for debugging purposes. The networked filesystem might in such cases be significantly larger than the target filesystem (which often resides on a very limited flash MTD of some kind). Thus, this filesystem may include many more optional binaries useful only during development, documentation, and updates to system software that can easily be copied over to, and tested on, the target system during various debugging sessions.

Types of Host/Target Debug Setups

There are basically three types of interfaces that developers use to link a target to a host for debugging: a serial line, a networking interface, and special debugging hardware. Each debugging interface has its own benefits and applications. We will discuss the detailed use of some of these interfaces in Chapter 11. This section will briefly review the benefits and characteristics of each type.

Using a serial link is the simplest way to debug a target from a host, because serial hardware is simple and is often found, in some form or another, in embedded systems. There are two potential problems with using a serial link, however. First, the speed of most serial links is rather limited. Second, if there's only one serial port in the embedded system or if the serial link is the embedded system's only external interface, it becomes impossible to simultaneously debug the system and interact with it using a terminal emulator. The absence of terminal interaction is not a problem in some cases, however. When debugging the startup of the kernel using a remote kernel debugger, for example, no terminal emulator is required, since no shell actually runs on the target until the kernel has finished booting.

 Although it can seem expensive to include additional serial hardware in your system design, note that you needn't include a full logical-level conversion (such as one of the popular MAXIM-TTL logic level conversion parts on the market), or even actually have an additional externally visible connector of any kind. All that it requires is a little logic in your design for the serial UART itself and some pads on the board, to which you can connect a logic level converter and external serial port connector during your debug sessions. Many manufacturers choose this option.

The use of a networking interface, such as TCP/IP over Ethernet, provides much higher bandwidth than a serial link. Moreover, the target and the host can use many networking connections over the same physical network link. Hence, you can continue to interact with the target while debugging applications on it. You can also debug over a networking link while interacting with the target using a terminal emulator over the embedded system's serial port. However, the use of a networking interface implies the presence of a networking stack. Since the networking stack is found in the Linux kernel, a networking link cannot be easily used to debug the kernel itself (although, to a certain extent, there are network diagnostics tools for the Linux kernel, such as *kdump*, which are useful for remotely capturing a crash). In contrast, kernel debugging can be, and often is, carried out over a serial link.

Both the use of a serial link and the use of a networking interface require some minimal software that recognizes the possibly primitive I/O hardware on the target. In some cases, such as when porting Linux to a new board or when debugging the kernel itself, such software is not present. In those cases, it is necessary to use a debugging interface that provides direct hardware control over the software. There are several ways to achieve this, but most are quite expensive.

Currently, the preferred way to obtain direct control over hardware for debugging purposes is to use a BDM or JTAG interface. These interfaces rely on special BDM or JTAG functionality embedded in the CPU. By connecting a special debugger (such as the BDI2000 family of popular debugger hardware devices, used by several of the authors in products that have been shipped) to the JTAG or BDM pins of the CPU, you can take complete control of its behavior. For this reason, JTAG and BDM are often used when bringing up new embedded boards or debugging the Linux kernel on such boards.

Though the BDM and JTAG debuggers are much less expensive and much less complicated in terms of their technical operation than in-circuit emulators (ICEs), they still require the purchase of special hardware and software. Often, this software and hardware are still relatively expensive because CPU manufacturers are not keen to share the detailed information regarding the use of the JTAG and BDM interfaces included in their products. Obtaining this information often involves establishing a trust relationship with the manufacturer and signing stringent NDAs. Consequently, you should not expect much change back from $1,000 U.S. (even on eBay) for a hardware debugging tool of this kind.

Though it would probably be too expensive to equip each member of an engineering team with her own BDM or JTAG debugger, we do highly recommend that you have at least one such debugger available throughout your project for debugging the very difficult problems that a serial or networking debugger cannot deal with appropriately, especially if you are porting Linux to an entirely new hardware platform. (If it's simply based on a standard reference platform, you might get away without the hardware-base debugger.) When selecting such a debugger, however, you may want to evaluate its compatibility with the GNU development toolchain. Some BDM and JTAG debuggers, for instance, require the use of specially modified *gdb* debuggers. A good BDM or JTAG debugger should be able to deal transparently with the standard GNU development toolchain, and the binary files generated using it.

Generic Architecture of an Embedded Linux System

Since Linux systems are made up of many components, let us take a look at the overall architecture of a generic Linux system. This will enable us to set each component in context and will help you understand the interaction between them and how to best take advantage of their assembly. Figure 2-4 presents the architecture of a generic Linux system with all the components involved. Although the figure abstracts to a high degree the content of the kernel and the other components, the abstractions presented are sufficient for this discussion. Notice that there is little difference in the following description between an embedded system and a workstation or server system, since Linux systems are all structured the same at this level of abstraction. In the rest of the book, however, emphasis will be on the details of the application of this architecture in embedded systems.

Hardware must meet some broad characteristics to run a Linux system:

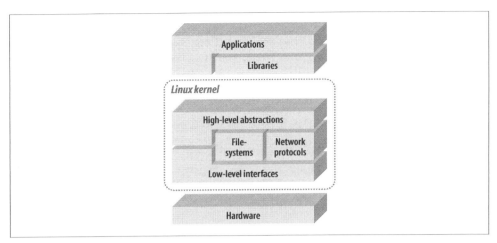

Figure 2-4. Architecture of a generic Linux system

- Linux normally requires at least a 32-bit CPU containing a memory management unit (MMU).[‡]

- A sufficient amount of RAM must be available to accommodate the system. Requirements will be laid out in later chapters.

- Minimal I/O capabilities are required if any development is to be carried out on the target with reasonable debugging facilities. This is also very important for any later troubleshooting in the field.

- The kernel must be able to load a root filesystem through some form of permanent storage, or access it over a network.

See "Types of Embedded Linux Systems in Chapter 1 for a discussion of typical system configurations.

Immediately above the hardware sits the kernel, the core component of the operating system. Its purpose is to manage the hardware in a coherent manner while providing familiar high-level abstractions to user-level software (such as the POSIX APIs and the other de facto, industry-standard APIs against which applications are generally written). As with other Unix-like kernels, Linux drives the devices, manages I/O access, controls process scheduling, enforces memory sharing, handles the distribution of signals, and tends to other administrative tasks. It is expected that applications using the APIs provided by a kernel will be portable among the various architectures supported by this kernel with little or no changes. This is usually the case with Linux, as can be seen by the body of applications uniformly available on all architectures it supports.

[‡] As we'll see, the official Linux kernel includes the fruits of a project known as uClinux which runs on some CPUs that aren't equipped with full MMUs. However, the development of applications for Linux on such processors differs sufficiently from standard Linux application development to require a separate discussion. Because of this, plus a relative lack of widely available software for such systems, we do not cover the use of Linux on MMU-less architectures.

Within the kernel, two broad categories of layered services provide the functionality required by applications. The low-level interfaces are specific to the hardware configuration on which the kernel runs and provide for the direct control of hardware resources using a hardware-independent API. That is, handling registers or memory pages will be done differently on a PowerPC system and on an ARM (Advanced RISC Machine) system (and perhaps even differently within the ARM and PowerPC families), but will be accessible using a common API to higher-level components of the kernel, with some rare exceptions. Typically, low-level services handle CPU-specific operations, architecture-specific memory operations, and basic interfaces to devices. These are then abstracted to higher level code through headers, macros, and wrapper functions.

Above the low-level services provided by the kernel, higher-level components provide the abstractions common to all Unix systems, including processes, files, sockets, and signals. Since the low-level APIs provided by the kernel are common among different architectures, the code implementing the higher-level abstractions is almost constant, regardless of the underlying architecture. There are some rare exceptions, as stated earlier, where the higher-level kernel code will include special cases or different functions for certain architectures.

Between these two levels of abstraction, the kernel sometimes needs what could be called *interpretation components* to understand and interact with structured data coming from or going to certain devices. Filesystem types and networking protocols are prime examples of sources of structured data the kernel needs to understand and interact with in order to provide access to data going to and coming from these sources.

Disk devices have been and still are the main storage media for computerized data. And in the embedded world, flash-based devices tend to provide the same functionality—even using compatible interfaces, in many cases. Yet disk devices, and all other storage devices for that matter, themselves contain little structure. Their content may be addressable by referencing the appropriate sector of a cylinder on a certain disk (or the erase block number of the NAND flash, logical block number of the CompactFlash, etc.), but this level of organization is quite insufficient to accommodate the ever-changing content of files and directories. File-level access is achieved using a special organization of the data on the disk where file and directory information is stored in a particular fashion so that it can be recognized when it is read again. This is what filesystems are all about.

During the evolution of operating systems, many different incompatible filesystems have seen the light of day. To accommodate these existing filesystems as well as new ones in development, the kernel has a number of filesystem engines that can recognize a particular disk structure and retrieve or add files and directories from this structure. The engines all provide the same API to the upper layers of the kernel through the Linux Virtual File System (VFS) abstraction so that accesses to the various filesystems are identical even though accesses to the lower-layer services vary according to the structure of the filesystem. The same API is provided to the virtual filesystem layer of the kernel by, for instance, the FAT filesystem and the ext3 filesystems, but the operations the filesystems conduct on the block device driver differ according to the respective structures used by FAT and ext3 to store data on disk (which are very different indeed!).

 In fact, disk vendors are increasingly heading toward higher level abstraction, even at the "hardware" level. By the time you read this, it is quite possible that disk devices will be on the market that deal solely with logical extents—chunks of data ("files"), streams, and similar information—rather than the old-fashioned sector-based approach with which you may be familiar. Linux will, at that point, use these new capabilities within the modern "extent"-based filesystems to store large amounts of data much more efficiently than ever before, with even less logic needed within the kernel itself for controlling the disk. Nonetheless, this is tangential to the current topic of conversation.

During its normal operation, the kernel requires at least one properly structured filesystem, the root filesystem. From this filesystem, the kernel loads the first application to run on the system. It also normally relies upon this filesystem for certain further operations, such as loading modules and providing each process with a working directory (though these activities might take place on other filesystems mounted within the tree that begins with the root filesystem). The root filesystem may be either stored and operated on from a real hardware storage device, or loaded into RAM during system startup and operated on from there. As we'll see later, the former is becoming much more popular than the latter with the advent of facilities such as the JFFS2, YAFFS2, LogFS, and other journaled flash filesystems.

You might expect that right above the kernel you would find the regular applications and utilities making up and running on the operating system. Yet the services exported by the kernel are often unfit to be used directly by applications. Instead, applications rely on libraries and special system daemons to provide familiar APIs and abstract services that interact with the kernel on the application's behalf to obtain the desired functionality. The main library used by most Linux applications is the GNU C library, *glibc*. For embedded Linux systems, substitutes to this library can be used (as we'll see later) to compensate for the GNU C library's main deficiency: its size. Other than the C library, libraries such as Qt, XML, or MD5 provide various utility and functionality APIs serving all sorts of purposes. Meanwhile, important system processes ("daemons") provide services exploited by applications. For instance, the udev device filesystem manager manages devices in */dev*, such as when USB storage devices are added to and removed from the system.

Libraries are typically linked *dynamically* with applications. That is, they are not part of the application's binary, but are rather loaded into the application's memory space during application startup. This allows many applications to use the same instance of a library instead of each having its own copy. The C library found on a system's filesystem, for instance, is loaded only once in the system RAM, and this same copy is usually shared among all applications that use this library.

But in some situations involving embedded systems, *static linking*, whereby libraries are part of the application's binary, is preferred to dynamic linking. When only part of a library is used by one or two applications, for example, static linking helps avoid the need to store the entire library on the embedded system's storage device. This issue becomes even more complex when linking proprietary applications with certain libraries covered only by a strict GPL license rather than the LGPL. Licensing issues were discussed in Chapter 1—for further information, consult your attorney.

System Startup

Three main software components participate in system startup: the bootloader, the kernel, and the init process. The bootloader is the first software to run upon startup and is highly dependent on the target's hardware. As we'll see in Chapter 9, many bootloaders are available for Linux. The bootloader performs low-level hardware initialization and then jumps to the kernel's startup code.

The early kernel startup code differs greatly between architectures and conducts initialization of its own before setting up a proper environment for the running of C code. Once this is done, the kernel jumps to the architecture-independent start_kernel( ) function, which initializes the high-level kernel functionality, mounts the root filesystem, and starts the init process. As part of the higher-level kernel initialization, various callbacks are made into platform-specific code, which varies by supported architecture. For example, some PowerPC systems take this opportunity to set up special memory mappings and mimimal versions of serial diagnostic functions, prior to the kernel bringing its usual memory and device management functionality online. This is useful mainly for debugging.

We will not cover the details of the kernel's internal startup and initialization, because they have already been covered in detail in *Linux Device Drivers* by Jonathan Corbet et al. (O'Reilly). Also, Appendix A of Daniel Bovet and Marco Cesati's *Understanding the Linux Kernel* (O'Reilly) provides a lengthy description of the startup of PC-based systems from the initial power-on to the execution of the init process. That discussion covers the kernel's internal startup for the x86, which is similar in concept to that used on other architectures, although the specifics do actually vary quite considerably. When it comes down to it, you will learn more about this in reading through the code, experimenting, performing your own kernel ports, and keeping up with the Linux kernel mailing lists than you will from any (quickly outdated) book.

The rest of the system startup is conducted in user space by the *init* program found on the root filesystem. We will discuss the setup and configuration of the init process in Chapter 6.

Types of Boot Configurations

The type of boot configuration chosen for a system greatly influences the selection of a bootloader, its configuration, and the type of software and hardware found in the host. A network boot configuration, for example, requires that the host provide some types of network services to the target. In designing your system, you first need to identify the boot configurations you are likely to use during development and in the final product. Then, you need to choose a bootloader or a set of bootloaders that will cater to the different types of boot setups you are likely to use. Not all bootloaders, for example, can boot kernels from disk devices. In the following discussion, we will cover the possible boot configurations. Let us start, nevertheless, by reviewing some boot basics.

All CPUs fetch their first instruction from an address preassigned by their manufacturer (occasionally with some design flexibility between a few alternative addresses—determined by strapping lines on the CPU). Any system built using a CPU has one form or another of a solid-state storage device at that location. Traditionally, the storage device was a masked ROM, but flash chips are increasingly the norm today. The software on this storage device is responsible for bootstrapping the system. The level of sophistication of the boot software and the extent to which it is subsequently used as part of the system's operation greatly depend on the type of system involved.

Masked ROMs continue to be used when devices are produced in very large quantities. Consumer gaming devices such as consoles, for example, often use masked ROMs.

Some higher-end FPGA platforms running Linux don't even use regular memory at all. They create special block RAM devices with "hard-wired" jump instructions at the regular CPU reset vector, designed to force it to jump to bootloader code preloaded into RAM by the same special hardware device that also loaded the FPGA configuration itself. Such an approach is extremely popular in designs based upon the Xilinx Virtex family of FPGAs. In this case, a mere five hardcoded PowerPC instructions are all that are required to be "hard-wired" into synthetic block RAM at the reset vector, sufficient to jump into a preloaded bootloader.

On most workstations and servers, the boot software is responsible only for loading the operating system from disk and for providing basic hardware configuration options to the operator. In contrast, there are very few agreed upon purposes, if any, for boot software in embedded systems, because of the diversity in purposes of embedded applications. Sometimes, the boot software will run throughout the system's lifetime. The boot software may also be a simple monitor that loads the rest of the system software. Such monitors can then provide enhanced debugging and upgrading facilities.

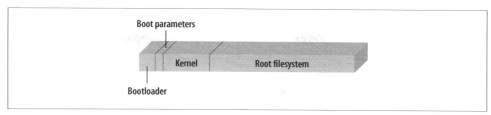

Figure 2-5. Typical solid-state storage device layout

The boot software may even load additional bootloaders, as is often the case with x86 PCs.

Embedded Linux systems are as diverse as their non-Linux counterparts. They are characterized, nevertheless, by the requirement to load a Linux kernel and its designated root filesystem. How these are loaded and operated largely depends on the system's requirements and sometimes on the state of its development, as described earlier in "Types of Host/Target Development Setups."

There are three different setups used to bootstrap an embedded Linux system: the solid-state storage media setup, the disk setup, and the network setup. Each setup has its own typical configurations and uses. The following subsections will discuss each setup in detail.

In Chapter 9, we will discuss the setup and configuration of specific bootloaders for each applicable setup.

Solid-State Storage Media

In this setup, a solid-state storage device holds the initial bootloader, its configuration parameters, the kernel, and the *root* filesystem. Although the development of an embedded Linux system may use other boot setups, depending on the development stage, most production systems contain a solid-state storage media to hold all the system's components. Figure 2-5 shows the most common layout of a solid-state storage device with all the system components.

No memory addresses are shown in Figure 2-5, because the ranges vary greatly. Intuitively, you may think that addresses are lower on the left and grow toward the right. However, there are cases where it is the inverse, and the bootloader is at the top of the storage device address range instead of the bottom. For this reason, many flash devices are provided in both top- and bottom-boot configurations. Depending on the configuration, the flash region where the bootloader is found often has special protection mechanisms to avoid damage to the bootloader if a memory write goes astray. In top-boot flash devices, this protected region is located at the top of the device's address range, whereas in bottom-boot flash devices, it is located in the bottom of the device's address range.

Although Figure 2-5 shows the storage device separated into four different parts, it may contain fewer parts. The boot parameters may be contained within the space reserved for the bootloader. The kernel may also be on the root filesystem (as is the case in popular devices, such as the OLPC "$100 laptop," which uses an OpenFirmware filesystem-aware bootloader). This, however, requires that the bootloader be able to read the root filesystem. Also, the kernel and the root filesystem could be packaged as a single image that is uncompressed in RAM before being used (in fact, 2.6 Linux kernels make this process particularly easy, if desired).

Depending on the capabilities provided by your bootloader, there may even be other possible configurations, each with its advantages and disadvantages. Usually, a setup can be categorized along a set of four criteria: flash memory use, RAM use, ease of upgrading, and bootup time.

Boot storage media are initially programmed using a device programmer—for example, in mass-produced devices on a large yield production line—or the CPU's integrated debug capabilities, such as JTAG or BDM. Once the device is initially programmed, it can be reprogrammed by the system designer using the bootloader, if it provides this capability, or using Linux's MTD subsystem (MTD stands for "memory technology device"). The system may also contain software that enables the user to easily update the storage device. We will discuss the programming of solid-state storage media in Chapter 7.

Disk

This is the setup you are probably most familiar with because of its widespread use in workstations and servers. Here, the kernel and the root filesystem are located on a disk device. The initial bootloader (which is normally resource constrained; for example, PC-based systems require that it fit into a 512-byte "boot sector") either loads a larger and more powerful secondary bootloader from the disk or fetches the kernel itself directly from the disk. One of the filesystems on the disk is then used as the root filesystem.

During development, this setup is particularly attractive if you would like to have a large number of kernel and root filesystem configurations for testing. If you plan to develop your embedded system using a customized mainstream distribution, for instance, this setup is convenient. If you are using a hard disk or a device mimicking a hard disk, such as CompactFlash, in your production system, this boot setup is probably the best choice.

Because this is a well-known and well-documented scheme, we will discuss it only briefly in Chapter 9. You will be able to find a wealth of documentation on this process from various Linux vendors, as well as from online resources.

Network

In this setup, either the root filesystem or both the kernel and the root filesystem are loaded via a network link. In the first case, the kernel resides on solid-state storage media or a disk, and the root filesystem is mounted via NFS. In the second case, only the bootloader (perhaps a very minimal bootloader, with just enough support to load a kernel image over a local network connection) resides on a local storage media. The kernel is then downloaded via TFTP, and the root filesystem is mounted via NFS. To automate the location of the TFTP server, the bootloader may also use BOOTP/DHCP. In that case, the target does not need any preset IP addresses to find either the TFTP server or the NFS server.

This setup is ideal in early stages of development or during debugging because it enables the developer to share data and software rapidly between his workstation and the target without having to reprogram the target. Software updates can then be compiled on the host and tested immediately on the target. In contrast, few production systems use this setup, because it requires the presence of a server. In the case of the control systems described in Chapter 1, however, this setup actually can be used for some of the devices, because the SYSM module already provides network services.

Obviously, this setup involves configuring the server to provide the appropriate network services. We discuss the configuration of these network services in Chapter 9.

System Memory Layout

To best use the available resources, it is important to understand the system's memory layout, and the differences between the physical address space and the kernel's virtual address space.§ Most importantly, many hardware peripherals are accessible within the system's physical address space, but have restricted access or are completely "invisible" in the virtual address space.

To best illustrate the difference between virtual and physical address spaces, let's take a look at an example. The venerable HP iPAQ remains popular with some embedded Linux enthusiasts, and is now cheaply available on eBay. Since its memory layout is fairly typical of many devices available, we'll use it as an example in Figure 2-6.

The physical map of a system is usually available with the technical literature accompanying your hardware. In the case of the iPAQ, the *SA-1110 Developer's Manual* is available on Intel's website.

The physical map is important because it provides you with information on how to configure the kernel and how to develop custom drivers. During the kernel's configuration, for instance, you may need to specify the location of the flash devices in your

---

§ What we call here a "virtual address" is known in x86 jargon as a "logical address" and can have other names on other architectures.

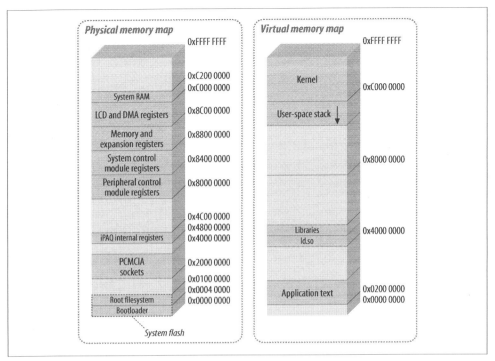

Figure 2-6. Physical and virtual memory maps for the Compaq iPAQ

system. During development, you may also need to write a driver for a memory-mapped peripheral. You will also need to provide your bootloader with information regarding the components it has to load. For these reasons, it is good practice to take the time to establish your system's physical memory map before starting software development.

On the iPAQ, the flash storage is divided in two. The first part contains the bootloader and starts at the lowest memory address available. Given the bootloader's size, this region is rather small. The rest of the flash storage space is occupied by the system's root filesystem, which in the case of Familiar is a JFFS2 filesystem. In this case, the kernel is actually on the root filesystem. This is possible because the bootloader has enough understanding of JFFS2 to find the kernel on the filesystem.

Upon startup, the bootloader reads the kernel from the root filesystem into the system's RAM and jumps to the kernel's start routines. From there on, the rest of the system startup is carried out by Linux.

Once Linux is running,[||] the programs use virtual addresses. In contrast to the physical memory map, the layout of the virtual memory map is of secondary importance for kernel configuration or device driver development. For device driver development, for

---

[||] As mentioned near the beginning of this chapter, we assume you are using MMU-equipped hardware.

instance, it is sufficient to know that some information is located in kernel space and other information in user space, and that appropriate functions must be used to properly exchange data between the two.

The virtual memory layout is mostly important in helping you understand and debug your applications. As you can see in Figure 2-6, the kernel occupies a quarter of the virtual address space, starting from address 0xC0000000. This region is also known as "kernel space." The rest of the address space is occupied by application-specific text, data, and library mappings. This is also known as "user space." Whereas the kernel is always located above the 0xC0000000 mark for all applications, the applications' memory maps may differ even on the same system.

To reconstruct a process of the virtual memory map, you need to look at the *maps* file in the process's pid entry in the /proc filesystem. For more details on how to get this information, see *Understanding the Linux Kernel*.

## CHAPTER 3

Hardware Support

Having covered the basics of embedded Linux systems, including generic system architecture, we will now discuss the embedded hardware Linux supports. First, we'll cover the processor architectures Linux supports that are commonly used in embedded systems. Next, we will cover the various hardware components involved, such as buses, I/O, storage, general-purpose networking, industrial-grade networking, and system monitoring. Although we will include many different components, we have omitted those not typically used in embedded configurations.

Note that the following discussion will not attempt to analyze the pros and cons of one hardware component or another. Hardware development is moving forward far too quickly for us to be in the business of doing such things. Use this chapter, instead, as a starting point for your research in either identifying the components to include in your system or judging the amount of effort needed to get Linux to run on the hardware you have already chosen.

A Word of Caution on the Use of Proprietary Device Drivers

Please note that the following sections will not cover the software made available by the various hardware vendors to support their hardware (unless that software has been made available through the upstream open source community). We will cover only hardware supported by the open source and free software communities. Some vendors may provide closed-source drivers for their hardware. If you intend to use such hardware, keep in mind that you will have no support from the open source and free software development community, members of which can be very vocal in their dislike of proprietary drivers. You will have to refer to the component vendor directly for any problems related to or caused by their closed-source drivers. Open source and free software developers have repeatedly refused to help anyone that has problems when using closed-source drivers, so please do not be under any false expectation that your case will be handled any differently.

Processor Architectures

Linux runs on a large and ever-growing number of machine architectures, but not all these architectures are actually used in embedded configurations, as already mentioned. A quick look at the *arch* subdirectory of the Linux kernel sources shows 24 architectures supported in the official kernel at the time of this writing, with others maintained by developers in separate development trees, possibly making it into a future release of the official kernel. Of those 24 architectures, we will cover 8 that are used in embedded Linux systems (in alphabetical order): ARM, AVR32, Intel x86, M32R, MIPS, Motorola 68000, PowerPC, and Super-H. The following discussion will look at each of these architectures in terms of the support provided by Linux to the CPUs belonging to that architecture and the boards built around those CPUs. It will also cover the intricacies of Linux's support as well as some of the possible caveats.

MMU-Less Linux Systems Running uClinux

In addition to the eight architectures mentioned previously, Linux also runs on uClinux-based systems—such as those based on the Blackfin from Analog Devices—and the Microblaze soft-synthesizable IP core from Xilinx used in a growing number of newer FPGA-based devices running Linux. These systems don't feature a traditional MMU (memory management unit), a defining characteristic of modern Unix-like systems and the hardware support for the operating system concept of virtual memory abstraction. These processors are typically intended as an alternative to older 8-bit microcontrollers in low-cost devices where cost sensitivity or FPGA fabric gate utilization still precludes use of a processor with an MMU. uClinux-based systems have included commercial printing solutions, home entertainment devices, and the original iPodLinux port. (Modern iPhones and iPods are based around more powerful ARM processors that include a full MMU and so eventually will be able to run the official Linux kernel, once the port is complete.) uClinux is feature complete and is supported in the official Linux kernel.

We will not cover the MMU-less architectures supported by uClinux in this chapter (even though such support has now been integrated into the official 2.6 series Linux kernel) because this book is primarily concerned with 32-bit (and higher) systems featuring a full MMU, but also because more and more processors that you are likely to encounter are now able to have an MMU. Few new architectures are being seriously considered that don't provide at least a basic MMU (and many are also now beginning to feature complete virtualization technologies—even in the embedded space). The bottom line: if you are interested in learning more about uClinux, we suggest that you first read this section, and then investigate one of the texts available on that subject, or consult *http://www.uclinux.org*.

ARM

ARM, which stands for Advanced RISC Machine, is a family of processors maintained and promoted by ARM Holdings Ltd. In contrast to other chip manufacturers such as IBM, Freescale, and Intel, ARM Holdings does not manufacture its own processors. Instead, it designs complete CPU cores for its customers based on the ARM core, charges customers licensing fees on the design, and lets them manufacture the chip wherever they see fit. This offers various advantages to the parties involved, but it does create a certain confusion to the developer approaching this architecture for the first time, as there is no central producer of ARM chips. There is, though, one unifying characteristic that is important to remember: all ARM processors share the same ARM instruction set, which makes all variants supporting a particular revision of the ARM instruction set fully software compatible.

This doesn't mean that all ARM CPUs and boards can be programmed and set up in the same way, only that the assembly language and resulting binary codes are identical for all ARM processors meeting a certain revision of the architecture. Revisions of the architecture in current use include ARMv4T (introduced the Thumb instruction set), ARMv5TE (the basis for "Xscale" parts), ARMv6 (TI-OMAP-based devices from Nokia, and the like, as well as the ARMv6KZ-based Apple iPhone), and ARMv7. Each of these architectural revisions enhances features within a "family" of ARM processors—ARM7TDMI, ARM9E, Xscale, ARM11, and so on. Naming gets slightly more complex in reality, because revisions of the architecture include letters or "flags" indicating adding features. For example, the ARMv4T introduced a condensed version of the instruction set ("Thumb") that aims to use less memory for instruction storage, while maintaining an adequate level of performance. There are also ARM processors with enhanced DSP performance ("E"), Java bytecode support ("J"), virtualization capabilities, and a growing number of other flags.

Currently, ARM CPUs are manufactured by Marvell (formerly Intel, under the "Xscale" brand), Toshiba, Samsung, and many others. The ARM architecture is very popular in many fields of application, from cell phones and PDAs to networking equipment, and there are hundreds of vendors providing products and services around it. It is highly likely that, as you read this, you are surrounded by devices featuring at least one (if not several) ARM cores.

At the time of this writing, Linux supports 40 distinct ARM CPUs, and a total of 1,832 different machine types. Given the quantity and variety of information involved, as well as the pace with which ARM Linux is developing, we refer you to the complete and up-to-date list of ARM systems supported and their details at *http://www.arm.linux.org.uk/ developer/machines*. Suffice it to say that Linux supports most mainstream CPUs and boards, such as the Texas Instruments OMAP CPUs used by Nokia in its well-known Linux Internet Tablets, and the IXP network processors used in many different networking devices. In case you need it, there is a way to add support for new hardware, although it is highly likely that support for your development reference board is already in the ARM Linux tree. Generally, for any information regarding the Linux ARM port, consult the project's website at *http://www.arm.linux.org.uk*.

For information regarding the ARM architecture itself and its instruction set, consult the *ARM Architecture Reference Manual* edited by David Seal (Addison-Wesley), and Steve Furber's *ARM System-on-Chip Architecture* (Addison-Wesley), as well as the materials available on the ARM website at *http://www.arm.com*.

AVR32

AVR32 is a newcomer to the industry (2006). It is a 32-bit microprocessor architecture designed by the Atmel corporation, which also produces the AVR 8-bit microcontroller devices used in deeply embedded situations. Although AVR32 and AVR are similar in name, they are unrelated except for sharing the same original design center. AVR32 comprises several subarchitectures and can additionally support the usual DSP and Java acceleration instructions one has come to expect from recent embedded processors. AVR32 provides for several modes of CPU operation; both fixed width 16-bit instructions and "extended" 32-bit instructions are supported. In some ways, the condensed format 16-bit width instructions are similar in purpose to the ARM Thumb instruction set mentioned in the previous section. Both processors compress instruction memory usage without losing the benefit of being a 32-bit device, although it has been suggested that AVR32 is actually more efficient in terms of code density (memory footprint used by code, etc.) and overall performance. AVR32 is exclusively used in Atmel's own products at the time of this writing.

The initial port of Linux to AVR32 was announced in a posting to the Linux Kernel Mailing List in early 2006. At the time of this writing, a single machine type (at32ap) is supported in the official Linux kernel, as well as several development boards. For more information about AVR32 Linux, refer to the website at *http://avr32linux.org*, as well as the community-maintained *http://www.avrfreaks.net*.

Intel x86

The x86 family starts with the 386 introduced by Intel in 1985 and goes on to include all the descendants of this processor, including the 486, the Pentium family, the Net-Burst (P6), Xeon, Core, and Core 2, along with compatible processors by other vendors such as National Semiconductor and AMD (which first popularized the *x86_64* 64-bit extensions of the x86 over Intel's redesigned Itanium, often simply called the "Itanic" by Linux developers for its lack of widespread adoption outside of a few niche markets). Intel remains, though, the main reference in regards to the x86 family and is still the largest distributor of processors of this family. Lately, a new trend is to group traditional PC functionality with a CPU core from one of the 386 family processors to form a System-on-Chip (SoC). AMD Geode family, which AMD bought from National Semiconductor, is a prime example of this trend; it is used in the OLPC's first generation XO laptop. There are many more SoCs on the market.

Although x86 is the most popular and most publicized platform to run Linux, it represents a small fraction of the traditional embedded systems market. In most cases, designers prefer ARM, MIPS, and PowerPC processors to i386 for reasons of complexity, power utilization (though this is changing), and overall cost.

That said, i386 remains the most widely used and tested Linux platform. Thus, it profits from the largest base of software available for Linux. Many applications and add-ons start their lives on the i386 before being ported to the other architectures supported by Linux. The kernel itself was in fact written for the i386 first before being ported to any other architecture. After many years of high-profile resistance from Linus Torvalds, the x86 architecture also finally has its own built-in debugger within the official Linux kernel, as opposed to the debugger being an intrusive add-on.

Since most, if not all, i386 embedded systems are very similar, or identical to the workstation and server counterparts in terms of functionality and programmability, the kernel makes little or no difference between the various x86 CPUs and related boards. When needed, a few `#ifdef` statements are used to accommodate the peculiarities of a certain CPU or board, but these are rare.

One exception to this is Voyager support. Voyager is a long defunct platform that ordinarily would have also long since ceased to be supported by mainstream Linux, were it not for the efforts of one man. James Bottomley (Linux SCSI maintainer and Voyager enthusiast) continues to keep this venerable platform alive. He even rewrote various parts of the low-level x86 architectural support code to handle Voyager's various oddities. Never say that Linux kernel engineers aren't enthusiastic, determined, or a even a little quirky from time to time.

The i386-based PC architecture is the most widely documented architecture around. There are several books and online documents in many languages discussing the intricacies of this architecture, in addition to the documents available from the various processor vendors, some of which are very complete. To get an idea of the scope of the existing documentation, try searching for "pc architecture" in the book section of Amazon.com.

It would be hard to recommend a single source of information regarding the i386 and PC architecture. *Intel Architecture Software Developer's Manual, Volume 1: Basic Architecture*, *Volume 2: Instruction Set Reference*, and *Volume 3: System Programming Guide*, published by Intel, are traditional sources of information about how to program the i386s and are quite rich, albeit limited to Intel's products. The availability of these documents may vary. At some point, hardcopies were not available from Intel's literature center. During that time, however, the documents were available in PDF format online. At the time of this writing, the manuals are available in electronic PDF downloadable form from Intel's literature center.

M32R

M32R is another recent (2003) 32-bit microprocessor architecture, designed by Renesas Technology and implemented both in silicon and as an FPGA synthesized soft-logic core. Unlike many other FPGA-based systems running Linux, the M32R actually implements a full MMU and can therefore run a stock Linux kernel without using uClinux's user space utilities. M32R has been used in a variety of applications, ranging from consumer electronics devices such as PDAs, cameras, and the like to engine control units. The Linux port supports nearly a dozen platforms based upon M32R.

For further information about the port, refer to the website at *http://www.linux-m32r.org*.

MIPS

MIPS is the brain child of John Hennessey—mostly known by computer science students all over the world for his books on computer architecture written with David Patterson—and is the result of the Stanford *Microprocessor without Interlocked Pipeline Stages* project (MIPS). MIPS is famed for once having been the basis of the workstations and servers sold by SGI and of gaming consoles such as Nintendo's 64-bit (N64) system and the Sony Playstations 1 and 2. It was also used in the Series 2 TiVo and in countless other consumer electronics devices. The company steering this processor, MIPS Technologies Inc., licenses CPU cores to third parties much like ARM. Unlike ARM, however, there are in fact many instruction set implementations, which differ from each other to various degrees. 32-bit MIPS implementations are available from manufacturers such as IDT, Toshiba, RMI (Alchemy), NXP (formerly Philips), and LSI. 64-bit implementations are available from IDT, LSI, NEC, NXP (formerly Philips), Broadcom, and Toshiba. There is also a growing market for synthesizable MIPS IP cores for use in soft-logic FPGA devices, and the like. Just as with ARM, we can only touch the surface of what is available based upon MIPS.

The initial port of Linux to MIPS was mainly done to support MIPS-based workstations, although these are now largely defunct (there aren't any MIPS workstations being made any more). Eventually, the port also came to include development boards and embedded systems that were based on MIPS. To accommodate the various CPUs and systems built around them, the layout of the MIPS portion of the kernel is divided into directories based on the type of system the kernel will run on. Similarly, kernel configuration for a given MIPS system is mainly influenced by the type of board being used. The actual type of MIPS chip on the board is much less important than the type of environment in which it is placed (the specifics of the board itself).

Support for Linux on MIPS is more limited than for other architectures such as the Intel x86 or the PowerPC. In fact, few of the main distributions have actually been ported to MIPS. When available, commercial vendor support for MIPS is mostly limited to embedded architectures. Nevertheless, there is a Debian port to both big- and little-endian MIPS, several community embedded distributions can target MIPS, and embedded Linux vendors such as MontaVista actively support MIPS, too. Also, many PDA and development board manufacturers actively support Linux ports on their own MIPS-based hardware. As with some other ports, MIPS lacks a few of the things you might have come to expect from using a desktop Linux environment on an Intel-like x86 system, but it is sufficient for many embedded Linux needs.

For more information regarding the MIPS port of Linux in general, take a look at the official home of the Linux MIPS port at *http://www.linux-mips.org*. The website contains a list of supported systems, documentation, links, and other useful resources. Because MIPS is divided into multiple platforms, you will need to refer to the data provided by your system's manufacturer to evaluate or implement Linux support. One general resource that is recommended on MIPS Technologies Inc.'s own website is *See MIPS Run* by Dominic Sweetman (Morgan Kaufmann Publishers). You can also get PDFs on MIPS's website. MIPS provides 32- and 64-bit editions of its *MIPS Architecture for Programmers* three-volume series, made up of *Volume I: Introduction to the MIPS Architecture*, *Volume II: The MIPS Instruction Set*, and *Volume III: The MIPS Privileged Resource Architecture*.

Motorola 68000

The Motorola 68000 family is known in Linux jargon as m68k. The MMU-equipped varieties have been supported under Linux for quite some time, and the MMU-less varieties have been supported starting with the 2.6 kernel.

m68k came in second only to the Intel x86 as a popular 1980s architecture. Apart from being used in many mainstream systems by Atari, Apple, and Amiga, and in popular workstation systems by HP, Sun, and Apollo, the m68k was also a platform of choice for embedded systems development. Recently, though, interest has drifted away from the m68k to newer architectures, such as ARM, MIPS, SH, and PowerPC, for embedded systems design. Nonetheless, from time to time new boards appear that are based upon this venerable architecture.

Linux supports many systems based on m68k, starting with the mainstream and workstation systems already mentioned and including VME systems from Motorola and BVM. Because these systems are completely different, the kernel tree is built to accommodate the variations and facilitate the addition of other m68k-based systems. Each system has its own set of specific modules to interface with the hardware. An example of this is the interrupt vector tables and related handling functions. Each system has a different way of dealing with these, and the kernel source reflects this difference by having a different set of functions to deal with interrupt setup and handling for each type of system.

Since the MMU versions of m68k are seldom used nowadays in new, cutting-edge designs, they lag behind in terms of software support. There is, for instance, no real Java support (but this may change due to the open sourcing of Sun's Java Virtual

Machine), nor is the processor architecture listed among supported architectures for some other user-level applications. For up-to-date information regarding the port, the supported hardware, and related resources, refer to the m68k Linux port home page at *http://www.linux-m68k.org*. One distribution that has done a lot work for m68k is Debian, so check out its documentation and mailing lists if you plan to deploy an m68k Linux system.

Since there is no standard m68k-based platform such as the PC for the Intel x86, there is no single reference covering all m68k-based systems. There are, however, many textbooks and online resources that discuss the traditional use of the m68k and its programming. Motorola provides the *68000 Family Programmer's Reference Manual* and the *M68000 8-/16-/32-Bit Microprocessors User's Manual* free through its literature center. Other, more elaborate, texts that include examples and applications can be found by searching for "68000" on any online bookstore.

PowerPC

PowerPC (PPC) architecture was the result of a collaboration between Apple, IBM, and Motorola (now Freescale)—the "AIM alliance." It inherited ideas from work done by the three firms, especially IBM's Performance Optimization With Enhanced RISC (POWER) architecture, which still exists and is heavily used as a 64-bit workhorse in IBM's many server offerings. PowerPC is mostly known for its original use in Apple's Macs, but there are other PowerPC-based workstations from IBM and other vendors, as well as many PowerPC-based embedded systems. The popular TiVo system, for instance, was based on an embedded PowerPC processor, for which TiVo actually did the original work required to get Linux running on such PowerPC variants. This was not a trivial task, since the embedded variants can be quite different at the OS level—including a replacement of the regular virtual memory implementation with a special soft-programmable one that requires the kernel to do much more work.

Along with i386 and ARM, the PowerPC is the best supported architecture in Linux, which is partly evident from the large number of PPC CPUs and systems on which Linux runs. Although it is clear that PowerPC Linux has benefited from some big players being behind it, it has also been successful because of a small but very dedicated number of core PowerPC developers. Several of these (for example, Benjamin Herrenschmidt) work for IBM. But others, notably Tom Rini and Matt Porter (along with others from Embedded Alley) got into PowerPC as a sideline, personal interest and wound up working at embedded Linux companies like MontaVista. Obviously, no description of PowerPC Linux support would be complete without mentioning its maintainer, Paul Mackerras, who originally started the "pmac" (Powermac, i.e. Apple) development back in the last century and who now maintains overall coordination of Linux PowerPC development, both 32- and 64-bit.

Thanks in part to sponsorship, bounties, and other, related development efforts of IBM (and other players), a great number of applications that run on the Intel x86 are available for PowerPC, including Java. The PPC Linux community is active in many areas of development ranging from workstation to embedded systems. The main PPC Linux site is *http://penguinppc.org*. Community members maintain it; is not affiliated with any particular vendor. It contains valuable documentation and links and should be considered the starting point for any Linux development on PPC.

A number of distributions support PowerPC, some exclusively. Yellow Dog Linux, for example, provides Linux only for PowerPC machines. There are also traditional mainstream distributions that provide support for PowerPC as part of their support for other architectures. These include Debian, OpenSuSE, Fedora, and Ubuntu. Note that PowerPC is often considered a "secondary" (community-maintained) architecture.

If you intend to use PowerPC in your embedded application and want to be in touch with other folks using this architecture in their systems, be sure to subscribe to the very active *linuxppc-embedded* list. Most problems are recurring, so there is probably someone on that list who has had your problem before. If not, many people will be interested in seeing your problem solved, as they may encounter it, too. The list is hosted on linuxppc.org, which also hosts many other PPC-related lists.

SuperH

In an effort to enhance its 8- and 16-bit H8 line of microcontrollers, Hitachi introduced the SuperH (SH) line of processors in the early 1990s. These manipulate 32-bit data internally and offer various external bus widths. Later, Hitachi formed SuperH Inc. (now Renesas Technology) with STMicroelectronics (formerly SGS-Thomson Microelectronics). Renesas licenses and steers development of the SuperH much the same way ARM Holdings Ltd. does for ARM and MIPS Technologies Inc. does for MIPS. The early implementations of the SuperH, such as the SH-1, SH-2, and their variants, did not have an MMU. Starting with the SH-3, however, all SuperH processors include an MMU. The SuperH is used within Hitachi's own products, in many consumer-oriented embedded systems such as PDAs, and in some older game consoles, too.

Because the early SuperH (SH) processors did not include MMUs, Linux does not support them. Currently, Linux supports some SH-3, SH-4, and SH-5 systems, but not all, because these chips have many variations with various capabilities. Support for the SuperH outside the kernel is rather limited for the moment. There is no support for Java, for instance. The architecture does have a kernel debugger. A few distributions provide SH support, such as MontaVista and Debian, whereas others such as Fedora have been recompiled successfully by community developers from time to time, but not on a permanent basis. A complete list of all supported versions of SuperH, along with links to distributions and the like, is available on the Linux SuperH community maintained website at *http://www.linux-sh.org*.

As there is no standard SH architecture, you will need to refer to your hardware's documentation for details about the layout and functionality of the specific hardware devices available in any reference board design. There are, nonetheless, manuals that describe the operations and instruction sets of the various processors.

Buses and Interfaces

The buses and interfaces are the fabric that connects the CPU to the peripherals on the system. Each bus and interface has its own intricacies, and the level of support Linux provides them varies accordingly. A rundown follows of some of the many different buses and interfaces found in typical embedded systems, and the level of support Linux provides them. Linux supports many other buses, and we couldn't hope to cover all of them in the space of just one chapter. Some of these other buses are used in older systems, are workstation- or server-centric, or are just a little too quirky to go into here. In addition, some buses are proprietary to a specific system vendor, or are not yet heavily adopted. We won't discuss buses that lack widespread adoption, nor will we cover so-called third generation buses such as HyperTransport in any detail, since they are usually used only semitransparently as a CPU-level root bus. But we will mention InfiniBand (and the OpenIB stack in particular).

If you're designing a new embedded system from scratch, you might have no enumerable, higher-level bus structure for certain devices. Instead, these may sit solely within the CPU's memory map as memory-mapped devices. Linux provides explicit support for just this kind of embedded situation, through the use of "platform devices." This abstraction allows the kernel to support devices that it cannot simply enumerate when it scans the available bus topology during bootup. Such devices are detected either through the use of special platform-specific code or may be mentioned in the system bootloader/kernel interface—for example, the flattened device tree passed between the bootloader and the kernel on PowerPC platforms.

For additional information about buses and device support, refer to *Linux Device Drivers* by Jonathan Corbet et al. (O'Reilly).

PCI/PCI-X/PCIe

The Peripheral Component Interconnect (PCI) bus, managed by the PCI Special Interest Group (PCI-SIG), is the most popular bus currently available. Designed as a replacement for the legacy Intel PC ISA bus, PCI is now available in two forms: the traditional parallel slot form factor using 120 (32-bit PCI) or 184 (64-bit PCI-X) I/O lines, and the newer (and also potentially much faster) PCI Express (commonly called PCIe or PCI-E) packet-switched serial implementation as used in most recent designs. Whether conventional PCI, 64-bit PCI-X, or serial PCI-Express, PCI remains software compatible between the different implementations, because the physical interconnect used underneath is generally abstracted by the standard itself. Linux support is very good indeed, but for those times when special support quirks are needed, Linux offers PCI "quirks" too.

PCI requires software support in order for it to be used by device drivers. The first part of this support is required to initialize and configure the PCI devices upon bootup (called PCI enumeration). On PC systems, this is traditionally done by the BIOS, and if the BIOS has carried out the initialization, the kernel will browse the BIOS's table to retrieve the PCI information. However, the kernel is capable of carrying out the initialization and configuration itself. In both cases, the kernel provides an API to device drivers, so they can access information regarding the devices on the PCI bus and act on these devices. There are also a number of user tools for manipulating PCI devices (for example, *lspci* lists all PCI buses and devices). In short, the level of support for PCI in Linux is fairly complete and mature.

Linux Device Drivers provides very good insight into PCI development in Linux and how the PCI bus operates in general. *PCI System Architecture* by Tom Shanely and Don Anderson (Addison-Wesley) gives in-depth information on the PCI bus for software developers. Of course, you can always get the official PCI specification from the PCI-SIG. Official specifications, however, tend to make very dry reading material. Finally, there is the Linux PCI-HOWTO, available from the Linux Documentation Project (LDP) at *http://www.tldp.org*, which discusses the caveats of using certain PCI devices with Linux and the support Linux provides to PCI devices in general.

ExpressCard (Replaces PCMCIA's PC Card)

Modern laptop and embedded devices replace the legacy PC Card first standardized by the Personal Computer Memory Card International Association (PCMCIA) with a higher speed standard based upon more recent technology, known as ExpressCard. Like the PC Card before it, ExpressCard is intended to allow for easy addition of internal peripheral devices to embedded devices in situations where, perhaps, using another bus such as USB is not desirable or practical. This can be true for laptops, where a given device should be added permanently without needing to constantly attach and detach it as the laptop is used or put away for safe storage. Unlike PC Card (which is based around its own unique bus design), ExpressCard simply provides both PCI-Express and USB 2.0 through a convenient interface card format. ExpressCard supports two form factors: ExpressCard/34 (34 mm wide) and ExpressCard/54 (54 mm wide, supports also the ExpressCard/34). Both are used depending upon device application requirements.

Since ExpressCard is functionally an implementation of both the PCI-Express and USB 2.0 standards (themselves well supported by Linux), ExpressCard already has good Linux support, and a growing number of systems are beginning to deploy it. Of course, at the same time, the legacy PCMCIA PC Card interface, which provides a modified form of 32-bit, 33 MHz PCI known as CardBus, continues to be used in some designs. Linux support for CardBus is (and has been for a long time) extremely good, in spite of the standard's various quirks and complexities. The Linux PCMCIA and hotplug mechanisms underwent a complete overhaul during the development of the 2.6 series

Linux kernel, and they continue to evolve. Still, we hope your designs won't need to make use of legacy PCMCIA.

There is extensive documentation available concerning the use and implementation of PCMCIA in the 2.6 series Linux kernel at *http://kernel.org/pub/linux/utils/kernel/ pcmcia/pcmcia.html*. For more modern ExpressCard systems, your first point of call as far as Linux is concerned should be the reference documentation on USB 2.0 or PCI-Express, depending upon which ExpressCard devices you plan to use.

PC/104, PC/104-Plus, PCI-104, and PCI/104-Express

Although many embedded devices today make use of regular desktop and server buses such as PCI and PCI Express, certain applications demand that they be hosted in a more robust form. This is the *raison d'etre* for the PC/104 embedded computer standard. PC/ 104 defines a form factor for stackable computer processor boards (and other boards) and serves a similar purpose in the space of industrial-grade computing to that of the ATX (and its variants) in the consumer and enterprise computing environment. In addition to being a different size, PC/104 systems have differing electrical and me-chanical tolerances intended to enhance extensibility and increase ruggedness. There are several forms of PC/104 depending upon whether a PCI or PCI-Express bus is provided for use by other components within the stack. These forms of the standard are commonly known as PCI/104 and PCI/104-Express, and are managed by the PC/ 104 Consortium. The original plain PCI/104 and PCI/104-Plus are seldom seen in new designs, because they rely upon the long since defunct ISA bus used in the original Intel PC.

Since the PCI/104 and PCI/104-Express standards both implement standard Linux-supported buses such as PCI and PCI-Express, devices built using the PC/104 form factor are supported by Linux. This does not, of course, mean that a given device will have a driver available, nor does it mean that you may not encounter problems, only that the potential for good support of your hardware is in place so long as the other necessary driver components are available.

CompactPCI/CompactPCIe

The CompactPCI specification was initiated by Ziatech and developed by members of the PCI Industrial Computer Manufacturer's Group (PICMG), which oversees the specification and promotes the use of CompactPCI. The CompactPCI specification provides an open and versatile platform for high-performance, high-availability applications. Its success is largely based on the technical choices its designers made. First, they chose to reuse the Eurocard form-factor popularized by older standards, such as VME. Second, they chose to make the bus PCI-compatible, hence enabling CompactPCI board manufacturers to reuse low-cost PCI chips already available in the mainstream market.

Technically, the CompactPCI bus is electrically identical to the PCI bus. Instead of using slot connections, as found in most workstations and servers, pin connectors are used to connect the vertically loaded CompactPCI boards to the CompactPCI backplane. As with PCI, CompactPCI requires a single bus master.* Consequently, CompactPCI requires the permanent presence of a board in the system slot. It is this board that arbitrates the CompactPCI backplane, just as a PCI chipset arbitrates a PCI bus in a workstation or a server.

In addition, the CompactPCI specification allows for the implementation of the *hot swap* specification, which describes methods and procedures for runtime insertion and removal of CompactPCI boards. This specification defines three levels of hot swapping. Each level implies a set of hardware and software capabilities. Here are the available levels and their requirements:

Basic hot swap

> This hot swap level involves console intervention by the system operator. When a new card is inserted, she must manually inform the OS to power it up and then configure and inform the software of its presence. To remove a card, she must tell the OS that the board is about to be removed. The OS must then stop the tasks that are interacting with the board and inform the board to shut down.

Full hot swap

> In contrast to basic hot swap, full hot swap does not require console intervention by the operator. Instead, the operator flips a microswitch attached to the card injector/ejector to notify the OS of the impending removal. The OS then performs the necessary operations to isolate the board and tell it to shut down. Finally, the OS lights an LED to notify the operator that the board can now be removed. On insertion, the OS receives an insertion signal and carries out the inverse operations.

---

* The term "bus master" can mean different things in different contexts. In this particular instance, "bus master" designates the device that sets up and configures the PCI bus. There can be only one such device on a PCI bus, though more than one may actually be able to access the memory regions exported by other PCI devices.

High availability

In this level, CompactPCI boards are under complete software control. A hot swap controller software manages the state of all the boards in the system and can selectively reverse these individual boards according to the system's state. If a board fails, for example, the controller can shut it down and power up a duplicate board that is present within the same chassis for this very purpose. This hot swap level is called "high availability," because it is mostly useful in what are known as high-availability applications,[†] such as telecommunications, where downtime must be minimal.

In addition to the regular CompactPCI standard, which is widely used, an ongoing standardization effort is leading up to the adoption of CompactPCIe, a PCI-Express variant of CompactPCI. CompactPCIe provides many of the same features as CompactPCI, including hot swap and high availability, while also offering increased throughput and other benefits of the more modern PCI-Express.

Linux accommodates various levels of the CompactPCI standard, including hotplugging, depending upon which tools are installed on your target embedded device. Several of the embedded Linux vendors have also developed enhancements (especially via the Carrier Grade Linux specification efforts) that allow for more complete control over the high availability aspects of CompactPCI. Further information about the Carrier Grade Linux specification and the level to which a given distribution supports the standard is available at *http://www.linuxfoundation.org/en/Carrier_Grade_Linux*.

SCSI/iSCSI

Shugart Associates introduced the Small Computer Systems Interface (SCSI), which eventually evolved into a series of standards developed and maintained by a series of standard bodies, including ANSI, ITIC, NCITS, and T10. Although mainly thought of as a high-throughput interface for hard drives for high-end workstations and servers, SCSI is a both a general software interface and a set of electrical specifications that can be used to connect various hardware peripherals. Only a small segment of embedded systems ever use SCSI devices, though. These systems are typically high-end embedded systems, such as ones providing an interface into NAS (network attached storage), and usually implement iSCSI, where the SCSI protocol is used over regular TCP/IP rather than as a traditional electrical bus within a machine.

Linux support for SCSI is extensive and well maintained, while iSCSI support varies depending upon whether you wish to implement an initiator (client), target (device), or both. Discussion of the kernel's SCSI device drivers architecture can be found on the

---

[†] To avoid any confusion, we will refer to this hot swap level as "high availability hot swap level" and will continue to use the "high-availability" adjective to refer to applications and systems that need to provide a high level of availability, regardless of whether they use CompactPCI or implement the "high availability hot swap level."

Linux SCSI mailing list (*linux-scsi*) at *http://vger.kernel.org*. The Open-iSCSI project provides a full implementation of an iSCSI Initiator for modern Linux kernels at *http://www.open-iscsi.org*. For iSCSI Target support, several open source projects are under development, as well as at least one proprietary implementation. You would be well advised to refer to the Open-iSCSI project as a starting point when implementing a Linux iSCSI target.

USB

The Universal Serial Bus (USB) was developed and is maintained by a group of companies that form the USB Implementers Forum (USB-IF). Initially developed to replace such fragmented and slow connection interfaces as the parallel and serial ports traditionally used to connect peripherals to PCs, USB has rapidly established itself as the interface of choice for peripherals, because of its low cost, ease of use, and high-speed throughput. Although mostly a mainstream device-oriented bus, USB is increasingly appearing in hardware used in embedded systems, such as SBCs and SoCs from several manufacturers, especially now that the USB On-The-Go (OTG) chipsets featuring both client and device side support in a single chipset are available to system manufacturers.

USB devices are connected in a tree-like fashion. The root is called the *root hub* and is usually the main board to which all USB devices and nonroot hubs are connected. The root hub is in charge of all the devices connected to it, directly or through secondary hubs. A limitation of this is that computers cannot be linked in any form of networking using direct USB cabling.‡

Support within Linux for USB devices is very good, especially as a result of the ongoing efforts of developers such as Greg Kroah-Hartman (Greg K-H) who is trying to actively engage device vendors in supporting as many devices as possible. As with other hardware components, many Linux drivers have instead been developed in spite of their manufacturers' unwillingness to provide the relevant specifications. The main component of Linux's USB support is provided by the USB stack in the kernel. The kernel also includes drivers for the USB devices supported by Linux. User tools are available to manage USB devices and they, along with a complete list of supported devices, are available through the Linux USB project website at *http://www.linux-usb.org*.

Linux Device Drivers provides guidelines on how to write Linux USB drivers. There are a number of books that discuss USB, which you can find at the various online bookstores. However, the consensus among developers and online book critics seems to indicate that the best place to start, as well as the best reference, is the original USB specification available online from the USB-IF.

---

‡ Some manufacturers actually provide a form of host-to-host link via USB, but the standard was not intended to accommodate this type of setup. There are also USB network adapters, including Ethernet adapters, that can be used to connect the computers to a common network.

IEEE1394 (FireWire)

FireWire is a trademark owned by Apple for a technology they designed in the late 1980s and early 1990s. They later submitted their work to the IEEE and it formed the basis of what eventually became IEEE standard 1394. Much like USB, IEEE1394 enables devices to be connected using simple and inexpensive hardware interfaces. Because of their similarities, IEEE1394 and USB often used to be considered together, although it seems that USB has won the popularity contest over time, perhaps also due to the licensing terms involved in using Firewire. Even Apple is now shipping systems without Firewire support, in favor of using high-speed USB 2.0 instead.

In contrast to USB, IEEE1394 connections do not require a root node. Rather, connections can be made either in a daisy-chain fashion or using an IEEE1394 hub. Also, unlike SCSI, connections do not need any termination. It is also possible to connect two or more computers directly using an IEEE1394 link, which isn't really possible with USB. To take advantage of this capability, there is even an Internet RFC (Request For Comment, a form of Internet "standard") specifying how to implement IP over IEEE1394.

Linux's support for IEEE1394 used to be buggy and was certainly incomplete in comparison with other operating systems. IEEE1394 support was completely rewritten in the 2.6 series Linux kernel and is now widely considered to be very good. For further information, visit *http://www.linux1394.org*.

InfiniBand

InfiniBand is a high-performance switched fabric interface created as a result of merging two competing designs: Future I/O (HP, and IBM) and Next Generation I/O (Intel, Microsoft, and Sun). It is built upon a number (ranging from 1–12 or more) of high-speed, point-to-point and bidirectional serial links, and in some ways is similar to other newer buses such as PCI Express. Maximum data throughput ranges from 2 Gigabits to 96 Gigabits for a 12X (12 bonded serial links) Quad Data Rate (QDR) configuration. Two of InfiniBand's main selling points are its very low end-to-end latency (around 1 microsecond) and its support for performance enhancing optimizations such as RDMA (Remote DMA). These features have encouraged InifiniBand adoption for high-performance computing, especially in supercomputers.

Linux support for InfiniBand comes thanks to Open Fabrics Alliance (OFA), an industry consortium created to address the lack of a standard InfiniBand API. OFA maintains the OpenIB InfiniBand Driver Stack that is shipped with a growing number of Linux distributions. Visit *http://www.openfabrics.org* for more information.

GPIB

The General-Purpose Interface Bus (GPIB) has its roots in HP's HP-IB bus, which was born at the end of the 1960s and is still being used in engineering and scientific applications. In the process of maturing, GPIB became the IEEE488 standard and was revised as late as 1992. Many devices that are used for data acquisition and analysis are, in fact, equipped with a GPIB interface. With the advent of mainstream hardware in this field of application, many GPIB hardware adapters have been made available for such hardware and for PCs in particular.

GPIB devices are connected together using a shielded cable that may have stackable connectors at both ends. Connectors are "stackable" in the sense that a connector on one end of a cable has the appropriate hardware interface to allow for another connector to be attached to it, which itself allows another connector to be attached. If, for instance, a cable is used to connect a computer to device *A*, the connector attached to *A* can be used to attach the connector of another cable going from *A* to device *B*.

Linux support for GPIB is available thanks to the Linux GPIB kernel driver and library maintained at *http://linux-gpib.sourceforge.net*. The maintainer has stated that he doesn't currently have any plans to add new features beyond ensuring that the existing library continues to build and run against recent kernels. The package currently provides kernel drivers, a user space library compatible with National Instrument's own GPIB library, and language bindings for Perl and Python. The package supports hardware from HP, Keithley, National Instruments, and other manufacturers. The complete list of supported hardware is included in the *devices.txt* file found in the package's sources and on the project's website.

I²C

Initially introduced by Philips (now NXP) to enable communication between components inside TV sets, the Inter-Integrated Circuit (I²C) bus can be found in many embedded devices of all sizes and purposes. As with other similar small-scale buses such as SPI and MicroWire, I²C is a simple serial bus that enables the exchange of limited amounts of data among the IC components of an embedded system. There is a broad range of I²C-capable devices on the market, including LCD drivers, EEPROMs, and DSPs. Because of its simplicity and its hardware requirements, I²C can be implemented in both software and hardware.

Connecting devices using I²C requires only two wires, the serial clock line (SCL) with the clock signal and the serial data line (SDA) with the data. All devices on an I²C bus are connected using the same wire pair. The device initiating a transaction on the bus becomes the bus master and communicates with slaves using an addressing scheme. Although I²C supports multiple masters, most implementations have only one master.

The main kernel tree includes support for I²C, a number of devices that use I²C, and the related System Management Bus (SMBus). Due to the heavy use of I²C by hardware monitoring sensor devices, the I²C support pages are hosted on the Linux hardware monitoring project website at *http://www2.lm-sensors.org*. The site includes a number of links, documentation, and the most recent I²C development code. Most importantly, it contains a list of the I²C devices supported, along with the appropriate driver to use for each device.

Apart from the documentation included with the kernel about I²C and the links and documentation available on the hardware sensors website, information regarding the bus and related specification can be obtained from Philips's website at *http://www.nxp.com/products/interface_control/i2c*.

I/O

Input and output (I/O) are central to the role of any computerized device. As with other OSes, Linux supports a wide range of I/O devices. The following does not pretend to be a complete run-down of all of them. For such a compilation, you may want to read through the Hardware Compatibility HOWTO available from LDP. Instead, this section will concentrate on the way the different types of I/O devices are supported by Linux, either by the kernel or by user applications.

Some of the I/O devices discussed are supported in two forms by the kernel, first by a native driver that handles the device's direct connection to the system, and second through the USB layer to which the device may be attached. There are, for instance, PS/2 keyboards and (older) parallel port printers along with USB keyboards and USB printers. Because USB has already been discussed earlier, and an in-depth discussion of Linux's USB stack would require a lengthy text of its own, we will cover only the support Linux provides to the devices directly attached to the system. Note, however, that USB drivers for similar devices tend to rely on the infrastructure already available in Linux to support the native devices. A USB serial adapter driver, for example, relies on the same facilities as the traditional serial driver, in addition to the USB stack.

Serial Port

The serial port is arguably every embedded system developer's best friend (or her worst enemy, depending on her past experience with this ubiquitous interface). Many embedded systems are developed and debugged using an RS232 serial link between the host and the target. Sometimes, PCBs are laid out to accommodate a serial port, but only development versions of the boards ever include the actual connector, while production systems are shipped without it. The simplicity of the RS232 interface has encouraged its widespread use and adoption, even though its bandwidth is rather limited compared to other means of transmission. Note that there are other serial interfaces besides RS232, some of which are less noise-sensitive and therefore more adapted to industrial environments. The hardware serial protocol, however, isn't as important as the actual programming interface provided by the serial device's hardware.

Since RS232 is a hardware interface, the kernel doesn't need to support RS232 itself. Rather, the kernel includes drivers to the chips that actually enact RS232 communication, Universal Asynchronous Receiver-Transmitters (UARTs). UARTs vary from one architecture to another, although some UARTs, such as the 16550(A), are used on more than one architecture.

The main serial (UART) driver in the kernel is *drivers/char/serial.c*. Some architectures, such as the SuperH, have other serial drivers to accommodate their hardware. Some architecture-independent peripheral cards also provide serial interfaces. Nonetheless, serial devices in Linux are uniformly accessed as terminal devices, as in Unix systems, regardless of the underlying hardware and related drivers. The corresponding device entries start with */dev/ttyS0* and can go up to */dev/ttyS191*. In most cases, however, there is only a handful of serial device entries in a system's */dev* directory.

Serial port basics, setup, and configuration are discussed in the Serial HOWTO available from the LDP. Programming the serial port in Linux is discussed in the Serial Programming HOWTO from the LDP. Since serial port programming is actually terminal programming, any good reference on Unix systems programming would be a good start. Worthy of note is Richard Stevens and Stephen Rago's *Advanced Programming in the UNIX Environment* (Addison-Wesley), which is one of the most widely recognized works on the subject of Unix systems programming, including terminal I/O.

Parallel Port

In comparison to the serial port, the parallel port is seldom an important part of an embedded system. Unless the embedded system is actually a PC-style SBC, the parallel port is, in fact, rarely even part of the system's hardware. In some cases, it is used because the embedded system has to drive a printer or some sort of external device, but with the widespread adoption of USB and IEEE1394, this need has almost completely disappeared.

One area of embedded systems development where the parallel port fits quite nicely, however, is simple multibit I/O. When debugging, for instance, you can easily attach a set of LEDs to the parallel port's pins and use those LEDs to indicate a position in the code. The trick is to insert a set of parallel port output commands in different portions of the code and to use the LEDs to identify the last position reached prior to machine lockup. This is possible because the parallel port's hardware keeps the last value output to it unchanged regardless of the state of the rest of the system. *Linux Device Drivers* provides a more detailed description of how to use the parallel port as a simple I/O interface.

Modem

Embedded systems that use a modem to call a data center are quite common. Alarm systems, bank machines, and remote-monitoring hardware are all examples of embedded systems that need to communicate with a central system to fulfill their primary purposes. The goals are different, but many of these systems still use conventional modems to interface with the POTS (plain old telephone system) to access a remote host. Of course, there are higher speed devices with greater bandwidth available, but since modems work in a wide variety of environments—including very remote locations that don't have the latest cellular or computer networks—don't count them out any time soon.

Modems in Linux are seen as serial ports, which is very much the same way they are seen across a variety of operating systems, including Unix. As such, they are accessible through the appropriate */dev* serial device entry and are controlled by the same driver as the native serial UARTs, regardless of whether they are internal or external. This support, however, applies only to real modems.

Many newer "modem" devices are actually very low-cost circuits containing little more technology than the most basic sound card. These so called WinModems contain only the bare minimal hardware that make up a modem, and they are capable of providing real modem services only because of software that runs on the operating system. As the name implies, these modems are mainly targeted to systems running Windows. They work fine with that operating system, because their vendors provide the appropriate drivers. With Linux, however, they do not always work, because they don't contain real modem hardware and the kernel can't use its serial driver to operate them without additional support.

To provide support for these types of (handicapped) devices, a number of projects have sprung up to develop the necessary software packages. A central authority on these projects is the Linmodems website at *http://www.linmodems.org*. The site provides documentation, news, and links to the various WinModem support projects. At the time of this writing, however, there is no body of code that provides uniform support for the various WinModems.

Real modem setup and operation are described in the Modem HOWTO from the LDP. Linmodem setup and operation are described in the Linmodem HOWTO from the LDP. Since modems are serial ports, the documentation previously mentioned for serial ports also applies to modems.

Data Acquisition

Data acquisition (DAQ) is at the basis of any process automation system. Any modern factory or scientific lab is filled with DAQ equipment linked, in one way or another, to computers running data analysis software. Typically, as described earlier, the events occurring in the real world are measured by means of transducers, which convert a physical phenomenon into an electrical value. These values are then sampled using DAQ hardware and are thereafter accessible to software.

There is no standard interface in Unix, or any other operating system for that matter, for interfacing with data acquisition hardware.[§] Comedi, the Linux control and measurement device interface, is the main package for interfacing with DAQ hardware. Comedi is found at *http://www.comedi.org* and contains device drivers for a great number of DAQ boards. The complete list of boards supported is found in the *Supported hardware* section of the website.

Along with providing drivers for DAQ hardware, the Comedi project includes Comedilib, a user space library that provides a unified API to interface with all DAQ hardware, regardless of model or manufacturer. This is very useful, because it allows you to develop the analysis software independently of the underlying hardware and avoid being locked in to a particular vendor.

Similarly, Kcomedilib, a kernel module providing an API similar to Comedilib, provides access to the DAQ hardware to other kernel modules, which could be real-time tasks.

No discussion about DAQ would be complete without covering some of the most well-known commercial (proprietary) packages used along with it, such as LabVIEW, Matlab, and Simulink. Given the popularity of Linux in this field, their respective vendors have made all three packages available for Linux. Note, however, that a number of packages are in development that aim to provide open source replacements for these packages. Scilab and Octave, for instance, are Matlab replacements found at *http://www.scilab*.org and *http://www.octave.org*, respectively.

Documentation regarding the installation and configuration of Comedi can be found on the project's website along with examples. The site also includes a number of useful links to other Linux DAQ-related sites. Documentation regarding the closed-source packages can be found on their vendors' websites.

Although we haven't covered them, some DAQ hardware vendors do provide drivers for their hardware, either in open source form or under a proprietary license. When evaluating whether to use such drivers, it is important to ponder future vendor support so that you don't find yourself trapped with dead and unmaintained code. Even when source is available under an open source or free software license, be sure to evaluate its quality to ensure that you can actually maintain it if the vendor decides to drop its support.

[§] DAQ hardware may actually take a number of forms. It can be an Ethernet-enabled device or PCI card, or use some other type of connection. However, most DAQ devices used with workstations connect through some standard interface such as ISA, PCI, or PCMCIA.

Keyboard

Most embedded systems are not equipped with keyboards. Some may have a limited input interface, but keyboards are usually considered a luxury found only on traditional workstation and server configurations. In fact, the idea that an embedded system may have a keyboard would be viewed as awkward by most traditional embedded system designers. Nonetheless, recent breeds of web-enabled and consumer-oriented embedded systems have some form of keyboard attached to them (or perhaps a Bluetooth-based cordless keyboard for entering data, surfing the web, and similar purposes).

As with other Unix-like systems, communication with the user in Linux is done by means of a terminal, in the Unix tty sense, where a keyboard is used for input and a console for output. (This description is, of course, a simplification of the very complex world of Unix terminal I/O, but it will suffice for the current discussion.) Hence, all keyboard input is considered by the kernel as input to a terminal. The conversion from the actual data inputted by the user to terminal input seen by the operating system may involve many different layers of kernel drivers, but all keyboard input is eventually fed to the terminal I/O driver.

There are other ways to provide input to a terminal, apart from the use of a physically connected keyboard. Terminal input is also possible through remote login, serial-linking between computers, and—in the case of PDAs and Tablets—handwriting recognition software or the dasher predictive text graphical input utility, optimized for use by those with all manners of disabilities. In each case, program access to character input requires terminal I/O programming.

Mouse

Embedded systems that have a user interface often offer some form of touch-based interaction. Whether it be a bank terminal or a PDA, the input generated by the user's touch of a screen area is treated the same way as input from a conventional workstation mouse. In this sense, many embedded systems have a "mouse." In fact, there are many more embedded systems that provide a mouse-like pointer interface than there are that provide a keyboard interface.

Since traditional Unix terminals do not account for mouse input, information about the pointer device's input doesn't follow the same path as data about keyboard activity. Instead, the pointer device is seen on most Linux systems via the Input events layer located under */dev/input*. There are several different files within */dev/input* from which one can determine current state, including */dev/input/mice*. The device can be polled and read to obtain information regarding the pointer device's movements and events. Any programming that involves a pointer device would require an understanding of the protocol used by the device. Fortunately, a number of libraries and environments already implement this level of decoding, and easy-to-use APIs are provided to obtain and react to pointer input.

Display

Blinking lights, LEDs, and alphanumeric LCDs are the traditional visual apparel of embedded systems. With the growing incursion of embedded devices into many facets of our daily lives, including service automation, there is a push to replace such traditional display methods with visually rich interfaces. In other areas of embedded systems deployment, such as factory automation, avionics, PDAs, and Web Tablets, visually rich interfaces have been the norm for quite a while. With a visually rich environment comes the (not unreasonable) user expectation that the device also be easier to use, and have a range of graphical tools for configuration.

As mentioned earlier, traditional Unix systems provide output through terminal consoles. These are great if you're living in the 1970s on a slow modem connection to a central Unix server sitting some hundreds or even thousands of miles away from the phosphorous green display in your darkened room, but not so useful if you're interested in creating the next multimillion user Web Tablet, cell phone, or many other kinds of modern embedded Linux device. The standards behind Unix terminals have been updated as recently as 1998 (still a decade ago, but surprisingly recent) but few modern users are comfortable using a Unix terminal from the days of yore. Besides, such interfaces are too rudimentary for today's demands. If nothing else, consoles can output only text, and even there can struggle with internationalization. Other more elaborate interfaces are needed when building graphic interfaces, which may include some form of windowing system.

With Linux there are many ways to control and program a display. Some of these involve kernel support, but most rely mainly on code running in user space, which enhances system stability and facilitates modularity. The most common way to provide a graphical interface with Linux is, of course, the X Window System, but there are other packages that may be preferable in certain circumstances. The X Window System provides only the basic graphical windowing environment, not the higher level libraries and applications needed to create a visually rich user experience. For these, you will want to look to the GNOME and QT projects that run on X, and embedded enviornments built upon their respective GUIs (QTopia, Maemo, etc.). Several popular embedded Linux devices have implemented their own UI from scratch, but we don't recommend that you (needlessly) reinvent the wheel.

To find out more about the current state of the art in Linux graphics and windowing systems, visit the Free Desktop Project at *http://www.freedesktop.org*.

Sound

Beep, Beep, Beep...that's what Sputnik emitted and that's pretty similar to what many embedded systems still sound like. Even the very graphic-rich avionics and factory automation systems don't have more sound output, except maybe in terms of decibel level.

Sound-rich embedded systems are, however, becoming more and more popular with the proliferation of consumer- and service-oriented devices. Consumer-oriented devices feature complex audio and video codec support—including MP3, Ogg Vorbis, AAC, MPEG, MPEG4, and H264—and demand good support for audio. Good support means the capability to multiplex multiple audio streams out to the same device simultaneously, real-time performance free from substantive (and highly annoying) jitter, and other requirements.

Unix, however, was never designed to accommodate sound. Over the years, a number of schemes appeared to provide support for sound devices. These include the legacy Open Sound System (OSS) and the Advanced Linux Sound Architecture (ALSA) that has replaced it. In addition, various other projects provide *sound servers*: software that conceptually sits above the device interface and supports multiplexing, remote audio, and other fancy capabilities that aren't really the domain of the sound device driver itself. Two popular sound server daemons in use today are PulseAudio (PA), which is used on Fedora, and JACK, which is enjoyed by many high-end audio enthusiasts, especially in combination with the real-time patches that we will discuss later in this book. These higher level audio services either have their own API or (much more likely) support the standard ALSA API either directly, or through the use of a software wrapper. In the case of PulseAudio, once you have the PA libraries installed in place of the stock ALSA user libraries, applications will automatically use PA instead of ALSA, without any need to modify the application source code.

For further information about Linux audio, refer to the ALSA project website at *http:// www.alsa-project.org*, as well as the websites for specific sound daemons that you are looking at, such as PulseAudio and JACK.

Printer

As with many mainstream peripherals, printers don't usually grace embedded systems. There are, however, exceptions. An embedded web server that supports printing is an example of an embedded system that needs an operating system with printer support. Traditional embedded system developers would usually consider "embedded web server" to be an oxymoron, but devices that provide these types of packaged services are more and more common and involve development methods similar to those of more constrained embedded devices. In addition, home routers, office print servers, and even PDAs these days require some capability to talk to a remote printer, even if they don't directly support attaching a regular printer to a port on the embedded device itself.

Conventional Unix printer support is rather outdated in comparison to the support provided by many other operating systems. This also used to be largely true of Linux (one of the authors recalls many hours as a teenager spent configuring LPD and APS MagicFilter to print Postscript) but fortunately, a lot has changed since. These days, most Linux systems handle device configuration, printer management, and actual printing itself through Common Unix Printing System (CUPS), the same printing service Apple uses in its various shiny laptops and gadgets. CUPS is an extremely flexible, modern alternative to the ancient Unix *lpd* printer daemon. You can find out more about CUPS at the CUPS project website at *http://www.cups.org*, whereas more generic Linux printing issues and most of your documentation needs are addressed at the Linux Printing website, *http://www.linuxprinting.org*. Unless, of course, you want to dig out a copy of MagicFilter and while away the evening.

Storage

All embedded systems require at least one form of persistent storage to start even the earliest stages of the boot process. Most systems, including embedded Linux systems, continue to use this same initial storage device for the rest of their operation, either to execute code or to access data. In comparison to traditional embedded software, however, Linux's use imposes greater requirements on the embedded system's storage hardware, both in terms of size and organization.

The size requirements for embedded Linux were discussed in Chapter 1, and an overview of the typical storage device configurations in Chapter 2. We will discuss the actual organization further in Chapters 7 and 8. For the moment, let's take a look at the persistent storage devices supported by Linux. In particular, we'll discuss the level of support provided for these devices and their typical use with Linux.

Memory Technology Devices

In Linux terminology, memory technology devices (MTDs) include memory devices such as conventional ROM as well as modern NOR/NAND flash parts. Such devices have their own capabilities, particularities, and limitations. For example, although some flash parts can be directly memory mapped (NOR flash and ROM devices), they still use special out-of-band mechanisms to handle rewriting and other actions. In the case of NAND flash, there is no direct memory mapping, and the Linux kernel must use bounce buffers (copy data from the flash into RAM) before it is able to access the data contained within the flash. Hence, to program and use an MTD device in their systems, embedded system developers traditionally have had to use tools and methods specific to that type of device.

To avoid, as much as possible, having different tools for different technologies and to provide common capabilities among the various technologies, the Linux kernel includes the MTD subsystem. This provides a unified and uniform layer that enables a seamless combination of low-level MTD chip drivers with higher-level interfaces called *user modules*. These user modules should not be confused with kernel modules or any sort of user space software abstraction. The term "MTD user module" refers to software modules within the kernel that enable access to the low-level MTD chip drivers by providing recognizable interfaces and abstractions to the higher levels of the kernel or, in some cases, to user space.

In Chapter 7, we will continue our discussion of the MTD subsystem and will detail the setup and configuration instructions for using MTD devices in your embedded system.

PATA, SATA, and ATAPI (IDE)

The AT Attachment (ATA)[||] was developed in 1986 by three companies: Imprimis, Western Digital, and Compaq. It was initially used only by Compaq but eventually became quite popular when Conner Peripherals began providing its IDE drives through retail stores. By 1994, ATA was an ANSI standard. Different versions of the standard have since been developed allowing faster transfer rates and enhanced capabilities. Along the way, the ATA Packet Interface (ATAPI) was developed by CD-ROM manufacturers with the help of Western Digital and Oak Technology. ATAPI allows access to CD-ROM and tape devices through the ATA interface using SCSI-like command packets. ATA exists in both parallel (PATA) and serial (SATA) forms. Today, a growing number of systems use the newer, serial-based, SATA interface that supersedes (parallel) ATA.

In embedded Linux systems, IDE and most other types of disks are usually set up as in a workstation or server. Typically, the disk holds the operating system bootloader, the root filesystem, and possibly a swap partition. In contrast to most workstations and servers, however, not all embedded system monitors and bootloaders are ATA-capable. In fact, as we'll see in Chapter 9, most bootloaders are not ATA/IDE-capable. If you want to use an IDE disk in your system and an ATA-capable monitor or bootloader is not present in your system's flash, you need to have the kernel present in flash or in ROM with the boot monitor so that it may be accessible at system startup. You then have to configure your boot monitor to use this kernel on startup in order to have access to the IDE disk. In this case, you can still configure your root filesystem and swap partition to be on the IDE disk.

Linux's support for the both the legacy PATA and newer SATA interfaces is quite extensive and mature. You are extremely unlikely to encounter fundamental problems in getting a hard disk to work with Linux—but you might want to visit the Linux ATA website anyway at *http://linux-ata.org*.

Non-MTD Flash-Based devices

In addition to the MTD flash-based devices we have previously discussed, a growing number of embedded systems are making use of flash memory sticks, cards, and other external peripherals that happen to contain flash memory but provide an alternative interface to that flash. Examples of such devices include CompactFlash, Secure Digital (SD, a replacement for older MMC), and all the popular USB sticks of various shapes,

---

[||] Although it is often referred to as "IDE," which stands for Integrated Drive Electronics, "ATA" is the real name of this interface.

sizes, and even colors. These flash devices all share one thing: they all come in a pre-packaged form factor and are presented as a disk device upon which sits a regular (FAT16 or FAT32) filesystem.

Linux support for these add-on flash devices is very good, and the kernel, for example, has built-in generic USB storage drivers for this purpose.

General-Purpose Networking

An increasing number of embedded systems is attached to general-purpose networks. These devices, although more constrained than other computerized systems in many ways, are often expected to provide the very same network services found in many modern servers. Fortunately, Linux lends itself quite well to general-purpose networks, since it is often used in mainstream servers.

The following discussion will cover the networking hardware most commonly found in embedded systems. Linux supports a much wider range than we will discuss, but many of these networking interfaces are not typically used in embedded systems and are therefore omitted. Also, as many of these networking interfaces have been extensively covered elsewhere, we will limit the discussion to the topics relevant to embedded Linux systems and will refer you to other sources for further information.

Network services will be discussed further in Chapter 10.

Ethernet

Initially developed at Xerox's PARC research center in Palo Alto, California, Ethernet is currently the most pervasive, best documented, and least expensive type of networking available. Its speed has kept up with the competition, growing geometrically over the decades. Given Ethernet's popularity and the increasing demand for embedded systems to be network enabled, many embedded development boards and production systems have been shipping with Ethernet hardware.

Linux supports a slew of 10 and 100 Megabit Ethernet devices and chips. It also supports a few Gigabit and even 10 Gigabit Ethernet devices. The kernel build configuration menu is probably the best place to start to see whether your particular hardware is supported, as it contains the latest drivers list.# At this point, there is almost certainly good Linux support for almost any network device you may be considering.

IrDA

The Infrared Data Association (IrDA) was established in 1993 by 50 companies with the mandate to create and promote a standard for low-cost, interoperable, infrared data

---

You may also want to use this list as the basis of your hardware design, as suggested earlier.

interconnections. The first IrDA specification was released in 1994 and continues to be maintained and developed by the association from which the specification takes its name. Today, IrDA hardware and software can still be found in certain consumer devices, although they have been largely displaced by other wireless communications such as WiFi (IEEE802.11) and Bluetooth.

There are two main types of protocols within the IrDA specification: mandatory and optional. A device must at least implement the mandatory protocols in order to be able to interoperate properly with other IrDA devices. The mandatory protocols are the physical signaling layer (IrPHY), the link access protocol (IrLAP), and the link management protocol (IrLMP). The last protocol also includes the Information Access Service (IAS), which provides service discovery capabilities.

IrDA devices can exchange data at rates of up to 4 Mbps within a one meter range. Unlike other wireless technologies, IrDA requires the devices involved in a communication to be directionally aligned (e.g., pointing a remote control device directly at the target). An obvious advantage of such a scheme is the increased security resulting from the requirement that IrDA users keep their devices pointing in each other's direction during the whole connection time: any intruder would have to be in direct view of the users involved in the communication.

Linux supports all the mandatory IrDA protocols and many of the optional protocols. In conjunction with the stack layers, you will need user space tools to operate Linux's IrDA capabilities. These tools are part of the IrDA Utils package, which is available, along with many other IrDA-related resources, from the Linux-IrDA project website at *http://irda.sourceforge.net*.

IEEE 802.11A/B/G/N (Wireless)

The 802.11 working group was set up by the IEEE 802 committee in 1990. The first 802.11 standard was published in 1997 and has been maintained and updated since then by the same group. The standard provides for wireless communication between computers using the 2.4 GHz (802.11b) and 5 GHz (802.11a) frequencies. Today, 802.11 (commonly refered to as "WiFi") is the wireless equivalent of Ethernet in terms of widespread adoption and mainstream support. It comes in the backward-compatible higher speed "G" form running at 54 Mbps (as opposed to the original 11 Mbps of 802.11B) and the new "N" form that can run up to 248 Mbps. Everything from PDAs, cell phones, and cameras to industrial automation, vehicles, and more use WiFi technology extensively to connect to the outside world.

Linux has strong support for 802.11B, G, and N hardware, as well as the various encryption standards used: WEP, WPA, and WPA2 are all well supported. And although WiFi network configuration in Linux is similar to configuring any other network device, additional graphical configuration tools such as the GNOME Project's NetworkManager help to make life much easier. It is also worth noting that the entire Linux softmac stack was rewritten during the course of series 2.6 to make it much easier to support the latest chipsets.

Bluetooth

Bluetooth was developed by Ericsson with help from Intel and was introduced in 1994. Ericsson, IBM, Intel, Nokia, and Toshiba formed a Bluetooth SIG. Today, the SIG has thousands of member companies, and a wide range of devices, such as PDAs and cell phones, are already Bluetooth-enabled with many more on the way.

Bluetooth operates on the 2.4 GHz band and uses spread spectrum frequency hopping to provide wireless connectivity to devices within the same *piconet*.* Some have called it a "cable replacement" and others have called it "wireless USB." In essence, it enables seamless wireless communication between devices. Hence, Bluetooth devices do not need any configuration to become part of a piconet. Rather, devices automatically detect each other and advertise their services so that the other devices in the piconet can in turn use these services.

The main Linux Bluetooth stack (the one present in the mainstream kernel source) is BlueZ. BlueZ was originally written by Qualcomm and is now an open source project available under the terms of the GPL from the project's website at *http://bluez.source forge.net*. The various BlueZ utilities are shipped in most Linux distributions, complete with graphical configuration tools, and the like.

Industrial-Grade Networking

As with other computerized applications, industrial control and automation rely increasingly on computerized networks. General-purpose networking or connectivity solutions such as regular Ethernet are, however, ill-adapted to the harsh and demanding environment (both electrically and otherwise) of industrial applications. Common Ethernet, for instance, is too vulnerable to EMI (electromagnetic interference) and RFI (radio frequency interference) to be used in many industrial environments with high reliability. This doesn't mean that Ethernet isn't being used in the form of "Industrial Ethernet," but because it was never designed for such uses, many manufacturers still choose to use one of the other available industrial networks instead.

Therefore, quite a few specialized, industrial-grade networking solutions have been developed over the years. In addition to being more adapted to industrial environments, these industrial networks, commonly known as *fieldbuses*, help reduce wiring, increase modularity, provide diagnostics capabilities, enable self-configuration, and facilitate the setup of enterprise-wide information systems.

---

* Piconets are wireless networks comprising Bluetooth devices. Since Bluetooth devices can belong to more than one piconet, piconets can overlap.

In the following sections, we will cover several industrial networks supported by Linux.

CAN

The Controller Area Network (CAN) is not only the most common fieldbus, but probably one of the most pervasive forms of networking ever used. CAN was introduced in 1986 by Robert Bosch GmbH. as a serial bus system for the automotive industry and has since been put to use in many other industries. CAN's development received early contributions from engineers at Mercedes-Benz and Intel, which provided the first CAN chip, the 82526. Today, more than 100 million new CAN devices are sold every year. Application fields range from middle- to upper-class cars (allowing for the many different systems within the car to communicate effectively, and for diagnostics), to factory automation networks.

CAN specifies a hardware interface and a communication mechanism. It is a multi-master serial networking protocol with error detection capabilities, where message identification is done through content rather than through identification of the receiver node or the transmitter node. The CAN in Automation (CiA) group manages and promotes CAN, which is subject to ISO standard 11898 published in 1993. It has been supported in the official Linux kernel starting with release 2.6.25, which as of this writing is a current release.

Since CAN is a low-level protocol, akin to Ethernet, many higher-level protocols have been put forward to complete it, including protocols such as J1939, DeviceNet, Smart Distributed System (SDS), and CANopen. J1939 was introduced and continues to be maintained by the Society of Automotive Engineers (SAE) and is very popular in the automotive industry, especially in diesel-powered applications. DeviceNet is another popular CAN-based higher-level protocol and is managed by the Open DeviceNet Vendor Association (ODVA). SDS was put forth by Honeywell and continues to be promoted and managed by the same company. CANopen was introduced and is managed by the same group that maintains CAN, the CiA. SDS has not been as popular as DeviceNet and J1939, because it was never standardized, while J1939, DeviceNet, and CANopen were.

For more information on CAN, CAN-related hardware, and CANopen, consult the CiA's website at *http://www.can-cia.org*. For more information about Linux kernel support of CAN, consult the documentation within the kernel itself.

Modbus

The Modbus Protocol was introduced by Modicon in 1978 as a simple way to transfer control data between controllers and sensors using RS232 in a master-slave fashion. Modicon was later acquired by Schneider Electric, which owns the Modbus trademark and continues to steer the development of the protocol and its descendants.

Since Modbus specifies a messaging structure, it is independent of the underlying physical layer. There are two formats used to transmit information with Modbus: ASCII and RTU. The first sends each byte as two ASCII characters, whereas the second sends each byte as two 4-bit hexadecimal characters. Modbus is usually implemented on top of a serial interface such as RS232, RS422, or RS485. In addition to Modbus, Schneider specifies the Modbus TCP/IP protocol, which uses TCP/IP and Ethernet to transmit Modbus messages.

Three open source projects provide Modbus capabilities to Linux:

jModbus

> This project aims to provide a Java implementation of Modbus RTU, Modbus ASCII, and Modbus TCP/IP. It resides at *http://jmodbus.sourceforge.net* and is distributed with documentation and examples under a BSD-style license.

libmodbus

> This is an active, up-to-date project that develops a C-based shared library for use in applications. Several existing projects use it, and it has the usual array of online Bazaar-based source versioning† and the like. It is licensed under version 3.0 of the GPL and is available at *http://copyleft.free.fr/wordpress/index.php/libmodbus*.

MAT LinuxPLC

> This is the same automation project mentioned earlier in "I/O." The MAT project now contains code implementing Modbus RTU and Modbus TCP/IP in its CVS repository. Although the source code is commented, there is little other documentation.

For more information about Modbus, read the Modbus specifications, available at *http://www.modbus.org*.

System Monitoring

Both hardware and software are prone to failure, sometimes drastically. Although the occurrence of failures can be reduced through careful design and runtime testing, they are sometimes unavoidable. It is the task of the embedded system designer to plan for such a possibility and to provide means of recovery. Often, failure detection and recovery is done by means of system monitoring hardware and software such as *watchdogs*.

Linux supports two types of system monitoring facilities: watchdog timers and hardware health monitoring. There are both hardware and software implementations of watchdog timers, whereas health monitors always require appropriate hardware. Watchdog timers depend on periodic reinitialization so as not to reboot the system. If the system hangs, the timer eventually expires and causes a reboot. Hardware health

---

† Bazaar is a software configuration management tool originally used by the Ubuntu project, an implementation and a fork of GNU Arch.

monitors provide information regarding the system's physical state. This information can in turn be used to carry out appropriate actions to signal or solve actual physical problems such as overheating or voltage irregularities.

The Linux kernel includes drivers for many watchdog timers. The complete list of supported watchdog devices can be found in the kernel build configuration menu in the Watchdog Cards submenu. The list includes drivers for watchdog timer peripheral cards, a software watchdog, and drivers for watchdog timers found in some CPUs such as the MachZ and the SuperH. Although you may want to use the software watchdog to avoid the cost of a real hardware watchdog, note that the software watchdog may fail to reboot the system in some circumstances. Timer watchdogs are seen as */dev/watchdog* in Linux and have to be written to periodically to avoid system reboot. This updating task is traditionally carried out by the watchdog daemon available from *ftp://metalab.unc.edu/pub/linux/system/daemons/watchdog*. In an actual embedded system, however, you may want to have the main application carry out the update instead of using the watchdog daemon, since the latter may have no way of knowing whether the main application has stopped functioning properly.

Finally, Linux supports quite a few hardware monitoring devices through the "Hardware Monitoring by lm_sensors" project found at *http://www.lm-sensors.org*. The project's website contains a complete list of supported devices along with extensive documentation on the installation and operation of the software. The lm_sensors package available from the project's website includes both device drivers and user-level utilities to interface with the drivers. These utilities include *sensord*, a daemon that can log sensor values and alert the system through the ALERT syslog level when an alarm condition occurs. The site also provides links to external projects and resources related to lm_sensors.

CHAPTER 4
Development Tools

Embedded system developers, like other software developers, need compilers, linkers, interpreters, integrated development environments (IDEs), and other such tools. The embedded developer's tools are different, however, in that they typically run on one platform while building applications for another. This is why these tools are often called *cross-platform development tools*, or *cross-development tools* for short.

Importance of a Dedicated Toolchain for Embedded Development

Even if you happen to be using the same architecture on both the development workstation and target board (such as x86 or x86_64), we still recommend using a different toolchain from the native one that comes with the Linux distribution you happen to be running on the development workstation. It is valuable to create a separate toolchain, thus providing a controlled development environment isolated from the workstation environment.

If you don't create a separate toolchain for the target, opting instead to use the native workstation toolchain, you might find your embedded application broken in subtle (and sometime not so subtle) ways by any future upgrade of the workstation software.

Furthermore, you'll be prohibited from rebuilding the toolchain with various certain configuration choices that could result in tools that are better optimized for use in embedded environments, such as an alternative C library.

It is therefore highly recommended that you use a custom cross-platform toolchain for building Linux embedded systems, even if the workstation architecture happens to match that of the target.

There are two ways to acquire the tools for embedded development: download the source code freely available on the Internet and build them yourself, or get binary versions compiled by another person, company, or project.

As mentioned in "Reasons for Choosing Linux in Chapter 1, several commercial vendors distribute integrated embedded Linux packages, including development environments. Two such offerings are MontaVista DevRocket and Wind River WorkBench. Some hardware and board vendors provide free compiled toolchains together with their hardware offerings. In addition, several community projects provide compiled toolchains for download over the Web, such as the Denx ELDK package at *http://www.denx.de/wiki/DULG/ELDK*.

Typically, such offerings include a ready-to-use toolchain, an Eclipse-based IDE, and sometimes proprietary "added value" plug-ins that extend Eclipse abilities and integrate them with hardware debuggers that are part of the offerings. Eclipse-based tools may allow configuration of the *root* filesystem and kernel within the Eclipse IDE, using a Java GUI that integrates well with the rest of the Eclipse IDE. This sample of enhancements gives you an idea of what prebuilt environments offer.

The value of an integrated, tested, and debugged toolchain and other development tools should not be taken lightly. Although all the development tools needed to build and develop for embedded Linux system are freely available, the tasks of integrating, building, and testing require time and come with a learning curve for the newly initiated embedded Linux developer. Thus, a prebuilt offering that fits your project's requirements can save time and help you and your team focus on their number-one priority: getting a successful product out the door.

As you might guess, however, using a prebuilt suite comes with the cost of locking you into the chosen suite. If you build the suite yourself—or at least understand what goes into the build process, which we will discuss in this chapter—you preserve your independence. An understanding of the process may let you have the best of both worlds: a ready-made and vendor-supported offering that saves time and manages risk, along with the ability to switch from one vendor to another or even migrate to a self-supported embedded Linux development environment.

This chapter, therefore, discusses the setup, configuration, and use of cross-platform development tools. First, we will suggest a layout for a practical project workspace. Then, we'll discuss the GNU cross-platform development toolchain, the C library alternatives, Java, Perl, Python, Ada, and other programming languages, IDEs, the GDB debugger, profilers, bounds checkers, terminal emulation programs, and system emulators.

Even if you opt to buy or download a ready-made toolchain, we recommend that you go through this chapter to get acquainted with the various terms and options involved in the process.

 Although debuggers, profilers, and bounds checkers may be be considered part of the development toolchain, these topics are large enough to deserve their own chapter, and therefore are covered in Chapter 11.

Throughout this chapter, we assume that you are using a Linux (or at least Unix-derived) development workstation. As previously mentioned in "Windows (Vista, XP, 2000, NT, 98, etc.) Workstation in Chapter 2, you run many of the procedures in this chapter to produce a working toolchain on the Windows platform as well, using the Cygwin compatibility library mentioned in Chapter 2. In addition, because Eclipse is a Java-based application, it can be deployed on a Windows platform just as easily as on Linux. It is worth noting, however, that some Cygwin-specific issues might complicate the effort of following this chapter's instructions, and so it is generally not recommended for developers taking their first steps with embedded Linux to use Cygwin.

A Practical Project Workspace

In the course of developing and customizing software for your target, you need to organize various software packages and project components in a comprehensive and easy-to-use directory structure. Table 4-1 shows a suggested directory layout that you may find useful. Of course, there is nothing special about the specific layout presented here and, in fact, some of the automated toolchain and *root* filesystem build tools we are about to describe use a different layout. Feel free to use whatever works for you. However, we will assume the layout shown in Table 4-1 in examples throughout the rest of this book.

 The directory layout presented here is aimed to host third-party packages you download from the Net as part of your project. We recommend highly that you separate your own code from the third-party code used to build the system, and we even go so far as to recommend that the two types of code reside in different source control modules. This will minimize any confusion regarding the source's ownership and licensing status and will make it easy to comply fully with the requirements of some of the open source packages we will use.

Table 4-1. Suggested project directory layout

Directory	Content
bootldr	The bootloader or bootloaders for your target
build-tools	The packages and directories needed to build the cross-platform development toolchain
debug	The debugging tools and all related packages
doc	All the documentation you will need for your project
images	The binary images of the bootloader, the kernel, and the *root* filesystem ready to be used on the target
kernel	The different kernel versions you are evaluating for your target
project	Your configuration files and settings for this project
rootfs	The *root* filesystem as seen by the target's kernel at runtime
sysapps	The system applications required for your target

Directory	Content
tmp	A temporary directory to experiment with and store transient files
tools	The complete cross-platform development toolchain and C library

Of course, each of these directories contains many subdirectories. We will populate the directories as we continue through the rest of the book.

The location of your project workspace is up to you, but we strongly encourage you *not* to use a system-wide entry such as */usr* or */usr/local*. Instead, assume as a general rule that the directory structure is being checked out of a source control system by each member of your development group into his own home directory.

 One common exception to this rule is the cross-platform development toolchain and related files, which some system builders prefer to keep in a system-wide (or even network-wide) location, as rebuilding them from source is time consuming.

Should you work on a project that supports multiple systems, create a separate directory layout for each component or board type.

For the example embedded control system, we will use the following layout:

```
$ ls -l ~/control-project
total 4
drwxr-xr-x   13 karim      karim           1024 Mar 28 22:38 control-module
drwxr-xr-x   13 karim      karim           1024 Mar 28 22:38 daq-module
drwxr-xr-x   13 karim      karim           1024 Mar 28 22:38 sysmgnt-module
drwxr-xr-x   13 karim      karim           1024 Mar 28 22:38 user-interface
```

Since they all run on different targets, each control system component has a separate entry in the *control-project* directory. Each entry has its own project workspace as described previously. Here is the *daq-module* workspace, for example:

```
$ ls -l ~/control-project/daq-module
total 11
drwxr-xr-x    2 karim      karim           1024 Mar 28 22:38 bootldr
drwxr-xr-x    2 karim      karim           1024 Mar 28 22:38 build-tools
drwxr-xr-x    2 karim      karim           1024 Mar 28 22:38 debug
drwxr-xr-x    2 karim      karim           1024 Mar 28 22:38 doc
drwxr-xr-x    2 karim      karim           1024 Mar 28 22:38 images
drwxr-xr-x    2 karim      karim           1024 Mar 28 22:38 kernel
drwxr-xr-x    2 karim      karim           1024 Mar 28 22:38 project
drwxr-xr-x    2 karim      karim           1024 Mar 28 22:38 rootfs
drwxr-xr-x    2 karim      karim           1024 Mar 28 22:38 sysapps
drwxr-xr-x    2 karim      karim           1024 Mar 28 22:38 tmp
drwxr-xr-x    2 karim      karim           1024 Mar 28 22:38 tools
```

Because you may need to provide the paths of these directories to some of the utilities you build and use, you may find it helpful to create a short script that sets appropriate environment variables. Here is such a script called *develdaq* for the DAQ module:

```
export PROJECT=daq-module
export PRJROOT=/home/karim/control-project/${PROJECT}
cd $PRJROOT
```

In addition to setting environment variables, this script moves you to the directory containing the project. You can remove the *cd* command if you would prefer not to be moved to the project directory right away. To execute this script in the current shell so that the environment variables are immediately visible, type:[*]

```
$ . develdaq
```

Future explanations will rely on the existence of the PROJECT and PRJROOT environment variables.

 Because the distribution on your workstation has already installed many of the same packages you will be building for your target, it is very important to clearly separate the two types of software. To ensure such separation, we strongly encourage you not to carry out any of the instructions provided in the rest of this book while logged in as root, unless we provide explicit instructions to the contrary. Among other things, logging in as an unprivileged user will avoid any possible destruction of the native GNU toolchain installed on your system and, most importantly, the C library most of your applications rely on. Therefore, instead of logging in as root, log in using a normal user account with no particular privileges.

GNU Cross-Platform Development Toolchain

A toolchain is a set of software tools needed to build computer software. Traditionally, these include a linker, assembler, archiver, C (and other languages) compiler, and the C library and headers. This last component, the C library and its headers, is a shared code library that acts as a wrapper around the raw Linux kernel API, and it is used by practically any application running in a Linux system.

Additional components in some toolchains include extra code libraries (such as the zlib library, which provides compression services) and more supplementary tools such as a debugger, profiler, and memory checker.

Last but not least, you might choose to work within an IDE that provides a frontend for these tools, although an IDE is not traditionally counted as part of the toolchain itself.

A cross-platform toolchain—or as it is commonly abbreviated, a *cross toolchain*—is built to run on one development platform (most commonly x86) but build programs that run on another platform, as is customary when developing for embedded systems.

---

[*] All commands used in this book assume the use of the *sh* or *bash* shell, because these are the shells most commonly used. If you use another shell, such as *csh*, you may need to modify some of the commands.

The cross toolchain we will discuss in this chapter includes the binary utilities, such as the *ld* linker, the *gas* assembler, gcc compilerthe *ar* archiver, the *gcc* compiler collection, and either glibc or an alternative C library.

In addition, we will touch upon acquiring and building the GDB source-level symbolic debugger, the Valgrind memory checker, and the Eclipse graphical integrated developer environment.

Most of the components of the toolchain are part of the GNU project and can be downloaded from the FSF's FTP site, either at *ftp://ftp.gnu.org/gnu* or any of its mirrors. The binutils package is in the *binutils* directory, the GCC package is in the *gcc* directory, and the glibc package is in the *glibc* directory. For any components we discuss in this chapter that are not part of the GNU project, we will describe their creators and how to obtain them.

Note that all the targets discussed in Chapter 3 are supported by the GNU toolchain.

Introduction to Building a GNU Toolchain

Configuring and building an appropriate GNU toolchain is a complex and delicate operation that requires a good understanding of the dependencies between the different software packages and their respective roles, the status of different software packages versions, and a lot of tedious work. The following section will provide a high-level walk-through of the various components, terms, and choices involved in creating a cross toolchain.

Terms and GNU configuration names

As our first step, we will introduce some terms describing the various systems that participate in building and using a cross toolchain:

build
> The build system is the one on which you build your toolchain.

host
> The host system is the one on which you host your toolchain.

target
> The target system is the one for which your cross toolchain will produce binaries.

For standard, nonembedded uses, all three are the same (although some people download binaries and don't care what the build system is). In most embedded scenarios, the build and the host will be the same machine—the workstation on which the developers work—whereas the target will be the embedded board for which you are developing an application.[†]

When you build software using the GNU configure and build system, as we do here for the various toolchain components, you specify the build, host, and target systems through names in GNU configuration files, which follow a standardized format:

```
cpu-manufacturer-kernel-os
```

The *kernel* component, being a later addition, is optional. In fact, triplets containing only the *cpu*, *manufacturer*, and *os* are still quite common. The various components specify:

cpu

> The system's chip architecture. Where both a big-endian and little-endian variant exists, it is customary to denote the little-endian variant by appending el to the architecture name.

manufacturer

> A specific maker or family of boards using the aforementioned CPU. As this rarely has any effect on the toolchain itself, it is not uncommon to specify an unknown machine type or simply to omit the machine description altogether.

kernel

> Used mainly for GNU/Linux systems, and even in that case it is sometimes omitted for brevity.

os

> The name of the operating system (or ABI) used on the system. Configuration names may be used to describe all sorts of systems, including embedded systems that do not run any operating system; in those cases, this field indicates the object file format, such as Elf or COFF.

Some examples of possible host, target, or build triplets follow:

i386-pc-linux-gnu

> A PC-style x86 Linux system

powerpc-8540-linux-gnu

> A Freescale 8540 PowerQuickIII Linux system

[†] It's so rare to use a different build system and host system that the situation has earned its own informal name: a "Canadian Cross" toolchain. A Canadian Cross build is most frequently used when building programs to run on a non-Unix system, such as DOS or Windows. It may be simpler to configure and build on a Unix system than to support the non-Unix system's configuration machinery. The unusual name springs from the historical coincidence that Canada had three national political parties at the time developers wanted to invent a name for this procedure.

mips-unknown-linux
    A big-endian MIPS Linux system from an unspecified manufacturer

mipsel-linux
    A little-endian MIPS Linux system from an unspecified manufacturer

xscale-unknown-linux
    An XScale (formely StrongARM) Linux system from an unspecified manufacturer

Typically, cross toolchain component names are prefixed with the target triplet. Thus, for example, a cross-compiler for a Freescale 8541 PowerQuickIII Linux system will be called *powerpc-8540-linux-gnu-gcc* (*gcc* being the executable name for the GNU Compiler Collection), whereas the linker for a little-endian MIPS Linux system might be named *mipsel-linux-ld*, (*ld* being the executable name of the GNU linker).

Linux kernel headers

The first component required for building a toolchain is the set of the Linux kernel headers. Because the C library, which is part of the toolchain, is a wrapper that presents a more palatable API to the application programmer for the raw Linux kernel system calls, compiling the library requires a subset of the Linux kernel header files that describes the kernel API.

In theory, one should always build the toolchain using the Linux kernel headers from the exact same Linux kernel version that will be used on the target. In practice, however, this is rarely done. Because the ABI of the Linux kernel rarely changes (or more correctly, the parts of it described by the headers rarely changes), using the headers from a different, but similar, kernel version is commonplace.

In Linux kernel releases prior to the 2.6 series, C library builds were based on a verbatim copy of the headers found in the Linux kernel directories *include/asm-architecture* and *include/linux*. Since the release of Linux 2.6, however, this is no longer supported, as the kernel headers contain much code that is unsuitable for inclusion in user space applications and can easily break the build of user programs, including the C library. Instead, builds use a sanitized version of the Linux kernel headers, suitable for use by user space code such as the C library. As of version 2.6.23 of the Linux kernel, the kernel source is equipped with an automated Make target for building such a "sanitized" version of the Linux kernel headers.

 For earlier versions, you can use the external utility available at *http://headers.cross-lfs.org* to accomplish the same task.

From the kernel source directory, simply issue the following commands, replacing *ppc* with your architecture and *headers/* with the path to the directory where you would like the sanitized headers installed:

```
$ make ARCH=ppc headers_check
$ make ARCH=ppc INSTALL_HDR_PATH=headers/ headers_instal;
```

Binutils

Another important component of the toolchain is the binutils package. This package includes the utilities most often used to manipulate binary object files. The two most important utilities in the package are the GNU assembler, *as*, and the linker, *ld*. Table 4-2 contains the complete list of utilities found in the binutils package.

Table 4-2. Utilities found in the binutils package

Utility	Use
as	GNU assembler
ld	GNU linker
gasp	GNU assembler pre-processor
ar	Creates and manipulates archive content
nmu	Lists the symbols in an object file
objcopy	Copies and translates object files
objdump	Displays information about the content of object files
ranlib	Generates an index to the content of an archive
readelf	Displays information about an ELF format object file
size	Lists the sizes of sections within an object file
strings	Prints the strings of printable characters in object files
strip	Strips symbols from object files
c++filt	Converts low-level, mangled assembly labels resulting from overloaded C++ functions to their user-level names
addr2line	Converts addresses into line numbers within original source files

Although *as* supports many processor architectures, it does not necessarily recognize the same syntax as other assemblers available for a given architecture. The syntax recognized by *as* is actually a machine-independent syntax inspired by BSD 4.2 assembly language.

The C library

The standard C library most often used with current day Linux systems is thein GNU C library, often abbreviated as glibc. glibc is a portable, high-performance C library supporting all relevant standards (ISO C 99, POSIX.1c, POSIX.1j, POSIX.1d, Unix98, and the Single Unix Specification). It also supports internationalization, sophisticated name resolution, time zone information, and authentication through the use of the NSS, the Name Service Switch, and PAM, the Pluggable Authentication Modules architecture.

The main website for the glibc development project, containing links to the development source tree, bug database, and many resources, can be found at *http://www.gnu.org/software/libc*. A list of all platforms the library supports can be found at *http://www.gnu.org/software/libc/ports.html*, and the library itself can be downloaded from the mirrors found at *http://ftp.gnu.org/gnu/glibc*.

 For recent glibc releases, supported architectures are separated into those supported by the core maintainers (x86, PowerPC, SPARC, SuperH, and their 64-bit counterparts are currently the most interesting to embedded system developers) and those supported by volunteers outside the main glibc core group (currently Arm and MIPS). Code for the latter architectures is in a separate glibc-ports package, which can be downloaded from the same location.

glibc is truly a robust, complete, and modern C library, and it can fit very well in many system designs. Indeed, many embedded Linux systems, especially in the telephony and networking market segments, are based on it. However, because it was never designed to be used in an embedded system context, developers building embedded Linux systems with more limited resources, such as consumer electronic devices, often find its resource usage less compelling.

Being rich and full-featured, glibc is huge. To compound the problem for embedded systems, it is not very modular: removing features is a cumbersome and sometimes even impossible job. Additionally, glibc's designers and implementors have traditionally optimized for performance instead of resource use. For instance, they have optimized for speedier operation at the expense of RAM utilization.

How much of a burden does the size of glibc impose? First of all, the various library files in a minimal glibc take up as much as 2 MB of storage space. But this is by no means the full extent of the problem. Keep in mind that almost every application is compiled against the C library headers. So, the C library also affects the size of application executable files and other libraries.

Executables built with alternative C libraries can be as little as one half the size as those built with glibc, depending on the actual program code and the compiler version used. Savings of 50 percent are quite rare, though; the difference varies widely and occasionally executables end up just as large as they would with glibc.

A similar effect, although usually much less dramatic, can be seen on application runtime RAM usage.

As a rule of thumb, glibc can be a good fit for projects with Flash storage sizes of 16 MB or more. If your project requires smaller RAM, however, you might want to consider popular embedded alternatives such as uClibc and diet libc, which we will describe in the upcoming sections.

The first decision facing a builder of a new toolchain, therefore, is which C library to use. Because the C library is a component in both the toolchain (both as part of the compiler, for support of C++ and other languages, and in the form of library headers) and the runtime image (the code library itself and the allocation code that is compiled to use it), it is impossible to change this decision later without affecting the entire system.

The threading library

Threads are a popular modern programming technique involving several independent, asynchronous tasks residing in the same process address space. The Linux kernel, prior to the 2.6 series, provided very little support for threads. To fill the gap, a few different threading libraries were developed that implemented much of the required support in user space with minimal kernel assistance. The most common was the LinuxThreads library, which was an implementation of the POSIX Threads standard and was distributed as a glibc add-on until Linux version 2.5. LinuxThreads was a noble and useful project, but it suffered from problems with scalability and adherence to standards, due to limitations imposed by the weakness of support for threads in the Linux kernel at that time. For example, both the `getpid()` system call and signal handling in LinuxThreads are non-compliant vis-à-vis the POSIX standard, on account of kernel-imposed limitations.

The release of the Linux 2.6 series was accompanied by a new thread implementation called the New POSIX Threading Library (NPTL). NPTL relies on Linux kernel supports for threads. A key piece of the implementation, known as a fast user space mutex (futex), provides a robust, POSIX-compliant threading implementation that scales up to thousands of threads. NPTL is now the supported Linux threading library and is distributed as part of recent versions of glibc.

For any new project making use of recent kernel versions and glibc releases, NPTL is the threading library of choice. However, because all Linux kernel releases prior to 2.6.16 contain bugs affecting the threading library, and because it is not unheard of for embedded system builders to base systems on older kernel and glibc releases (mainly due to vendor support issues), LinuxThreads can still be a valid option, especially if your system is only expected to make very limited use of threads.

You can also start off with LinuxThreads and migrate to NPTL, because both conform (at least roughly) to the POSIX standard.

The `confstr()` function can be used to test which threading library implemention is in use at runtime:

```
#define _XOPEN_SOURCE
#include <unistd.h>
#include <stdio.h>

int main(void)
{
```

```
    char name[128];
    confstr (_CS_GNU_LIBPTHREAD_VERSION, name, sizeof(name));
    printf ("Pthreads lib is: %s\n", name);
    return 0;
}
```

Component versions

The first step in building the toolchain is to select the version of each component you will use: GCC, glibc, and binutils. Because these packages are maintained and released independently, not all versions of one package will build properly when combined with different versions of the other packages. You can try using the latest versions of each, but this combination is not guaranteed to work either.

To select the appropriate versions, you have to test a combination tailored to your host and target. You may be lucky and find a previously tested combination. If not, start with the most recent stable version of each package and replace it with successively older versions if it fails to build.

 In some cases, the version with the highest version number may not have had the time to be tested enough to be considered "stable." At the time glibc 2.3 was released, for example, it may have been a better choice to keep using glibc 2.2.5 until 2.3.1 became available.

At the time of this writing, for instance, the latest version of binutils is 2.18, the latest version of GCC is 4.2.2, and the latest version of glibc is 2.7. Most often, binutils will build successfully and you will not need to change it. Hence, let us assume that GCC 4.2.2 fails to build even though all the appropriate configuration flags have been provided. In that case, we would revert to GCC 4.2.1. If that failed, we would try 4.2, and so on.

You must understand, however, that you cannot go back like this indefinitely, because the most recent package versions expect the other packages to provide certain capabilities. You may, therefore, have to go back to older versions of packages that you successfully built if the other packages down the line fail to build. Using the versions just mentioned, for example, if we had to go back to glibc 2.6.0, it might be appropriate to change back to GCC 4.1 and binutils 2.17, even if the most recent GCC and most recent binutils may have compiled perfectly.

In addition, it is quite common to apply patches to some versions to get them to build correctly for your target. The websites and mailing lists provided for each processor architecture in Chapter 3 are good places to find such patches and package versions suggestions.

Whenever you discover a new version combination that compiles successfully, make sure you test the resulting toolchain to ensure that it is indeed functional. Some version combinations may compile successfully and still fail when used. Version 2.2.3 of glibc, for example, builds successfully for a PPC target on an x86 host using GCC 2.95.3. The resulting library is, nevertheless, broken and will cause a core dump when used on the target. In that particular setup, you can obtain a functional C library by reverting to glibc 2.2.1.

There are also cases where a version combination was found to work properly on certain processors within a processor family while failing to work on other processors of the same family. Versions of glibc earlier than 2.2, for example, worked fine for most PPC processors, except those that were part of the MPC8xx series. The problem was that glibc assumed 32-byte cache lines for all PPC processors, whereas the processors in the MPC8xx series have 16-byte cache lines. Version 2.2 fixed this problem by assuming 16-byte cache lines for all PPC processors.

Additional build requirements

To build a cross-platform development toolchain, you will need a functional native toolchain. Most mainstream distributions provide this toolchain as part of their packages. If it was not installed on your workstation or if you chose not to install it to save space, you will need to install it at this point, using the procedure appropriate to your distribution. With a Red Hat distribution, for instance, you will need to install the appropriate RPM packages.

Build overview

With the appropriate tools in place, let's take a look at the procedure used to build the toolchain. The five main steps involve setting up:

1. Linux headers
2. Binary utilities
3. The bootstrap compiler
4. The C library
5. The full compiler

The first thing that you probably noticed is that the compiler seems to be built twice. This is normal and required, because some languages supported by GCC, such as C++, require glibc support. Hence, a bootstrap compiler is built with support for C only, and a full compiler is built once the C library is available.

Although we listed the Linux headers as the first step, the headers will not be used until the C library setup. Hence, you could alter the steps and set up the Linux headers right before the C library setup.

Each of the steps involves many iterations of its own. Nonetheless, the steps remain similar in several ways. Most toolchain build steps involve carrying out the following actions:

1. Unpack the package.
2. Configure the package for cross-platform development.
3. Build the package.
4. Install the package.

Some toolchain builds differ slightly from this sequence. The Linux headers, for instance, do not require you to build or install the kernel, as we have already seen. Also, because the compiler will have already been unpacked for the bootstrap compiler's setup, the full compiler setup does not require unpacking the GCC package again.

Workspace setup

According to the workspace directory layout suggested earlier, the toolchain will be built in the ${PRJROOT}/build-tools directory, while the components built will be installed in the ${PRJROOT}/tools directory. To this end, we need to define some additional environment variables. They ease the build process and are based on the environment variables already defined. Using the same example project as before, here is the new develdaq script with the new variables:

```
export PROJECT=daq-module
export PRJROOT=/home/gby/bels/control-project/${PROJECT}
export TARGET=powerpc-unknown-linux
export HOST=i686-cross-linux-gnu
export PREFIX=${PRJROOT}/tools
```

```
export TARGET_PREFIX=${PREFIX}/${TARGET}
export PATH=${PREFIX}/bin:${PATH}
cd $PRJROOT
```

The TARGET variable defines the type of target for which your toolchain will be built. It is expressed as a host/target/build triplet, as explained earlier.

The HOST variable defines the type of host on which the toolchain will run, namely your workstation type. Note that we have slightly modified the host triplet and, instead of using i686-pc-linux-gnu, actually use i686-cross-linux-gnu. The reason for this is that it is possible and sometimes desirable to be able to build a cross toolchain for an x86-based system, such as a PC104 platform. If that was done, the host and target triplets could have been identical, which would have caused a regular toolchain to be created. Although no such issue exists in our earlier example, because its toolchain runs on x86 but builds binaries for a PowerPC system, we still use this convention for good measure.

The PREFIX variable provides the component configuration scripts with a pointer to the directory where you would like the target utilities to be installed. Conversely, TARGET_PREFIX is used for the installation of target-dependent header files and libraries. To have access to the newly installed utilities, you also need to modify the PATH variable to point to the directory where the binaries will be installed.

Some people prefer to set PREFIX to *usr/local*. This installs the tools and libraries within the *usr/local* directory, where any user can access them. We don't find this approach useful for most situations, however, because even projects using the same target architecture may require different toolchain configurations.

If you need to set up a toolchain for an entire development team, instead of sharing tools and libraries via the *usr/local* directory, we recommend that you build the toolchain within a directory shared by all project members, such as a subdirectory of *opt* or a directory on a shared network.

If you choose to set PREFIX to *usr/local*, you will also have to issue the commands shown later while logged in as the superuser, with all the risks this entails. You could instead set the permission bits of the *usr/local* directory to allow yourself or your user group to issue the commands without requiring root privileges.

Notice that TARGET_PREFIX is set to *${PREFIX}/${TARGET}*, which is a target-dependent directory. Thus, successive installations of development toolchains for different targets will place the libraries and header files of each installation in different subdirectories of *${PREFIX}*.

Regardless of the value you give to PREFIX, the *${PREFIX}/${TARGET}* combination is the configuration the GNU toolchain utilities expect to find during their configuration and installation. Hence, we strongly suggest that you use this value for TARGET_PREFIX. The following explanations may require changes if you modify TARGET_PREFIX's value.

Again, you can remove the *cd* command from the script if you would prefer not to move directly to the project directory.

Resources

Before proceeding to the actual building of the toolchain, let's look at some resources you might find useful in case you run into problems during the build process.

First and foremost, each package comes with its own documentation. Although the binutils package is the leanest in terms of installation documentation, it is also the least likely to cause any problems. The GCC and glibc packages, however, are amply documented. Within the GCC package, you will find an FAQ file and an *install* directory containing instructions about how to configure and install GCC. This includes an extensive explanation of the build configuration options. Similarly, the glibc package contains *FAQ* and *INSTALL* files. The *INSTALL* file covers the build configuration options and the installation process, and it provides recommendations for compilation tool versions.

In addition, you may want to try using a general search engine such as Google to look for reports by other developers who may have already encountered and solved problems similar to yours. Often, this will be the most effective way to solve a build problem with a GNU toolchain.

One extremely useful resource is the Cross-Compiled Linux From Scratch website (*http://trac.cross-lfs.org*), mentioned earlier. The combination of component versions used in the example toolchain build in the following section has been taken mostly from this resource.

Finally, you can check the crosgcc mailing list, hosted by Red Hat, at *http://sources.red hat.com/ml/crossgcc*. You will find this mailing list quite useful if you ever get stuck, because many people on this list have a great deal of experience with the process of building cross-platform development toolchains. Often, just searching or browsing the archive will immediately help you locate answers to your questions.

Building the Toolchain

As must be obvious by now, building a cross toolchain is a delicate and complicated process. It requires arcane knowledge concerning versions, patches, and tweaks of the various toolchain components for various architectures—knowledge that is not only scattered among many locations, but also changes from version to version of the components. It is certainly not a task for the novice, or even intermediate, embedded Linux system builder to tackle unassisted.

In fact, this is how Dan Kegel, the main author of Crosstool, described the process of building a cross toolchain manually:

"Building a [...] cross-toolchain for use in embedded systems development [is] a scary prospect, requiring iron will, days if not weeks of effort, lots of Unix and Gnu lore, and sometimes willingness to take dodgy shortcuts."

Manually building a toolchain

If you are truly brave of heart or happen to have a lot of free time on your hands and desire to learn the process of cross toolchain inside and out, the authors highly recommend following the Cross Linux From Scratch project (*http://trac.cross-lfs.org*) as a reference. Otherwise, skip to the next section, where we will describe Crosstool, an automated cross toolchain build system.

Version 1.0.0 of the Cross LFS guide, covering the x86, PPC, MIPS, and Sparc V8 architectures, is available at *http://cross-lfs.org/view/1.0.0*.

The development branch of the guide—with more updated information but possibly less reliable—can be found at *http://cross-lfs.org/view/svn*.

Automated cross toolchain build systems

Although it is certainly possible and educational to build a toolchain using a step-by-step manual process, it is not the recommended way to build one for a production system. Instead, we recommend an automated cross toolchain build system, which has the following advantages:

Reproducible
> Because the build is done in an automated fashion, it can be exactly repeated should that be necessary to update a component or fix an error. There is no danger of accidentally omitting an important step.

Documented
> Practically all automated cross toolchain build systems use some sort of configuration file to document the build components, versions, and other choices related to producing the toolchain. This configuration file becomes a form of "executable documentation" for the toolchain and its build process.

Sharable
> This advantage follows from the previous two. Because the cross toolchain build process can be reproduced from a configuration file, you can publish the configuration file to share with other developers.

> Indeed, all automated cross toolchain build systems that we will cover come bundled with several pretested components and version combinations that are known to produce working toolchains for specific architectures. This enables novice and intermediate embedded Linux system builders to build working toolchains easily,

without needing to become experts on the states of various toolchain components versions.

We'll describe several automated cross toolchain build systems later in this section.

Crosstool

Crosstool is a set of scripts that build and test several versions of GCC and glibc for most architectures supported by glibc. Crosstool will even download and patch the original tarballs for you. The resulting script and associated patches, and the latest version of the documentation, are available at *http://kegel.com/crosstool*.

It originated as a script by Bill Gatliff called crossgcc, which Dan Kegel generalized and hacked on until it took its current shape.

Crosstool comes with a set of patches for the toolchain components, which are required to build cross toolchain combinations. It supports the Alpha, ARM, i686, ia64, MIPS, PowerPC, PowerPC64, SH4, SPARC, SPARC64, s390, and x86_64 architectures. Supported software includes GCC versions gcc-2.95.3 through gcc-4.0.0 and glibc versions glibc-2.1.3 through glibc-2.3.5.

It is portable and can be used to build cross toolchains that run on Linux, Mac OS X, Solaris, and Cygwin for building Linux binaries.

Grab the Crosstool archive and unpack it as follows:

```
$ cd $PRJROOT/tools-build/
$ wget http://kegel.com/crosstool/crosstool-0.43.tar.gz
$ tar -xzvf crosstool-0.43.tar.gz
$ cd crosstool-0.43
```

Crosstool is comprised of a couple of shell scripts and data files used by those scripts. The following are the major scripts:

crosstool.sh
> The main script, containing the logic to compile GCC and glibc.

getandpatch.sh
> This script is in charge of downloading, unpacking, and patching the various toolchain components' source packages.

crosstest.sh
> This script can run the GCC and glibc regression tests remotely on your target machine. It can be very useful to verify that the toolchain you have just created is indeed working.

testhello.sh
> This script tries to build a trivial "Hello World" program using the newly generated toolchain as a sanity check.

---

mkdistcc.sh and mkdistcclinks.sh

These scripts contain Crosstool support for building DistCC-supported cross toolchains.

 DistCC achieves faster build times by distributing the build work across a cluster of computers. It is outside the scope of this book, but if you are interested, we recommend the DistCC website at *http://distcc.samba.org.*

demo-cpu.sh

Example scripts that serve as starting points. One exists for each supported architecture (e.g., *demo-i686.sh*).

demo.sh

A big demo file that runs all the architecture demo files. Used mainly for testing Crosstool itself.

clean.sh

As the name implies, a script that cleans up a Crosstool working directory.

all.sh

The script that actually generates a toolchain; an example of its use appears later in this section. It is a general control script that has the logic to invoke all other scripts in order, according to the parameters supplied. Parameters include:

`--nounpack`

Instructs the script not to run *getandpatch.sh*. Useful for quickly restarting a build.

`--nobuild`

Instruct the script not to run *crosstool.sh*. Useful for downloading the sources for a later build or for running the regression tests.

`--notest`

Instructs the script not to run *crosstest.sh*, thus skipping the regression suite tests.

These scripts are mostly architecture- and version-generic. The information pertaining to different architectures and tool versions is stored in separate data files:

cpu .dat

One such file exists for each supported architecture (e.g., *arm.dat*) or specific CPU (e.g., *ppc-8540.dat*). The file contains the information needed to configure Crosstool for a specific architecture. It sets the GNU target name and additional related options.

gcc- version -glibc- version .dat

One such file exists for each combination of GCC and GLibc versions (e.g., *gcc-3.4.0-glibc-2.3.2.dat*). The file contains the information needed to configure

Crosstool for that combination. It sets the binutils, GCC, glibc versions, and related options.

patches/ program /*.patch

These are patch files required to properly build various components' versions. The *program* is the name of the program and version the patch is intended for. Each patch file header contains comments about what it is for and has links to any associated discussion.

Using Crosstool is very simple and straightforward: create a shell script to set up some important shell variables and invoke the build script. For the purpose of the following example, we'll assume we named the file *mytoolchain.sh*.

 Use one of the example scripts included with Crosstool as a starting point and adapt it to your needs.

Here are the first lines of our script:

```
TARBALLS_DIR=download        # where it will save source tarballs
RESULT_TOP=$PRJROOT/tools/    # where it will install the tools
GCC_LANGUAGES="c,c++"        # which languages it will make compilers for
```

To build the cross toolchain, create an architecture description file and a description file for the GCC and glibc versions. Then invoke the build script.

For example, to build a toolchain based on gcc-3.4.0 and glibc-2.3.2 for i686, add the following line to the *mytoolchain.sh* script:

```
eval `cat i686.dat gcc-3.4.0-glibc-2.3.2.dat`  sh all.sh --notest
```

Then execute the script:

```
$ sh mytoolchain.sh
```

At this point, the script will run for quite some time as it downloads each and every toolchain component, patches them, configures them, and builds them.

When the script finishes, the new toolchain will be ready and you can run the newly created compiler from *$PRJROOT/tools/gcc-3.4.0-glibc-2.3.2/i686-unknown-linux-gnu/bin/i686-unknown-linux-gnu-gcc*. Of course, you might need to replace *gcc-3.4.0-glibc-2.3.2* and *i686-unknown-linux-gnu* with your actual GCC and glibc versions and architecture.

Your toolchain is ready for use now, but the long pathname of its location is not very convenient to use. As our last step, therefore, we will create a shortcut by making a soft link from the *tools* directory to the *bin* directory of the toolchain:

```
$ ln -s $PRJROOT/tools/gcc-3.4.0-glibc-2.3.2/i686-unknown-linux-gnu/bin \
    $PRJROOT/tools/bin
```

Henceforth, you can access the toolchain at *$PRJROOT/tools/bin/i686-unknown-linux-gnu-gcc*, and if you have added this directory to your run path in your workspace setup script, you can use simply *686-unknown-linux-gnu-gcc*.

Ptxdist

Ptxdist is a build system for userlands started by the German company Pengutronix e.K. It is maintained as an open source project under a GPL, with the active participation of Pengutronix, which also sells commercial support for it under the brand name OSE-LAS. The project website can be found at *http://www.pengutronix.de/software/ptxdist/index_en.html*.

Ptxdist overview. Much more then just an automated cross toolchain building framework, Ptxdist can be considered "executable documentation." It builds a cross toolchain, then uses this toolchain to build a Linux kernel image and *root* filesystem for the target, which it then packs as a binary image in one of many available formats.

In this section, however, we will cover Ptxdist just for use as an automated cross toolchain build system. Later in the chapter, we'll use it as an automated build system for an entire embedded Linux project.

The process for building a cross toolchain with Ptxdist has two phases. First, we'll download and install the core Ptxdist package and the Ptxdist patches packages. Then, we'll download an example Ptxdist project that can generate a few different cross toolchain variants.

Installing Ptxdist. First, grab the latest version of the project from its website and install it. At the time of this writing, the latest version is 1.0.1:

```
$ wget http://www.pengutronix.de/software/ptxdist/download/v1.0/ptxdist-1.0.1.tgz
$ wget http://www.pengutronix.de/software/ptxdist/download/v1.0/ptxdist-1.0.1-
  patches.tgz
```

Next, unpack the compressed tar archives and move to the project's directory:

```
$ tar zxvf ptxdist-1.0.1.tgz
$ tar zxvf ptxdist-1.0.1-patches.tgz
$ cd ptxdist-1.0.1
```

Now, configure Ptxdist for use on your system, build it, and install it:

```
$ ./configure --prefix=$PRJROOT/build-tools/
$ make
$ make install
```

Setting up Ptxdist. After Ptxdist has been installed, you can set it up to build a toolchain. Although the default configuration works quite well in most cases, local network and security policies might require a good deal of configuration.

To set up your new Ptxdist installation, issue the following command:

```
$ ptxdist setup
```

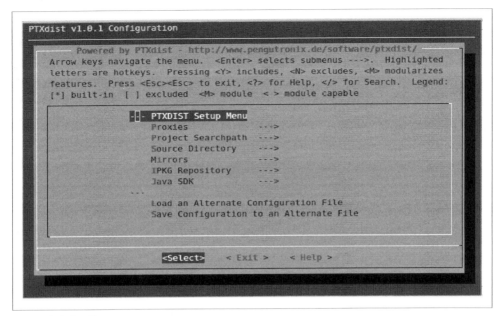

Figure 4-1. Ptxdist setup menu

It presents the Ptxdist setup menu, shown in Figure 4-1.

The setup menu allows you to configure many options. You can obtain information regarding each option using the ? key. This displays a paragraph explaining how the current option is used and provides its default values.

The following submenus are available:

Proxies

Set up HTTP and FTP proxy servers for Ptxdist to use when downloading source packages from the Internet.

Project Searchpath

Choose a default project working directory. Set this to your project *tools* directory.

Source Directory

Choose a directory into which all source packages will be downloaded. Set this to a subdirectory under your project *build-tools* directory.

Mirrors

Allows you to specify places to download Debian, GNU, and Xorg source packages. Normally, there is no reason to change this, but if some source packages fail to load due to an unavailable server, you may try to specify a different mirror for the appropriate project.

IPKG Repository

> IPKG is a binary packaging format used in many Linux-based embedded system distributions. Ptxdist can create a custom IPKG repository for you from the packages it builds. For a toolchain building project, leave this at the default value.

JAVA SDK

> Ptxdist allows you to build some Java-based packages. This submenu can be used to point to the relevant Java SDK required to build Java programs. You can leave this as the default value for a toolchain building project.

 If the configuration menu did not show up, make sure that your executable path is set correctly (for example, by running the development environment setup script described earlier) and that your terminal has at least 19 lines by 80 columns.

When you finish, choose the < Exit > button and press Enter, and then choose the < Yes > button to save your new configuration.

Creating a toolchain project. Ptxdist is organized around the concept of a *project*, a set of configuration files and patches required to build a certain set of software. To start building our cross toolchain using the Ptxdist framework, we'll download an example toolchain Ptxdist project from the Ptxdist website and uncompress the archive:

```
$ wget http://www.pengutronix.de/oselas/toolchain/download/OSELAS.Toolchain-1.1.1.tar.bz2
$ tar jxvf OSELAS.Toolchain-1.1.1.tar.bz2
$ cd OSELAS.Toolchain-1.1.1/
```

Now pick a sample toolchain to build from the included examples. Each toolchain example is represented by a configuration file in the *ptxconfigs* directory:

```
$ ls ptxconfigs/
arm-1136jfs-linux-gnueabi_gcc-4.1.2_glibc-2.5_linux-2.6.18.ptxconfig
armeb-xscale-linux-gnueabi_gcc-4.1.2_glibc-2.5_linux-2.6.18.ptxconfig
armeb-xscale-linux-gnu_gcc-4.0.4_glibc-2.3.6_linux-2.6.17.ptxconfig
arm-ep93xx-linux-gnueabi_gcc-4.1.2_glibc-2.5_linux-2.6.18.ptxconfig
arm-iwmmx-linux-gnueabi_gcc-4.1.2_glibc-2.5_linux-2.6.18.ptxconfig
arm-v4t_hardfloat-linux-gnu_gcc-4.0.4_glibc-2.3.6_linux-2.6.18.ptxconfig
arm-v4t-linux-gnueabi_gcc-4.1.2_glibc-2.5_linux-2.6.18.ptxconfig
arm-v4t-linux-gnu_gcc-4.0.4_glibc-2.3.6_linux-2.6.18.ptxconfig
arm-xscale_hardfloat-linux-gnu_gcc-4.0.4_glibc-2.3.6_linux-2.6.17.ptxconfig
arm-xscale-linux-gnueabi_gcc-4.1.2_glibc-2.5_linux-2.6.18.ptxconfig
arm-xscale-linux-gnu_gcc-4.0.4_glibc-2.3.6_linux-2.6.17.ptxconfig
i586-unknown-linux-gnu_gcc-4.1.2_glibc-2.5_linux-2.6.18.ptxconfig
i686-unknown-linux-gnu_gcc-4.1.2_glibc-2.5_linux-2.6.18.ptxconfig
mips-r6000-linux-gnu_gcc-4.1.2_glibc-2.5_linux-2.6.18.ptxconfig
powerpc-603e-linux-gnu_gcc-4.1.2_glibc-2.5_linux-2.6.18.ptxconfig
powerpc64-970-linux-gnu_gcc-4.1.2_glibc-2.5_linux-2.6.18.ptxconfig
```

To build one of the example toolchains, you need to tell Ptxdist which configuration file you want to use and then tell it to build the toolchain according to the instructions in the configuration file.

As an example, let's build a cross toolchain for the a ARM Xscale EABI, using GCC 4.1.2 and glibc 2.5 with kernel headers from version 2.6.18, including NPTL support. The example file you will use will therefore be *ptxconfigs/arm-xscale-linux-gnuea bi_gcc-4.1.2_glibc-2.5_linux-2.6.18.ptxconfig*.

Before you do so, however, you must make a small change in the example configuration file in order to use it, because the example configuration files were generated using an earlier version of the Ptxdist framework. The version number of that earlier version is embedded in the configuration file, which will cause Ptxdist to fail with an error message if you try to use the example configuration as is.

Luckily, the configuration files are simple text files. You can simply edit the configuration file and update the version number to match the latest version you use. While this can easily be done manually with a text editor, the following shell hackery does the trick very well:

```
$ sed s/PTXCONF_CONFIGFILE_VERSION=.*/PTXCONF_CONFIGFILE_VERSION="1.0"/ \
    ptxconfigs/arm-xscale-linux-gnueabi_gcc-4.1.2_glibc-2.5_linux-2.6.18.ptxconfig > \
    ptxconfigs/arm-xscale-linux-gnueabi_gcc-4.1.2_glibc-2.5_linux-2.6.18.ptxconfig.tmp
$ mv ptxconfigs/arm-xscale-linux-gnueabi_gcc-4.1.2_glibc-2.5_linux-2.6.18.ptxconfig.tmp \
    ptxconfigs/arm-xscale-linux-gnueabi_gcc-4.1.2_glibc-2.5_linux-2.6.18.ptxconfig
```

After running this command, instruct Ptxdist to use your "patched" configuration file through the following command:

```
$ $PRJROOT/build-tools/bin/ptxdist select \
    ptxconfigs/arm-xscale-linux-gnueabi_gcc-4.1.2_glibc-2.5_linux-2.6.18.ptxconfig
```

Now you can customize our chosen example toolchan project configuration. Issue the following command:

```
$ ptxdist menuconfig
```

You will be presented with the Ptxdist toolchain project menu, shown in Figure 4-2.

The menu contains the following options and submenus:

Project Name
    A text box to enter a long name for the project. Useful if you are maintaining several different Ptxdist toolchain projects.

glibc
    This submenu allows you to specify the glibc version, any extra configuration options you might wish to pass to the package configuration script, a file list, a series of patches to apply to the library source before the build, the minimum supported kernel version, extra environment variables you might want to pass to the glibc configuration script, which threading library to use (NPTL or LinuxThreads), and whether the resulting glibc will support thread-local storage.

glibc-ports
    This submenu lets you list a series of patches to apply to glibc from the glibc-ports archive, which contains patches for glibc originating outside the glibc core team.

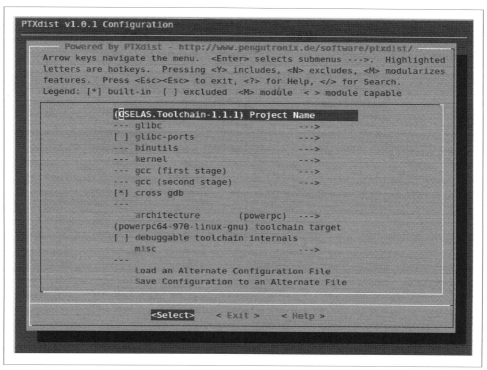

```
 PTXdist v1.0.1 Configuration

 ┌── Powered by PTXdist - http://www.pengutronix.de/software/ptxdist/ ──┐
 │ Arrow keys navigate the menu.  <Enter> selects submenus --->.  Highlighted  │
 │ letters are hotkeys.  Pressing <Y> includes, <N> excludes, <M> modularizes  │
 │ features.  Press <Esc><Esc> to exit, <?> for Help, </> for Search.          │
 │ Legend: [*] built-in  [ ] excluded  <M> module  < > module capable          │
 │ ┌───────────────────────────────────────────────────────────────────────┐ │
 │ │ (OSELAS.Toolchain-1.1.1) Project Name                                   │ │
 │ │ --- glibc                                             --->              │ │
 │ │ [ ] glibc-ports                                       --->              │ │
 │ │ --- binutils                                          --->              │ │
 │ │ --- kernel                                            --->              │ │
 │ │ --- gcc (first stage)                                 --->              │ │
 │ │ --- gcc (second stage)                                --->              │ │
 │ │ [*] cross gdb                                                           │ │
 │ │ ---                                                                     │ │
 │ │     architecture        (powerpc)  --->                                │ │
 │ │ (powerpc64-970-linux-gnu) toolchain target                             │ │
 │ │ [ ] debuggable toolchain internals                                     │ │
 │ │     misc                              --->                              │ │
 │ │ ---                                                                     │ │
 │ │     Load an Alternate Configuration File                               │ │
 │ │     Save Configuration to an Alternate File                            │ │
 │ └───────────────────────────────────────────────────────────────────────┘ │
 │                                                                             │
 │              <Select>      < Exit >      < Help >                           │
 └─────────────────────────────────────────────────────────────────────────┘
```

Figure 4-2. Ptxdist toolchain menu

binutils

> This submenu lets you pick which binutils package version to include in the toolchain built.

kernel

> This submenu sets the kernel version and the configuration file for the Linux kernel headers required to build the toolchain. It also lets you specify whether or not to use sanitized headers. For more on kernel configuration, see "Configuring the Kernel in Chapter 5.

gcc (first stage)

> This submenu lets you specify the GCC version to use for the first stage (bootstrap) compiler, as well as a patch series file and extra options to provide to the GCC configuration script.

gcc (second stage)

> This submenu allows you to choose which programming languages the newly created toolchain will support. The languages supported depend on the GCC version, but all versions support C and C++.

cross gdb

This checkbox can be checked to ask PTxdist to build a cross debugger as part of the toolchain.

architecture

This drop-down box lets you specify the toolchain's target architecture. Currently ARM, MIPS, PowerPC, and x86 are supported.

toolchain target

This text box allows you to set your toolchain GNU configuration string (e.g., *powerpc64-970-linux-gnu*).

debuggable toolchain internals

This checkbox allows you to specify whether full debugging information should be generated for the toolchain's glibc and libstdc++ libraries. Selecting this checkbox lets you step into functions defined in these basic libraries, but it will make your toolchain about 500 MB bigger. (It does not affect the target filesystem size, though.)

misc

The misc submenu allows you to specify the version of Ptxdist that is compatible with the current toolchain project, as well as set the filesystem prefixes into which the generated filesystem will be installed. Set the first prefix to the *tools* directory under the project root, and leave the second prefix field blank.

After you finish configuring these items, choose the < Exit > button and press Enter , then choose the < Yes > button to save your configuration.

Building the toolchain. Finally, you are ready to let Ptxdist build your toolchain. In the process, Ptxdist will automatically download, configure, patch, build, and install all required components. To start the build process, issue the following command:

```
$ ptxdist go
```

 The build process can take from one to a few hours, depending on the speed of your workstation and Internet connection.

When the build finishes, the new toolchain will be ready in the *tools/bin* directory of your project root.

Using the Toolchain

The steps in the previous sections should have created a fully functional cross-development toolchain, which you can use much as you would a native GNU toolchain; you just need to prepend the target name to every command. For instance, instead of invoking *gcc* and *objdump* for your target, you will need to invoke something such as *i386-linux-gcc* and *i386-linux-objdump*.

A *Makefile* for the control daemon on the DAQ module follows, which provides a good example of the cross-development toolchain's use:

```
# Tool names
CROSS_COMPILE = ${TARGET}-
AS            = $(CROSS_COMPILE)as
AR            = $(CROSS_COMPILE)ar
CC            = $(CROSS_COMPILE)gcc
CPP           = $(CC) -E
LD            = $(CROSS_COMPILE)ld
NM            = $(CROSS_COMPILE)nm
OBJCOPY       = $(CROSS_COMPILE)objcopy
OBJDUMP       = $(CROSS_COMPILE)objdump
RANLIB        = $(CROSS_COMPILE)ranlib
READELF       = $(CROSS_COMPILE)readelf
SIZE          = $(CROSS_COMPILE)size
STRINGS       = $(CROSS_COMPILE)strings
STRIP         = $(CROSS_COMPILE)strip

export AS AR CC CPP LD NM OBJCOPY OBJDUMP RANLIB READELF SIZE STRINGS \
       STRIP

# Build settings
CFLAGS        = -O2 -Wall
HEADER_OPS    =
LDFLAGS       =

# Installation variables
EXEC_NAME     = command-daemon
INSTALL       = install
INSTALL_DIR   = ${PRJROOT}/rootfs/bin

# Files needed for the build
OBJS          = daemon.o

# Make rules
all: daemon

.c.o:
        $(CC) $(CFLAGS) $(HEADER_OPS) -c $<

daemon: ${OBJS}
        $(CC) -o $(EXEC_NAME) ${OBJS} $(LDFLAGS)

install: daemon
        test -d $(INSTALL_DIR) || $(INSTALL) -d -m 755 $(INSTALL_DIR)
        $(INSTALL) -m 755 $(EXEC_NAME) $(INSTALL_DIR)

clean:
        rm -f *.o $(EXEC_NAME) core

distclean:
```

```
rm -f *~
rm -f *.o $(EXEC_NAME) core
```

The first part of the *Makefile* specifies the names of the toolchain utilities we are using to build the program. The name of every utility is prepended with the target's name. Hence, the value of CC will be *i386-linux-gcc*, the cross-compiler we built earlier. In addition to defining the name of the utilities, we also export these values so that subsequent Makefiles called by this Makefile will use the same names. Such a build architecture is quite common in large projects that have one main directory containing many subdirectories.

The second part of the Makefile defines the build settings. CFLAGS provides the flags to be used during the build of any C file.

As we saw in the previous section, the compiler is already using the correct path to the target's libraries. The linker flags variable, LDFLAGS, is therefore empty. If the compiler wasn't pointing to the correct libraries or was using the host's libraries (which shouldn't happen if you followed the instructions provided earlier), you would have to tell the compiler which libraries to use by setting the link flags as follows:

```
LDFLAGS       = -nostdlib -L${TARGET_PREFIX}/lib
```

If you wish to link your application statically, you need to add the *-static* option to LDFLAGS. This generates an executable that does not rely on any shared library. But given that the standard GNU C library is rather large, this will result in a very large binary. A simple program that uses printf() to print "Hello World!", for example, is less than 12 KB in size when linked dynamically and around 350 KB when linked statically, even when stripped.

The variables in the installation section indicate what, where, and how to install the resulting binary. In this case, the binary is being installed in the *bin* directory of the target's *root* filesystem.

In the case of the control daemon, we currently have only one file to build. Hence, the program's compilation requires only this single file, but had you used the *-nostdlib* option in LDFLAGS (which you should not normally need to do) you would also need to change the section describing the files required for the build and the rule for generating the binary:

```
STARTUP_FILES = ${TARGET_PREFIX}/lib/crt1.o \
                ${TARGET_PREFIX}/lib/crti.o \
                ${PREFIX}/lib/gcc-lib/${TARGET}/2.95.3/crtbegin.o
END_FILES     = ${PREFIX}/lib/gcc-lib/${TARGET}/2.95.3/crtend.o \
                ${TARGET_PREFIX}/lib/crtn.o
LIBS          = -lc
OBJS          = daemon.o
LINKED_FILES  = ${STARTUP_FILES} ${OBJS} ${LIBS} ${END_FILES}
...
daemon: ${OBJS}
        $(CC) -o $(EXEC_NAME) ${LINKED_FILES} $(LDFLAGS)
```

The preceding Makefile excerpt adds five object files to the one it generates from our own C file: *crt1.o*, *crti.o*, *crtbegin.o*, *crtend.o*, and *crtn.o*. These are special startup, initialization, constructor, destructor, and finalization files, respectively, which are usually automatically linked to your applications. It is through these files that your application's `main( )` function is called, for example. Since we told the compiler not to use standard linking in this case, we need to explicitly mention the files. If you disable standard linking but forget to explicitly mention the files, the linker will complain about a missing `_start` symbol and fail. The order in which the object files are provided to the compiler is important because the GNU linker, which is automatically invoked by the compiler to link the object files, is a one-pass linker.

The *make* rules themselves are very much the same ones you would find in a standard, native Makefile. We added the `install` rule to automate the install process. You may choose not to have such a rule but to copy the executable manually to the proper directory.

With the Makefile and the source file in your local directory, all you need to do is type *make* to build your program for your target. If you want to build your program for native execution on your host to test your application, for example, you could use the following command:

```
$ make CROSS_COMPILE=""
```

C Library Alternatives

Given the constraints and limitations of embedded systems, the size of the standard GNU C library makes it an unlikely candidate for use on our target. Instead, we need to look for a C library that will have sufficient functionality while being relatively small.

Over time, a number of libraries have been implemented with these priorities in mind. In this section, we will discuss the two most important C library alternatives: uClibc and diet libc. For each library, we'll provide background information, instructions on how to build the library for your target, and instructions on how to build your applications using the library.

uClibc

The uClibc library originates from the uClinux project, which provides a Linux that runs on processors lacking a memory management unit (MMU).[‡] The library, however, has since become a project of its own and supports a number of processors, including ones that have an MMU. In fact, at the time of this writing, uClibc supports all the processor architectures discussed in-depth in Chapter 3.

[‡] Processors without MMUs are low-end, and Linux is increasingly used on embedded systems with MMUs. With special treatment, it can run on MMU-less systems, with the drawback that several features will not work (such as memory protection).

Although it does not rely on the GNU C library, uClibc provides most of the same functionality. It is, of course, not as complete as the GNU library and does not attempt to comply with all the standards with which the GNU library complies. Functions and function features that are seldom used, for instance, are omitted from uClibc. Even so, most applications that can be compiled against the GNU C library will also compile and run using uClibc. To this end, uClibc developers focus on maintaining compatibility with C89, C99, and SUSv3.§ They regularly run extensive test suites to ensure that uClibc conforms to these standards.

uClibc is available for download as a tar-gzipped or tar-bzip2'd archive or by using CVS from the project's website at *http://uclibc.org*. The library is distributed under the terms of the LGPL. An FAQ is available on the project's website, and you can subscribe to the uClibc mailing list or browse the mailing list archive if you need help. In the following description, we will use version 0.9.29 of uClibc, but the explanation should apply to subsequent versions as well. Versions earlier than 0.9.16 depended on a different configuration system and are not covered in the following discussion.

Buildroot

Because the C library is one of the major components of a toolchain, and uClibc is an alternative C library for embedded Linux systems, using it requires building a custom cross toolchain. Just as with glibc cross toolchains, the best way to build a uClibc-based cross toolchain is to use an automated build framework to do the heavy lifting. The uClibc distribution includes its own framework called Buildroot.

 Older versions of uClibc provided a wrapper around various toolchain components that allowed you to build applications against uClibc without the need for a custom toolchain.

Alas, this approach has been discontinued, as the wrappers have proved to introduce more complications than assistance.

Download Buildroot from the *http://buildroot.uclibc.org* website and extract the compressed tar archive:

```
$ cd $PRJROOT/build-tools/
$ wget http://buildroot.uclibc.org/downloads/snapshots/buildroot-snapshot.tar.bz2
$ tar jxvf buildroot-snapshot.tar.gz
$ cd buildroot/
```

Run the configuration menu utility:

```
$ make menuconfig
```

You will be presented with Buildroot configuration menu, shown in Figure 4-3. As in the Ptxdist menu, you can obtain information regarding each option using the ? key.

---

§ Single UNIX Specification, version 3.

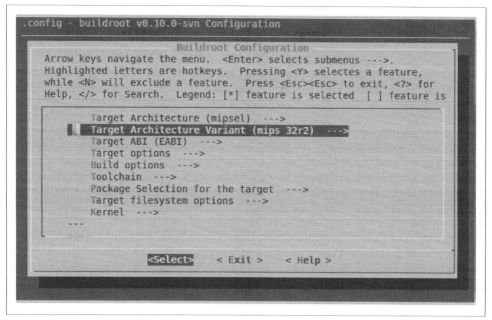

Figure 4-3. *uClibc Buildroot main menu*

Indeed, both Ptxdist and Buildroot share the same configuration system, which uClibc, the Linux kernel, and many other projects also use.

The Buildroot main menu includes the following options:

Target Architecture
Lets you choose the target architecture for which the cross toolchain creates binaries.

Target Architecture Variant (optional)
Configures a subarchitecture or generation to build for, such as 386, 486, or 686 for the x86 family, if applicable.

Target ABI (MIPS only)
The target ABI option, which is offered only for the MIPS architecture, controls which of three available Application Binary Interfaces to use. Most embedded systems builders are likely to choose the new embedded targeted API, called EABI.

Target options
This submenu controls several settings of interest only to people using Buildroot to build the entire root filesystems. They do not affect cross toolchain compilation.

Build options
This submenu allows you to set several different options concerning the cross toolchain build process:

- The commands used to perform such tasks as retrieving files from FTP and websites, checking out source code from Subversion and Git source control repositories, and uncompressing Gzip and Bzip2 archives, as well as any special command-line options to pass to the *tar* command. The defaults provided are quite sensible and will work out of the box for most modern Linux systems.

- Mirrors and download locations for components such as the Linux kernel, GNU software (such as GCC, binutils, and GDB packages), and a Debian project mirror (used to fetch additional packages). Leaving the defaults is safe, but if you happen to know the URL of a nearby mirror, you may save considerable time by configuring it here.

- The directory into which the cross toolchain and header files will be installed. Change this to the directory we have configured as *$PRJROOT/tools/*.

 Due to the way these configuration options are used, you cannot actually use the $PRJROOT environment variable here and will have to enter its value.

- The _nofpu suffix on the names of executables that support targets with no hardware floating point.

- The custom prefix and suffix for build directories' names to allow the building of several architectures in a single location. Use of these options is not recommended.

- An optional, custom GNU target suffix. You can use this to "brand" your cross toolchain.

- A version of the *strip* utility. The traditional *strip* command is recommended, rather then the newer *sstrip*.

- An option to configure the toolchain to use static libraries, rather then dynamic, loadable ones. Not recommended for novice users.

- Several other options related to the use of Buildroot for building root filesystems, which are not relevant for toolchains.

Toolchain

This submenu, shown in Figure 4-4, controls several key configuration options for Buildroot-based toolchain builders:

- Select whether you wish to use an external toolchain or build a new one. Use the default, called "Buildroot toolchain," because you should have Buildroot generate a toolchain and not rely on an externally supplied toolchain.

- Select a kernel headers version. Pick the version that most closely matches your target kernel version.

- Choose a uClibc library version. Choosing one of the latest released versions (rather than the daily snapshot) is recommended.

- Configure the location of the uClibc library configuration file. Leave it as the default at the moment; we will describe how to customise uClibc configuration in the next section.

- Support internationalization (i18n). Not normally useful for embedded systems.

- Pick a threading library implementation. NPTL is recommended.

- Control whether to build the threading library with debug symbols. Most people will want to say "Yes" here.

- Set an option to support the GNU "program invocation name" extension, which is used by some third-party programs (such as GNU *tar*) but not generally required. Choose "Yes" here.

- Pick the version of the binutils package. Pick the most recent version offered.

- Set additional options to pass when building the bintuils packages. Normally this is left empty.

- Pick the GCC compiler version. Older versions usually produce smaller code but support fewer features and have known issues.

- Enable your cross toolchain to use a custom sysroot, separate from the system's. It is important to enable this option to separate the cross toolchain cleanly from the native toolchain and libraries that might be installed on your workstation.

- Implement exception handling using setjmp/longjmp, rather then the more orthodox stack unwinding, to overcome issues with stack unwinding code. Choose "No" unless exceptions do not work correctly.

- Set additional options to pass during the GCC build. Leave this empty.

- Configure whether to build C++, FORTRAN, and Objective-C compiler and runtime support, in addition to C support.

- Build and install a shared library version of libgcc, the GCC runtime code library. Most people will choose "Yes" here.

- Build a toolchain supporting the *ccache* compiler cache tool.

- Set options for building and installing GDB, the GNU debugger, as part of the toolchain. See additional discussion of GDB in "Building and Installing gdb Components in Chapter 11.

- Support the FLT format, which is used with uClinux systems (Linux for systems with no MMU support).

- Choose whether to build and install *sstrip* (an enhanced version of the *strip* utility for editing ELF binary sections). As this is a useful tool, it is recommended that you set this option.

- Choose whether to build and support libraries that support multiple target ABIs. Not usually needed or recommended.

- Support files larger then 2 GB. Enabling this will require more runtime resources.

- Enable support for the IPv6 and RPC network protocols in the uClibc library.

- Support wide characters, or WCHAR, which is needed by some third-party software packages.

- Select whether to include software floating-point emulation in the toolchain. Useful for targets with no FPU, and preferred over using Linux-kernel-based emulation on these systems for performance reasons.

- Choose whether to install some useful target binaries (such as the debugger agent) in the toolchain directory.

- Configure additional options related to the use of Buildroot to generate root filesystems.

Package Selection for the target

As the name implies, this submenu allows one to ask Buildroot to fetch, build, and package additional software packages for the target filesystem using the cross tool-chain. Although this is a very useful option, it is of not interest to us at this time. Unmark all the options in this menu. The next chapter discusses building the target filesystem.

Target filesystem options

This submenu allows you to configure how Buildroot will package the root file-system it builds. As explained in the previous entry, you should unmark all the options in this submenu at this time.

Kernel

This submenu allows you to configure a Linux kernel version and configuration file to be automatically fetched and built by Buildroot using the cross toolchain. As before, leave all options unmarked at this time.

When finished, choose the < Exit > button and press Enter, then choose the < Yes > button to save your configuration.

Next, run *make* to let Buildroot fetch, patch, configure, build, and install your new uClibc-based cross toolchain:

```
$ make
```

 This stage can take quite some time and requires a working Internet connection.

The resulting toolchain will be installed in the *$PRJROOT/tools/bin* directory when the build completes.

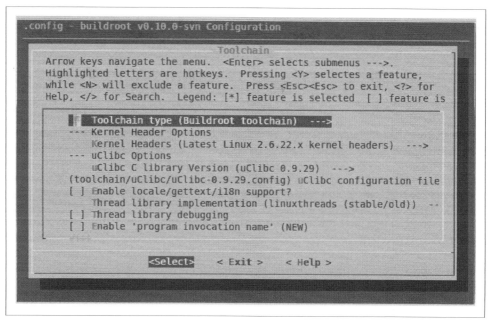

```
.config - buildroot v0.10.0-svn Configuration
                            Toolchain
  Arrow keys navigate the menu.  <Enter> selects submenus --->.
  Highlighted letters are hotkeys.  Pressing <Y> selectes a feature,
  while <N> will exclude a feature.  Press <Esc><Esc> to exit, <?> for
  Help, </> for Search.  Legend: [*] feature is selected  [ ] feature is

          Toolchain type (Buildroot toolchain)  --->
      --- Kernel Header Options
          Kernel Headers (Latest Linux 2.6.22.x kernel headers)  --->
      --- uClibc Options
          uClibc C library Version (uClibc 0.9.29)  --->
      (toolchain/uClibc/uClibc-0.9.29.config) uClibc configuration file
      [ ] Enable locale/gettext/i18n support?
          Thread library implementation (linuxthreads (stable/old))  --
      [ ] Thread library debugging
      [ ] Enable 'program invocation name' (NEW)


           <Select>    < Exit >    < Help >
```

Figure 4-4. uClibc Buildroot toolchain menu

Customizing the uClibc configuration

The previous section used Buildroot to build a uClibc-based toolchain, using the default uClibc options for our target architecture. These default options are very reasonable, and it is recommended you stick with them, at least in your first attempt to build a uClibc-based system.

Having said that, we recognize it is sometimes desirable to fine-tune and optimize certain options in the uClibc configuration itself. This can be done through Buildroot, after it is configured using the procedure outlined in the previous section, by issuing the following command:

```
$ make uclibc-menuconfig
```

You will be presented with the uClibc configuration menu, which includes the following submenus and options:

- Target Architecture
- Target Architecture Features and Options
- General Library Settings
- Advanced Library Settings
- Networking Support
- String and Stdio Support

- Big and Tall
- Library Installation Options
- Security Options
- uClibc Development/Debugging Options

Note that many options in the uClibc configuration menu (such as the architecture type and installation path) will already be set according to your previous choices in the Buildroot configuration menu.

Let us now take a look at the options found in each configuration submenu. As mentioned earlier, you can use the ? key to obtain more information about each option from the configuration system. Because some options depend on the settings of other options, some of the options listed here may not be displayed in your configuration. While most options are binary choices (either enabled or disabled), others are text fields.

The Target Architecture option designates the target architecture for which uClibc will be built. The Buildroot configuration menu we described earlier set this option already.

The Target Architecture Features and Options submenu includes the following options:

Target Processor Type
   Which model of the specific architecture to optimize for.

Target file format
   Which executable file format to use. For targets using an MMU, the option is preset to ELF. For non-MMU-based targets, a choice of binary file types is available. For a discussion of the various formats and their relative weak and strong points, see *http://www.linuxdevices.com/articles/AT3186625227.html*.

Target CPU has a memory management unit (MMU)
   Specifies whether the specified target CPU has an MMU. If you chose a specific target model in the Target Processor Type option, this field may be preset for you.

Do you want to utilize the MMU?
   Even when hardware supports an MMU, you might want to conserve RAM and CPU cycles by not using it.

Enable floating-point number support
   This option allows you to omit all floating-point number support from uClibc. This will cause floating-point functions such as strtod() to be omitted from uClibc. Other floating-point functions, such as printf() and scanf(), will still be included in the library, but will not contain support for floating-point numbers.

Target CPU has a floating-point unit (FPU)
   If your target CPU does not have a floating-point unit (FPU) or a kernel FPU emulator, but you still wish to support floating-point functions, uClibc can be

compiled with soft floating-point support (using the *-msoft-float* option to the GCC). Unsetting this option will turn this behavior on.

Enable full C99 math library support
> If you want the uClibc math library to contain the full set of C99 math library features, set this option. If you leave it unset, the math library will contain only the math functions listed in the POSIX/IEEE 1003.1b-1993 standard, thus saving a couple of tens of kilobytes from the library size, depending on your architecture.

Linux kernel header location
> This field contains the kernel headers path and is preset by the Buildroot system.

The General Library Settings submenu includes the following options:

Generate position-independent code (PIC)
> Build uClibc entirely as position-independent code, even the static parts (shared library parts are always built as PIC code). This option is useful only if you want to statically link uClibc inside a shared library, and is very rarely turned on.

Enable support for shared libraries
> Unless you are building a static library only system, you should enable this option.

Only load shared libraries which can share their text segment
> This option will prevent the shared library loader from loading shared libraries that modify the program's code section during the load in order to support relocations (thus requiring additional memory for each user of the shared library). Such modifications normally take place when a shared library is been compiled without the -*fPIC* or *-fpic* options, which enforce position-independent code.

> Because building a shared library without position-independent code is rarely a good idea, this option can trap build mistakes that would otherwise cause a needless waste of RAM.

Native 'ldd' support
> Enables all the code needed to support the traditional *ldd*, which executes the shared library loader to resolve all dependencies and then displays a list of shared libraries that are required for an application to function. Disabling this option makes uClibc's shared library loader a little bit smaller, but makes debugging certain link problems harder.

Enable library loader cache (ld.so.conf)
> Enable this to make use of */etc/ld.so.conf*, the shared library loader cache configuration file, to support nonstandard library paths, similar to the equivalent behavior in glibc.

Enable library loader preload file (ld.so.preload)
> Enable this to make use of */etc/ld.so.preload*. This file contains a whitespace-separated list of shared libraries to be loaded before the program. It also has an equivalent in glibc.

Shared library loader naming prefix

Sets a custom prefix for all shared library loader files. Required only if you plan to support glibc and uClibc on the same system, which should practically never happen in a production embedded system, so leaving the default is recommended.

Link ldconfig statically

Enable this option to statically link the ldconfig binary (thus making it a little bit bigger), which is useful if you are trying to debug shared library linkage problems. Otherwise, you might not be able to run the *ldconfig* tool, because it too is dependent upon a shared library. If space requirements permit, you should enable this option.

Enable ELF RUNPATH tag support

The ELF executable format supports a dynamic RPATH/RUNPATH tag that allows it to dynamically override the default search path of shared libraries on an executable-by-executable basis. Use of this feature is not very common, so disabling support for it is a good way to lower the shared library's loader size and the load time of shared libraries.

Support global constructors and destructors

If you have no plan to use C++ or GNU extension constructor and destructor attributes (using the __attribute__((constructor)) and __attribute__((destructor)) syntax), you can leave out support for them entirely, making each executable in the system a little smaller.

POSIX threading support

Enabling this option adds support for POSIX threads, which will increase the size of uClibc as well as have a slight impact on runtime performance, because locking primitives will be added to protect internal critical uClibc data structures. Enable this option unless you never plan to make use of threads.

Build pthreads debugging support

Enabling this option will build the libthread_db shared library, which is necessary to debug multithreaded applications. Unless you never plan to debug multithreaded code on your target, you should enable this option.

 GDB must also be built with uClibc to make multithreaded debugging possible.

Use the older (stable) version of LinuxThreads

Currently, uClibc supports only the legacy (LinuxThreads) threading library, although experimental support for NPTL is also available.

However, there are two versions of LinuxThreads supported by uClibc. The older (stable) version has been in uClibc for quite a long time but hasn't seen too many updates other than bug fixes. The new version has not been tested much, and lacks ports for architectures glibc does not support (such as Blackfin and FRV), but is based on the latest code from glibc, so it may be the only choice for the newer ports (such as Alpha, AMD64, and HPPA).

Large file support

Enabling this option allows uCLibc to support files larger then 2 GB, at the expense of a bigger footprint.

Malloc implementation

This submenu allows a choice between three `malloc()` implementations, ranging from a simplistic implementation suitable for systems with smaller RAM and allocations up to a standard implementation equivalent to the one found in glibc.

Malloc returns live pointer for malloc(0)

This option controls the behavior of `malloc()` when asked to return an allocation of zero size. Enable this option for full glibc compatibility.

Dynamic atexit() support

Controls whether to support multiple dynamic `atext()` callbacks. Required for proper C++ support.

Old (visible) atexit support

An outdated option included for backward compatibility with older releases of uClibc. Leave unset.

Enable SuSv3 LEGACY functions and enable SuSv3 LEGACY macros

Enable support for defunct functions and macros (`bcopy`, `bzero`, `bcmp`, `index`, and `rindex`) that some software packages might still need.

Shadow password support

Enable support for keeping the user password in a shadow file, separate from the master user database, for better security. This option is recommended.

Support for program_invocation_name and support for __progname

These options enable support for very rarely used aliases to the `argv[0]` argument containing a program name. Some software packages (notably GNU *tar* and coreutils) use these aliases to provide extra useful output. It is normally safe to leave this option unset.

Supports only Unix 98 PTYs

Unsetting this option enables legacy support for non-Unix 98 PTYs. Unless you are going to use older applications, it is safe to leave this set.

Assume that /dev/pts is a devpts or devfs filesystem

Enabling this option assumes that the devpts virtual filesystem is used to keep track of pseudoterminal devices. This is normally true for modern Linux systems. But if you choose this option, enable devpts support in the kernel configuration.

Various additional time related options

The last options in this menu control the handling of time and time zones in uClibc. For full glibc compatibility and best performance, you should turn on all these options.

The Advanced Library Settings submenu contains advanced options that allow expert developers to tweak the sizes of various buffers used internally in uClibc.

The Networking Support submenu includes the following options:

IP version 6 support
Enables support for IPv6 in networking system calls.

Remote Procedure Call (RPC) support
Enables RPC support. Unless you plan to make use of NFS, it is safe to unset this option.

Full RPC support
Full-featured RPC support. Not required for NFS. Unless you have a very specific need for full RPC support, you can safely unset this option.

Reentrant RPC support
Provides reentrant versions of the RPC calls. Required for some programs (such as *exportfs*).

Use netlink to query interfaces
Query network devices via the newer Netlink interface rather then the old ioctl interface. Usually not recommended, as the newer Netlink interface requires a larger footprint but can be turned on to resolve issues with newer network device drivers that do not support the old interface.

Support res_close() (bsd-compat)
Turns on the BSD-compatible network API. Usually not required.

The String and Stdio Support submenu includes various options to tweak and configure the behavior of functions related to strings and files. The major options are the following:

Wide character support
Enables wide character support. This will make uClibc much larger. It is required for locale support (the next option), so this option is recommended only if you must support languages using characters greater than 8 bits in length.

Locale support
Turns on full ANSI/ISO C99 locale support (except for `wcsftime()` and collating items in regular expressions).

Enabling this option will make uClibc much larger; used with the default set of supported locales (169 UTF-8 locales and 144 locales for other codesets) will enlarge uClibc by around 300 KB. Use this only if internationalization support at the system library level is a must.

Include the errno message text in the library, Include the signum message text in the library
Enable these options to display verbose error messages and signal descriptions at the cost of about 3.5 KB in uClubc library size. These options alter the displays shown by `strerror()` and `strsignal()`. Recommended for most systems.

Additional miscellaneous options and submenus allow you to change other, less critical string and file handling in uClibc.

The Big and Tall submenu provides several options allowing you to drop rarely used functionality from uClibc. As a general rule, the defaults are recommended.

The Library Installation Options submenu specifies several installation paths and prefixes used by the uClibc installer. The Buildroot environment will have already chosen the values of the options in this section; you shouldn't change them.

The Security Options submenu provides options to turn on several security features, allowing you to harden the uCLibc installation against security attacks at the cost of runtime performance. It is safe to leave all these options unset.

The uClibc Development/Debugging Options submenu accesses some options that can be useful when debugging uClibc and uClibc-based applications, such as debug symbols for the library and runtime assertions in the uClibc library code for debugging uClibc itself. You would not normally ship a finished product with these debug options enabled, however.

After using the menus just described to adapt the uClibc configuration to your needs, copy the .config file to *toolchain/uClibc/uClibc.config* or *toolchain/uClibc/uClibc.config-locale*. The former is used if you haven't selected locale support in the Buildroot configuration, and the latter if you have selected it.

```
$ cp toolchain_build_arm/uClibc-0.9.29/.config toolchain/uClibc/uClibc.config
```

Now rebuild Buildroot:

```
$ make clean
$ make
```

Diet libc

The diet libc project was started and is maintained by Felix von Leitner. Its goals are similar to uClibc. In contrast with uClibc, however, diet libc did not grow from previous work on libraries but was written from scratch with an emphasis on minimizing size and optimizing performance. Hence, diet libc compares quite favorably to glibc in terms of footprint and speed. In comparison to uClibc, though, we have not noticed any substantial difference.

Diet libc does not support all the processor architectures discussed in Chapter 3; it supports the ARM, MIPS, x86, and PPC. Also, the authors of diet libc favor static linking over dynamic linking. So, although diet libc can be used as a shared library on some platforms, it is intended to be used as a static library.

One of the most important issues to keep in mind while evaluating diet libc is its licensing. In contrast to most other libraries, including uClibc, which are usually licensed under the LGPL, diet libc is licensed under the terms of the GPL. As we explained in Chapter 1, this means that by linking your code to diet libc, you make the resulting binary a derived work and can distribute it only under the terms of the GPL. A commercial license is available from the package's main author if you wish to distribute non-GPL code linked with diet libc.[||] If, however, you would prefer not to have to deal with such licensing issues, you may want to use uClibc instead.

Diet libc is available for download both as a tar-bzip2'd archive or using CVS from the project's website at *http://www.fefe.de/dietlibc/*.[#] The package comes with an FAQ and installation instructions. In the following examples, we will use version 0.21 of diet libc, but the explanations should apply to other versions as well.

Library setup

As with uClibc, the first step to setting up diet libc is to download it into your *${PRJROOT}/build-tools* directory. Here, too, you will build the library within the package's source directory and not in another directory, as was the case for the GNU toolchain. No configuration is required for diet libc. Instead, you can proceed with the build stage immediately.

Once the package is extracted, move into the *diet libc* directory for the setup:

```
$ cd ${PRJROOT}/build-tools/dietlibc-0.31
```

Before building the package for your target, build it for your host. This is necessary to create the *diet* utility, which is required to build diet libc for the target and later to build applications against diet libc:

```
$ make
```

In the setup used for this example, this command creates a *bin-ppc* directory containing a PPC diet libc. You can now compile diet libc for your target:

```
$ make ARCH=i386 CROSS=i386-linux-
```

You will see even more warnings than with the other packages, but you can ignore them. Here, you must tell the Makefile both the architecture for which diet libc is built and the prefix of the cross-platform development tools.

With the package now built, you can install it:

```
$ make ARCH=i386 DESTDIR=${PREFIX}/dietlibc prefix="" install
```

This installs diet libc components in *${PREFIX}/dietlibc*. Again, as when building the package for your target, you must specify the architecture. Also specify the install destination using the DESTDIR variable, and reset the Makefile's internal prefix variable, which is different from the capital PREFIX environment variable.

[||] It is not clear whether this license covers the contributions made to diet libc by developers other than the main author.

[#] Notice the final "/". If you omit this slash, the web server will be unable to locate the web page.

Diet libc has now been installed in the proper directory. There is, however, one correction you may need to make to the installation. Because the example shown here installed the x86 version of diet libc, it also installed the x86 version of the *diet* utility in *${PREFIX}/dietlibc/bin*. Since we intend to compile our applications on the host, we need to overwrite this with the native *diet* utility we built earlier:

```
$ cp bin-ppc/diet ${PREFIX}/dietlibc/bin
```

Usage

In order to use diet libc, you must first modify your system PATH variable, and then make use of a special diet libc wrapper when making calls to the various build tools.

First, change your path to include the directory containing the diet libc binary:

```
$ export PATH=${PREFIX}/dietlibc/bin:${PATH}
```

Again, you will also want to change your development environment script. For example, the path line in our *develdaq* script becomes:

```
export PATH=${PREFIX}/bin:${PREFIX}/dietlibc/bin:${PATH}
```

Notice that we assume you won't be using both uClibc and diet libc at the same time. Hence, the path line has only diet libc added. If you would like to have both diet libc and uClibc on your system during development, you need to add both paths.

To compile the control daemon with diet libc, use the following command line:

```
$ make CROSS_COMPILE="diet i386-linux-"
```

Because diet libc is mainly a static library, this will result in a statically linked binary by default and you don't need to add `LDFLAGS="-static"` to the command line. Using the same "Hello World!" program as earlier, we obtained a 24 KB binary when linked with diet libc.

Java

Since Sun introduced it in 1995, Java has become one of the most important programming languages around. Today, it is found in every category of computerized systems, including embedded systems. Although still not as popular as C in the embedded programming world, it is nonetheless turning up in an ever-increasing number of designs.

As Sun has released most of the source of Java under the GPL version 2 license, with a clause excusing code using the Java runtime classes from the requirement to be licensed under the GPL, the Sun Java reference implementation is now (mostly) a true open source project. It can be downloaded and compiled like any other open source program, making it the most natural candidate for a Java runtime for an embedded Linux system.

Having said that, before Sun elected to release Java under an open source license, several other open source Java packages were created, and some of them were successfully used in embedded Linux systems.

In this chapter, we will briefly review some of these options and provide pointers to the various projects' websites.

 There also exist numerous commercial, proprietary Java VMs for Linux. However, we will not cover them here.

Sun Java Micro Edition

Sun Java Micro Edition, also known as J2ME, is a subset of the Java platform that aims to provide a certified collection of Java APIs for the development of software for embedded and mobile devices, mostly mobile phones.

As of December 2006, the Sun reference specification of J2ME is available from Sun under the GNU GPL, under the PhoneME moniker from the Mobile and Embedded community web page on the Sun website at:

http://community.java.net/mobileandembedded

The source code for the latest releases and prebuilt binaries for Linux x86 and ARM-platforms are available at *https://phoneme.dev.java.net/downloads_page.html#feature*. A very detailed guide for building a current MR2 release of phoneME is available at *https://phoneme.dev.java.net/content/mr2/index_feature.html*.

Because Sun PhoneME is the reference Java platform for mobile devices, it is most compatible with the Java standard. However, it is not necessarily the one with the best performance or smallest footprint. One can hope that, with its release under an open source license, this might change in the future.

Non-Sun-Related Open Source Virtual Machines

Because Sun Java was released under an open source license only in late 2006, a number of older projects exist that provide open source, fully functional JVMs without using any of Sun's source code. Since there isn't any consensus on the feasibility of using any of the various open source VMs as the main JVM in an embedded Linux project, we will only mention the VMs briefly and will not provide any information regarding their use. You are invited to look at each VM and follow the efforts of the individual teams.

The Kaffe Java Virtual Machine (*http://www.kaffe.org*) is based on KaffePro VM, a product sold commercially by Transvirtual, Inc., and is a clean-room implementation of the JVM.[*] Although no new releases of the project have been made since July 2000, and although this VM is not 100 percent compatible with Sun's VM (according to the project's website), it is still the main open source alternative to Sun's VM.

---

[*] That is, it was written from scratch without using any of Sun's Java source code.

There are other projects that may eventually become more important, such as Japhar (*http://www.japhar.org*), Kissme (*http://kissme.sourceforge.net*), Aegis (*http://ae gisvm.sourceforge.net*), and Sable VM (*http://www.sablevm.org*). For a complete list of open source VM projects, see the list provided by the Kaffe project at *http:// www.kaffe.org/links.shtml*.

See each project's respective website and documentation for information on how to install and operate the VM.

The GNU Java Compiler

As part of the GNU project, the GNU Compiler for the Java programming language (GCJ) is an extension to GCC that can handle both Java source code and Java bytecode. In particular, GCJ can compile either Java source code or Java bytecode into native machine code. In addition, it can also compile Java source into Java bytecode. It is often referred to as an ahead-of-time (AOT) compiler, because it can compile Java source code directly into native code, in contrast with popular just-in-time (JIT) compilers that convert Java bytecode into native code at runtime. GCJ does, nevertheless, include a Java interpreter equivalent to the JDK's *java* command.

GCJ is a fairly active project, and most core Java class libraries are already available as part of the GCJ runtime libraries. Although most windowing components, such as AWT, are still under development, the compiler and its runtime environment can already be used to compile and run most command-line applications.

As with other GNU projects, GCJ is fairly well documented. A good starting place is the project's website at *http://gcc.gnu.org/java*. In its documentation section, you will find a compile HOWTO, a general FAQ, and instructions on how to debug Java applications with *gdb*. You should be able to use the compilation HOWTO in conjunction with our earlier instructions regarding the GNU toolchain to build GCJ for your target.

Perl

Larry Wall introduced Perl in 1987, and it has since become a world of its own. If you are interested in Perl, have a look at *Programming Perl* by Larry Wall, Tom Christiansen, and Jon Orwant or *Learning Perl* by Randal Schwartz, Tom Phoenix, and brian d foy (both O'Reilly). Briefly, Perl is an interpreted language whose compiler, tools, and libraries are all available as open source under the terms of the Perl Artistic License and the GNU GPL from the Comprehensive Perl Archive Network (CPAN) at *http:// www.cpan.org*. Because there is only one Perl toolset, you will not need to evaluate different toolsets to figure out which one best suits your needs.

The main component you will need to run Perl programs on your target is a properly compiled Perl interpreter. Unfortunately, at the time of this writing, Perl is not well adapted to cross-compilation, and it is currently not possible to cross-compile a full Perl package.

However, two build options for cross-compiling small versions of the full Perl package do exist: microperl and miniperl. Note that both options are part of the same package, available on CPAN, and you do not need to download any other package.

Microperl

Simon Cozens implemented the microperl build option, based on an idea by Ilya Zakhareivh. It is the absolute bare minimum build of Perl, with no outside dependencies other than ANSI C and the *make* utility. Unlike the other builds, microperl does not require that you run the *Configure* script, which performs a great deal of tests on the installation machine before generating the appropriate files for the package's build. Instead, microperl provides default configuration files with minimal settings that allow the core Perl interpreter to build properly. None of the language's core features is missing from this interpreter. Of course, it does not support all the features of the full interpreter, but it is sufficient to run basic Perl applications. Because this code is considered "experimental," for the moment you will need to evaluate most of microperl's capabilities on your own.

We have successfully built a microperl for our DAQ module using the toolchain set up earlier, uClibc, and Perl 5.7.3. The resulting interpreter was able to adequately execute all Perl programs that did not have any outside references. It failed, however, to run programs that used any of the standard Perl modules.

To build microperl for your target, you must first download a Perl version from CPAN and extract it into the *${PRJROOT}/sysapps* directory. Place the package in the *sysapps* directory, because it will run only on the target and will not be used to build any of the other software packages for your target. After extracting the package, move into its directory for the build (here, you cannot use a different build directory, as we did for the GNU toolchain, because Perl does not support this build method):

```
$ cd ${PRJROOT}/sysapps/perl-5.10.0
```

Since microperl is a minimal build of Perl, you do not need to configure anything. Build the package using the appropriate Makefile and instructing it to use the uClibc compiler wrapper instead of the standard GCC compiler:

```
$ make -f Makefile.micro CC=i386-uclibc-gcc
```

This will generate a *microperl* binary in the package's root directory. This binary does not require any other Perl components and can be copied directly to the */bin* directory of your target's root filesystem, *${PRJROOT}/rootfs*.

When dynamically linked with either glibc or uClibc and stripped, the *microperl* binary is about 1.5 MB in size.

For more information on how microperl is built, have a look at the *Makefile.micro* Makefile and the *uconfig.sh* script. As work continues on microperl, it is expected that more documentation will become available.

Miniperl

Miniperl is less minimalistic than microperl and provides most of what you would expect from the standard Perl interpreter. The main component it lacks is the Dyna-Loader XS module, which allows Perl subroutines to call C functions. It is therefore incapable of loading XS modules dynamically. This is a minor issue, however, given the type of system miniperl will be running on.

As with the main Perl build, miniperl requires that you run the *Configure* script to determine the system's capabilities. Since the system for which Perl must be built is your target, the script requires you to specify information about how to communicate with that target: a hostname, a remote username, and a target-mapped directory. The script uses this information to run its tests on your target and generate the proper build files.

The main caveat concerning this method is that it requires a direct network link between the host and the target. In essence, if your target does not have some form of networking, you will be unable to build miniperl for it.

The installation methodology for miniperl is explained well in the *INSTALL* file provided with the 5.10.0 Perl package, under the "Cross-compilation" heading.

Cross-Compiling the Impossible

As we've just seen with Perl, not all packages cross-compile easily. As a matter of fact, a great number of packages have not been designed to allow cross-compilation. We've mentioned a few of these, but certainly can't list them all.

Besides trying to modify build scripts and using compilation tricks to force packages to compile for another architecture, sometimes the only realistic solution is to actually build the package on the target where it is supposed to run. At first, this may seem unfeasible for most embedded systems because of their limited storage space. As we shall see in Chapter 9, however, it is possible to mount a system's *root* filesystem on a server using NFS. By using an NFS-mounted *root* filesystem, the target can access as much storage space as the server allows.

In such a setup, it is therefore possible to cross-compile the GCC compiler itself for the target, and then use this compiler to natively compile any package directly on the target in exactly the same way the package's build scripts expect to operate. Once the package has been compiled, the resulting binaries and libraries can thereafter be copied to a small *root* filesystem tailored for the target's internal storage device, and used in the field like any other target application. Obviously, there is no need to package the cross-compiled GCC with the rest of the system in the field.

Python

Guido van Rossum introduced Python to the world in 1991. It has since gathered many followers and, as with Perl, is a world of its own. If you are interested in Python, read Mark Lutz's *Programming Python* or his *Learning Python* (both O'Reilly). Python is routinely compared to Perl, because it often serves the same purposes, but because this is the subject of yet another "holy war," we will not go any further. Instead, feel free to browse the main Python website at *http://www.python.org* for more information. The Python package, which includes the Python interpreter and the Python libraries, is available from that website under the terms of a composite license called the Python license, which is an approved open source license.

As with Perl, you will need a properly configured interpreter to run Python code on your target. Although the main Python distribution does not support cross-compilation, a patch by Christopher Lambacher that allows cross-compilation of Python 2.5 is available at *http://whatschrisdoing.com/~lambacck/Python2.5_xcompile.patch*. A blog post by Lambacher at *http://whatschrisdoing.com/blog/2006/10/06/howto-cross-compile-python-25* explains in detail how to get Python to cross-compile with this patch.

Follow the instructions, substituting the appropriate names for your target in the place of the `arm-linux` target used in the instructions. To follow the same project workspace organization that we established earlier, download and extract the Python package into the *${PRJROOT}/sysapps* directory. Also, instead of building Python directly in its source directory, you can use a *build-python* directory, as we did with the GNU tools, because Python supports this build method. In addition, use the *--prefix=${PREFIX}/${TARGET}/usr* option instead of the values provided by the HOWTO. All the Python material will thereby be installed in the *${PREFIX}/${TARGET}/usr* directory. You can then customize this directory and copy it onto the target's root filesystem.

There are a couple of observations to make about the resulting package. First, you will not be able to build Python with diet libc; use either glibc or uClibc. This means that glibc or uClibc will have to be on your target's root filesystem. When storage space on your target is limited, we recommend you use uClibc instead of glibc.

Second, Python has installed many libraries in the *${PREFIX}/${TARGET}/usr/lib/python2.2* directory, and many of those are large. You may want to trim down the content of this directory by deleting the components you are unlikely to use. By itself, the dynamically linked and stripped Python interpreter is 725 KB in size.

Nevertheless, Python's size and dependencies have not stopped developers from using it. A number of projects, including the OLPC's entire "Sugar" environment, make heavy use of Python. And a growing number of major Linux distributions are now even requiring a minimal python interpreter in order to even boot normally.

Finally, you may see some warnings and failures during the build. This is because some libraries and applications are missing from your target. The Tkinter interface to *libtk.a* and *libtcl.a* will fail to build, for instance, unless you cross-compiled and installed Tcl/Tk for your target. This doesn't mean the Python build has failed. Rather, it is an indication that one of the Python components has not built successfully. You will still be able to install and use the Python interpreter and the modules that built properly on your target.

Other Programming Languages

Linux, of course, supports many more programming languages. Whether you are looking for programming in Ada, Forth, Lisp, or FORTRAN, a short search on the Net with your favorite search engine should yield rapid results. A good starting point is the "Other Languages" section in Chapter 13 of *Running Linux* by Matthias Dalheimer and Matt Welsh (O'Reilly).

The cross-compiling and cross-development capabilities of the various language tools will need to be evaluated on a tool-tool basis, since few compilers and interpreters lend themselves well to cross-platform development.

Eclipse: An Integrated Development Environment

As we have seen in previous sections, the development tools for embedded Linux are a collection of standalone command-line programs. It has long been the preference of die-hard Unix and Linux developers to create software using a simple file editor and a command-line shell to invoke the development tool. However, most embedded software developers prefer to work in an IDE that provides a common graphical interface to all the functions of the development tools.

The Eclipse project, which IBM originally created in November 2001, and which has been an independent nonprofit corporation since 2004, provides an open development platform comprised of extensible frameworks, tools, and runtimes for building, deploying, and managing software. Its popularity, openness, and rich features make it an excellent choice as an IDE for embedded Linux development. A typical display by Eclipse appears in Figure 4-5.

Instead of a monolithic IDE, Eclipse provides a modular framework on which many IDEs can be built by combining a common base and a plethora of plug-ins for various functionalities, such as the CDT plug-in for C/C++ developers and the Remote System Explorer for target management. You can read more about Eclipse on the project website at *http://www.eclipse.org*.

Although several other IDEs exist for Linux, no other such tool enjoys the widespread adoption of Eclipse, which is used by both commercial vendors (who base development environments on Eclipse and provide many plug-ins and extensions) and the open source community, which has extended Eclipse to support practically every need.

We will cover the installation, adaptation, and use of Eclipse in the following sections.

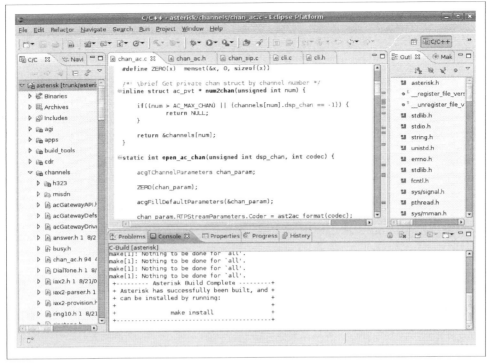

Figure 4-5. Typical Eclipse project workspace

Installing Eclipse

Eclipse is a Java application, which makes it cross-platform. However, that means you need a Java runtime virtual machine (JVM) to run it. Most current Linux distributions come with a preinstalled JVM called GCJ. Unfortunately, although Eclipse does run on the GCJ, it is not one of the referenced JVMs on which it is regularly tested. We therefore recommend that you first install a free JVM for Linux from the Sun Java download website at *http://www.java.com/en/download/manual.jsp*.

 The Sun Java JV can peacefully coexist with GCJ, so you should not worry about trashing your current JVM installation.

After successfully installing the Sun JVM, proceed to download Eclipse from the project download page at *http://www.eclipse.org/downloads*. You will want to download the Eclipse IDE for C/C++ Developers edition, which integrates the basic common Eclipse core with the CDT plug-in for C/C++ developers.

After downloading the compressed tar archive, change into the directory to which you wish to install Eclipse and decompress the tar archive.

 You can install Eclipse in any location you wish, including your home directory, but if you wish to share the Eclipse installation with others using the same computer (such as a shared networked server), we recommend you open the archive in a location that is accessible to all users. This may require you to uncompress the archive as the superuser.

```
$ cd $PRJROOT/tools
$ tar zxvf $PROJROOT/build-tools/eclipse-cpp-europa-fall2-linux-gtk-x86_64.tar.gz
```

Before you can run Eclipse, you need to configure the location of your alternative JVM. To do so, find the text file named *eclipse.ini* in the *$PRJROOT/tools/eclipse* folder, and make sure the following lines are present and point to the correct location where the Sun JVM has been installed:

```
...
-vm
/usr/lib/jvm/java-6-sun/jre/bin/java
...
```

 Do not try to put the path to the JVM in the same line as the -vm argument. The text must appear on two separate lines, as shown in the preceding excerpt.

Running Eclipse

Now you are ready to run Eclipse:

```
$ $PRJROOT/tools/eclipse/eclipse &
```

The first time you invoke it, you will be presented with a dialog box asking you to select a workspace (Figure 4-6). An Eclipse workspace is the location where development projects and Eclipse configuration information are saved. Either accept the default workspace location of a directory named *workspace* in your home directory, or provide an alternate location and click OK.

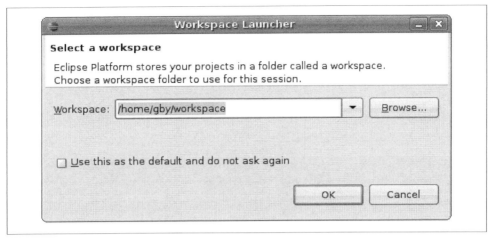

Figure 4-6. Eclipse Workspace Launcher

After Eclipse finishes loading, it presents you with a welcome screen.

Extending Eclipse

As we explained, Eclipse is a modular framework for building IDEs. Thus, apart from the common core framework, most Eclipse-based IDE functionalities are provided by plug-ins. Plug-ins allow Eclipse to support a wide range of languages, source control systems, targets, debugging facilities, and more.

As we chose to install the Eclipse IDE for C/C++ Developers edition, one plug-in is already installed in our new Eclipse installation: CDT, the C/C++ developer support plug-in. In order to make Eclipse a more useful developer environment for embedded Linux, we will add the the Target Management toolkit plug-in and the Subclipse Subversion source control integration plug-in.

 You can find many more plug-ins (more than a thousand are listed at the time of this writing) in the Eclipse Plugin Central website at *http://www.eclipseplugincentral.com*.

Installing a plug-in

Eclipse contains a generic infrastructure for installing and updating plug-ins. Installation of practically all Eclipse plug-ins, therefore, follows the same procedure.

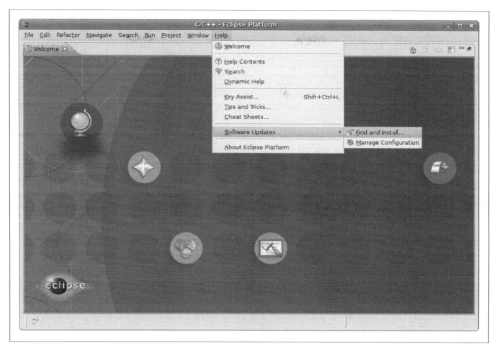

Figure 4-7. *Eclipse Software Updates menu*

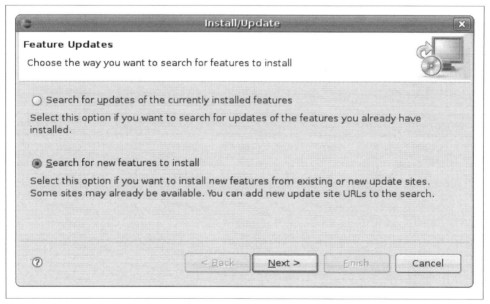

Figure 4-8. *Eclipse Install/Update dialog*

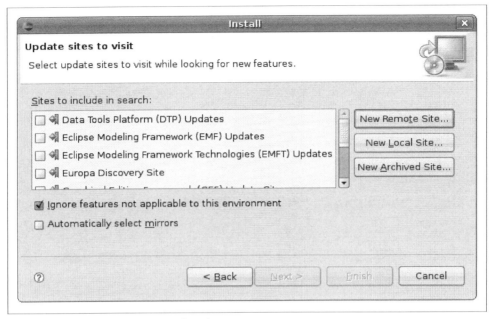

Figure 4-9. Eclipse Install dialog with update sites

First, locate the requested plug-in's update site URL. This is a web URL (e.g., *http:// download.eclipse.org/dsdp/tm/updates/2.0*) that hosts a specific plug-in download and future updates. The update site URL tells the Eclipse plug-in framework where to download both the plug-in and future updates to it. The update site URL for a specific plug-in version is usually published on the plug-in website.

Now configure the Eclipse plug-in framework to pull the plug-in from the update site as follows:

1. From the Help menu, choose the Software Updates entry (Figure 4-7).

2. In the Install/Update dialog that appears, choose "Search for new features to install" and click Next (Figure 4-8).

3. In the Install dialog, click on the "New Remote Site..." button, which displays a list of update sites (Figure 4-9).

4. Enter a descriptive name for the new update site (such as the plug-in name) and the update site URL from the plug-in website. Click OK.

5. The new site will be added to the list of available update sites. Make sure the checkbox next to the new site entry is marked and click Finish.

6. In the new Updates dialog that appears, check all the requested plug-ins from the available list.

7. Click on the Select Required button to automatically add any additional plug-ins that your chosen plug-ins depend upon.

8. Click Finish.

The new plug-in will be now be installed.

Target Management toolkit

The Target Management project creates data models and frameworks to configure and manage remote systems, their connections, and their services. It has been found useful on all kinds of remote systems, from mainframes down to embedded devices. The base toolkit includes a Remote Files subsystem, which allows you to work on remote computers transparently, just as if you were on the local system. It also includes a shell and processes subsystem, a lightweight terminal, and a Network Discovery framework.

You can read more about the Target Management project at the project website, *http://www.eclipse.org/dsdp/tm*. An online tutorial for the Target Management toolkit is available at *http://www.eclipse.org/dsdp/tm/tutorial*.

You can find the update site URL for the latest version of the Target Management toolkit on the project website and can install it using the procedure outlined earlier in "Installing a plug-in."

Subclipse

Subclipse is an Eclipse Team Provider plug-in that provides support for Subversion within the Eclipse IDE. You can read more about Subclipse at the project website, *http://subclipse.tigris.org*. The update site for the latest version of the Subclipse plug-in is available on the project website.

Working With Eclipse

Eclipse is a modern IDE supporting many types of languages and setups, and it is very customizable. The following sections will walk you through the setup of a new embedded software project.

Projects

Like many IDEs, Eclipse groups the development of related software in the context of a project. To start a new project, choose "New entry" from the file menu, and you will be presented with the New Project wizard dialog (Figure 4-10).

Choose a C (or C++) project and click on Next. You will be presented with the C Project configuration dialog (Figure 4-11). Its options involve a choice between two basic approaches: letting Eclipse manage the project build (called a managed project) or managing your own build system in the traditional fashion using your own Makefile.

In managed build projects, Eclipse automatically creates a set of Makefiles to build the project based on project properties that you define (e.g., the toolchain to use) and the

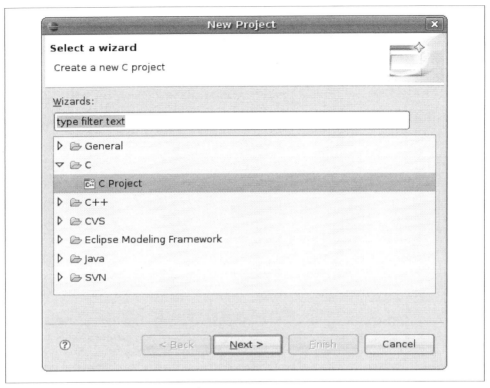

Figure 4-10. Eclipse New Project wizard

specific configuration (e.g., Debug versus Release). Eclipse builds the software by executing this automatically created Makefile.

Delegating the project build to Eclipse may seem very convenient, but it comes at a price: henceforth, you will be tightly dependent on the Eclipse IDE to build your project.

Indeed, such tasks as performing an automated nightly build may become much more complicated, and optimizing your build process might become much more difficult, if at all possible.

Consider carefully whether the time and effort saved by letting Eclipse create your Makefiles automatically might cost you extra time and effort later on.

If you are like most embedded systems developers, you'll prefer to have as much control as you can over the build process of your projects. The best way to accomplish this is to create your own custom Makefile. This also allows you to import software projects that already have an existing build system. Finally, it frees you from depending on Eclipse for building your project, which can come in handy under circumstances such as implementing nightly builds.

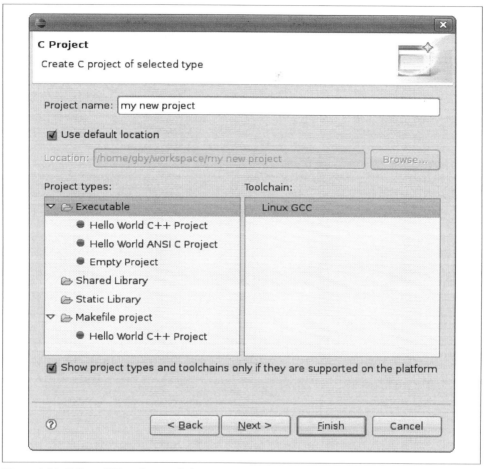

Figure 4-11. Eclipse C/C++ Project dialog

Managed build projects. If you wish to let Eclipse manage your project's build process, you must first tell Eclipse what kind of project you wish to create. The following are the available options:

Executable

This project will produce an executable binary image.

Shared library

This project will produce a dynamically loaded, shared library whose code can be shared between several processes at runtime.

Static library

This project will create a standard static code library, whose code is added to the code of the executable that makes use of it at build time.

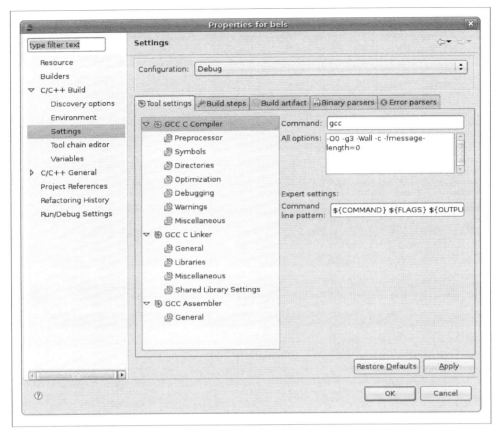

Figure 4-12. Eclipse Properties sheet

The same screen allows you to choose which toolchain you wish to work with. By default, Eclipse offers just the Linux GCC toolchain, the native toolchain installed by default on the host development machine. Choose this toolchain for now; we'll edit the configuration later to make use of our custom cross toolchain.

To continue, click on the Next button. You will be presented with the configuration selection screen, which will let you define which configurations you wish to support. By default, Eclipse offers the Debug and Release configurations.

By default, Eclipse will configure your project to use the native host toolchain. Since you wish to use a cross toolchain, you need to make some changes to this default configuration. Thus, in the same screen, choose the "Advanced settings..." button. In the project properties screen that will open, choose the Settings entry from the C/C++ Build submenu and replace the command fields of both the "GCC C compiler" and "GCC C linker" entries with the cross toolchain counterparts, such as `arm-linux-gcc`. See Figure 4-12.

Makefile projects.   To use your own Makefile, choose the "Hello World C++ Project" under the "Makefile project" entry in the "C/C++ Project" wizard dialog and click on the Finish button. Eclipse will create a template Makefile project for you with a single C++ file and a Makefile that builds it. You can then customize the Makefile.

Development

From the point where your new project has been created, the rest of the development cycle with Eclipse is no different from development with a native toolchain. Therefore, instead of documenting it here, we refer you to the Eclipse CDT website, where various Eclipse CDT functions and screens are documented: *http://www.eclipse.org/cdt/*.

Target management

One of the most convienient facilities Eclipse offers for embedded systems developers is the Remote System Explorer (RSE) subsystem, which is part of the Target Management toolkit plug-in we installed earlier. Features include:

Remote filesystems
> Browse, upload, and download files on the target board and remote server using SSH, FTP, or the dstore agent. dstore supports the seamless editing of remote files, including remote searches and comparisons.

Remote shell access
> Remote control of the target board.

Remote process control
> View the remote board tasks and state (requires a dstore agent running on the target).

Remote debugging
> This is offered through CDT, GDB, and the GDBServer proxy.

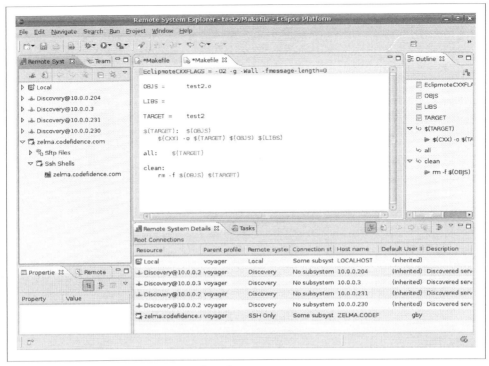

Figure 4-13. Eclipse Remote System Explorer browser

Defining remote connections. To use all the features the RSE framework has to offer, you must configure some remote machines or target boards to interact with. To do this, open the Open Perspective submenu in the Window menu and choose Remote Systems Prespective (Figure 4-13).

At the right of the screen, the Remote Systems list will open with a list of all previously configured remote systems. To create a new connection, right-click in the Remote Systems list window and choose New Connection. This displays a Remote System Type wizard (Figure 4-14).

If autodiscovery via DNS-SD Service Discovery (previously known as Zeroconf) is available, it will be automatically selected for you. Otherwise, you can manually configure a new remote connection.

After a connection has been created, you can browse the resources it provides via the Remote Systems view. Resources include remote files, remote shells, and views of remote processes, if available. Not all types of connections provide all the functionality, and some require the dstore agent to be running on the remote target.

In addition, once a connection has been defined in such a fashion, it will show up in the list of available connections in the C/C++ Remote Application menu in both the

Figure 4-14. Eclipse Remote System Type wizard

Run and Debug menus, allowing you to run and debug your application remotely on the target board.

For further discussion of debugging with Eclipse, see "Eclipse in Chapter 11.

Terminal Emulators

The most common way to communicate with an embedded system is to use a terminal emulation program on the host and communicate through an RS232 serial port with the target. Although there are a few terminal emulation programs available for Linux, not every one is fit for all uses. In the past, there have been well-know problems between minicom and U-Boot, for instance, during file transfers over the serial port. Hence, we recommend that you try more than one terminal application to communicate with your target. If nothing else, you are likely to discover one that best fits your personal preferences. Also, see your bootloader's documentation for any warnings regarding terminal emulators.

Three main terminal emulators are available in Linux: *minicom*, *cu*, and *kermit*. The following sections cover the setup and configuration of these tools, but not their uses. Refer to each package's documentation for its use.

Accessing the Serial Port

Before you can use any terminal emulator, you must ensure that you have the appropriate access rights to use the serial port on your host. In particular, you need read and write access to the serial port device, which is */dev/ttyS0* for permanently connected physical ports and */dev/ttyUSB0* for ports attached via USB. If you do not have these rights, any terminal emulator you use will complain at startup.[†]

To give your user account permission to access the serial port, add your username to the group of users with serial port access. The name of this group changes from one Linux distribution to another, so the easiest way to find it is to check the ownership on the serial port device file using the *ls* command:

```
$ ls -al /dev/ttyS0
crw-------    1 root      tty         4,  64 May  5  1998 /dev/ttyS0
```

In this example, the */dev/ttyS0* serial port device file is owned by the *root* user and the group named *tty* (the fourth field from the left). So, you will need to add your username to this group.

In addition, some terminal emulation applications also require your user to have access to the */var/lock* directory, for the purpose of creating a lock file, to protect the serial port from concurrent use. Although the use of lock files for this purpose is outdated, some programs still make use of it for backward compatibility. For this reason, you also need to check which group has access to the */var/lock* file and add your user to that group as well.

In similar fashion to our check with the serial port device file, you can examine the permission on the */var/lock* directory using the following command:

```
$ ls -ld /var/lock
drwxrwxr-x    5 root      uucp            1024 Oct  2 17:14 /var/lock
```

As you can see in this example, the required group is called *uucp*.

You will need, therefore, to add your user to both the *tty* and the *uucp* groups. The easiest way to add a user to a group is to use the appropriate graphical user interface tool provided by your distribution. The following are a couple of popular distributions that currently offer the commands described here:

[†] The actual changes required for your distribution may differ from those discussed in this section. Refer to your distribution's documentation in case of doubt.

Red Hat and Fedora
Systems based on these distributions can use the *redhat-config-users* tool:

```
$ redhat-config-users
```

Ubuntu
These distributions can use the *users-admin* tool with the gksu wrapper:

```
$ gksu users-admin
```

In addition, you can add a user to a group by editing the */etc/group* file using the *vigr* command. The command is tailored for editing that file and sets locks to ensure that only one user is accessing the file at any time. Because the command requires superuser access, you usually invoke it as follows:

Red Hat Enterprise Linux, Fedora, OpenSuSE, SLES, and Debian
Use the following command sequence:

```
$ su
Password:
# vigr
```

Ubuntu
Use the following alternate syntax:

```
$ sudo vigr
```

Once in *vigr*, locate the line that starts with the group name (such as tty) and add your username:

```
...
tty:x:5:karim
uucp:x:14:uucp,karim
...
```

See the *vigr* manpage for more information.

Finally, log out from superuser mode and from your own account, and log back into your account:

```
# exit
$ id
uid=501(karim) gid=501(karim) groups=501(karim)
$ exit

Teotihuacan login: karim
Password:
$ id
uid=501(karim) gid=501(karim) groups=501(karim),5(tty),14(uucp)
```

As you can see, you need to log out and then log back in for the changes to take effect. Opening a new terminal window in your GUI may have similar effects, depending on the GUI you are using and the way it starts new terminal windows. Even if it works, however, only the new terminal window will be part of the appropriate groups, but any other window opened before the changes will still be excluded. For this reason, it is preferable to exit your GUI, completely log out, and then log back in.

For more information on the setup of the serial interface, have a look at the Serial HOWTO available from the Linux Documentation Project and Chapter 3 of the *Linux Network Administrator's Guide* by Tony Bautts et al. (O'Reilly).

Eclipse Terminal

If you followed the instructions on the installation and configuration of the Eclipse IDE provided earlier in this chapter, a simple terminal is already installed as part of the Target Management toolkit plug-in. To use it, choose Show View from the Window menu and then choose the Terminal view.

A new terminal tab will open at the bottom of the screen and allow you to connect to any remote system via the Telnet protocol, the SSH protocol, or an RS232 serial connection. To connect to a remote system, simply choose the Connect button at the top of the tab.

The Telnet and SSH protocols do not require any additional installation. But to use a serial connection, a free third-party Java library called RXTX needs to be downloaded and installed.

The RXTX library is available at *ftp://ftp.qbang.org/pub/rxtx/rxtx-2.1.-7-bins.zip*. Install it as follows, replacing the string x86_64-unknown-linux-gnu in the example with the appropriate directory on your host system:

```
$ wget ftp://ftp.qbang.org/pub/rxtx/rxtx-2.1-7-bins.zip
$ cd rxtx-2.1-7-bins/
$ cp RXTXcomm.jar /usr/lib/jvm/java-6-sun/jre/lib/ext/
$ cp Linux/x86_64-unknown-linux-gnu/librxtxSerial.so /usr/lib/
```

Minicom

Minicom is the most commonly used terminal emulator for Linux. Most documentation about embedded Linux assumes that you are using minicom. However, as we said earlier, there are known file transfer problems between minicom and at least one bootloader, so it may not be right for you.

Minicom is a GPL clone of the Telix DOS program and provides ANSI and VT102 terminals. Its project website is currently located at *http://alioth.debian.org/projects/ minicom*. Minicom is also likely to be available through your distribution's software package management tool. To install it, use *yum install minicom* if you are using a distribution based on Red Hat or SUSE, and *apt-get install minicom* for a distribution based on Debian or Ubuntu.

Use the *minicom* command to start it:

```
$ minicom
```

The utility starts in full-screen mode and displays the following at the top of the screen:

```
Welcome to minicom 1.83.0

OPTIONS: History Buffer, F-key Macros, Search History Buffer, I18n
Compiled on Mar  7 2000, 06:12:31.

Press CTRL-A Z for help on special keys
```

To enter commands to Minicom, press Ctrl-A and then the letter of the desired function. As Minicom's welcome message states, use Ctrl-A Z to get help from Minicom. Refer to the package's manpage for more details about its use.

UUCP cu

Unix to Unix CoPy (UUCP) used to be one of the most popular ways to link Unix systems. Though UUCP is rarely used today, the *cu* command in the UUCP package can be used to "call up" other systems. The connection used to communicate to the other system can take many forms. In our case, we are mostly interested in establishing a terminal connection over a serial line to our target.

To this end, we must add the appropriate entries to the configuration files used by UUCP. In particular, this means adding a port entry in */etc/uucp/port* and a remote system definition to */etc/uucp/sys*. As the UUCP info page states, "a port is a particular hardware connection on your computer," whereas a system definition describes the system to connect to and the port used to connect to it.

Although UUCP is available from the GNU FTP site under the terms of the GPL, it is usually already installed on your system. On a system based on Red Hat or Fedora, enter *rpm -q uucp* to verify that it is installed.

Here is an example */etc/uucp/port* file:

```
# /etc/uucp/port - UUCP ports
# /dev/ttyS0
port      ttyS0        # Port name
type      direct       # Direct connection to other system
device    /dev/ttyS0   # Port device node
hardflow  false        # No hardware flow control
speed     115200       # Line speed
```

This entry states that there is a port called ttyS0 that uses direct 115200 bps connections without hardware flow control to connect to remote systems through */dev/ttyS0*. The name of the port in this case, ttyS0, is used only to identify this port definition for the rest of UUCP utilities and configuration files. If you've used UUCP before to connect using a traditional modem, you will notice that this entry resembles modem definitions. Unlike modem definitions, however, there is no need to provide a carrier field to specify whether a carrier should be expected. Setting the connection type to direct makes carrier default to false.

Here is an example */etc/uucp/sys* file that complements the */etc/uucp/port* file just shown:

```
# /etc/uucp/sys - name UUCP neighbors
# system: target
system  target   # Remote system name
port    ttyS0    # Port name
time    any      # Access is possible at any time
```

Basically, this definition states that the system called `target` can be called up at any time, using port ttyS0.

With those files in place, you can use *cu* to connect to the target:

```
$ cu target
Connected.
```

Once in a *cu* session, you can issue instructions using the ~ character, followed by another character specifying the actual command. For a complete list of commands, use ~?.

For more information on configuring and customizing UUCP for your system, look at Chapter 16 of the *Linux Network Administrator's Guide*, the UUCP HOWTO available from the Linux Documentation Project (LDP), and the UUCP info page.

C-Kermit

C-Kermit is one of the packages maintained as part of Columbia University's Kermit project (*http://www.columbia.edu/kermit*). C-Kermit provides a unified interface for network operations across a wide range of platforms. Although it features many capabilities, terminal emulation is the one we are most interested in.

Though you are free to download it for personal and internal use, C-Kermit is not open source software and its licensing makes it difficult for use in commercial distributions.[‡] C-Kermit is available for download at *http://www.columbia.edu/kermit/cker mit.html*. Follow the documentation in the *ckuins.txt* file included with the package to compile and install C-Kermit. In contrast with most other tools we discuss in this book, C-Kermit should be installed system-wide, not locally to your project workspace. Once installed, C-Kermit is started using the *kermit* command.

In terms of usability, *kermit* compares quite favorably to both Minicom and UUCP. Although it lacks the menus provided by Minicom, *kermit*'s interactive command language provides a very intuitive and powerful way of interacting with the terminal emulator. When you initiate a file transfer from the target's bootloader, for example, the bootloader starts waiting for the file. You can then switch to *kermit*'s interactive command line on the host using Ctrl-\ C and send the actual file using the *send* command.

Among other things, the interactive command line provides tab filename completion similar to that provided by most shells in Linux. Also, the interactive command line is

---

[‡] Although the license was changed lately to simplify inclusion in commercial distributions such as Red Hat, C-Kermit has yet to be included in most mainstream distributions.

capable of recognizing commands using the shortest unique character string that is part of a command name. The *set receive* command, for example, can be shortened to *set rec*.

To use the *kermit* command, you must have a *.kermrc* configuration file in your home directory. *kermit* runs this file at startup. Here is an example *.kermrc* file that one author uses on his workstation:

```
; Line properties
set modem type              none ; Direct connection
set line            /dev/ttyS0 ; Device file
set speed                 115200 ; Line speed
set carrier-watch            off ; No carrier expected
set handshake               none ; No handshaking
set flow-control            none ; No flow control

; Communication properties
robust                            ; Most robust transfer settings macro
set receive packet-length 1000 ; Max pack len remote system should use
set send packet-length    1000 ; Max pack len local system should use
set window                   10 ; Nbr of packets to send until ack

; File transfer properties
set file type             binary ; All files transferred are binary
set file names           literal ; Don't modify filenames during xfers
```

For more information about each of the settings, try the *help* command provided by *kermit*'s interactive command line. For more information regarding the *robust* macro, for example, enter *help robust*. In this case, *robust* must be used before *set receive*, because *robust* sets the maximum packet length to be used by the remote system to 90 bytes, whereas we want it set to 1,000 bytes.

After creating your configuration file, you can start *kermit*:

```
$ kermit -c
Connecting to /dev/ttyS0, speed 115200
 Escape character: Ctrl-\ (ASCII 28, FS): enabled
Type the escape character followed by C to get back,
or followed by ? to see other options.
----------------------------------------------------
```

If you are looking for more information about the use of C-Kermit and intend to use it more extensively, think about purchasing *Using C-Kermit* by Frank Da Cruz and Christine Gianone (Digital Press). Apart from providing information regarding the use of C-Kermit, sales of the book help fund the project. Although the book covers version 6.0, supplements for versions 7.0 and 8.0 are freely available on the project's website.

## CHAPTER 5

Kernel Considerations

The kernel is the most fundamental software component of all Linux systems. It is responsible for managing the bare hardware within your chosen target system and bringing order to what would otherwise be a chaotic struggle between each of the many various software components on a typical system.

In essence, this means the kernel is a resource broker. It takes care of scheduling use of (and mediating access to) the available hardware resources within a particular Linux system. Resources managed by the kernel include system processor time given to programs, use of available RAM, and indirect access to a multitude of hardware devices—including those custom to your chosen target. The kernel provides a variety of software abstractions through which application programs can request access to system resources, without communicating with the hardware directly.

The precise capabilities provided by any particular build of the Linux kernel are configurable when that kernel is built. Kernel configuration allows you to remove support for unnecessary or obscure capabilities that will never be used. For example, it is possible to remove support for the many different networked filesystems from an embedded device that has no networking support. Conversely, it is possible to add support for a particular peripheral device unique to a chosen target system. Depending on their function, many capabilities can also be built into optional, runtime-loadable, modular components. These can be loaded later when the particular capability is required.

Most desktop or enterprise Linux vendors ship prebuilt Linux kernels as part of their distributions. Such kernels include support for the wide range of generic hardware devices typically available within modern consumer-grade or enterprise-level computing systems. Many of these capabilities are built into runtime-loadable modules, which are demand loaded by a variety of automated tools as hardware devices are detected. This one-size-fits-all approach allows Linux vendors to support a wide range of target systems with a single prebuilt binary kernel package, at the cost of a certain amount of generalization and the occasional performance impact that goes alongside it.

Unlike their desktop, server, or enterprise counterparts, embedded Linux systems usually do not make use of such all-encompassing prebuilt, vendor-supplied kernels. The reasons for this are varied, but include an inability for generic kernels to handle certain embedded, target-specific customizations, as well as a general underlying desire to keep the kernel configuration as simple as possible. A simpler configuration is both easier to debug and typically requires a reduced resource footprint when compared with its more generic counterpart. Building an embedded system from scratch is tough enough already without worrying about the many kernel capabilities you will never use.

This chapter will cover some of the many considerations you will face when choosing a suitable Linux kernel for your target embedded system. Our discussion will include issues surrounding Linux kernel configuration, compilation, and installation as it pertains to such embedded use. We will not discuss using the Linux kernel in typical user systems at any considerable length. If you are interested in learning more about doing the latter, have a look at *Running Linux* by Matthias Dalheimer and Matt Welsh and *Linux Kernel in a Nutshell* by Greg Kroah-Hartman (both from O'Reilly).

Selecting a Kernel

As you begin to work more with Linux, you will quickly discover that more than one kernel is available to you. The "official" (also known as the "upstream" or "mainline") Linux kernel is always available for download at *http://www.kernel.org/*. There are several releases of the upstream kernel available for download. Those beginning 2.6.x or 2.6.x.y are the latest series at the time of this writing, and they are generally intended to be used in new Linux system deployments. An older 2.4 series is still in use in many devices and is occasionally updated with maintenance releases, but all new development should happen with the 2.6 kernel.

The kernel available from kernel.org is blessed by Linux creator Linus Torvalds, and a diverse assortment of volunteers spread across the globe are actively developing it. This is known as upstream development, and those working directly on the upstream Linux kernel are motivated by extending the state of the art. For a number of practical reasons, upstream kernel developers are likely to show more interest in issues related to using Linux on desktop and server class hardware with Intel or AMD x86 (i686) and x86_64 processors rather than on embedded devices, which few upstream developers have access to. But embedded developers are not ignored.

Where you get your Linux kernel from is largely determined by the architecture of your chosen target. Of course, this chapter will not address vendor-specific issues, but should you be using a vendor-supplied kernel in place of the official release, then you will want to contact your vendor for support. The kernel development community cannot be expected to know what additional features (patches) were added to the kernel supplied by another party.

Embedded Linux Kernels

Development of the Linux kernel for embedded devices tends to be split according to the processor architecture involved. For example, Russell King leads a group of developers who actively port Linux to ARM-based devices (via the *http://www.arm.li nux.org.uk/* website). The ARM developers base their work on the upstream Linux kernel as published by Linus Torvalds and develop ARM-specific patches for it. These source code patches enable new hardware support, fix existing bugs affecting the ARM architecture in the upstream kernel, and do many other things besides. From time to time, these patches are pushed back upstream; that is, Russell will ask Linus to merge his changes into the official kernel. The process is automated using the git SCM tool Linus wrote for just this purpose.

Historically, Linux kernel development for embedded devices was much more fragmented than it is today, and those who read the previous edition of this book will have seen this firsthand. Many embedded Linux developers often maintained their own entirely separate kernel source trees, only occasionally sending patches upstream to Linus or one of the other key kernel developers for inclusion in an arbitrary future release of the mainline kernel. The situation was so precarious that there were periods during 2.4 Linux kernel development when the official kernel wouldn't even boot on a wide variety of target platforms it *allegedly* supported. In fact, necessary support was typically in place, but the fixes required to make it work were not always correctly synchronized into the official Linux kernel.

During the development of the 2.6 series Linux kernel, various key failings of the 2.4 development process were identified and measures were put in place to address them. Of course, there are still a number of different groups within the wider Linux kernel development community maintaining their own patches to the official kernel, but these days the process for getting these fixes upstream and into the mainline kernel is much better defined. You will benefit directly from this enhanced development process because you will be able to track the official Linux kernel much more closely in your own embedded development. Today, you can (and typically should) simply use the official Linux kernel as much as possible in order to benefit from the collective strength of the entire kernel community.

Your first point of call when building a Linux kernel for your chosen target will be the website of the person (or group) that maintains the kernel on your chosen architecture —for example, Russell's ARM Linux website or Paul Mackerras's PowerPC Linux website. A list of such resources was given in Chapter 3. Even though you may not require any special version of the kernel, it pays to know who is responsible for the ongoing development of support for your architecture of choice and where to go for those architecture-specific issues that are bound to arise sooner or later. At the very least, you will want to join whatever developer mailing list is available to you.

2.4 Series Kernels

The 2.4 series Linux kernel is arguably no longer relevant for new embedded designs, as it has long since been replaced by the more recent (and much improved) 2.6 series. Although the 2.6 series kernel is known mostly for its improvements in the area of scalability—improvements aimed at large servers—it also adds a rich set of configurable options for resource-constrained embedded devices. Despite the many advantages of using a 2.6 kernel, it has taken much longer to reach a point where embedded developers are comfortable using the 2.6 kernel than might have reasonably been expected. This was largely due to the time required to bring third-party kernel source trees and drivers up-to-date.

At this point, you are extremely unlikely to begin a new project with the 2.4 Linux kernel. In fact, you are discouraged from doing so due to the declining support for the older kernel, coupled with the fact that ongoing development work exclusively involves the newer 2.6 series kernel. This means that fixes for subtle bugs—for example, a hardware vendor supplied workaround addressing an issue affecting a specific System on Chip (SoC)—are much more likely to be available for a 2.6 kernel than the older series. For this and other reasons, this chapter will not dwell on 2.4 kernel considerations. If you need to use a 2.4 kernel, you may wish to consult the previous edition of this book.

The 2.6 Series Linux Kernel

The mainstream, or official, 2.6 series Linux kernel is generally available from the kernel.org website. There are two ways in which you will usually obtain source code for this kernel:

- As a tarball, or archive, from which you can unpack a specific release of the kernel. These releases are self-contained and released whenever Linus Torvalds deems the current stage of development fit for release. For example, you might obtain the 2.6.20 release of the kernel in a file named *linux-2.6.20.tar.bz2*.
- Using the git kernel Software Configuration Management (SCM) tool to track day-to-day development, as well as official releases of the kernel. You can also visualize changes to the kernel using a variety of git add-on tools, such as the gtik graphical changeset tracking tool that allows you to visually track daily kernel development.

An official release of the kernel is generally preferred to a development snapshot when it comes to new embedded device designs, although you are also encouraged to track ongoing development and join the various community mailing lists in order to be aware of any changes that might later affect your work. The general goal of any Linux kernel developer is to have his modifications feed back into a later release of the official kernel so that they are immediately available to future projects or later updates to the current project.* Traditionally, embedded developers have chosen one specific release of the Linux kernel and stuck with it throughout the lifetime (or at least initial release) of their product. This is fine if you don't make any modifications to the kernel for your embedded project. However, if you find that you need to develop Linux kernel code for yourself, you are advised to track ongoing development in order to ensure that your modifications continue to work. This will prevent lengthy refactoring of existing code when you later decide to rebase to a newer version of the kernel.

Using a stable release tarball

Stable Linux kernel releases tend to happen roughly every 1–2 months, following phases of active development and prerelease stabilization of new features and other additions. Tarballs, or source archives, are made available on the kernel.org website. For example, following the 2.6.20 release, the front page of the website contained a link to this particular release, along with various changelog information and other related resources. You can always download the current release of the Linux kernel— just follow the links on the main kernel.org webpage.

Unpacking the kernel is as easy as unpacking any other source archive. Using regular GNU tar commands, you can extract the source tree, which will be in the form of either a conventional *.gz* tarball or a slightly more heavily compressed *.bz2* tarball. The appropriate extraction command will vary depending upon the type of archive. To extract a regular *.gz* tarball archive of the 2.6.20 kernel, you would run the following command:

```
tar xvfz linux-2.6.20.tar.gz
```

Whereas, for a bz2-compressed kernel, the command changes to:

```
tar xvfj linux-2.6.20.tar.bz2
```

This instructs GNU tar to extract the given file in a verbose mode. You can find out more about the available options for the tar command by referring to any standard Linux administration reference or by reading the tar man or info page. Once the kernel sources are unpacked, they are ready for configuration and compilation using the process described in the following sections.

---

* There really is little commercial advantage to be gained from keeping your fixes, device drivers, and other kernel code out of the official Linux kernel, especially as the GPL places a variety of legal obligations upon you to distribute such source modifications along with your embedded product. However, it does appear to be a common practice that certain patches are withheld until a product is released, for reasons of confidentiality. If this is your plan, try to get these patches into the official kernel at the earliest opportunity.

Tracking development with git

Day-to-day development of the Linux kernel is supported through extensive use of Linus Torvald's git SCM tool. git, the "stupid content tracker," was written by Torvalds in response to a sudden need to replace a proprietary version control system that had previously been in use for some time. It works by tracking changesets—related groups of changes to the kernel—rather than changes (patches) to individual source files. In this way, it is possible to see modifications in terms of their collective impact upon the kernel, rather than by wading through many patches. A variety of third-party tools, such as gitk, can be used to provide a visual representation of the changing state of a git repository. You can obtain a copy of git from your Linux distribution, or at *http://www.kernel.org/*.

You can download a private copy of the kernel git repository using the clone command:

```
git clone git://git.kernel.org/pub/scm/linux/git/torvalds/linux-2.6.git linus_26
```

This clones, or copies, the upstream Linux kernel repository (which Linus Torvalds maintains on the kernel.org site) and creates a local directory, in this case called *linus_26*, that reflects the current state of the art. The upstream kernel repository is frequently changing due to the many thousands of changesets that can make it into the kernel from one release to the next. If you're serious about tracking the Linux kernel, you will want to get into a daily habit of updating your local copy of Linus's repository. You can do this using the following command, from within the local repository:

```
git pull
```

Many more commands exist, along with a number of documents describing the kernel development process and how it involves git. You can find out more about git or download a copy (if your Linux distribution does not include it, or you are running another operating system for which git has been ported) at *http://git.or.cz/*.

Third-party kernel trees and patches

Rather than using the kernel available from the kernel.org website, you may also choose to use a third-party-supplied 2.6 kernel. This will typically be the case whenever you elect to use a specific embedded Linux distribution. Although these kernels are based on the upstream 2.6 Linux kernel, they are typically patched with a variety of additional features, bug fixes, and other modifications deemed useful by the vendor. Therefore, you should not place too much stock in the version of the kernel they claim to provide —you might think you have a 2.6.20 kernel, but in fact it may differ widely from the 2.6.20 kernel available from the kernel.org website. In any case, you should contact your vendor for support in the first instance; the kernel community, in general, does not support vendor kernels.

You may also want to try some of the various patches made available by some developers. Extra kernel functionality is often available as an independent patch before it is integrated into the mainstream kernel. Robert Love's kernel preemption patch, for instance, was maintained as a separate patch before Linus integrated it into the 2.5 development series. We will discuss a few kernel patches in Chapter 11. Have a look at *Running Linux* if you are not familiar with patches.

Configuring the Kernel

Configuration is the initial step in the build of a kernel for your target. There are many ways to configure the Linux kernel, and there are many options from which to choose. Regardless of the configuration method you use or the actual configuration options you choose, the kernel will generate a *.config* file at the end of the configuration and will generate a number of symbolic links and file headers that will be used by the rest of the build process.

We will limit our discussion to issues specifically affecting embedded systems. For general advice on kernel configuration and compilation, consult one of the previously mentioned texts on Linux kernel development or the documentation supplied inside the Linux kernel source tree itself; see the *Documentation* subdirectory.

Linux Kernel in a Nutshell (published by O'Reilly and also available online at *http://www.kroah.com/lkn*) provides a brief but thorough guide to configuring and building a kernel, along with explanations of some of the most popular configuration options. (It is not specially addressed to embedded systems developers, though.)

Configuration Options

It is during configuration that you will be able to select the options you want to see included in the kernel. Depending on your target, the option menus available will change, as will their content. Some options, however, will be available no matter which embedded architecture you choose. The following is a list of the main menu options available to all embedded Linux architectures:

- Code maturity level options
- General setup
- Loadable module support
- Block layer
- Networking
- Device drivers
- Filesystems
- Kernel hacking
- Security options
- Cryptographic options
- Library routines

This section will not cover each option individually, as the kernel configuration menu provides context-sensitive help that you can refer to as you perform the configuration. Many of the options are self-explanatory—for example, which device drivers will be built—while others are less obvious. For instance, the kernel can include a variety of strong security options as part of the SELinux stack implemented by the U.S. National Security Agency (NSA). Many of these options will make less sense to you if you are not familiar with the design of SELinux. This isn't a huge problem, however, since only a few embedded devices choose to make use of the extensive SELinux functionality in Linux.

One of the most important option menus is the one in which you choose the exact instance of the processor architecture that best fits your target. The name of this menu varies according to your architecture. Table 5-1 provides the system and processor selection option menu name, along with the correct kernel architecture name for several of the common architectures. When issuing *make* commands, you need to set the ARCH variable to the architecture name recognized by the kernel *Makefiles*.

Table 5-1. System and processor selection option and kernel architecture name according to processor architecture

Processor architecture	System and processor selection option	Kernel architecture name
x86	Processor type and features	i386
ARM	System Type	arm
PPC	Platform support	powerpc (or ppc for older targets)
MIPS	Machine selection/CPU selection	mips
SH	System type	sh
M68k	Platform-dependent support or processor type and features	m68k or m68knommu
AVR32	System Type and features	avr32

When browsing through the kernel configuration options for your target, bear in mind that it is possible to enable support for hardware you do not have. Indeed, the configuration menus may allow you to enable many kernel features that have never been tested for your target. There are many millions of possible kernel configuration combinations, and it is not possible for the kernel developers to test every configuration choice you may make. Typically, selecting support for a device that is not present won't prevent a system from booting, especially if it's simply a PCI device driver that won't be detected by the kernel anyway. But this isn't always the case on embedded systems, and it is still all too possible to create a kernel that will not boot on a particular target. Therefore, you are advised to verify your selections against the published documentation for your chosen target before building your target kernel.

Configuration Methods

The Linux kernel build system (Kbuild) includes support for a variety of configuration methods, including the following:

make config

> Provides a command-line interface where you are asked about each option one by one. If a *.config* configuration file is already present, it uses that file to set the default values of the options it asks you to set.

make oldconfig

> Feeds *config* with an existing *.config* configuration file and prompts you to configure only those options you have not previously configured. This contrasts with *make config*, which asks you about all options, even those you have previously configured. Developers often use this option to update their configuration as upstream configuration options change, without having to reconfigure the entire kernel.

make menuconfig

> Displays a curses-based terminal configuration menu. If a *.config* file is present, it uses it to set default values, as with *make config*.

make xconfig

> Displays a Tk-based X Window configuration menu. If a *.config* file is present, it uses it to set default values, as with *make config* and *make menuconfig*.

Any of these can be used to configure the kernel. They all generate a *.config* file in the root directory of the kernel sources. (This is the file that contains the full details of the options you choose.)

Few developers actually use the *make config* command to configure the kernel. Instead, most use *make menuconfig* to create an initial configuration or to tweak an existing one. You can also use *make xconfig*. Keep in mind, however, that *make xconfig* may have some broken menus in some architectures, as is the case for the PowerPC, for instance.

To view the kernel configuration menu, type the appropriate command at the command line with the proper parameters. For example, to cross compile the Linux kernel for use on an embedded ARM system, you might use the following command line (the exact cross-compiler name prefix may vary):

```
$ make ARCH=arm CROSS_COMPILE=arm-linux- menuconfig
```

Note that the CROSS_COMPILE prefix ends with a hyphen (this will be prepended to command names, such as "gcc", forming "arm-linux-gcc", and so on), and there is a space between that and the *menuconfig* command itself.

This presents a graphical configuration menu from which available options can be selected. Many features and drivers are available as modules, and it is possible to choose whether to build features into the kernel or as modules at this stage. Once the kernel has been configured, you can quit the kernel configuration menu via the Escape key or the Exit menu item. The kernel configuration system will ask whether to save the new configuration. Choosing Yes saves the new configuration into a new *.config* file. In addition to creating the *.config* file, a few header files and symbolic links are created. It is also possible to exit the kernel configuration without making any changes, just answer No to the question.

Apart from the main configuration options, the architecture support within the kernel often includes standard template configurations for certain targets. This is especially true for standard PowerPC and ARM targets. In those cases, the defaults provided with the kernel will be used to generate the *.config* file. For example, here is how to configure the kernel for a TQM860L ppc target:

```
$ make ARCH=ppc CROSS_COMPILE=powerpc-linux- TQM860L_config
$ make ARCH=ppc CROSS_COMPILE=powerpc-linux- oldconfig
```

Managing Multiple Configurations

It is often desirable to test different configurations using the same kernel sources. Changing the kernel's configuration, however, destroys the previous configuration, because all the configuration files are overwritten by the kernel's configuration utilities. To save a configuration for future use, you need to save the *.config* files created by the kernel's configuration. These files can later be reused to restore a previous kernel configuration.

The easiest way to back up and retrieve configurations is to use the kernel's own configuration procedures. The menus displayed by both the menuconfig and xconfig *Makefile* targets allow you to save and restore configurations. In each case, you need to provide an appropriate filename.

You can also save the *.config* files by hand. In that case, you need to copy the configuration file created by the kernel configuration utilities to an alternative location for future use. To use a saved configuration, you will need to copy the previously saved *.config* file back into the kernel's root directory and then use the *make* command with the oldconfig *Makefile* target to configure the kernel using the newly copied *.config* file. As with the menuconfig *Makefile* target, the oldconfig *Makefile* target creates a few headers files and symbolic links.

Whether you copy the files manually or use the menus provided by the various utilities, store the configurations in an intuitive location and use a meaningful naming scheme for saving your configurations. To identify each configuration file, prepend each filename with the kernel version it relates to, along with a small descriptive comment, a date, or both. Leave the *.config* extension as-is, nevertheless, to identify the file as a kernel configuration file.

Using the EXTRAVERSION Variable

If you are using multiple variants of the same kernel version, you will find the EXTRAVERSION variable to be quite useful in identifying each instance. The EXTRAVERSION variable is appended to the kernel's version number to give the kernel being built its final name. For example, if you need to add an additional patch from Russell King in order to add serial support for a given target to your 2.6.20 kernel, it might set EXTRAVERSION to -rmk1. The end result would be a kernel version of 2.6.20-rmk1. EXTRAVERSION is commonly used to identify prerelease kernels, too. For example, prior to the release of 2.6.21, the EXTRAVERSION in Linus's git repository was regularly set to -rc followed by a number, indicating multiple release candidate kernels, not an official release.

The final version number is also used to name the directory where the modules built for the kernel are stored. Hence, modules built for two kernels based on the same initial version but with different EXTRAVERSIONs will be stored in two different directories, whereas modules built for two kernels based on the same initial version but that have no EXTRAVERSION will be stored in the same directory.

You can also use EXTRAVERSION to identify variants based on the same kernel version. To do so, edit the *Makefile* in the main kernel directory and set EXTRAVERSION to your desired value. You will find it useful to rename the directory containing this modified source code using this same value. If, for example, the EXTRAVERSION of a 2.6.20 kernel is set to -motor-diff, the parent directory should be named *2.6.20-motor-diff*. The naming of the backup *.config* files should also reflect the use of EXTRAVERSION. The configuration file for the kernel with disabled serial support should therefore be called *2.6.20-motor-diff-no-serial.config* in this case.

Compiling the Kernel

Compiling the kernel involves a number of steps. These include building the kernel image and building the kernel modules. Each step uses a different *make* command and is described separately in this section. However, you could also carry out all these steps using a single command line.

The kernel build process has changed in the 2.6 series kernel. Prior to 2.6, it was necessary to carry out an additional dependency generation stage in which you would explicitly invoke the kernel build system to calculate all the necessary *Makefile* dependencies for a subsequent build. During the 2.6 development process, the entire kernel build system was overhauled and replaced with a newer, improved build system that does not require this additional step.

Building the Kernel

Building the kernel requires little more than a simple call to GNU *make*. Depending upon your chosen architecture, you might also need to specify what kind of image will be produced. For example, in the case of an ARM platform, you could use the following command to create a compressed image:

```
$ make ARCH=arm CROSS_COMPILE=arm-linux- zImage
```

The zImage target instructs the *Makefile* to build a kernel image that is compressed using the gzip algorithm.[†] There are, nevertheless, other ways to build a kernel image. The vmlinux target instructs the *Makefile* to build only the uncompressed image. Note that this image is generated even when a compressed image is requested.

On the x86, there is also the bzImage target. The "bzImage" name stands for "big zImage," and has nothing to do with the *bzip2* compression utility. In fact, both the bzImage and zImage *Makefile* targets rely on the gzip algorithm. The difference between the two *Makefile* targets is that the compressed kernel images generated using zImage cannot be larger than 512 KB, whereas those generated using bzImage are not bound by this limit. If you want more information regarding the differences between zImage and bzImage, have a look at the *Documentation/i386/boot.txt* file included in the kernel sources.

If you chose any options not supported by your architecture during the kernel configuration, or if some kernel option is broken, your build will fail at this stage. If all goes well, you should have a newly built kernel image within five minutes, at most, on any reasonably powerful development machine.

Verifying the Cross-Development Toolchain

Notice that the kernel build is the first real test for the cross-development tools we built in the previous chapter. If the tools you built earlier compile a functional kernel successfully, all the other software should build perfectly. Of course, you will need to download the kernel you built to your target to verify its functionality, but the fact that it builds properly is already a positive sign.

Building the Modules

With the kernel image properly built, you can now build the kernel modules:

```
$ make ARCH=arm CROSS_COMPILE=arm-linux- modules
```

The duration of this stage depends largely on the number of kernel options you chose to build as modules instead of having been linked in as part of the main kernel image.

---

† Though zImage is a valid *Makefile* target for all the architectures we discussed in depth in Chapter 3, there are other Linux architectures for which it isn't valid.

This stage is seldom longer than the build of the kernel image. As with the kernel image, if your configuration is inadequate for your target or if a feature is broken, this stage of the build may also fail.

With both the kernel image and the kernel modules now built, it is time to install them onto the target system. Before you do so, note that if you needed to clean up the kernel's sources and return them to their initial state prior to any configuration, dependency building, or compilation, you could use the following command:

```
$ make ARCH=arm CROSS_COMPILE=arm-linux- distclean
```

Be sure to back up your kernel configuration file prior to using this command, as *make distclean* erases all the files generated during the previous stages, including the *.config* file, all object files, and the kernel images.

Installing the Kernel

Ultimately, the kernel you just generated and its modules will have to be copied to your target to be used. The actual copying of the kernel and its modules is covered in Chapters 6 and 9. Meanwhile, the next few sections will discuss how to manage multiple kernel images and corresponding module installations. The configuration of the target's boot layout and its root filesystem depends on what you do after reading the following sections.

Managing Multiple Kernel Images

In addition to using separate directories for different kernel versions, you will find it useful to have access to multiple kernel images to test on your target. Since these images may be built using the same sources, you will need to copy them out of the kernel source and into a directory where they can be properly identified. For example, you might create an *images* directory containing each of the available kernel images for your embedded project.

For each kernel configuration, you will need to copy four files: the uncompressed kernel image, the compressed kernel image, the kernel symbol map, and the configuration file. The last three are found within the kernel source's root directory and are called *vmlinux*, *System.map*, and *.config*, respectively. The compressed kernel image file is found in the *arch/your_arch/boot* directory, where *your_arch* is the name of your target's architecture, and is called *zImage* or *bzImage*, depending on the *Makefile* target you used earlier. For the example ARM-based target, the compressed kernel image would be located in *arch/arm/boot/zImage*.

Some architectures, such as the PPC, have many boot directories. In those cases, the kernel image to use is not necessarily the one located at *arch/your_arch/boot/zImage*. In the case of the TQM board mentioned earlier, for example, the compressed kernel image that should be used is *arch/ppc/images/vmlinux.gz*. Have a look at the *arch/*

your_arch/*Makefile* for a full description of all the *Makefile* boot image targets for your architecture. In the case of the PPC, the type of boot image generated depends on the processor model for which the kernel is compiled.

To identify the four files needed, you can use a naming scheme similar to that of the kernel's version. For example, for a kernel built from the 2.6.20 source release, you might copy the kernel into a dedicated project directory:

```
$ cp arch/arm/boot/zImage ${PRJROOT}/images/zImage-2.6.20
$ cp System.map ${PRJROOT}/images/System.map-2.6.20
$ cp vmlinux ${PRJROOT}/images/vmlinux-2.6.20
$ cp .config ${PRJROOT}/images/2.6.20.config
```

where $PRJROOT represents the top directory of your embedded project.

You could also include the configuration name in the filenames. For example, suppose that you decided it was worthwhile having a build without any serial support (for whatever reason). To distinguish this special build of the kernel from any others, you might dutifully decide upon the following names: *zImage-2.6.20-no-serial*, *System.map-2.6.20-no-serial*, *vmlinux-2.6.20-no-serial*, and *2.6.20-no-serial.config*.

Installing Kernel Modules

The kernel *Makefile* includes the `modules_install` target for installing the kernel modules. By default, the modules are installed in the */lib/modules* directory. This is entirely appropriate for most desktop and enterprise Linux environments, but doesn't work so well when you're using a cross-development environment. In the case of cross-compilation, you specifically don't want to install the newly built kernel modules into your host */lib/modules* hierarchy (not unless you want to risk interfering with your host development system, anyway). Instead, you need to instruct make to use an alternate location.

Linux kernel modules are strongly dependent upon a particular build of the kernel—a particular kernel image. Because this is the case, you will usually install kernel modules in a directory similar in name to that of the corresponding prebuilt kernel image. In the case of the 2.6.20 kernel, you might install the modules in a directory named *${PRJROOT}/images/modules-2.6.20*. The content of this directory will later be copied to the target's */lib/modules* directory within its root filesystem for use with the corresponding kernel on the target.

To install the Linux kernel modules in an alternate directory, use this command:

```
$ make ARCH=arm CROSS_COMPILE=arm-linux- \
> INSTALL_MOD_PATH=${PRJROOT}/images/modules-2.6.20 \
> modules_install
```

The precise command will vary by target architecture, but the important part is that the `INSTALL_MOD_PATH` variable is used to set the alternate path for module installation. The kernel build system will take care of the rest, provided that it can write into the location that you have specified. The *modules-2.6.20* subdirectory will be created if it does not exist.

Once it is done copying the modules, the kernel build system will try to build the module dependencies needed for the module utilities during runtime. Since *depmod*, the utility that builds the module dependencies, is not designed to deal with cross-compiled modules, it will fail.

To build the module dependencies for your modules, you will need to use another module dependency builder provided with the BusyBox package. You will learn more than you could ever want to know about BusyBox (well, almost) in Chapter 6. For now, you can download, and then extract, a copy of the BusyBox archive from *http:// www.busybox.net* into a convenient location (for example, *${PRJROOT}/sysapps*).‡ From the BusyBox directory, copy the *scripts/depmod.pl* Perl script into the *${PREFIX}/ bin* directory.

You can now build the module dependencies for the target:

```
$ depmod.pl \
> -k ./vmlinux -F ./System.map \
> -b ${PRJROOT}/images/modules-2.6.20/lib/modules > \
> ${PRJROOT}/images/modules-2.6.20/lib/modules/2.6.20/modules.dep
```

The *-k* option is used to specify the uncompressed kernel image, the *-F* option is used to specify the system map, and the *-b* option is used to specify the base directory containing the modules for which you will need to build dependencies. Because the tool's output goes to the standard output, you will want to redirect it to the actual dependency file, which is always called *modules.dep*.

In the Field

Let's take a look at the kernel's operation once it's installed on your target and ready to run. Because the algorithms and underlying source code are the same for embedded and regular systems, the kernel will behave almost exactly the same as it would on a workstation or a server. For this reason, other books and online material on the subject, such as *Linux Device Drivers* by Jonathan Corbet et al. and *Understanding the Linux Kernel* by Daniel Bovet and Marco Cesati (both from O'Reilly), are much more appropriate for finding in-depth explanations of the kernel. There are, nevertheless, aspects particular to embedded Linux systems that warrant particular emphasis.

Dealing with Kernel Failure

The Linux kernel is a very stable and mature piece of software. This, however, does not mean that it or the hardware it relies on never fails. *Linux Device Drivers* covers issues such as "oops" messages and system hangs. In addition to keeping these issues in mind

‡ Download BusyBox version 0.60.5 or later.

during your design, you should think about the most common form of kernel failure: kernel panic.

When a fatal error occurs and the kernel catches it, it will stop all processing and emit a kernel panic message. There are many reasons a kernel panic can occur. One of the most frequent reasons is that you forgot to specify to the kernel the location of its root filesystem. In that case, the kernel will boot normally and will panic upon trying to mount its root filesystem.

The only means of recovery in case of a kernel panic is a complete system reboot. For this reason, the kernel accepts a boot parameter that indicates the number of seconds it should wait after a kernel panic to reboot. If you would like the kernel to reboot one second after a kernel panic, for instance, you would pass the following sequence as part of the kernel's boot parameters: panic=1.

Depending on your setup, however, a simple reboot may not be sufficient. In the case of our control module, for instance, a simple reboot may even be dangerous, since the chemical or mechanical process being controlled may get out of hand. For this reason, we need to change the kernel's panic function to notify a human operator who could then use emergency manual procedures to control the process. Of course, the actual panic behavior of your system depends on the type of application for which your system is being used.

The code for the kernel's panic function, panic(), is in the *kernel/panic.c* file in the kernel's sources. The first observation to be made is that the panic function's default output goes to the console.§ Since your system may not even have a terminal, you may want to modify this function according to your particular hardware. An alternative to the terminal, for example, would be to write the actual error string in a special section of flash memory that is specifically set aside for this purpose. At the next reboot, you would be able to retrieve the text information from that flash section and attempt to solve the problem.

Whether you are interested in the actual text message or not, you can register your own panic function with the kernel. This function will be called by the kernel's panic function in the event of a kernel panic and can be used to carry out such things as signaling an emergency.

The list that holds the functions called by the kernel's own panic function is panic_notifier_list. The notifier_chain_register function is used to add an item to this list. Conversely, notifier_chain_unregister is used to remove an item from this list.

---

§ The console is the main terminal to which all system messages are sent.

The location of your own panic function has little importance, but the registration of this function must be done during system initialization. In our case, we add a *mypanic.c* file in the *kernel* directory of the kernel sources and modify that directory's *Makefile* accordingly. Here is the *mypanic.c* for our control module:

```
#include <linux/kernel.h>
#include <linux/init.h>
#include <linux/notifier.h>

static int my_panic_event(struct notifier_block *,
                          unsigned long,
                          void *);

static struct notifier_block my_panic_block = {
        notifier_call:   my_panic_event,
        next:            NULL,
        priority:        INT_MAX
};

int _ _init register_my_panic(void)
{
        printk("Registering buzzer notifier \n");

        notifier_chain_register(&panic_notifier_list,
                        &my_panic_block);

        return 0;
}

void ring_big_buzzer(void)
{
        ...
}

static int my_panic_event(struct notifier_block *this,
                          unsigned long event,
                          void *ptr)
{
        ring_big_buzzer( );

        return NOTIFY_DONE;
}

module_init(register_my_panic);
```

The `module_init(register_my_panic);` statement ensures that the `register_my_panic` function is called during the kernel's initialization without requiring any modification of the kernel's startup functions. The registration function adds `my_panic_block` to the list of other blocks in the panic notifier list. The `notifier_block` structure has three fields. The first field is the function to be called, the second is a pointer to the next notifier block, and the third is the priority of this block. In our case, we want to have the highest possible priority. Hence the use of `INT_MAX`.

In case of kernel panic, `my_panic_event` is called as part of the kernel's notification of all panic functions. In turn, this function calls on `ring_big_buzzer`, which contains code to start a loud alarm to attract the human operator's attention to the imminent problem.

## CHAPTER 6

Root Filesystem Content

Michael Opdenacker

One of the last operations conducted by the Linux kernel during system startup is mounting the root filesystem. The Linux kernel itself doesn't dictate any filesystem structure, but user space applications do expect to find files with specific names in specific directory structures. Therefore, it is useful to follow the de facto standards that have emerged in Linux systems.

In this chapter, we will start by discussing the basic root filesystem structure. Then, we will explain how and where to install the system libraries, the kernel modules, kernel images, device nodes, main system applications, and custom applications. Finally, we will discuss how to configure the system initialization scripts.

At the end of this chapter, you will have a fully functional root filesystem for your target. In the following chapters, we will talk about how you can place this root filesystem on an actual filesystem type on a storage device for use in your target.

Basic Root Filesystem Structure

The "official" rules to build a root filesystem are contained in the Filesystem Hierarchy Standard (FHS) introduced in Chapter 1. The document is less than 30 pages long and is fairly easy to read. If you are looking for answers or clarifications regarding how to build a root filesystem, the FHS, along with related standards documentation from the Linux Foundation, are probably the best places to start.

Each of the top-level directories in the root filesystem has a specific purpose. Many of these, however, are meaningful only in multiuser systems in which a system administrator is in charge of many servers or workstations employed by different users. In most embedded Linux systems, where there are no users and no administrators, the rules for building a root filesystem can be loosely interpreted. This doesn't mean that all rules can be violated, but it does mean that breaking some of them will have little to no effect on the system's proper operation. Interestingly, even mainstream commercial distributions for workstations and servers sometimes deviate from the de facto rules for root filesystems.

Table 6-1 provides the complete list of root filesystem top-level directories and their content as specified by the FHS (note that /sys is not in the standard yet, and therefore doesn't appear in the table).

Table 6-1. Root filesystem top-level directories

Directory	Content
bin	Essential user command binaries
boot	Static files used by the bootloader
dev	Devices and other special files
etc	System configuration files, including startup files
home	User home directories
lib	Essential libraries, such as the C library, and kernel modules
media	Mount points for removable media
mnt	Mount points for temporarily mounted filesystems
opt	Add-on software packages
proc	Virtual filesystem for kernel and process information
root	Root user's home directory
sbin	Essential system administration binaries
sys	Virtual filesystem for system information and control (buses, devices, and drivers)
tmp	Temporary files
usr	Secondary hierarchy containing most applications and documents useful to most users, including the X server
var	Variable data stored by daemons and utilities

If you are using Linux for your day-to-day work, you are already familiar with some of these directories. Nevertheless, let's take a closer look at the content of a typical root filesystem for use in an embedded Linux system.

First, all the directories that pertain to providing an extensible multiuser environment, such as /home, /mnt, /opt, and /root, can be omitted. You could trim the root filesystem even further by removing /tmp and /var, but these omissions may jeopardize the operation of certain programs. We do not encourage such a minimalistic approach.

This choice of what to include in your root filesystem should be based on what's actually useful, not on size considerations, because omitting a directory entry has practically no effect on the resulting root filesystem's size. The reason we recommend the omission of /home, for example, is that it would be left empty in an embedded Linux system because its content, as prescribed by the FHS, is useful only in workstation and server setups.

Depending on your bootloader and its configuration, you may not need to have a /boot directory. This will depend on whether your bootloader can retrieve kernel images from your root filesystem before your kernel is booted. You will be able to decide whether you should use a /boot directory and how to use it for your target after you read Chapter 9. Of course, you can redesign the root filesystem later if need be.

The remaining directories—/bin, /dev, /etc, /lib, /proc, /sbin, /sys, and /usr—are essential.

At the extreme, you could decide to omit /proc and /sys, and configure the kernel without support for the corresponding virtual filesystems. However, access to the proc filesystem is required by very basic commands such as ps, mount, ifconfig, and modprobe. The sysfs filesystem is now also used by an increasing number of programs. So, unless your system has a very limited scope, be prepared to replace scripts with custom C programs directly accessing the kernel system call interface if you wish to do without proc and sysfs.

Two of the root directories, /usr and /var, have a predefined hierarchy of their own, much like that of the root directory. We will briefly discuss these hierarchies as we populate both directories in the steps below.

Confusing Similarities

One of the most confusing aspects of the root filesystem is the apparent similarity in purpose of some directories. In particular, newcomers often ask what difference there is between the various directories containing binaries and the various directories containing libraries.

There are four main directories for binaries in the root filesystem: /bin, /sbin, /usr/bin, and /usr/sbin. The directory in which a binary is placed largely depends on its role in the system. Binaries that are *essential* to both users and system administrators are in /bin. Binaries that are essential to system administration, but will never be used by ordinary users, are located in /sbin. In contrast, most nonessential user binaries are located in /usr/bin and most nonessential system administration tools are in /usr/sbin.

The rationale is similar for the location of libraries. The ones required to boot the system and run the most essential commands are located in /lib, while /usr/lib contains all the other libraries. Often, packages will create subdirectories in /usr/lib to contain their own libraries. The Perl 5.x packages, for instance, have a /usr/lib/perl5 directory that contains all the Perl-related libraries and modules.

A look at your Linux workstation's own root filesystem in these directories will show you actual examples of the application of these criteria by your distribution's designers.

To work on the root filesystem, let's move into the directory we created for this purpose:

```
$ cd ${PRJROOT}/rootfs
```

Now create the core root filesystem directories required for your system:

```
$ mkdir bin dev etc lib proc sbin sys tmp usr var
$ chmod 1777 tmp
```

Notice that we did not create */boot*. We will come back to it later and create it if it becomes necessary. Also, note that we changed the permissions for the */tmp* directory to turn the "sticky bit" on. This bit in the directory permissions field ensures that files created in the */tmp* directory can be deleted only by the user who created them. Though most embedded Linux systems are single-user systems, as mentioned already, there are cases in which embedded applications must not run with root privileges. The OpenSSH package we discuss in Chapter 10, for example, is such an application. Hence the need to follow some basic rules about root filesystem permission bits.

You can then proceed with the creation of the */usr* hierarchy:

```
$ mkdir usr/bin usr/lib usr/sbin
```

On a fully featured root filesystem, the */usr* directory usually contains many more entries. You can easily demonstrate this by typing *ls -al /usr* (perhaps adding a *-r* for recursive output) on your workstation. You will find directories that are useful on non-embedded systems for routine user activity, such as *man*, *src*, and *local*. The FHS contains a section addressing the layout of this directory in detail. For the purposes of most embedded Linux systems, however, the three directories we created will suffice.

The last entries to create are in the */var* directory:

```
$ mkdir var/lib var/lock var/log var/run var/tmp
$ chmod 1777 var/tmp
```

Here, too, this directory contains many more entries on nonembedded systems. Directories such as *cache*, *mail*, and *spool* are useful for a workstation or a server, but few embedded systems need those directories. The directories we created are the bare minimum required for the normal operation of most applications found in an embedded Linux system. Of course, if you need functionality such as serving web pages or printing, you may want to add some of the additional directories required by the applications providing this functionality. See the FHS and the documentation provided with your application to find out your actual requirements.

With the root filesystem skeleton now ready, let's place the various software components in their appropriate locations.

Running Linux with a Different Root Filesystem Structure

As we said in the previous discussion, the rules for building a root filesystem are in the FHS. Although most Linux applications and distributions depend on these rules, they are not enforced by the Linux kernel itself. In fact, the kernel source code makes very few assumptions regarding the structure of the root filesystem. It follows from this that you could build an embedded Linux system with a very different root filesystem structure. You would then have to modify the defaults of most software packages to make

---

them comply with your new structure. Indeed, certain regular "desktop" oriented distributions have attempted to mimic the Apple filesystem layout. Some have taken an even more extreme approach by building embedded Linux systems without any root filesystem at all.

Needless to say, we don't encourage you to go down this path. The root filesystem rules we outlined earlier are recognized and agreed upon by all open source and free software developers working on Linux systems. Building your embedded Linux system using other rules would cut you off from most open source and free software packages and their developers, and you would be needlessly ignoring a useful de facto standard in the process.

Libraries

In Chapter 4, we discussed how to build, install, and use the GNU C library and its alternatives for application development. Here, we will discuss how to install those same libraries on the target's root filesystem so that the applications you develop can use them at runtime. We will not discuss diet libc, because it is mainly used as a static library.

glibc

As we said earlier, the glibc package contains a number of libraries. Look in your *${TARGET_PREFIX}/lib* directory for the entire list of libraries installed during the package's build process. This directory contains mainly four types of files:

Actual shared libraries

These files' names are formatted as *libLIBRARY_NAME-GLIBC_VERSION.so*, where *LIBRARY_NAME* is the name of the library and *GLIBC_VERSION* is the version of the glibc package you are using. For instance, the name of the math library for glibc 2.3.6 is *libm-2.3.6.so* (the name of the math library is simply "m").

Many people do not know that *.so* files are also executable ELF binaries that can return useful information. For example:

```
/lib/libc-2.5.so
GNU C Library stable release version 2.5, by Roland McGrath et al.
Copyright (C) 2006 Free Software Foundation, Inc.
This is free software; see the source for copying conditions.
There is NO warranty; not even for MERCHANTABILITY or FITNESS FOR A
PARTICULAR PURPOSE.
Compiled by GNU CC version 4.1.2 (Ubuntu 4.1.2-0ubuntu4).
Compiled on a Linux >>2.6.15.7<< system on 2007-04-04.
Available extensions:
        crypt add-on version 2.1 by Michael Glad and others
        GNU Libidn by Simon Josefsson
        GNU libio by Per Bothner
        NIS(YP)/NIS+ NSS modules 0.19 by Thorsten Kukuk
```

```
Native POSIX Threads Library by Ulrich Drepper et al
BIND-8.2.3-T5B
Thread-local storage support included.
For bug reporting instructions, please see:
<http://www.gnu.org/software/libc/bugs.html>.
```

Major revision version symbolic links

Major revision versions do not follow the same numbering as the actual glibc version. The major revision version for the actual shared C library in glibc 2.3.6, *libc-2.3.6.so*, is 6, not 2 as the name suggests. In contrast, the major revision version for *libdl-2.3.6.so* truly is 2. The names of the symbolic links for the major revision version are formatted as *libLIBRARY_NAME.so.MAJOR_REVISION_VERSION*, where *MAJOR_REVISION_VERSION* is the major revision version of the library. For the actual C library, for instance, the symbolic link is *libc.so.6*. For libdl, it is *libdl.so.2*. Once a program has been linked to a library, it will refer to this symbolic link. At startup, the loader will therefore look for this file before loading the program.

Version-independent symbolic links to the major revision version symbolic links

The role of these links is to provide a universal entry for all the programs that need to link with a particular library, regardless of the actual major revision or the version of glibc involved. These symbolic links are typically formatted as *libLIBRARY_NAME.so*. For example, *libm.so* points to *libm.so.6*, which itself points to the actual shared library, *libm-2.3.6.so*. The only exception to this is *libc.so*, which, as we said in Chapter 4, is a link script. The version-independent symbolic link is the one used when linking programs.

Static library archives

These archives are used by applications that choose to link statically with a library. The names of these archives are formatted as *libLIBRARY_NAME.a*. The static archive for libdl, for instance, is *libdl.a*.

You will also find some other types of files in *${TARGET_PREFIX}/lib*, such as *crti.o* and *crt1.o*, but you will not need to copy them to your target's root filesystem. These files are used by the GNU Linker *ld* when producing executable binaries that need to "bootstrap" themselves (load themselves into memory and initialize). Thus, their role is finished after linking, and they are not used at runtime.

Out of the four types of files just described, you need only two for each library: the actual shared libraries and the major revision version symbolic links. The other two file types are needed only when linking executables and are not required for the runtime operation of your applications.

In addition to the library files, you need to copy the dynamic linker and its symbolic link. The dynamic linker itself follows the naming convention of the various glibc libraries and is usually called *ld-GLIBC_VERSION.so*. In what is probably one of the most bizarre aspects of the GNU toolchain, however, the name of the symbolic link to the dynamic linker differs depending on the architecture for which the toolchain has been built. If the toolchain is built for the i386, the ARM, the SuperH, or the m68k, the symbolic link to the dynamic linker is usually called *ld-linux.so.MAJOR_REVI-SION_VERSION*. If the toolchain is built for the MIPS or the PowerPC, the symbolic link to the dynamic linker is usually called *ld.so.MAJOR_REVISION_VERSION*.

Before you actually copy any glibc component to the target's root filesystem, however, you need to select the glibc components required for your applications. Table 6-2 provides the description of all the components in glibc[*] and provides inclusion guidelines for each component. In addition to our guidelines, you will need to evaluate which components your programs need, depending on how they are linked.

Table 6-2. Library components in glibc and root filesystem inclusion guidelines

Library component	Content	Inclusion guidelines
ld	Dynamic linker.[a]	Compulsory. Needed to use any shared libraries. Theoretically not necessary if using only a statically built root filesystem—although this is quite rare, unless you are only using BusyBox, for example.
libBrokenLocale	Fixup routines to get applications that have broken locale features to run. Overrides application defaults through preloading. (Need to use LD_PRELOAD.)	Rarely used.
libSegFault	Routines for catching segmentation faults and doing backtraces.	Rarely used.
libanl	Asynchronous name lookup routines.	Rarely used.
libbsd-compat	Dummy library for certain BSD programs that are compiled with -lbsd-compat.	Rarely used.
libc	Main C library routines.	Compulsory.
libcrypt	Cryptography routines.	Required for most applications involved in authentication.
libdl	Routines for loading shared objects dynamically.	Required for applications that use functions such as dlopen().
libm	Math routines.	Required for math functions.
libmemusage	Routines for heap and stack memory profiling.	Rarely used.
libnsl	NIS network services library routines.	Rarely used.
libnss_compat	Name Switch Service (NSS) compatibility routines for NIS.	Loaded automatically by the glibc NSS.[b]
libnss_dns	NSS routines for DNS.	Loaded automatically by the glibc NSS.
libnss_files	NSS routines for file lookups.	Loaded automatically by the glibc NSS.
libnss_hesiod	NSS routines for Hesiod name service.	Loaded automatically by the glibc NSS.
libnss_nis	NSS routines for NIS.	Loaded automatically by the glibc NSS.

[*] See the glibc manual for a complete description of the facilities provided.

Library component	Content	Inclusion guidelines
libnss_nisplus	NSS routines for NIS plus.	Loaded automatically by the glibc NSS.
libpcprofile	Program counter profiling routines.	Rarely used.
libpthread	POSIX 1003.1c threads routines for Linux.	Required for threads programming.
libresolv	Name resolver routines.	Required for name resolution.
librt	Asynchronous I/O routines.	Rarely used.
libthread_db	Thread debugging routines.	Loaded automatically by gdb when debugging threaded applications. Never actually linked to by any application.
libutil	Login routines, part of the user accounting database.	Required for terminal connection management.

a This library component is not itself a library. Instead, *ld.so* is an executable invoked by the ELF binary format loader to load the dynamically linked libraries into an application's memory space.

b See Chapter 4 for details.

If you wish to find out which dynamic libraries a given application uses, the usual way is with the *ldd* command. In a cross-platform development environment, however, your host's *ldd* command will fail when provided with target binaries. Instead, you could use the cross-platform *readelf* command you installed in Chapter 4 to identify the dynamic libraries that your application depends on. Here is an example using *readelf* to retrieve the BusyBox utility's dependencies:

```
$ powerpc-linux-readelf -a ${PRJROOT}/rootfs/bin/busybox | \
> grep "Shared library"
 0x00000001 (NEEDED)                    Shared library: [libc.so.0]
```

Ideally, however, if you installed uClibc, you should use the *ldd*-like command installed by uClibc, which has cross-platform capabilities. For our control module target, which is based on a PowerPC board, the command's name is *powerpc-uclibc-ldd*. This way, you can build the list of libraries your target binaries depend on. Here are the dependencies of the BusyBox utility, for example (one line has been wrapped to fit the page):

```
$ powerpc-uclibc-ldd ${PRJROOT}/rootfs/bin/busybox
        libc.so.0 => /home/karim/control-project/control-module/tools/uclibc/lib/
            libc.so.0
/lib/ld-uClibc.so.0 => /lib/ld-uClibc.so.0
```

Having determined the library components you need, you can copy them and the relevant symbolic links to the */lib* directory of the target's root filesystem. Here is a set of commands that copy the essential glibc components:

```
$ cd ${TARGET_PREFIX}/lib
$ for file in libc libcrypt libdl libm \
> libpthread libresolv libutil
> do
> cp $file-*.so ${PRJROOT}/rootfs/lib
> cp -d $file.so.[*0-9] ${PRJROOT}/rootfs/lib
```

```
> done
$ cp -d ld*.so* ${PRJROOT}/rootfs/lib
```

The first *cp* command copies the actual shared libraries, the second one copies the major revision version symbolic links, and the third one copies the dynamic linker and its symbolic link. All three commands are based on the rules outlined earlier in this section regarding the naming conventions of the different files in *${TARGET_PREFIX}/lib*. The -*d* option is used with the second and third *cp* commands to preserve the symbolic links as-is. Otherwise, the files that the symbolic links point to are copied in their entirety.

Of course, you can remove the libraries that are not used by your applications from the list in the set of commands shown. If you would rather have the complete set of libraries included in glibc on your root filesystem, use the following commands:

```
$ cd ${TARGET_PREFIX}/lib
$ cp *-*.so ${PRJROOT}/rootfs/lib
$ cp -d *.so.[*0-9] ${PRJROOT}/rootfs/lib
$ cp libSegFault.so libmemusage.so libpcprofile.so \
> ${PRJROOT}/rootfs/lib
```

If you have applications that use the glibc NSS, don't forget to copy the *libnss_SERVICE* libraries you need to your target's root filesystem. *libnss_files* and *libnss_dns* are the ones most often used. You will also need to copy the sample *nsswitch.conf* provided with glibc to your target's */etc* directory and customize it to your setup:[†]

```
$ cp ${PRJROOT}/build-tools/glibc-2.2.1/nss/nsswitch.conf \
> ${PRJROOT}/rootfs/etc
```

Whether you copy all or part of the glibc libraries, you will notice that some of these libraries are large. To reduce the size of the libraries installed, you can use the cross-platform *strip* utility you built in Chapter 4. Be careful not to strip the original libraries, because you would have to install them all over again. Strip the libraries only after you copy them to the root filesystem:

```
$ powerpc-linux-strip ${PRJROOT}/rootfs/lib/*.so
```

On our control module, the *${PRJROOT}/rootfs/lib* directory with all the glibc libraries weighs around 10 MB before stripping. Stripping all the libraries reduces the directory size to 2.5 MB.

The glibc components have now been installed on the target's root filesystem and are ready to be used at runtime by your applications.

[†] Have a look at *Linux Network Administrator's Guide* by Tony Bautts, Terry Dawson, and Gregor Purdy (O'Reilly) for details about the customization of the *nsswitch.conf* file.

uClibc

As with glibc, uClibc contains a number of libraries. Look in your *${PREFIX}/uclibc/lib* directory for the entire list. It contains the same four different types of files as the glibc directory.

Because uClibc is meant to be a glibc replacement, the names and uses of the uClibc components are identical to the glibc components. Hence, you can use Table 6-2 (shown previously) to research uClibc components. Note, however, that not all glibc components are implemented by uClibc. uClibc implements only *ld, libc, libcrypt, libdl, libm, libpthread, libresolv,* and *libutil*. Use the same method as described for glibc to identify the uClibc components you will need on your target.

Having determined the list of components you need, you can now copy them and their relevant symbolic links to the */lib* directory of your target's root filesystem. The following set of commands copies the essential uClibc components:

```
$ cd ${PREFIX}/uclibc/lib
$ for file in libuClibc ld-uClibc libc libdl \
> libcrypt libm libresolv libutil
> do
> cp $file-*.so ${PRJROOT}/rootfs/lib
> cp -d $file.so.[*0-9] ${PRJROOT}/rootfs/lib
> done
```

The commands are likely to report that two files haven't been found:

```
cp: libuClibc.so.[*0-9]: No such file or directory
cp: libc-*.so: No such file or directory
```

This is not a problem, because these files are not supposed to exist. The set of commands just shown is meant to be easy to type in, but you could add conditional statements around the *cp* commands if you prefer not to see any errors.

As with glibc, you can modify the list of libraries you copy according to your requirements. Note that, in contrast to glibc, you will not save much space by copying only a select few uClibc components. For the control module previously mentioned, for instance, the root filesystem's */lib* directory weighs only around 300 KB when *all* the uClibc components are copied. The following commands copy all uClibc's components to your target's root filesystem:

```
$ cd ${PREFIX}/uclibc/lib
$ cp *-*.so ${PRJROOT}/rootfs/lib
$ cp -d *.so.[*0-9] ${PRJROOT}/rootfs/lib
```

There is no need to strip uClibc components, since they were already stripped by uClibc's own build scripts. You can verify this using the *file* command.

Kernel Modules

In Chapter 5, we built the kernel modules and installed them in a temporary directory, *${PRJROOT}/images*. We are now ready to copy these modules to their final destination in the target's */lib* directory.

Since you may have compiled many kernels to test for your target, you now need to select which set of kernel modules to copy to the root filesystem. In the case of our control module, for example, we chose a 2.6.20 kernel for the target. The following command copies that kernel's entire *modules* directory to the root filesystem:

```
$ cp -a ${PRJROOT}/images/modules-2.6.20/* ${PRJROOT}/rootfs
```

We use *cp*'s *-a* option here to copy the files and directories in archive mode. This has the effect of preserving file attributes and links, and copying directories recursively. Note that there is no need to explicitly append the */lib/modules* path to *${PRJROOT}/ rootfs* in the previous command because of the way we installed the modules in the *${PRJROOT}/images/modules-2.6.20* directory in Chapter 5.

That's it; the kernel modules are now ready for use on your target. You may also need to add a */etc/modprobe.conf* file to specify special module parameter values, to manually override modules, or to do anything else that alters *modprobe*'s default behavior. See the *modprobe.conf* manpage for details.

Kernel Images

As we said earlier, the presence of the actual kernel image on your root filesystem largely depends on your bootloader's capabilities. If you anticipate that your bootloader's set-up will boot a kernel from the root filesystem, you may copy the kernel image to your target's root filesystem at this time:

```
$ mkdir ${PRJROOT}/rootfs/boot
$ cd ${PRJROOT}/images
$ cp zImage-2.6.20 ${PRJROOT}/rootfs/boot
```

In addition to the kernel image, you may want to make it a standard practice to copy the configuration file used to create the kernel so that you can service units for which the original project workspace may be lost:

```
$ cp 2.6.20.config ${PRJROOT}/rootfs/boot
```

Because we discuss the actual bootloader setup in Chapter 9, there is nothing more to be done here about the kernel's setup for now. We will continue the kernel image's setup later.

Device Files

Following Unix tradition, every object in a Linux system is visible as a file, including devices.[‡] All the device files (a.k.a. device "nodes") in a Linux root filesystem are located in the */dev* directory. Once more, having device files in */dev* is not dictated by the kernel, but by standard applications such as interactive shells that expect to find device files there.

In generic Linux systems, managing device files is a complex task, because devices can change from one computer to another, and external devices can also change at any moment. Therefore, such systems need a way to keep track of connected devices to make sure that the corresponding device files exist and that the corresponding drivers are loaded. Fortunately, many custom embedded systems always run with the same devices and just need fixed device files.

Static Device Files

These device files are called *static* because they just need to be created once in the filesystem. They are special files characterized by a type, *character* or *block*, and a *major* and *minor* number. Whereas user space applications distinguish device files by their names, the kernel just relies on their type and their major and minor numbers to find which driver manages each device. Therefore, two different device files with the same type, major number, and minor number will be processed in the same way.

The official source of information for static device major and minor numbers is the *Documentation/devices.txt* file in the kernel sources. You can consult this file whenever you are uncertain about the name or numbering of a certain device. Another, easier option is to read the numbers of device files on your Linux workstation.

For example, listing */dev/console* shows that it is a character device (because the first character on the line is c), with major number 5 and minor number 1:

```
$ ls -l /dev/console
crw------- 1 root root 5, 1 2007-05-10 07:05 /dev/console
```

Similarly, */dev/ram0* (the first ramdisk) is a block device, (listed with a b character), with major number 1 and minor number 0:

```
$ ls -l /dev/ram0
brw-rw---- 1 root disk 1, 0 2007-05-04 13:20 /dev/ram0
```

Table 6-3 lists the essential entries you need in your */dev* directory. Depending on your particular setup, you will probably need to add a few extra entries. In some cases, you may even need to use entries other than the ones listed in the table. On some systems, for example, the first serial port is not *ttyS0*. Such is the case of SuperH-based systems,

---

[‡] The notable exception to this is networking interfaces, such as Ethernet cards, for which there are no device files.

for instance, where the first serial port is *ttySC0* (major number: 204, minor number: 8), and StrongARM-based systems where the first serial port is *ttySA0* (major number: 204, minor number: 5).

Table 6-3. Basic /dev entries

Filename	Description	Type	Major number	Minor number	Permission bits
mem	Physical memory access	char	1	1	600
null	Null device	char	1	3	666
zero	Null byte source	char	1	5	666
random	Nondeterministic random number generator	char	1	8	644
tty0	Current virtual console	char	4	0	600
tty1	First virtual console	char	4	1	600
ttyS0	First UART serial port	char	4	64	600
tty	Current TTY device	char	5	0	666
console	System console	char	5	1	600

Matthias Dalheimer and Matt Welsh's *Running Linux* (O'Reilly) explains how to create device files. Essentially, you need to use the *mknod* command for each entry to be created. In contrast to most other commands we have used up until now, you need to be logged in as *root* to use this one. Remember to log out from the *root* user mode once you are done creating the device files.

Here is a simple example showing the creation of the first few entries in Table 6-3:

```
$ cd ${PRJROOT}/rootfs/dev
$ su -m
Password:
# mknod -m 600 mem c 1 1
# mknod -m 666 null c 1 3
# mknod -m 666 zero c 1 5
# mknod -m 644 random c 1 8
...
# exit
```

In addition to the basic device files, a few symbolic links, which are described in Table 6-4, have to be part of your */dev* directory. As with other symbolic links, you can use the *ln -s* command to create these links.

Table 6-4. Compulsory /dev symbolic links

Link name	Target
fd	/proc/self/fd
stdin	fd/0
stdout	fd/1

Link name	Target
stderr	fd/2

We have now prepared a basic */dev* directory for our target. We will come back to this directory later to create some additional entries for some types of storage devices. You can consult *Linux Device Drivers* by Jonathan Corbet et al. (O'Reilly) for a more complete discussion about device files and device drivers in general.

Creation of /dev Entries Without Root Privileges

Creation tools for the EXT2 and JFFS2 filesystems have been extended by Erik Andersen to allow the creation of */dev* entries on the fly using a device table file. With such a file, it is no longer necessary to log in as *root*, mount the newly created filesystem, and use the *mknod* command to create the device files. Instead, the file creation tool parses the device table file and creates the entries while it builds the rest of the filesystem, without requiring *root* login.

The *device_table.txt* file in the MTD tools package explains how to write device tables. Here is an example table for basic devices:

```
#<name>          <type>    <mode>    <uid>     <gid>     <major>    <minor>    <start>
<inc>    <count>
/dev           d    755    0    0    -    -    -    -    -
/dev/mem       c    640    0    0    1    1    0    0    -
/dev/kmem      c    640    0    0    1    2    0    0    -
/dev/null      c    640    0    0    1    3    0    0    -
/dev/zero      c    640    0    0    1    5    0    0    -
/dev/random      c    640    0    0    1    8    0    0    -
/dev/urandom     c    640    0    0    1    9    0    0    -
/dev/tty       c    666    0    0    5    0    0    0    -
/dev/tty       c    666    0    0    4    0    0    1    6
/dev/console     c    640    0    0    5    1    0    0    -
/dev/ram       b    640    0    0    1    1    0    0    -
/dev/ram       b    640    0    0    1    0    0    1    4
/dev/loop      b    640    0    0    7    0    0    1    2
```

To create a JFFS2 filesystem using such a device table, you just need the standard *mkfs.jffs2* command, found in the MTD tools package. For EXT2, however, you need to use *genext2fs* instead of *mkfs.ext2*. *genext2fs* supports the same specification table format. You can find *genext2fs* at *http://genext2fs.sourceforge.net*.

---

udev

The first edition of this book and Red Hat 9.0 were released in the same year. Red Hat 9.0 had over 18,000 files in */dev*. We were still in the Linux 2.4 days, and static device files had reached their climax. The */dev* directory in all distributions contained entries for all the possible devices the system could support, and continued to grow, whenever the need arose for some kind of new device—not such a rare occurrence!

Things are very different now, as we release the new edition of this book. We have been using Linux 2.6 for four years, and newly installed Linux systems (for example, in this case, an Ubuntu 7.04 system) might have only 700 device files in the /dev directory. Indeed, if you were to mount the / directory from another system, /dev might even be an empty directory, which means that there aren't any static device files. We are now entering what might be eventually described as "the golden days" of dynamic device files. We've been here before, of course—with devfs—but this time, the solution seems more practical, and built to last, too.

The rise and fall of static device files is easy to explain: it was difficult to implement dynamic device files in the Linux 2.4 days. We'll discuss how Linux 2.6 and udev made dynamic device files easy to implement in today's Linux systems. We will then look at why you want to use udev if your embedded system has to support external devices (and perhaps even just because it's a better design decision, period).

The need for dynamic devices

Back in the Linux 2.4 days and the proliferation of /dev static device files, the main problem for user space applications was that they couldn't tell whether a device was present on the system by looking at the contents of the /dev directory. All they could do was try to open a particular device file, and if this operation failed, assume that the corresponding device was not present.

This situation called for the use of dynamic device files, which cause /dev to contain only devices files that are ready to use. This removes some unwanted complexity from user space applications (of course, error handling is still needed, just in case!). As device information is primarily managed by the kernel, the first dynamic device files were implemented in Linux 2.3 with devfs.

Even though it had a long life, devfs was never fully adopted by the community, largely because of major shortcomings. First, there was no flexibility in device names. For example, the first IDE disk device had to be named either /dev/hda or /dev/ide/hd/c0b0t0u0. Device driver developers also had to modify their code to add support for devfs. Last but not least, devfs stored the device-naming policy in kernel memory. This was a very serious offense, as kernel code usually stays in RAM forever, even if it is used just once (for a kernel module, at least for the whole time the module is loaded; in certain other cases, until the kernel specifically frees it—for example, at boot time when the kernel frees unneeded "init" memory used during early kernel initialization). In addition, in the common mechanism/policy design philosophy, the kernel is supposed to implement only the mechanism, and it leaves policy up to user space.

In early Linux 2.6, Greg Kroah-Hartman created a new solution called udev. As suggested by the *u* character in its name, udev is completely implemented in user space. It doesn't have the limitations and shortcomings that any in-kernel implementation would have.

In the beginning, udev took advantage of new kernel services, namely sysfs and the hotplug infrastructure. sysfs, usually mounted in */sys*, makes device, system, and driver information available to user space. For example, you can enumerate all devices on the USB bus, and for each device, read its vendor and device ID. Hotplug was introduced in Linux 2.4 to support USB devices. Whenever a device was inserted or removed, the kernel executed the */sbin/hotplug* program to notify user space programs. For each subsystem (USB, PCI, etc.), */sbin/hotplug* then ran scripts (agents) identifying the hardware and inserting or removing the right driver modules. udev was just one of these scripts.

The implementation of udev had to evolve because of limitations in the hotplug infrastructure. First, hotplug processes sometimes executed in the wrong order. For example, they might not realize that events for partitions in an inserted disk had to be processed after the disk event itself.

Out-of-memory failures also happened when hotplug got too hot and ran too many udev processes in a very short time. To overcome these issues, udev had to take over several parts of the hotplug infrastructure, and eventually completely replaced it. Today, this means that udev manages not just device file creation and naming, but also tasks previously handled by hotplug, such as loading or removing drivers, loading firmware, and notifying user space programs of events.

Building udev

You can obtain udev sources from the project's web page (*http://kernel.org/pub/linux/ utils/kernel/hotplug/udev.html*), and extract them into your *${PRJROOT}/sysapps* directory. We tested this section of the chapter with udev version 110. Let's start out in the source directory:

```
$ cd ${PRJROOT}/sysapps/udev-110
```

You have to use variables in Guinea hensudev's *Makefile* to configure udev features and the way udev is built. Here are the most useful ones:

DESTDIR
> Specifies the root directory in which to install the udev directory structure. Be sure to set this variable, because udev installs itself by default in /. You may overwrite the udev software and settings of your workstation distribution if you run **make install** without specifying *DESTDIR*. This could make your workstation stop working properly.

CROSS_COMPILE
> Specifies a cross-compiler prefix, for use when you build udev for a different processor architecture or C library. This variable has exactly the same usage as in Linux kernel compilation.

USE_STATIC

> Set this to `true` if you want to build udev without dynamic libraries. The default value is `false`.

Now compile and install udev. The following command does this for a PowerPC target with glibc:

```
$ make CROSS_COMPILE=powerpc-linux- DESTDIR=${PRJROOT}/rootfs install
```

Starting udev

Near the beginning of your system startup script, or in one of the first system services that you start, mount */dev* as a tmpfs filesystem (tmpfs is a kind of in-memory RAM-based filesystem backed by kernel virtual memory):

```
$ mount -t tmpfs udev /dev
```

Then, populate */dev* with static device files, contained in */lib/udev/devices*:

```
$ cp -a -f /lib/udev/devices/* /dev
```

For example, here are static device files used in Ubuntu 6.10:

```
$ ls -la /lib/udev/devices
crw-------  1 root root    5,  1 2007-01-31 04:18 console
lrwxrwxrwx  1 root root       11 2007-01-31 04:18 core -> /proc/kcore
lrwxrwxrwx  1 root root       13 2007-01-31 04:18 fd -> /proc/self/fd
crw-r-----  1 root kmem    1,  2 2007-01-31 04:18 kmem
brw-------  1 root root    7,  0 2007-01-31 04:18 loop0
lrwxrwxrwx  1 root root       13 2007-01-31 04:18 MAKEDEV -> /sbin/MAKEDEV
drwxr-xr-x  2 root root     4096 2007-01-31 04:18 net
crw-------  1 root root    1,  3 2007-01-31 04:18 null
crw-------  1 root root  108,  0 2007-01-31 04:18 ppp
drwxr-xr-x  2 root root     4096 2006-10-16 14:39 pts
drwxr-xr-x  2 root root     4096 2006-10-16 14:39 shm
lrwxrwxrwx  1 root root       24 2007-01-31 04:18 sndstat -> /proc/asound/oss/sndstat
lrwxrwxrwx  1 root root       15 2007-01-31 04:18 stderr -> /proc/self/fd/2
lrwxrwxrwx  1 root root       15 2007-01-31 04:18 stdin -> /proc/self/fd/0
lrwxrwxrwx  1 root root       15 2007-01-31 04:18 stdout -> /proc/self/fd/1
```

The next thing to do is to start */sbin/udevd*, the udev daemon. This daemon first reads and parses all the rules found in */etc/udev/rules.d* and keeps them in memory. Whenever rules are added, removed, or modified, udevd receives an inotify[§] event and updates its ruleset in memory.

udev's operation

udevd waits for *uevents* from the kernel core (such as the USB and PCI core drivers), which are messages sent whenever a device is inserted or removed. When it receives such an event, udevd starts a process to:

[§] The inotify mechanism lets user space programs subscribe to notifications of filesystem changes. See *http://en.wikipedia.org/wiki/Inotify* for details.

- Try to match an event against udev rules, using information found in the message itself or extracting device information from */sys*. Rules are processed in lexical order.

- When a matching naming rule is found, create or remove device files.

- When a matching rule is found, execute a specified command, such as loading or removing a driver module, or notifying user space programs.

The kernel uses *netlink sockets* to carry uevents. Unlike other means of communication between kernelspace and user space (system calls, ioctls, */proc* or */sys*), these sockets are asynchronous. They are queued and the receiver can choose to process the messages at its convenience. This lets udevd limit the number of processes it starts, to avoid out-of-memory issues. With netlink sockets, sending a message to multiple recipients is also possible (*multicasting* in networking language).

You can use the *udevmonitor* command to visualize the driver core events and the corresponding udev event processes. The following sequence was obtained after inserting a USB mouse:

```
UEVENT[1170452995.094476] add@/devices/pci0000:00/0000:00:1d.7/usb4/4-3/4-3.2
UEVENT[1170452995.094569] add@/devices/pci0000:00/0000:00:1d.7/usb4/4-3/4-3.2/4-3.2:1.0
UEVENT[1170452995.098337] add@/class/input/input28
UEVENT[1170452995.098618] add@/class/input/input28/mouse2
UEVENT[1170452995.098868] add@/class/input/input28/event4
UEVENT[1170452995.099110] add@/class/input/input28/ts2
UEVENT[1170452995.099353] add@/class/usb_device/usbdev4.30
UDEV  [1170452995.165185] add@/devices/pci0000:00/0000:00:1d.7/usb4/4-3/4-3.2
UDEV  [1170452995.274128] add@/devices/pci0000:00/0000:00:1d.7/usb4/4-3/4-3.2/4-3.2:1.0
UDEV  [1170452995.375726] add@/class/usb_device/usbdev4.30
UDEV  [1170452995.415638] add@/class/input/input28
UDEV  [1170452995.504164] add@/class/input/input28/mouse2
UDEV  [1170452995.525087] add@/class/input/input28/event4
UDEV  [1170452995.568758] add@/class/input/input28/ts2
```

Each line gives time information measured in microseconds. By a simple subtraction you can measure the elapsed time between a given uevent (a *UEVENT* line), and the completion of the corresponding udev process (the matching *UDEV* line).

With *udevmonitor --env*, you can see the kind of information each event carries, which can be matched against udev rules:

```
UDEV  [1170453642.595297] add@/devices/pci0000:00/0000:00:1d.7/usb4/4-3/4-3.2/4-3.2:1.0
UDEV_LOG=3
ACTION=add
DEVPATH=/devices/pci0000:00/0000:00:1d.7/usb4/4-3/4-3.2/4-3.2:1.0
SUBSYSTEM=usb
SEQNUM=3417
PHYSDEVBUS=usb
DEVICE=/proc/bus/usb/004/031
PRODUCT=46d/c03d/2000
TYPE=0/0/0
INTERFACE=3/1/2
```

```
MODALIAS=usb:v046DpC03Dd2000dc00dsc00dp00ic03isc01ip02
UDEVD_EVENT=1
```

udev rules

Rather than describing udev rules extensively, let's just review typical rules that demonstrate udev matching capabilities. A full reference is available at *http://www.reacti vated.net/writing_udev_rules.html*. The *udev* manual page on your Linux workstation is a good reference, too.

The first types of rules are *naming rules*. iSuch rules make it possible to choose a device filename from a label or serial number, from a bus device number, from a location on the bus topology, from a kernel driver name, or from the output of a program:

```
# Naming testing the output of a program
BUS=="scsi", PROGRAM="/sbin/scsi_id", RESULT=="OEM 0815", NAME="disk1"

# USB printer to be called lp_color
BUS=="usb", SYSFS{serial}=="W09090207101241330", NAME="lp_color"

# SCSI disk with a specific vendor and model number will be called boot
BUS=="scsi", SYSFS{vendor}=="IBM", SYSFS{model}=="ST336", NAME="boot%n"

# sound card with PCI bus id 00:0b.0 to be called dsp
BUS=="pci", ID=="00:0b.0", NAME="dsp"

# USB mouse at third port of the second hub to be called mouse1
BUS=="usb", PLACE=="2.3", NAME="mouse1"

# ttyUSB1 should always be called pda with two additional symlinks
KERNEL=="ttyUSB1", NAME="pda", SYMLINK="palmtop handheld"
```

As an example of a way to manipulate this data, you can use serial numbers to mark the difference between two identical color printers, such as one with photo-quality cartridges and one with regular cartridges for ordinary documents.

udev rules can also be used to control the group and permissions of the device files created:

```
BUS=="usb",                         GROUP="plugdev"
SUBSYSTEM=="sound",                 GROUP="audio"
KERNEL=="ttyLTM[0-9]*",             GROUP="dialout", MODE="0660"
```

Last but not least, udev rules can be used to identify the right driver module to load or remove. Here are some example *modprobe* rules:

```
SUBSYSTEM!="ide", GOTO="ide_end"
IMPORT{program}="ide_media --export $devpath"
ENV{IDE_MEDIA}=="cdrom",  RUN+="/sbin/modprobe -Qba ide-cd"
ENV{IDE_MEDIA}=="disk",   RUN+="/sbin/modprobe -Qba ide-disk"
ENV{IDE_MEDIA}=="floppy", RUN+="/sbin/modprobe -Qba ide-floppy"
ENV{IDE_MEDIA}=="tape",   RUN+="/sbin/modprobe -Qba ide-tape"
LABEL="ide_end"
SUBSYSTEM=="input", PROGRAM="/sbin/grepmap --udev", \
            RUN+="/sbin/modprobe -Qba $result"
```

```
# Load drivers that match kernel-supplied alias
ENV{MODALIAS}=="?*", RUN+="/sbin/modprobe -Q $env{MODALIAS}"
```

In the case of our USB mouse, *modprobe* is run with the value of the MODALIAS environment variable. To identify the driver module to load, it tries to find a matching line in the */lib/modules/kernel-version/modules.alias* file.

How does it work? PCI or USB drivers announce the devices they support, denoting them by vendor IDs, product IDs, or device classes. When modules are installed, such information is stored in *modules.alias*. In this file, you can see that the line corresponding to the USB mouse driver can match several product and vendor IDs:

```
alias usb:v*p*d*dc*dsc*dp*ic03isc01ip02* usbmouse
```

When our USB mouse is inserted, you can see from the output of *udevmonitor --env* that the MODALIAS environment variable matches the previous line from the file:

```
MODALIAS=usb:v046DpC03Ed2000dc00dsc00dp00ic03isc01ip02
```

Coldplugging

What about device files for devices that were already present when the system was started? udev offers an elegant solution to this scenario. After starting the udev daemon, you can use the *udevtrigger* utility to have the kernel emit uevents for all devices present in */sys*.

Thanks to *udevtrigger*, legacy and removable devices are handled and named in exactly the same way. Whether a device has been hotplugged or not is completely transparent to user space.

Kernel configuration

udev's operation requires a kernel compiled with several settings. Here are the ones needed in a 2.6.20 kernel:

Hotplugging support

```
# General setup
CONFIG_HOTPLUG=y
```

Networking support, for netlink sockets

```
# Networking, networking options
CONFIG_NET=y
CONFIG_UNIX=y
CONFIG_NETFILTER_NETLINK=y
CONFIG_NETFILTER_NETLINK_QUEUE=y
```

Pseudofilesystems, to manage /dev

```
# Pseudofilesystems
CONFIG_PROC_FS=y
CONFIG_SYSFS=y
```

```
CONFIG_TMPFS=y
CONFIG_RAMFS=y
```

Of course, support for kernel core subsystems (such as USB and PCI) and drivers should be added, too.

Lightweight udev implementation: BusyBox mdev

Embedded system makers found that udev wasn't always well suited for very small systems. The main reason is that, although udev executables are small C executables, the *udevd* daemon can consume more than 1 MB of RAM, probably because it keeps its rules in memory.

The BusyBox toolset, covered in the next section, offers a lightweight implementation of udev called mdev. You may be interested in mdev if saving 1 MB of RAM matters to your system.

Here's a typical system startup scheme using mdev:

1. Mount */sys*:

    ```
    mount -t sysfs none /sys
    ```
2. Mount a tmpfs filesystem on */dev*:

    ```
    mount -t tmpfs mdev /dev
    ```
3. Instruct the kernel to call */bin/mdev* every time a hotplug event happens:

    ```
    echo /bin/mdev > /proc/sys/kernel/hotplug
    ```
4. Populate */dev* with devices already found in */sys*:

    ```
    mdev -s
    ```

Note that mdev relies on the original hotplug infrastructure, as udev used to do. Because it doesn't use netlink sockets, mdev doesn't have to stay running, and therefore doesn't consume RAM permanently. This is another advantage for very small systems.

mdev doesn't have the sophisticated naming capabilities of udev; it just uses raw device information found in */sys* to name device files. However, an */etc/mdev.conf* file lets you control the permissions and ownership of device files. For each entry in this file, a dedicated script can also be specified, for example, to rename device files or to notify user space processes.

Extra details about BusyBox mdev can be found in the *docs/mdev.txt* file in BusyBox sources.

Main System Applications

Beyond the kernel's functionality and the root filesystem's structure, Linux inherits Unix's very rich command set. The problem is that a standard workstation or server distribution comes equipped with thousands of command binaries, each providing its own set of capabilities. Obviously, developers cannot be expected to cross-compile such a large amount of binaries one by one, nor do most embedded systems require such a large body of binaries.

There are, therefore, two possibilities: choose a few select standard commands, or try to group as many commands as possible into a very few trimmed-down applications that implement the essential overall functionality. We will start by discussing the first approach, but we don't favor it because it is tedious at best. Instead, we will mostly focus on the second approach and the various projects that implement it. In particular, we will discuss BusyBox (including TinyLogin) and embutils, which are the main packages used for this purpose.

Complete Standard Applications

If you would like to selectively include some of the standard applications found in mainstream distributions, your best bet is to start with the Linux From Scratch project, located at *http://www.linuxfromscratch.org*. This project aims to provide explanations and links to packages to help you build your own custom distributions. *Linux From Scratch*, available through the project's website, is its main documentation. It includes instructions and links to build each application one by one. For each package, the instructions provide build-time and disk-space estimates.

Alternatively, you can download applications off the Net one by one and follow each package's instructions for compiling and cross-compiling. Because few packages include full cross-compilation instructions, you may need to look in the packages' *Make files* to determine the appropriate build flags or make the proper modifications for the packages to cross-compile adequately.

BusyBox

The BusyBox project was initiated by Bruce Perens in 1996 to help build install disks for the Debian distribution. In December 1999, Eric Andersen, the maintainer of uClibc, revived the project, first as part of Lineo's open source efforts and then as a vendor-independent project. Since then, the embedded Linux market has exploded in growth and the BusyBox project has grown dramatically in features and user base. Busybox can now be found in most embedded Linux systems and in all embedded Linux distributions, and it has a very active user community. The project's location is *http://www.busybox.net*. The website includes documentation, downloads, links, and a mailing list archive. BusyBox is available under the GNU GPL.

Enthusiasm for BusyBox stems from the functionality it provides while still remaining a very small-size application. BusyBox implements most Unix commands through a single executable that is less than 1 MB (statically linked with glibc) or less than 500 KB (statically linked with uClibc). BusyBox even includes a DHCP client and server (*udhcpc* and *udhcpd*), package managers (*dpkg* and *rpm*), a *vi* implementation with most of its features, and last but not least, a web server. This server should satisfy the typical needs of many embedded systems, as it supports HTTP authentication, CGI scripts, and external scripts (such as PHP). Configuring support for this server with all its features adds only 9 KB to BusyBox 1.5.0 (dynamically linked to glibc on i386).

You can save an enormous amount of storage space—perhaps tens of megabytes—using BusyBox instead of the standard versions of the utilities it contains. You'll also save a lot of time and find it easier to implement a simple system, because you don't have to configure and build the sources of each tool.[||]

Although BusyBox does not support all the options provided by the commands it replaces, the subset it provides is sufficient for most typical uses. The *docs* directory of the BusyBox distribution contains its documentation in a number of different formats.

BusyBox supports all the architectures covered in Chapter 3. It can be linked both statically and dynamically to glibc or uClibc.

Setup

First, you need to download a copy of the BusyBox package from the project's website and into your *${PRJROOT}/sysapps* directory. We will be using BusyBox 1.4.2 for the example in this section.

Once the package is extracted, move into its directory for the rest of the setup:

```
$ cd ${PRJROOT}/sysapps/busybox-1.4.2
```

Since version 1.3, BusyBox uses exactly the same configuration tools as the Linux 2.6 kernel. Hence, the *Config.in* files describing configuration parameters have the same syntax as the kernel *Kconfig* ones. Likewise, all configuration settings are stored in a *.config* file in the root source directory, which can be created with the same configuration commands:

make xconfig
> This command starts the *qconf* Qt-based graphical interface, used for configuring the Linux kernel. However, the BusyBox releases do not include the *qconf* version from the latest kernel releases. For example, BusyBox 1.4.2 *qconf* shipped without the search functionality that appeared in the Linux version available at that time.

make gconfig
> This command starts the GTK equivalent of *qconf*.

[||] Some people insist on using the term *GNU/Linux* instead of just *Linux* to stress the huge contribution of the GNU project and insist on its core values. While the GNU development toolchains are still essential, many embedded Linux systems using BusyBox and the uClibc library no longer include any GNU components at all. Such systems could thus be called *BusyBox/Linux*.

make menuconfig

This text-based interface, based on the *ncurses* library, is the one most BusyBox users are familiar with. It had been the friendliest configuration tool available in the years before the kernel configuration interface was introduced.

make defconfig

This command gives a generic configuration to BusyBox. It enables most common options and can be used as an initial configuration for people trying BusyBox for the first time.

make allnoconfig

This command configures BusyBox with only a strict minimum of options enabled. It is typically run before one of the configuration interfaces, because it helps build an embedded system containing only the features the system needs.

make oldconfig

Do not be confused by the name of this command. It is not an old way of configuring BusyBox. Instead, it is meant to process an existing *.config* file, typically from an older version. Whenever a new parameter is introduced, this command-line interface asks the user to choose a value, rather than silently picking a default one, as *make xconfig*, *make gconfig*, or *make menuconfig* do.

Using this command is also essential after making manual changes in the *.config* file. Many configuration options have dependencies on others, so when you enable a given option, it may require new ones. For example, once you enable support for the *ls* command, you need to set each of the optional features for this command to y or n. *make oldconfig* prompts you for values for undefined options, and therefore avoids failures in compilation.

make help

This is not a configuration command, but it explains all the available *Makefile* targets, such as *make clean*, *make mrproper*, and *make install*. You can use this command on newer versions of BusyBox to learn about new *Makefile* capabilities.

Because the *.config* file contains *Makefile* variable definitions included by the main *Makefile*, it is also possible to define configuration settings on the *make* command line.

Compilation

BusyBox has several configuration options to control the way it is built. The main one is CONFIG_STATIC. By default, BusyBox is dynamically linked with the C library. However, in small systems using only BusyBox and a few small extra binaries, it can make sense to compile everything statically (by setting CONFIG_STATIC=y for BusyBox). This way, the whole C library is no longer needed in the filesystem, making the system simpler and often smaller because unused parts of the C library symbols are not included.

Since version 1.3, the choice of a compiler or a cross-compiler is no longer made in the configuration file, but instead in the same way as in the Linux kernel, with the same ARCH and CROSS_COMPILE settings. This was explained in detail in Chapter 5.

Once BusyBox is configured, you can compile and install it. When linking with glibc, use the following command:

```
$ make ARCH=ppc CROSS_COMPILE=powerpc-linux- \
> CONFIG_PREFIX=${PRJROOT}/rootfs install
```

CONFIG_PREFIX is set to the root filesystem base directory. The *Makefile* will install all BusyBox's components within this directory.

To build BusyBox with uClibc instead of the GNU C library, use the following command:

```
$ make ARCH=ppc CROSS_COMPILE=powerpc-uclibc- \
> CONFIG_PREFIX=${PRJROOT}/rootfs install
```

BusyBox is now installed on your target's root filesystem and ready to be used.

Usage

To understand how best to use BusyBox, let's first take a look at the components BusyBox's build process installs on the target's root filesystem. As expected, only one executable was installed, */bin/busybox*. This is the single binary with support for the configured commands. This binary is never called directly, however; instead, symbolic links bearing the original commands' names have been created to */bin/busybox*. Such symbolic links have been created in all the directories in which the original commands would be found, including */bin*, */sbin*, */usr/bin*, and */usr/sbin*.

When you type a command during the system's normal operation, the *busybox* command is invoked via the symbolic link. In turn, *busybox* determines the actual command you were invoking, using the name being used to run it. */bin/ls*, for instance, points to */bin/busybox*. When you type *ls*, the *busybox* command is called and it determines that you were trying to use the *ls* command, because *ls* is the first argument on the command line.[#]

Although this scheme is simple and effective, it means you can't use arbitrary names for symbolic links. Creating a symbolic link called */bin/dir* to either */bin/ls* or */bin/busy box* will not work, because *busybox* does not recognize the *dir* command.

Note that, although symbolic links are the usual way of linking commands to */bin/busybox*, BusyBox can also be instructed to create hard links instead of symbolic ones during its installation. Its behavior at runtime is the same, regardless of the type of links used.

[#] Like any other application, *busybox*'s main() function is passed to the command line used to invoke it.

The documentation on the project's website, which is also provided with the package, describes all the options available for each command supported. In most cases, the options supported by BusyBox have the same functions as the options provided by the original commands. For instance, using the -al options with BusyBox's *ls* will have the same effect as using the same options with the original *ls*.

When using one of the shells provided in BusyBox, such as *ash*, *hush*, *lash*, or *msh*, you will find it convenient to use a */etc/profile* file to define a few global variables for all shell users. Here is a sample */etc/profile* file for a single-user target:

```
# Set path
PATH=/bin:/sbin:/usr/bin:/usr/sbin
export PATH
```

In addition to setting the path, you could set the LD_LIBRARY_PATH environment variable, which is used during the startup of each application to locate the libraries it depends on. Though the default location for libraries is */lib*, your system may have libraries located in other directories. If that is the case, you can force the dynamic linker to look for the other libraries by adding the appropriate directory paths to LD_LIBRARY_PATH. As with the PATH environment variable, you can add more directories to the library path by placing colons between directory paths.

Note that on a workstation or a server, LD_LIBRARY_PATH would actually be used only as a temporary holding place for new library paths. To permanently add another library path, the administrator would edit */etc/ld.so.conf* and run the *ldconfig* command to consult that file and generate */etc/ld.so.cache*, which is itself read by the dynamic linker to find libraries for dynamically linked applications. Although *ldconfig* was generated when we compiled glibc in Chapter 4, it is a target binary and cannot be run on the host to generate a target *ld.so.cache*. So, you can expect many embedded systems to have no */etc/ld.conf* and instead rely on the LD_LIBRARY_PATH technique.

TinyLogin: BusyBox logging utilities

TinyLogin used to be another collection of utilities maintained by the developers of BusyBox. A single binary like BusyBox, it implemented the following commands: *addgroup*, *adduser*, *delgroup*, *deluser*, *getty*, *login*, *passwd*, *su*, *sulogin*, and *vlock*.

There were several reasons to keep the TinyLogin functionality separate from BusyBox. The main one was that many of the commands implemented in TinyLogin had to run with root privileges, which in turn required that the TinyLogin binary file belong to the *root* user and have its "set user" permission bit enabled, a configuration commonly known as "setuid root." Since TinyLogin used symbolic links in the same way BusyBox does, a single binary containing the functionality of both packages would also result in having commands such as *ls* and *cat* run as *root*, which increased the likelihood that a programming error in any one command could be exploited to gain root privileges.

However, as you can see from the original TinyLogin website, *http://tinylogin.busy box.net*, the project hasn't been updated since 2003. These logging utilities are now actively maintained in BusyBox.

To address the setuid security issues, BusyBox drops its *root* privileges for applets that don't require *root* access. It can also be configured to check the */etc/busybox.conf* configuration file specifying those privileged applets. For the most paranoid users, the safest solution is still to build two separate BusyBox binaries, one for privileged applets and one for unprivileged applets.

Among the options you can configure, pay special attention to the CONFIG_FEATURE_SHADOWPASSWD, CONFIG_USE_BB_SHADOW, and CONFIG_USE_BB_PWD_GRP configuration options, which are documented in the configuration interface. The most important one is CONFIG_FEATURE_SHADOWPASSWD, which adds support for passwords encrypted in a separate */etc/shadow* file.

Traditionally, */etc/passwd* could be read by anyone in the system, and this in turn became a security risk as more and more programs for cracking passwords were available. Hence, the use of so-called *shadow passwords* became the norm. When in use, the password fields in */etc/passwd* contain only filler characters. The real encrypted passwords are stored in */etc/shadow*, which can be read only by a process running with root privileges. Note that if you configure uClibc without shadow password support, enabling CONFIG_FEATURE_SHADOWPASSWD and linking with uClibc will result in a failed build.

You should enable CONFIG_USE_BB_SHADOW to let BusyBox use its own shadow functions for accessing shadow passwords, unless you plan to use glibc's NSS libraries with a properly configured */etc/nsswitch.conf* file.

If you enable CONFIG_USE_BB_PWD_GRP, the logging utilities will directly use the */etc/ passwd* and */etc/group* files instead of using the password and group functions provided by glibc. Otherwise, you will also need the C library NSS libraries and a */etc/ nsswitch.conf* file.

Note that you will not need to create and manage the */etc/group*, */etc/passwd*, and */etc/ shadow* files by hand, as the *addgroup*, *adduser*, *delgroup*, and *deluser* commands take care of creating or updating these files.

For more information on the creation and manipulation of group, password, or shadow password files, as well as system administration in general, see the *Linux System Administrator's Guide* (O'Reilly, also available from the Linux Documentation Project [LDP]), *Running Linux*, and the *Linux From Scratch* book (mentioned earlier in "Complete Standard Applications").

embutils

embutils is another set of miniaturized and optimized replacements for mainstream Unix commands. Although embutils groups some of the commands in a single binary, its main approach is to provide one small binary for each command. embutils was written and is maintained by Felix von Leitner, the author of diet libc, with goals very similar to those of diet libc. embutils is available at *http://www.fefe.de/embutils/*.[*]

Though it supports many of the most common Unix commands, embutils is still far from being as exhaustive as BusyBox. For example, at the time of this writing, version 0.18 still lacks *fbset*, *find*, *grep*, *ifconfig*, *ps*, and *route*. It doesn't offer any shell command either.

As with BusyBox, not all the options provided by the full commands are supported, but the subset provided is sufficient for most system operations. In contrast to BusyBox, however, embutils must be statically linked with diet libc. It can't be linked to any other library. Because diet libc is already very small, the resulting command binaries are reasonably small, too. This can make embutils a better choice than BusyBox when just a few binaries are needed, because the overall size is smaller.

Setup

Before you start the setup, you will need to have diet libc installed on your host system, as described in Chapter 4. Then, download embutils and extract it into your *${PRJROOT}/sysapps* directory. For this example, we use embutils 0.18. You can move into the package's directory for the rest of the setup:

```
$ cd ${PRJROOT}/sysapps/embutils-0.18
```

There is no configuration capability for embutils. You can, therefore, build the package right away:

```
$ make ARCH=ppc CROSS=powerpc-linux- all
```

You can then install embutils:

```
$ make ARCH=ppc DESTDIR=${PRJROOT}/rootfs prefix="" install
```

The options and variables used in the build and installation of embutils have the same meaning as those used for diet libc.

Usage

The embutils installation procedure copies quite a few statically linked binaries to your target root filesystem's */bin* directory. In contrast to BusyBox, this is the only directory where binaries are installed.

A BusyBox-like all-in-one binary has also been installed, *allinone*. This binary reacts the same way as BusyBox when proper symbolic links are created to it. Note that unlike BusyBox, you need to create these symbolic links manually, because they are not created automatically by the installation scripts. *allinone* supports the following commands, as revealed by the *allinone.c* file:

---

[*] As with diet libc, the trailing slash ("/") is important.

arch	pwd
basename	sleep
clear	sync
chvt	tee
dirname	true
dmesg	tty
domainname	uname
echo	which
env	whoami
false	yes
hostname	

Custom Applications

There are many places in the root filesystem where you can put your own application, depending on the number and types of components it has. Usually, it is preferable to follow the FHS's guidelines.

If your application consists of a relatively small number of binaries, placing them in /bin is probably the best choice. This is the actual installation path used for the control daemon in Chapter 4.

If your application consists of a complex set of binaries, and possibly datafiles, consider adding an entry in the root filesystem for your project. You may either call this new directory *project* or name it after your own project. In the case of our control module, this directory could be *control-module*.

The custom directory can contain a hierarchy of its own that you can customize to best suit your needs. You may have to set the PATH environment variable on your target to include the custom directory if your binaries are placed there.

Note that the addition of a custom entry in the root filesystem is contrary to the FHS. This is a forgivable violation of the standard, however, because your filesystem is custom built for your target and is unlikely to become a distribution of its own.

System Initialization

System initialization is yet another particularity of Unix systems. As explained in Chapter 2, the kernel's last action during initialization is to start the *init* program. This program is in charge of finalizing system startup by spawning various applications and starting some key software components. In most Linux systems, *init* mimics System V *init* and is configured much the same way. In embedded Linux systems, the flexibility of System V *init* is overkill, because they rarely run as multiuser systems.

There is no actual requirement for you to have a standard *init* program, such as System V *init*, on your root filesystem. The kernel itself doesn't really care. All it needs is an application it can start once it's done initializing the system. For instance, you can add an init=*path_to_your_init* boot parameter to tell the kernel to use your main application as its *init*. There are, however, drawbacks to this approach, because your application will be the one and only application the kernel ever starts. Your application would then be responsible for starting other applications on the system. Furthermore, if your application unexpectedly dies, its exit will cause a kernel panic followed by a system reboot, as would an unexpected exit of System V *init*. Though this may be the desired behavior in some cases, it would usually render an embedded system useless. For these reasons, generally it is much safer and useful to actually have a real *init* on your root filesystem.

The following subsections cover the standard *init* package found in most Linux distributions, the BusyBox *init*, and Minit, a miniature *init* provided by the author of embutils and diet libc.

As with other issues in Unix, *init* is a broad subject. There are quite a few documents that discuss Linux *init* at length. *Running Linux* describes the mainstream workstation and server *init* setups. Alessandro Rubini wrote a very interesting piece about *init* that goes into the nuances of the various initialization schemes, available at *http://www.li nux.it/kerneldocs/init*.

Standard System V init

The standard *init* package found in most Linux distributions was written by Miquel van Soorenburg and is available at *ftp://ftp.cistron.nl/pub/people/miquels/sysvinit*. Using this package gives you the same flexibility to configure your target's startup that you would have configuring the startup of a workstation or a server. However, the extra functionality and flexibility require additional space. Also, it requires that you keep track of the development of yet another software package. The 2.86 version of the package includes the following commands:

bootlogd	*poweroff*
halt	*reboot*
init	*runlevel*
killall5	*shutdown*
last	*sulogin*
mesg	*telinit*
mountpoint	*utmpdump*
pidof	*wall*

The package can be cross-compiled easily. First, download the package and uncompress it into your *${PRJROOT}/sysapps* directory. For our control module, we used sysvinit version 2.86. Then, move into the package's source directory and build it:

```
$ cd ${PRJROOT}/sysapps/sysvinit-2.86/src
$ make CC=powerpc-linux-gcc
```

Replace the value of CC to match the cross-compiler for your target. With the package now built, you can install it on the target's root filesystem:

```
$ make BIN_OWNER="$(id -un)" BIN_GROUP="$(id -gn)" \
> ROOT=${PRJROOT}/rootfs install
```

This command will install all the binaries in the target's root filesystem, but it will fail afterward because the *Makefile* tries to install the manpages on the root filesystem as well. You can modify the *Makefile* to avoid this, but you can also ignore the failure message.

The previous command sets the BIN_OWNER and BIN_GROUP variables to be that of your own current user. By default, the *Makefile* attempts to install the various components and set their ownership to the *root* user. Since you aren't logged in as *root*, the *Makefile* would fail. The ownership of the binaries matters little on the target, because it generally isn't a multiuser system. If it is, however, you need to log in as *root* and run the *make install* command. Be very careful, in any case, to appropriately set the value of ROOT to point to your target's root filesystem. Otherwise, you may end up overwriting your workstation's *init* with a target binary. Alternatively, to avoid having to log in as *root*, you could still run the installation command using your normal user privileges and then use the *chown* command as *root* to change the privileges on each file installed. This, however, involves going through the *Makefile* to find each installed file and its destination.

With *init* installed on your target's root filesystem, you will need to add the appropriate */etc/inittab* file and fill the */etc/rc.d* directory with the appropriate files. In essence, */etc/inittab* defines the runlevels for your system, and the files in */etc/rc.d* define which services run on each runlevel. Table 6-5 lists *init*'s seven runlevels and their typical uses in a workstation and server distribution.

Table 6-5. System V init runlevels

Runlevel	Description
0	System is halted.
1	Only one user on system; no need for *login*.
2	Multiuser mode without NFS, command-line *login*.
3	Full multiuser mode, command-line *login*.
4	Unused.
5	X11, graphical user interface *login*.
6	Reboot the system.

Each runlevel corresponds to a certain set of applications. When entering runlevel 5 on a workstation, for example, *init* starts X11 and the user is prompted to enter his username and password using a graphical *login*. When switching between runlevels, the services started in the previous runlevel are shut down and the services of the new runlevel are started.

In this scheme, runlevels 0 and 6 have a special meaning: they are used for stopping the system safely. This may involve, for example, remounting the root filesystem in read-only mode—to avoid filesystem corruption when the system is halted—and unmounting all the other filesystems.

On most workstations, the default runlevel at system startup is 5. For an embedded system, it can be set to 1 if no access control is necessary. The system's runlevel can be changed after system startup using either *init* or *telinit*, which is a symbolic link to *init*. In both cases, the newly issued *init* command communicates with the original *init* through the */dev/initctl* FIFO. To this end, we need to create a corresponding entry in our target's root filesystem:

```
$ mknod -m 600 ${PRJROOT}/rootfs/dev/initctl p
```

For more information on the format of */etc/inittab* and the files found in */etc/rc.d*, refer to the resources mentioned earlier.

BusyBox init

Among the commands it supports by default, BusyBox provides *init*-like capabilities. BusyBox *init* is particularly well adapted to embedded systems because it provides most of the *init* functionality an embedded system typically needs without dragging the weight of the extra features found in System V *init*. Also, because BusyBox is a single package, there is no need to keep track of an additional software package when developing or maintaining your system. There are cases, however, where BusyBox *init* may not be sufficient, for example, it does not support multiple runlevels.

Since we already described how to obtain, configure, and build BusyBox, we will limit this discussion to the setup of the *init* configuration files.

Because */sbin/init* is a symbolic link to */bin/busybox*, BusyBox is the first application to run on the target system. BusyBox identifies that the command being invoked is *init* and immediately jumps to the *init* routine.

BusyBox's *init* routine carries out the following main tasks in order. (Action types are defined in the *inittab* file, described later in this section.)

1. Sets up signal handlers for *init*.
2. Initializes the console. By default, it uses the device specified with the kernel's console boot option. If no console was specified to the kernel, BusyBox tries to use */dev/console*.
3. Parses the *inittab* file, */etc/inittab*.

4. Runs the system initialization script. (*/etc/init.d/rcS* is the default for BusyBox.)

5. Runs all the *inittab* commands that block (action type: `wait`).

6. Runs all the *inittab* commands that run only once (action type: `once`).

After completing these steps, the *init* routine loops forever, carrying out the following tasks:

1. Runs all the *inittab* commands that have to be respawned (action type: `respawn`).

2. Runs all the *inittab* commands that have to be asked for first (action type: `askfirst`).

3. Waits for child processes to exit.

After having initialized the console, BusyBox checks for the existence of an */etc/init tab* file. If no such file exists, BusyBox uses a default *inittab* configuration. Mainly, it sets up default actions for system reboot, system halt, and *init* restart. Also, it sets up actions to start shells on the console and on the virtual consoles from */dev/tty2* to */dev/tty4*, although it will skip consoles without complaining if you haven't created the virtual console device entries.

If an */etc/inittab* file is found, it is parsed, and the commands it contains are recorded inside internal structures to be carried out at the appropriate time. The format of the *inittab* file as recognized by BusyBox is well explained in the documentation included in the BusyBox package, which also includes an elaborate example *inittab* file.

Each line in the *inittab* file follows this format:

```
id:runlevel:action:process
```

Although this format resembles that of traditional System V *init*, take note that the meaning of `id` is different in BusyBox *init*. Mainly, the `id` is used to specify the controlling tty for the process to be started. If you leave this entry empty, BusyBox *init* will use the system console, which is fine when the process to be started isn't an interactive shell, or when you start a shell on the console. BusyBox completely ignores the `runlevel` field, so you can leave it blank. The `process` field specifies the path of the program to run, along with its command-line options. The `action` field is one of eight recognized actions to be applied to `process`, as described in Table 6-6.

Table 6-6. Types of inittab actions recognized by BusyBox init

Action	Effect
sysinit	Provides *init* with the path to the initialization script.
respawn	Restarts the process every time it terminates.
askfirst	Similar to respawn, but is mainly useful for reducing the number of terminal applications running on the system. It prompts *init* to display "Please press Enter to activate this console." at the console and waits for the user to press Enter before starting the process.
wait	Tells *init* that it has to wait for the process to complete before continuing.
once	Runs the process only once without waiting for its completion.

Action	Effect
ctrlaltdel	Runs the process when the Ctrl-Alt-Delete key combination is pressed.
shutdown	Runs the process before shutting the system down.
restart	Runs the process when *init* restarts. Usually, the process to be run here is *init* itself.

The following is a simple *inittab* file for our control module:

```
::sysinit:/etc/init.d/rcS
::respawn:/sbin/getty 115200 ttyS0
::respawn:/control-module/bin/init
::restart:/sbin/init
::shutdown:/bin/umount -a -r
```

This *inittab* file does the following:

1. Sets */etc/init.d/rcS* as the system initialization file.
2. Starts a login session on the serial port at 115200 bps.
3. Starts the control module's custom software initialization script.
4. Sets */sbin/init* as the program to execute if *init* restarts.
5. Tells *init* to run the *umount* command to unmount all filesystems it can at system shutdown and set the others as read-only to preserve the filesystems.

However, none of these actions takes place until *init* runs the system initialization script. This script can be quite elaborate and can actually call other scripts. Use it to set all the basic settings and initialize the various components of the system that need special handling. Particularly, this is a good place to:

- Remount the root filesystem in read-write mode.
- Mount additional filesystems.
- Initialize and start networking interfaces.
- Start system daemons.

Here is the initialization script for the control module:

```
#!/bin/sh

# Remount the root filesystem in read-write (requires /etc/fstab)
mount -n -o remount,rw /

# Mount /proc filesystem
mount /proc

# Start the network interface
/sbin/ifconfig eth0 192.168.172.10
```

This initialization script depends on the existence of an */etc/fstab* file in the target's root filesystem. We won't discuss the contents and use of this file, because it is already explained in many documentation sources, such as the *fstab* manpage and *Running*

Linux. Nevertheless, here's the */etc/fstab* file used for the development of my control module:

```
# /etc/fstab
# device      directory    type    options
#
/dev/nfs      /            nfs     defaults
none          /proc        proc    defaults
```

In this case, we mount the target's root filesystem on NFS to simplify development. Chapter 8 discusses filesystem types, and Chapter 9 discusses NFS mounts.

Minit

Minit is part of the miniaturized tools developed by Felix von Leitner, such as diet libc and embutils, and is available at *http://www.fefe.de/minit/*.[†] As with the other tools distributed by Felix, Minit requires a properly configured diet libc.

Minit's initialization procedure is a complete departure from the traditional System V *init*. Instead of using */etc/inittab*, for instance, Minit relies on the existence of a properly built */etc/minit* directory. Firdtjof Busse provides a description of how Minit operates at *http://www.fbunet.de/minit.shtml*. He also provides pointers to example */etc/minit* directories.

By default, Minit's *Makefile* installs Minit components in the host's root filesystem. You can use the DESTDIR *Makefile* variable to install Minit in another directory:

```
$ make DESTDIR=${PRJROOT}/rootfs install
```

[†] As with the other tools available from *fefe.de*, the last slash ("/") is important.

## CHAPTER 7

Storage Device Manipulation

David Woodhouse

The storage devices used in embedded systems are often quite different from those used in workstations and servers. Embedded systems tend to use solid-state storage devices, such as flash chips and flash disks. As with any other component of the Linux system, these devices must be properly set up and configured to be used by the kernel. Because these storage devices differ greatly from typical workstation and server disks, the tools to manipulate them (for partitioning, copying files, and erasing, for instance) are also different. These tools are the subject of this chapter.

In this chapter, we will discuss the manipulation of embedded storage devices for use with Linux. We will start with our primary topic: the manipulation of devices supported by the memory technology device (MTD) subsystem. We'll also briefly cover the manipulation of disk devices. If you intend to use a conventional disk device as part of your system, however, we recommend that you look at one of the books that discusses Linux system maintenance, such as O'Reilly's *Running Linux* by Matthias Dalheimer and Matt Welsh for more extensive coverage. The last section of this chapter will cover the use of swap in embedded systems.

MTD-Supported Devices

As we saw in "Memory Technology Devices in Chapter 3, the MTD subsystem is rich and elaborate. To use it on your target, you will need a properly configured kernel and the MTD tools available from the project's website. We will discuss both of these issues.

As with other kernel subsystems, the development of the MTD subsystem is closely linked with the upstream kernel, and the best way to ensure you have the latest functionality and bug fixes is to make sure you run the latest Linux kernel. For bleeding-edge requirements, there is a git repository at *git://git.infradead.org/mtd-2.6.git* that contains the latest changes due for inclusion in the next development cycle of the Linux kernel. It is also often helpful to follow the MTD mailing list or peruse its archive.

In the following sections, we will discuss the basic use of the MTD subsystem. We'll cover issues such as configuring the kernel, installing the required utilities, and creating appropriate entries in the /dev device directory. We will then focus on the use of the MTD subsystem with the solid-state storage devices most commonly used in embedded Linux systems: native common flash interface (CFI)-compliant NOR flash and NAND flash. We will also briefly cover the popular DiskOnChip devices.

MTD Usage Basics

Having already covered the detailed architecture of the MTD subsystem, we can now concentrate on the actual practical use of its components. First, we will discuss how MTD storage devices are presented to user space, including the /dev entries required for MTD abstractions. Second, we will discuss the basic MTD kernel configuration options. Third, we will discuss the tools available to manipulate MTD storage devices in Linux. Finally, we will describe how to install these tools both on the host and on the target.

MTD /dev entries

Traditional Unix knows two types of devices: character and block. Memory technology devices are not a perfect match for either of these abstractions, since they share characteristics of both and have their own unique limitations.

The primary method of access to "raw" devices from user space is through a character device, /dev/mtdN. This offers basic read and write functionality, along with ioctl access to the erase function and other functionality, such as locking.

For compatibility with device node registration, which predates the MTD infrastructure, there are also read-only versions of the same devices, /dev/mtdrN. These devices serve no particular purpose except to confuse users by ensuring that there is not a 1:1 mapping between the device name and the minor device number. Each *mtdN* device has minor number *N*2*, while the corresponding read-only device *mtdrN* has minor number *N*2 + 1*.

Additionally, there are various types of "translation layers" that allow flash devices to be used as if they were standard block devices. These translation layers are forms of pseudofilesystems that plays tricks to pretend to be a normal hard drive with individually overwritable 512-byte sectors. They are generally designed for compatibility with existing devices in the field, and usually provide some form of wear levelling and power-fail resilience, as well as mapping out bad blocks on NAND flash.

The most naïve implementation of a translation layer is the mtdblock driver, which provides /dev/mtdblockN devices, with a 1:1 mapping between logical and physical sectors. The illusion of being able to overwrite 512-byte sectors individually is provided by reading an entire erase block into RAM, modifying the changed sectors, and then erasing and rewriting the flash. This, obviously, provides no reliability in the face of power loss or kernel crashes—and not only are the sectors being modified likely to be lost, but also a large amount of data surrounding them. However, the mtdblock driver is useful for purely read-only access, in conjunction with "normal" filesystems such as Cramfs.

When mounting a JFFS2 or other MTD-aware filesystem, it is also possible to refer to MTD devices by number or name, in which case, the MTD user modules don't have to be loaded. For example:

```
# mount -tjffs2 mtd0 /mnt
# mount -tjffs2 mtd:jffs2 /mnt
```

Note that if you use this method with the **root=** option to mount the root filesystem, you must also specify **rootfstype=jffs2**.

It is also possible to mount JFFS2 using the */dev/mtdblockN* device, although in this case the device is not actually used; it simply serves as a way to tell the kernel which internal MTD device to use.

There are six types of MTD */dev* entries and seven corresponding MTD user modules. Table 7-1 describes each type of MTD */dev* entry and the corresponding MTD user modules, and Table 7-2 provides the minor number ranges and describes the naming scheme used for each device type.

Note that there are two user modules that provide the */dev/mtdblockN* devices: the mtdblock driver and the mtdblock_ro driver. As the name implies, the latter driver provides read-only access, lacking the read-modify-erase-write functionality of the former.

Table 7-1. MTD /dev entries, corresponding MTD user modules, and relevant device major numbers

/dev entry	Accessible MTD user module	Device type	Major number
mtdN	char device	char	90
mtdrN	char device	char	90
mtdblockN	block device, read-only block device, JFFS, and JFFS2	block	31
ftlLN	FTL	block	44
nftlLN	NFTL	block	93
inftlLN	INFTL	block	96
rfdLN	RFD FTL	block	256
ssfdcLN	SmartMedia FTL	block	257

Table 7-2. MTD /dev entries, minor numbers, and naming schemes

/dev entry	Minor number range	Naming scheme
mtdN	0 to 32 per increments of 2	$N = minor / 2$
mtdrN	1 to 33 per increments of 2	$N = (minor - 1) / 2$
mtdblockN	0 to 16 per increments of 1	$N = minor$

/dev entry	Minor number range	Naming scheme
nftlLN	0 to 255 per sets of 16	L = set;[a] N = minor - (set - 1) × 16; N is not appended to the entry name if its value is zero.
inftlLN	0 to 255 per sets of 16	Same as NFTL.
ftlLN	0 to 255 per sets of 16	Same as NFTL.
rfd_ftlLN	0 to 255 per sets of 16	Same as NFTL.
ssdfcLN	0 to 255 per sets of 8	N = minor - (set - 1) * 8

a As with other partitionable block device entries in /dev, device sets are identified by letters. The first set is "a," the second set is "b," the third set is "c," and so on.

The use of each type of MTD /dev entry is as follows:

mtd N
> Each entry is a separate MTD device or partition. Remember that each MTD partition acts as a separate MTD device.

mtdr N
> Each entry is the read-only equivalent of the matching */dev/mtdN* entry.

mtdblock N
> Each entry is the block device equivalent of the matching */dev/mtdN* entry.

nftl LN
> Each set is a separate NFTL device, and each entry in a set is a partition on that device. The first entry in a set is the entire device. */dev/nftlb*, for instance, is the second NFTL device in its entirety, while */dev/nftlb3* is the third partition on the second NFTL device.

inftlLN, ftlLN, rfd_ftlLN, and ssfdcLN
> Same as NFTL.

As we'll see later, you don't need to create all these entries manually on your host. Unless you use udev, however, you will need to create some of these entries manually on your target's root filesystem to use the corresponding MTD user module.

Configuring the kernel

As mentioned in Chapter 5, the configuration of the MTD subsystem is part of the main menu of the kernel configuration options. Whether you are configuring the kernel using the curses-based terminal configuration menu or through the graphical X Window configuration menu, you will need to enter the MTD submenu to configure the MTD subsystem for your kernel.

The MTD submenu contains a list of configuration options that you can choose to build as part of the kernel, build as separate modules, or disable completely. Here are the main options you can configure in the MTD submenu:

MTD support, `CONFIG_MTD`

> Enable this option if you want to include core MTD subsystem support. If you disable this option, this kernel will not have any MTD support. When this option is set to be built as a module, the resulting functionality is found in the module called *mtdcore.ko*.

MTD concatenating support, `CONFIG_MTD_CONCAT`

> Enable this option if you want to combine multiple MTD devices or partitions into a single logical device, for example, to combine space from two or more separate devices into a single filesystem. If you compile this as a module, the module's filename will be *mtdconcat.ko*.

MTD partitioning support, `CONFIG_MTD_PARTITIONS`

> Enable this option if you want to be able to divide your MTD devices into separate partitions. If you compile this as a module, the module's filename is *mtdpart.ko*. Note that MTD partitioning does not apply to partitions within the "translation layer" used on DiskOnChip devices. These devices are partitioned using conventional disk partitioning tools.

Direct char device access to MTD devices, `CONFIG_MTD_CHAR`

> This is the configuration option for the char device MTD user module that is visible as */dev/mtdN* and */dev/mtdrN*. If you configure this as a module, the module's filename will be *mtdchar.ko*.

Caching block device access to MTD devices, `CONFIG_MTD_BLOCK`

> This is the configuration option for the read-write block device MTD user module that is visible as */dev/mtdblockN*. If you configure this as a module, the module's filename will be *mtdblock.ko*.

Read-only block device access to MTD devices, `CONFIG_MTD_BLOCK_RO`

> This is the configuration option for the read-only block device MTD user module that is visible using the same */dev* entries as the read-write block device. If you configure the read-only block device user module as a module, the module's filename will be *mtdblock_ro.ko*.

FTL (Flash Translation Layer) support, `CONFIG_FTL`

> Set this option if you would like to include the FTL user module in your kernel. When configured as a module, the module's filename is *ftl.ko*. The FTL user module is accessible through the */dev/ftlLN* device entries.

NFTL (NAND Flash Translation Layer) support, `CONFIG_NFTL`

> Set this option if you would like to include the NFTL user module in your kernel. When configured as a module, the module's filename is *nftl.o*. The NFTL user module is accessible through the */dev/nftlLN* device entries.

Write support for NFTL, `CONFIG_NFTL_RW`

> You must enable this option if you want to be able to write to your NFTL-formatted devices. This will only influence the way the NFTL user module is built and is not a separate user module in itself.

Notice that only one of the two block device MTD user modules can be built in the kernel, although both can be configured as modules (*mtdblock.ko* and *mtdblock_ro.ko*). In other words, if you set the read-write block device user module to be built into the kernel—not as a module—you will not be able to configure the read-only block device user module, either built-in or as a module. As we saw earlier, both block device MTD user modules use the same */dev* entry and cannot therefore be active simultaneously.

The preceding list is primarily made up of the user modules described earlier. The remaining MTD user modules, JFFS and JFFS2, are not configured as part of the MTD subsystem configuration, rather, they are configured within the "Filesystems" submenu. Nevertheless, you will need to enable MTD support to enable support for either JFFS or JFFS2.

The MTD submenu also contains four submenus to configure support for the actual MTD hardware device drivers. Here are the submenus found in the MTD submenu and their descriptions:

RAM/ROM/Flash chip drivers
Contains configuration options for CFI-compliant flash, JEDEC-compliant flash, old non-CFI flash, RAM, ROM, and absent chips.

Mapping drivers for chip access
Contains configuration options for mapping drivers. Includes one generic mapping driver that can be configured by providing the physical start address of the device and its size in hexadecimal notation, and its bus width in octets. This submenu also contains one entry for each board for which there is an existing mapping driver included in the kernel.

Self-contained MTD device drivers
Contains configuration options for standalone drivers that are not part of the NOR, NAND, or OneNAND frameworks. This includes test drivers such as the memory-backed test device, "loopback" block device driver, and legacy drivers for the DiskOnChip devices.

NAND Flash Device Drivers
Contains configuration options for NAND flash devices, including the supported DiskOnChip modules.

OneNAND Flash Device Drivers
Contains configuration options for Samsung OneNAND flash devices.

Before configuring your kernel's MTD subsystem, make sure you have read the MTD subsystem discussion in Chapter 3, since many of the options described here were amply covered there.

When configuring the kernel for your host, you will find it useful to configure all the MTD subsystem options as modules, since you will be able to test different device setup combinations. For your target, however, you will need to compile all the options required to support your solid-state storage device as part of your kernel, rather than as modules. Otherwise, your target will not be able to mount its root filesystem from its solid-state storage device. If you forget to configure your target's kernel so that it can mount its root filesystem from the MTD device, your kernel will panic during startup and complain about its inability to mount its root filesystem with a message similar to the following:

```
Kernel panic: VFS: unable to mount root fs on ...
```

The MTD utilities

Because the MTD subsystem's functionality is different from that of other kernel subsystems, a special set of utilities is required to interact with it. We will see in the next sections how to obtain and install these utilities. For now, let's take a look at the available tools and their purposes.

The MTD utilities are powerful tools. Make sure you understand exactly the operations a tool performs before using it. Also, make sure you understand the particularities of the device on which you are using the tools. DiskOnChip devices, for example, require careful manipulation. You can easily damage your DiskOnChip device if you do not use the MTD tools appropriately.

Within the MTD tool set, there are different categories of tools, each serving a different MTD subsystem component. Here are the different tool categories and the tools they contain:

Generic tools

These are the tools that can be used with all types of MTD devices:

flash_info device

Provides information regarding a device's erase regions.

flash_erase device start_address number_of_blocks

Erases a certain number of blocks from a device starting at a given address.

flash_eraseall [options] device

Erases the entire device. The *-j* option is often used to write JFFS2 "clean-markers" to each erase block after erasing. This informs the JFFS2 filesystem that the block was completely erased, and prevents JFFS2 from erasing each block again for itself when first mounted.

flash_unlock device

Unlocks[*] all the sectors of a device.

---

[*] Some devices can be protected from accidental writes using write "locks." Once a device, or some portion of it, is locked, it cannot be written to until it is unlocked.

flash_lock `device offset number_of_blocks`
> Locks a certain number of blocks on a device.

flashcp [options] `filename flash_device`
> Copies a file to a flash device.

doc_loadbios `device firmware_file`
> Writes a bootloader to the device's boot region. Though this command is usually used with DiskOnChip devices only, it is not DiskOnChip-specific.

mtd_debug operation [operation_parameters]
> Provides useful MTD debugging operations.

Filesystem creation tools
> These tools manipulate the filesystems that are later used by the corresponding MTD user modules:

mkfs.jffs2 [options] `-r directory -o output_file`
> Builds a JFFS2 filesystem image from a directory.

sumtool [options] `-i input_file -o output_file`
> Processes a JFFS2 filesystem image, adding summary information to each erase block. This works in conjunction with the `CONFIG_JFFS2_SUMMARY` support in the kernel to speed up mounting JFFS2 filesystems. By storing a summary at the end of each erase block, JFFS2 avoids the need to scan every node in the block.

jffs2dump [options] `image`
> Dumps the contents of a binary JFFS2 image, and also allows endian conversion.

NFTL tools
> These tools interact with NFTL partitions:

nftl_format device [start_address [size]]
> Formats a DiskOnChip device for use with the NFTL or INFTL user module.

nftldump device [output_file]
> Dumps the content of an NFTL partition to a file. This utility does not presently support INFTL.

FTL tools
> These tools interact with FTL partitions:

ftl_format [options] device
> Formats a NOR flash device with FTL.

ftl_check [options] device
> Checks and provides information regarding an FTL device.

NAND chip tools
> These tools are provided for manipulating NAND chips:

nandwrite `device input_file start_address`
> Writes the content of a file to a NAND chip.

nandtest device
> Tests NAND chips, including those in DiskOnChip devices.

nanddump device output_file [offset] [number_of_bytes]
> Dumps the content of a NAND chip to a file.

Most of these tools are used on */dev/mtdN* devices, which are the char device interfaces to the various MTD devices. I will describe the typical uses of the most important MTD tools over the next few chapters, covering the actual MTD hardware in this chapter, preparation of the root filesystem in Chapter 8, and the boot setup in Chapter 9.

Installing the MTD utilities for the host

The MTD utilities are maintained in the git tree at *git://git.infradead.org/mtd-utils.git*, also viewable through gitweb at *http://git.infradead.org/mtd-utils.git*. Release tarballs are downloadable from *ftp://ftp.infradead.org/pub/mtd-utils*, and distributions such as Fedora include relatively recent versions of the tools. Therefore, it is likely that you will need to build the tools for your host only if you need bleeding-edge features or bug fixes.

To build the latest MTD utilities for your host, first clone the GIT tree in your *${PRJROOT}/build-tools* directory:

```
$ cd ${PRJROOT}/build-tools/
$ git-clone git://git.infradead.org/mtd-utils
Initialized empty Git repository in /tmp/mtd-utils/.git/
remote: Counting objects: 1838, done.
remote: Compressing objects: 100% (554/554), done.
remote: Total 1838 (delta 1254), reused 1828 (delta 1244)
Receiving objects: 100% (1838/1838), 809.16 KiB | 80 KiB/s, done.
Resolving deltas: 100% (1254/1254), done.
$ cd mtd-utils
```

The MTD utilities do not use autoconf; you simply use the provided *Makefile* to build them:

```
$ make
```

To build the *mkfs.jffs2* utility you will need to have the development packages for *libacl*, *lzo*, and *zlib* installed. If you don't need to build JFFS2 images, you can edit the *Make file* and remove *mkfs.jffs2* from the RAWTARGETS variable.

With the utilities built, you can now install them in your *tools* directory:

```
$ make DESTDIR=${PREFIX} install
```

This will install the utilities in *${PREFIX}/usr/sbin*. You will need to add this directory to your path if it's not already part of it. See the earlier explanation in Chapter 4 about installing uClibc's utilities for a complete description of how to add a new directory to your development path.

If your MTD devices are accessible on the host because you are using the removable storage setup or the standalone setup we discussed in Chapter 2, you are ready to manipulate your MTD devices immediately. If you are using the linked setup or want to use the MTD utilities on your target in a removable storage setup, read the next section for instructions on how to build the MTD utilities for your target.

Installing the MTD utilities for the target

To install the MTD utilities for your target, you need to first download and install *zlib*, *lzo*, and *libacl* in the sys-root of your cross-compiler. Although you will need to build *libz* and *liblzo2*, you need only the Zlib from *http://www.gzip.org/zlib*, LZO from *http://www.oberhumer.com/opensource/lzo*, and libacl from *http://oss.sgi.com/projects/xfs*. You need to build *libz* and *liblzo*, but we need only the *<sys/acl.h>* header file from *libacl*.

Download the *zlib* tarball and extract it in your *${PRJROOT}/build-tools* directory. You can then move to the library's directory to prepare its compilation:

```
$ cd ${PRJROOT}/build-tools/zlib-1.2.3
$ CC=i386-linux-gcc LDSHARED="i386-linux-ld -shared" \
> ./configure --shared
```

By default, the zlib build process generates a static library. To build zlib as a shared library, you must set the LDSHARED variable and provide the - -*shared* option when invoking *configure*. With the *Makefile* created, you can compile and install the library:

```
$ make
$ make prefix=${TARGET_PREFIX} install
```

As with the other target libraries we installed earlier, we install *zlib* in *${TARGET_PRE FIX}/lib*. Once the library is installed, you can install it on your target's root filesystem:

```
$ cd ${TARGET_PREFIX}/lib
$ cp -d libz.so* ${PRJROOT}/rootfs/lib
```

Next, build *lzo* in a similar fashion:

```
$ cd ${PRJROOT}/build-tools/lzo-2.03
$ CC=i386-linux-gcc ./configure --enable-shared
$ make
$ make prefix=${TARGET_PREFIX} install
$ cp -d ${TARGET_PREFIX}/lib/liblzo.so* ${PRJROOT}/rootfs/lib
```

Finally, extract the *libacl* tarball and simply copy its *acl.h* in place:

```
$ tar xfz acl_2.2.47-1.tar.gz
$ cp acl-2.2.47/include/acl.h ${TARGET_PREFIX}/usr/include/sys
```

As before, if you don't need to build *mkfs.jffs2*, you can simply edit the *Makefile* and remove it from the RAWTARGETS variable.

You are now ready to build the MTD utilities. Download the MTD snapshot into your *${PRJROOT}/sysapps* and extract it, or use git to clone it there. Now move into the utilities directory and build the tools:

```
$ cd ${PRJROOT}/sysapps/mtd-utils*
$ make CROSS=i386-linux-
```

With the utilities built, you can now install them in your target's root filesystem:

```
$ make DESTDIR=${PRJROOT}/rootfs install
```

This will install the utilities in *${PRJROOT}/rootfs/sbin*. Unless your target is using udev, you will also need to create appropriate device nodes. We will see in the following sections how to create just the devices needed on the target's root filesystem.

How NOR and NAND Flash Work

Flash devices, including NOR flash devices such as CFI flash chips and NAND flash devices such as the DiskOnChip, are not like disk storage devices. They cannot be written to and read from arbitrarily. To understand how to operate flash chips properly, we must first look at how they operate internally. Flash devices are generally divided into *erase blocks*. Initially, an empty block will have all its bits set to 1. Writing to this block amounts to clearing bits to 0. Once all the bits in a block are cleared (set to 0), the only possible way to erase this block is to set *all* of its bits to 1 simultaneously. With NOR flash devices, bits can be set to 0 individually in an erase block until the entire block is full of 0s. NAND flash devices, on the other hand, have their erase blocks divided further into pages, typically of 512 bytes, which can be written only to a certain number of times—typically fewer than 10 times—before their content becomes undefined. Pages can then only be reused once the blocks they are part of are erased in their entirety. Newer NAND flash chips known as MLC or Multi Level Cell flash reduce the number of writes per page to only one.

Native CFI Flash

Most recent small- to medium-size non-x86 embedded Linux systems are equipped with some form of CFI flash. Setting up CFI flash to be used with Linux is relatively easy. In this section, we will discuss the setup and manipulation of CFI devices in Linux. We will not discuss the use of filesystems on such devices, however, since these will be covered in the next chapter. The order of the subsections follows the actual steps involved in using CFI flash devices with Linux as much as possible. You can, nevertheless, use these instructions selectively according to your current manipulation.

Kernel configuration

You will need to enable kernel support for the following options to use your CFI flash device:

- MTD support
- MTD partitioning support if you would like to partition your flash device
- Direct char device access to MTD devices
- Caching block device access to MTD devices
- In the "RAM/ROM/Flash chip drivers" submenu, detect flash chips by CFI probe

- In the "Mapping drivers for chip access" submenu, the CFI flash device-mapping driver for your particular board

You may also choose to enable other options, but these are the bare minimum. Also, remember to set the options to "y" instead of "m" if you intend to have the kernel mount its root filesystem from the CFI device.

Partitioning

Unlike disk devices (or those that pretend to be a disk, such as a DiskOnChip using NFTL), CFI flash cannot be partitioned using tools such as *fdisk* or *pdisk*. Those tools are for block devices only. Instead, partition information is often hardcoded in the mapping driver, or the board's device tree, and registered with the MTD subsystem during the driver's initialization. In this case, the actual device does not contain any partition information whatsoever. You will, therefore, have to edit the mapping driver's C source code or its OpenFirmware device tree to modify the partitions.

Take TQM8xxL PPC boards, for instance. Such boards can contain up to two 4 MiB flash banks. Each 32-bit-wide memory-addressable flash bank is made of two 16-bit-wide flash chips. To define the partitions on these boards, the boards' mapping driver contains the following structure initializations:

```
static struct mtd_partition tqm8xxl_partitions[  ] = {
    {
        name:   "ppcboot",                      /* PPCBoot Firmware */
        offset: 0x00000000,
        size:   0x00040000,                     /* 256 KiB */
    },
    {
        name:   "kernel",                       /* default kernel image */
        offset: 0x00040000,
        size:   0x000C0000,
    },
    {
        name:   "user",
        offset: 0x00100000,
        size:   0x00100000,
    },
    {
        name:   "initrd",
        offset: 0x00200000,
        size:   0x00200000,
    }
};

static struct mtd_partition tqm8xxl_fs_partitions[  ] = {
    {
        name:   "cramfs",
        offset: 0x00000000,
        size:   0x00200000,
    },
    {
```

```
            name:   "jffs2",
            offset: 0x00200000,
            size:   0x00200000,
    }
};
```

In this case, `tqm8xxl_partitions` defines four partitions for the first 4 MiB flash bank, and `tqm8xxl_fs_partitions` defines two partitions for the second 4 MiB flash bank. Three attributes are defined for each partition: `name`, `offset`, and `size`.

A partition's `name` is an arbitrary string meant only to facilitate human usability. Neither the MTD subsystem nor the MTD utilities uses this name to enforce any sort of structure on said partition, although it can be used to mount MTD-based filesystems (such as JFFS2) by name, as we saw earlier in this chapter.

The `offset` is used to provide the MTD subsystem with the start address of the partition, while the `size` is self-explanatory. Notice that each partition on a device starts where the previous one ended; no padding is necessary. Table 7-3 presents the actual physical memory address ranges for these partitions on a TQM860L board where the two 4 MiB banks are mapped consecutively starting at address 0x40000000.

Table 7-3. Flash device partition physical memory mapping for TQM860L board

Device	Start address	End address	Partition name
0	0x40000000	0x40040000	ppcboot
0	0x40040000	0x40100000	kernel
0	0x40100000	0x40200000	user
0	0x40200000	0x40400000	initrd
1	0x40400000	0x40600000	cramfs
1	0x40600000	0x40800000	jffs2

During the registration of this device's mapping, the kernel displays the following message:

```
TQM flash bank 0: Using static image partition definition
Creating 4 MTD partitions on "TQM8xxL Bank 0":
0x00000000-0x00040000 : "ppcboot"
0x00040000-0x00100000 : "kernel"
0x00100000-0x00200000 : "user"
0x00200000-0x00400000 : "initrd"
TQM flash bank 1: Using static filesystem partition definition
Creating 2 MTD partitions on "TQM8xxL Bank 1":
0x00000000-0x00200000 : "cramfs"
0x00200000-0x00400000 : "jffs2"
```

You can also see the partitions by looking at */proc/mtd*. Here is its content for my control module:

```
# cat /proc/mtd
dev:    size    erasesize   name
```

```
mtd0: 00040000 00020000 "ppcboot"
mtd1: 000c0000 00020000 "kernel"
mtd2: 00100000 00020000 "user"
mtd3: 00200000 00020000 "initrd"
mtd4: 00200000 00020000 "cramfs"
mtd5: 00200000 00020000 "jffs2"
```

Notice that the partitions are on erase size boundaries. Because flash chips are erased by block, not by byte, the size of the erase blocks must be taken into account when creating partitions. In this case, erase blocks are 128 KB in size, and all partitions are aligned on 128 KB (0x20000) boundaries.

Some types of boot firmware, such as RedBoot, AFS, and TI AR7, do store information on the flash itself about how it is divided into separate images or regions. When appropriately configured, the MTD subsystem is capable of interpreting such information to provide an automatic partition of the flash.

As you see, the concept of MTD partitioning is not exposed to user space in the same way that partitioning on block devices is. The separate partitions of a single flash chip appear to user space as entirely separate MTD devices (*mtd0*, *mtd1*, etc.).

Another Way to Provide MTD Partition Information

For some time now, the MTD subsystem has been able to accept partition information as part of the kernel boot options. The iPAQ's Familiar distribution uses this capability to provide the iPAQ's kernel with the partition information for the device's CFI flash chips.

Here is an example boot option line used to provide the kernel with the same partition information provided in the previous section for the TQM8xxL board (it must be written as a single line):

```
mtdparts=0:256k(ppcboot)ro,768k(kernel),1m(user),-(initrd);1:2m(cramfs),-(jffs2)
```

Required /dev entries

You need to create */dev* entries for the MTD character devices, and potentially also for the block device MTD user modules, to access your CFI flash device. Create as many entries for each type of user module as you have partitions on your device. For example, the following commands create root filesystem entries for the six partitions of my TQM860L board:

```
$ cd ${PRJROOT}/rootfs/dev
$ su -m
Password:
# for i in $(seq 0 5)
> do
> mknod mtd$i c 90 $(expr $i + $i)
> mknod mtdblock$i b 31 $i
> done
# exit
```

Here are the resulting entries:

```
$ ls -al mtd*
crw-rw-r--  1 root    root    90,  0 Aug 23 17:19 mtd0
crw-rw-r--  1 root    root    90,  2 Aug 23 17:20 mtd1
crw-rw-r--  1 root    root    90,  4 Aug 23 17:20 mtd2
crw-rw-r--  1 root    root    90,  6 Aug 23 17:20 mtd3
crw-rw-r--  1 root    root    90,  8 Aug 23 17:20 mtd4
crw-rw-r--  1 root    root    90, 10 Aug 23 17:20 mtd5
brw-rw-r--  1 root    root    31,  0 Aug 23 17:17 mtdblock0
brw-rw-r--  1 root    root    31,  1 Aug 23 17:17 mtdblock1
brw-rw-r--  1 root    root    31,  2 Aug 23 17:17 mtdblock2
brw-rw-r--  1 root    root    31,  3 Aug 23 17:17 mtdblock3
brw-rw-r--  1 root    root    31,  4 Aug 23 17:17 mtdblock4
brw-rw-r--  1 root    root    31,  5 Aug 23 17:17 mtdblock5
```

Erasing

Before you can write to a CFI flash device, you need to erase its content. You can do this with one of the two erase commands available as part of the MTD utilities, *flash_erase* and *flash_eraseall*.

Before updating the initial RAM disk on my control module, for example, I need to erase the "initrd" partition:

```
# eraseall /dev/mtd3
Erased 2048 Kibyte @ 0 -- 100% complete.
```

Writing and reading

Whereas flash filesystems such as JFFS2 take advantage of their capability to continue clearing bits to 0 in an erase block to allow transparent read and write access, you cannot usually use user-level tools to write to an MTD device more than once. This is mostly because the tools usually will want to replace an image wholesale, and thus would want to set some bits from 0 to 1, which is not possible with erasing. If you want to update the content of an MTD device or partition using its raw char */dev* entry, for example, you generally must erase this device or partition before you can write new data to it.

Although writing to a raw flash device can be done using traditional filesystem commands such as *cat* and *dd*, it is better to use the MTD utilities—*flashcp* for NOR flash and *nandwrite* for NAND—because they are more suited to the task. The *flashcp* command will erase flash before writing, and will read back the contents afterward to verify correct programming. The *nandwrite* command will detect bad blocks on a NAND flash device, and skip over them as appropriate. To write a new initial RAM disk image to the "initrd" partition on my control module, for example, I use the following command:

```
# flashcp /tmp/initrd.bin /dev/mtd3
```

In this case, my target's root filesystem is mounted via NFS, and I am running the MTD commands on my target.

Reading from a CFI MTD partition is no different from reading from any other device. The following command on my control module, for instance, will copy the binary image of the bootloader partition to a file:

```
# dd if=/dev/mtd0 of=/tmp/ppcboot.img
```

Since the bootloader image itself may not fill the entire partition, the *ppcboot.img* file may contain some extra unrelated data in addition to the bootloader image.

DiskOnChip

DiskOnChip devices used to be quite popular in x86-based embedded Linux systems, and the MTD subsystem goes a long way in providing support for them. I use it, for example, in my DAQ module. It remains that the DiskOnChip is a peculiar beast that requires an attentive master. The reasons for such a statement will become evident shortly.

The DiskOnChip is simply a NAND flash device with a clever ASIC that performs ECC calculations in hardware. On that NAND flash, we use a special "translation layer" called NFTL, which works as a kind of pseudofilesystem that is used to emulate a normal hard drive. The underlying raw flash device is exposed as */dev/mtdN* devices, while the emulated disk is exposed as */dev/nftlX*. It is this dichotomy that often causes confusion.

Like all NAND flash devices, DiskOnChip devices can contain a certain number of manufacturing defects that result in bad blocks. Before a DiskOnChip is shipped from the factory, a *Bad Block Table* (BBT) is written on it. Although this table is not write-protected, it is essential to the operation of all software that reads and writes to the device. As such, M-Systems's DiskOnChip software is capable of reading this table and storing it to a file. Linux *should* manage to preserve this table, but the tools are not particularly well tested.

There are two ways to install a bootloader on the DiskOnChip (DOC) and format it for NFTL. The first, which is most recommended by the MTD maintainer because it is guaranteed to preserve the Bad Block Table, is to use M-Systems's *dformat* DOS utility. The second, which gives you the greatest degree of control over your DOC device from within Linux, is to use the *doc_loadbios* and *nftl_format* MTD utilities.

M-Systems's DOS DOC tools and related documentation used to be available from the company's website at *http://www.m-sys.com*. However, Sandisk bought M-Systems, and the website now redirects to the parent company. I have been unable to find the DiskOnChip tools on the new site.

When experimenting with a DiskOnChip, it is useful to save the Bad Block Table before you manage to destroy it. You can do this using the DOS *dformat* tool:

```
A:\>dformat /win:d000 /noformat /log:docbbt.txt
DFORMAT Version 5.1.0.25 for DOS
Copyright (C) M-Systems, 1992-2002

DiskOnChip 2000 found in 0xd0000.
32M media, 16K unit

OK
```

The *dformat* command is usually used to format the DOC for use with DOS. In this case, we use the */noformat* option to instruct *dformat* not to format the device. In addition, we instruct it to record the BBT of the device starting at segment 0xD000[†] to the *docbbt.txt* file. Once *dformat* finishes retrieving the BBT, store a copy of *docbbt.txt* in a safe repository, since you may have to restore it if you erase the entire DOC device in Linux. Have a look at the M-Systems *dformat* documentation for information on how to restore a lost BBT.

Note that your DOC device may be free of bad blocks. In that case, the *docbbt.txt* will be empty and you will not need to worry about restoring the BBT if you erase the device completely.

Kernel configuration

You will need to enable kernel support for the following options to use your DiskOnChip device:

- MTD support
- MTD partitioning support if you would like to partition your flash device
- Direct char device access to MTD devices
- NAFT (NAND Flash Translation Layer) support
- Write support for NFTL (BETA)
- NAND Device Support
- DiskOnChip 2000, Millennium and Millennium Plus (NAND reimplementation) (EXPERIMENTAL)

Although the DiskOnChip devices used to have a dedicated driver, we now make use of the generic NAND flash infrastructure for DiskOnChip. It is even possible to use JFFS2 on the DiskOnChip instead of NFTL, although it is harder to boot from it that way.

As with CFI flash, you may choose to select other options. If you compile the options just listed as modules, the DiskOnChip support will require a number of modules. Issuing a *modprobe diskonchip* command should load all necessary modules

---

[†] "Real-mode" addresses on the PC are represented using a segment and offset couple in the following way: *segment:offset*. It's usually shorter to provide just the segment whenever the offset is null. In this case, for example, segment 0xD000 starts at address 0xD0000, as is displayed by *dformat* in its output.

automatically. Whether it is part of the kernel or loaded as a module, the DiskOnChip driver will probe all potential memory addresses for DOC devices. Here is an example of output from the driver on my DAQ module:

```
DiskOnChip found at 0xd0000
DiskOnChip 2000 responds to DWORD access
NAND device: Manufacturer ID: 0x98, Chip ID: 0x73 (Toshiba NAND 16MiB 3,3V 8-bit)
Found DiskOnChip ANAND Media Header at 0x10000
Found DiskOnChip ANAND Media Header at 0x18000
```

The M-Systems DOC Driver

M-Systems provides a DOC driver for Linux as part of its Linux tools packages. This driver, however, is not under the GPL, and you can use it only as a loadable kernel module. Distributing a kernel with this driver built-in, or any combined or collective work comprised of both this module and a Linux kernel, is a violation of the GPL. Hence, if you want to boot from a DOC with a kernel that uses the M-Systems driver, you need to use an init RAM disk to load the binary driver and ship it separately from the kernel. Also, postings on the MTD mailing list suggest that the driver uses a lot of system resources and can sometimes cause data loss on the serial port. For these reasons, I recommend that you avoid using the M-Systems Linux DOC driver. Instead, use the GPL MTD drivers, as I describe here.

Required /dev entries

You need to create /dev entries for the char device and the NFTL MTD user modules in order to access your DOC device. Create as many char device entries and sets of NFTL entries as you have DOC devices in your system. For each NFTL set, create as many entries as you will create partitions on your device. For my DAQ module, for instance, I have one DOC device with only one main partition. I use the following commands to create the relevant entries:

```
$ cd ${PRJROOT}/rootfs/dev
$ su -m
Password:
# mknod mtd0 c 90 0
# mknod nftla b 93 0
# mknod nftla1 b 93 1
# exit
```

Here are the resulting entries:

```
$ ls -al mtd* nftl*
crw-rw-r--    1 root      root       90,   0 Aug 29 12:48 mtd0
brw-rw-r--    1 root      root       93,   0 Aug 29 12:48 nftla
brw-rw-r--    1 root      root       93,   1 Aug 29 12:48 nftla1
```

Erasing

Erasing a DOC device is done in very much the same way as other MTD devices, using the *erase* and *eraseall* commands. Before using any such command on a DOC device,

---

make sure you have a copy of the BBT, because an erase of the device will wipe out the BBT it contains.

To erase the entire DOC device in my DAQ modules, for instance, I use the following command on my DAQ module:

```
# eraseall /dev/mtd0
Erased 32768 Kibyte @ 0 -- 100% complete.
```

Typically, you will need to erase a DOC device only if you want to erase the bootloader and the current format on the device. If you installed a Linux bootloader, for example, and would like to revert back to an M-Systems SPL, you will need to use the *eraseall* command before you can install the M-Systems SPL with M-Systems tools. Whenever you erase the entire device, however, you need to use the M-Systems tools to restore the BBT.

Installing bootloader image

If your target does not boot from its DOC device, you can skip this step. Otherwise, you need to build the bootloader, described in Chapter 9, before going any further. But first, let's see how a system boots from the DOC.

During system startup on x86 systems, the BIOS scans the memory for BIOS extensions. When such an extension is found, it is executed by the BIOS. DOC devices contain a ROM program called the *Initial Program Loader* (IPL) that takes advantage of this characteristic to install another program called the *Secondary Program Loader* (SPL), which acts as a bootloader during system startup. By default, the SPL is provided by M-Systems' own firmware. To boot Linux from a DOC device, however, the SPL must be replaced with a bootloader able to recognize the format used by Linux on a DOC. We will discuss the various DOC-capable Linux bootloaders in Chapter 9. For now, let us take a look at how we can install our own SPL on a DOC.

Here is the command I use to install the GRUB bootloader image, *grub_firmware*, on the DOC in Linux:

```
# doc_loadbios /dev/mtd0 grub_firmware
Performing Flash Erase of length 16384 at offset 0
Performing Flash Erase of length 16384 at offset 16384
Performing Flash Erase of length 16384 at offset 32768
Performing Flash Erase of length 16384 at offset 49152
Performing Flash Erase of length 16384 at offset 65536
Performing Flash Erase of length 16384 at offset 81920
Writing the firmware of length 92752 at 0... Done.
```

Here is the command I use to install the GRUB bootloader image on the DOC in DOS:

```
A:\>dformat /win:d000 /bdkf0:grub_firmware
DFORMAT Version 5.1.0.25 for DOS
Copyright (C) M-Systems, 1992-2002
WARNING: All data on DiskOnChip will be destroyed. Continue ? (Y/N)y

DiskOnChip 2000 found in 0xd0000.
```

```
32M media, 16K unit

Formatting               2042
Writing file to BDK 0    92752
OK
Please reboot to let DiskOnChip install itself.
```

As with updating the firmware version earlier, you need to power cycle your system after using *doc_loadbios* or *dformat* for the firmware to be installed properly. That said, do not use *doc_loadbios* or *dformat* before reading the explanations in Chapter 9 pertaining to its use with a bootloader.

NFTL formatting

Currently, the only way to use DOC devices in Linux is to format them for NFTL. Once we format a DOC device for NFTL, we can use conventional block device tools and filesystems in conjunction with the device.

If you would like to boot from the DOC, read the sections in Chapter 9 regarding x86 bootloaders before carrying out any further operations on your DOC.

If you used the *dformat* utility earlier to install GRUB on the DOC, your DOC is already formatted for NFTL. If you used *doc_loadbios* in Linux, you must use the *nftl_format* command to format the device for NFTL.

The following MTD command formats the entire DOC device for NFTL:

```
# nftl_format /dev/mtd0
$Id: ch07.xml,v 1.5 2004/04/16 20:29:01 chodacki Exp $
Phase 1. Checking and erasing Erase Zones from 0x00000000 to 0x02000000
        Checking Zone #2047 @ 0x1ffc000
Phase 2.a Writing NFTL Media Header and Bad Unit Table
Phase 2.b Writing Spare NFTL Media Header and Spare Bad Unit Table
Phase 3. Writing Unit Control Information to each Erase Unit
```

This command takes some time to go through the various zones on the DOC. If *nftl_format* encounter bad blocks on the DOC, it outputs the following message:

```
Skipping bad zone (factory marked) #BLOCK_NUM @ 0xADDRESS
```

The *BLOCK_NUM* and *ADDR* values output by *nftl_format* should match the values found in the *docbbt.txt* file generated earlier.

A Word of Caution on Flash Translation Layers and Formatting

For the *nftl_format* command to operate properly, it needs to have total control and exclusive access over the raw DOC device it is formatting. Total control is guaranteed by the fact that the commands provided earlier use the */dev/mtdX* device entries. Because these entries are handled by the char device MTD user module, there is no conversion layer between the operations conducted on these devices and the actual hardware. Hence, any operation carried out by *nftl_format* has a direct effect on the hardware.

Exclusive access to the raw DOC device is a little trickier, however, because of the NFTL driver. Basically, once the NFTL driver recognizes a DOC device, it assumes that it has total control over the device. Consequently, no other software, including *nftl_format*, should attempt to manipulate a DOC device while the NFTL driver controls it. There are a few ways to avoid this type of conflict, depending on the configuration of the kernel you are using.

If the NFTL driver was configured as a module, unload the module before running *nftl_format*. You can reload it once *nftl_format* is done formatting the device. If the NFTL driver was built-in, you can either use another kernel or build one, if need be, that doesn't have the NFTL driver built-in. If you want to continue to use the same kernel that has the NFTL driver built-in, you can use the *eraseall* command to erase the device entirely. The next time you restart your system after the erase, the built-in NFTL driver will not recognize the DOC and therefore will not interfere with the operations of *nftl_format*. Finally, if you are carrying out these instructions for the first time, because the NFTL driver should not be able to recognize any format on the DOC device at this stage, it should not cause any problems.

If you have installed a Linux bootloader on the DOC using *doc_loadbios*, you need to skip the region where the bootloader was written and start formatting at its end. To do so, you need to provide an offset to *nftl_format*. Here is the command I use to format my DOC for NFTL in the case where I had already installed GRUB as the SPL:

```
# nftl_format /dev/mtd0 98304
$Id: ch07.xml,v 1.5 2004/04/16 20:29:01 chodacki Exp $
Phase 1. Checking and erasing Erase Zones from 0x00018000 to 0x02000000
        Checking Zone #2047 @ 0x1ffc000
Phase 2.a Writing NFTL Media Header and Bad Unit Table
Phase 2.b Writing Spare NFTL Media Header and Spare Bad Unit Table
Phase 3. Writing Unit Control Information to each Erase Unit
```

The 98304 offset is determined by the output of the *doc_loadbios* command shown earlier. The last erase message output by the command reported erasing 16,384 bytes at offset 81920. 98304 is therefore the first address following the last region erased for the bootloader.

With the DOC device formatted for NFTL, reboot the system as a precautionary step. When the NFTL driver is activated, either at kernel startup or when loading the *nftl.o* module, it should output a message similar to the following:

```
NFTL driver: nftlcore.c $Revision: 1.5 $, nftlmount.c $Revision:…
Cannot calculate an NFTL geometry to match size of 0xfea0.
Using C:1018 H:16 S:4 (= = 0xfe80 sects)
```

If the NFTL driver can see a DOC device but is unable to recognize its format, it will output this message instead:

```
Could not find valid boot record
Could not mount NFTL device
```

Although this message is normal if you have not yet used *nftl_format* on the DOC device, it is a sign that an error occurred if you already used *nftl_format* on the DOC.

There are many reasons why you may encounter these messages. None of them is your fault if you have followed the instructions here, as well as those in Chapter 9.

Whenever you encounter such a message, review your manipulations and make sure you have faithfully followed the steps in the discussion. If it is not a manipulation error, you can choose to dig deeper and use your hacking skills to figure out the problem on your own. It is often a good idea to consult the MTD mailing list and search its archive, because others may have encountered a similar problem and already solved it. When sending a message to the MTD mailing list (or any other mailing list, for that matter), try to be as verbose as possible. It is very frustrating for mailing list subscribers to receive pleas for help that have little or no detail. Specifically, provide the versions of all the software components involved, explain the exact steps you followed, and provide the output of all the tools you used.

Partitioning

With the DOC device formatted for NFTL, you can now partition the device using *fdisk*. Here is the transcript of an *fdisk* session in which I created one partition on my NFTL device:

```
# fdisk /dev/nftla
Device contains neither a valid DOS partition table, nor Sun or S...
Building a new DOS disklabel. Changes will remain in memory only,
until you decide to write them. After that, of course, the previous
content won't be recoverable.


Command (m for help): p

Disk /dev/nftla: 16 heads, 4 sectors, 1018 cylinders
Units = cylinders of 64 * 512 bytes

    Device Boot    Start      End    Blocks   Id  System

Command (m for help): d
Partition number (1-4): 1

Command (m for help): n
   e   extended
   p   primary partition (1-4)
p
Partition number (1-4): 1
First cylinder (1-1018, default 1):
Using default value 1
Last cylinder or +size or +sizeM or +sizeK (1-1018, default 1018):
Using default value 1018

Command (m for help): p
```

```
Disk /dev/nftla: 16 heads, 4 sectors, 1018 cylinders
Units = cylinders of 64 * 512 bytes

     Device Boot    Start      End    Blocks   Id  System
/dev/nftla1                1     1018     32574   83  Linux

Command (m for help): w
The partition table has been altered!

Calling ioctl( ) to re-read partition table.

WARNING: If you have created or modified any DOS 6.x
partitions, please see the fdisk manual page for additional
information.
Syncing disks.
```

Note that we delete the first partition before creating it again. This is because the use of *dformat* to install the bootloader and format the DOC also results in the creation of a single FAT partition spanning the entire device. If you had used the Linux *doc_load-bios*, *fdisk* would have displayed the following error message regarding the partition deletion, which you can ignore:

```
Warning: partition 1 has empty type
```

Also, note that instead of using a single partition on the DOC, or any other storage device for that matter, you could delete all partitions and store your filesystem on the entire device.

See Chapter 3 of *Running Linux* for a full description of how to use *fdisk*. With the DOC partitioning done, you can manipulate the newly created partitions like any conventional disk partition. Among other things, you can format and mount the NFTL partitions. We will discuss these issues in detail in Chapter 8.

Disk Devices

Manipulating disk devices[‡] for use in embedded Linux devices is similar to what you do in Linux workstations or servers. In the following sections, we will concentrate only on those aspects that differ from conventional disk manipulations. I encourage you to consult other documents discussing Linux system maintenance in general, such as *Running Linux*, to get the rest of the details.

CompactFlash

A CompactFlash (CF) card is accessible in Linux in two ways: either as an IDE disk, when plugged in a CF-to-IDE or a CF-to-PCMCIA adapter, or as a SCSI disk when accessed through a USB CF reader. In practice, it is often convenient to use a USB reader

---

[‡] I use the term "disk devices" here to designate all devices that, in one way or another, appear as magnetic disk devices to the Linux kernel. This includes CompactFlash devices, which appear as ATA (IDE) disks.

to program the CF card on the host while using a CF-to-IDE or a CF-to-PCMCIA adapter in the target to access the device. Hence, the CF card is visible as a SCSI disk on the host, but is seen by the target as an IDE disk. To complicate matters further, recent kernels have started to access IDE (or "PATA") disks through the SCSI subsystem using *libata*, so IDE drives appear as */dev/sdX* just as SCSI disks do.

The fact that the same CF card can be accessed through two very different kernel disk subsystems can be problematic, however, as we'll see during the configuration of LILO for a CF card in Chapter 9. Of course, there would be no problem if a CF device were always be accessed through the same disk subsystem.

To access the CF card through a USB CF reader on the host, you must have kernel support for USB storage devices. Most distributions are shipped with USB device support built as modules, and should load them automatically. Therefore, all you need to do is plug the USB device into your host.

When the device is attached, you can look at the appropriate entries in */proc* to see your CF reader. For example, this is how the SCSI subsystem sees the SanDisk SDDR-31 reader I have on my PC host:

```
# cat /proc/scsi/scsi
Attached devices:
Host: scsi0 Channel: 00 Id: 00 Lun: 00
  Vendor: SanDisk  Model: ImageMate II    Rev: 1.30
  Type:   Direct-Access                   ANSI SCSI revision: 02
# cat /proc/scsi/usb-storage-0/0
   Host scsi0: usb-storage
       Vendor: SanDisk Corporation
      Product: ImageMate CompactFlash USB
Serial Number: None
     Protocol: Transparent SCSI
    Transport: Bulk
         GUID: 078100020000000000000000
     Attached: Yes
```

In this case, because the reader is the first device on the SCSI bus, it can be accessed as */dev/sda*. Therefore, I can partition, format, and mount the CF card the same way I would partition, format, and mount a conventional SCSI disk:

```
# fdisk /dev/sda
...
# mkdir /mnt/cf
# mke2fs /dev/sda1
# mount -t ext2 /dev/sda1 /mnt/cf
```

Be careful, however; recent Linux distributions may automatically mount such removable devices for you, and even ask if you want to import photos from them, assuming that they come from a digital camera. You can disable this behavior in the GNOME or KDE settings, or manually unmount the devices when they appear on your desktop. If you attempt to repartition the device while it is mounted, *fdisk* will report an error:

```
Command (m for help): w
The partition table has been altered!

Calling ioctl() to re-read partition table.

WARNING: Re-reading the partition table failed with error 16: Device or resource busy.
The kernel still uses the old table.
The new table will be used at the next reboot.
Syncing disks.
```

The partitions you put on the CF card and the use of the various partitions depends largely on your target. If your target is an x86 PC derivative, you can use a single partition. If your target is PPC using the U-Boot bootloader, you need to have a few small partitions to hold kernel images and one large partition to hold your root filesystem. This is because U-Boot can read CF device partitions and the data on those partitions, but it does not recognize any filesystem organization. Hence, kernel images must be written to raw partitions to be loadable by U-Boot. We will discuss example uses of CF cards as boot devices in Chapter 9.

Floppy Disk

If you intend to use a floppy disk as your main storage device for your embedded Linux project, have a look at the "Putting them together: Making the diskette(s)" section of Tom Fawcett's Linux Bootdisk HOWTO, available from the Linux Documentation Project (LDP). Tom explains in detail how to create a bootable floppy using either LILO or the kernel alone. Although you do not need to read other sections of the HOWTO, the instructions assume that you have created a RAM disk image containing your root filesystem. See Chapter 8 for an explanation of how to create this RAM disk image.

We will not discuss the use of floppy disks in embedded Linux systems any further, because they are very seldom used in production systems and also the Linux Bootdisk HOWTO already covers the issues quite well.

Hard Disk

When configuring a hard disk for use in an embedded Linux system, the most convenient setup to bootstrap the target is to attach the hard disk destined for the target to the host's own disk interface. In this way, the target's hard disk can be manipulated directly on the host. If using a host that has the same CPU architecture as the target, it is even possible to perform a normal installation of a standard Linux distribution, to serve a base for the target filesystem.

If the host already has one IDE disk that is seen as /dev/hda, for example, the target's IDE disk may be seen as hdb or hdc, depending on the host's setup. We can then format and mount this drive as we would any other hard disk. The only difference, however, is that the target's disk, seen on the host as a secondary disk such as */dev/hdb* or */dev/*

hdc, will very likely be seen as hda on the target. This poses certain problems when configuring bootloaders. We will discuss these issues further in Chapter 9.

To Swap or Not To Swap

Swapping is an essential component of most Linux workstation and server installations. It enables the system to address more memory than is physically available by emulating the additional memory on a storage device. Most embedded storage devices, such as flash and DOC devices, however, are ill-adapted to this use, because they have limited erase and write cycles. Since your application has little control over the kernel's use of swapping, it is possible to accelerate the wear on the storage device used for swapping. With this in mind, I encourage you to find alternatives to swapping. Try reducing your applications' memory usage and having only the minimal set of binaries required for your system's proper behavior loaded at any time.

Of course, if your storage device is a real hard disk—not a CF card—swapping is a viable option. Using swap may, however, result in slower response times.

## CHAPTER 8

Root Filesystem Setup

Having built the files for our root filesystem and prepared the target's storage device, we are now ready to set up the root filesystem on the target as well as any additional filesystems we may wish to use. First, we need to select a filesystem type for each of the filesystems. Then, we need to pack the filesystem's content (the files and directories) in the selected format. Finally, we need to write those filesystems to a storage device on the target.

Because Linux supports quite a few different filesystem types and an embedded-Linux-based system typically uses several of them, we will need to understand what types exist and how they can be put to use in our embedded device.

We shall begin, therefore, with a short overview of important properties that Linux filesystems offer to embedded devices. Then, we will continue with a guide to deciding on a filesystem type, and describe how they can be combined to fulfill different roles in the embedded device. Last but not least, we'll cover the issue of upgrading embedded system software. As we shall see, this last topic ties in closely with the types and uses of the filesystems you choose to employ.

Filesystem Types for Embedded Devices

This section will highlight the features and potential pitfalls to think about when selecting a filesystem and how these play out in some of the more popular filesystems used on Linux embedded devices.

Characterizing Filesystems

To select the best filesystem or best combination of filesystems for an embedded device, it's useful to compare them along a coherent set of characteristics. The following sections will present general filesystem properties that we will use later to characterize the current filesystems that are appropriate for embedded systems.

Online write support

Most filesystems support online updates: adding, deleting, and altering files. However, some filesystems lack the ability to do updates online while they are in use, usually for the purpose of achieving a more compact storage device representation or allowing a simpler implementation.

Such filesystems are useful for content that rarely, if ever, changes—which includes most embedded system software. These filesystems can still be updated by rewriting the whole filesystem image on the storage device. But this action is not only time-consuming but also dangerous if not handled correctly, because a power failure during such an update may corrupt the filesystem and render it unusable.

Persistence

Most filesystems have some sort of storage device representation, which enables the content of the filesystem to be preserved between system reboots. However, some filesystems keep all of their data or metadata in system RAM alone, which means it is not persistent. Should the system be shut down or restarted, all the information stored on the filesystem will be lost.

Nonpersistent filesystems are useful to store temporary runtime information that either loses its meaning once the system is restarted (for instance, /proc and /sys) or can be recreated or recomputed by some other means.

Don't confuse the nonpersistent filesystems discussed here—which offer no facility to store the filesystem content on a permanent storage device at all—with the storage of a persistent filesystem on a nonpersistent storage device, such as a RAM disk. Although the end result is the same, these are two different cases. Later we'll explain more about the effect of the storage device on the properties of the filesystem being stored.

Power-down reliability

One of the most salient characteristics of embedded systems, at least in our eyes, is that they are not managed by a professional system administrator. Thus, it is prudent not to expect that your embedded system will be shut down properly via an appropriate system facility. In fact, the most common way of shutting down an embedded device in the field is to simply yank out its power cord or battery.

In light of this, the programmer should take care to assure that the information and metadata stored in a filesystem used in an embedded device will not become corrupted in the event of this common scenario, even if the filesystem content is in the process of being updated just as the power goes down.

Some filesystems employ special means to support power-down reliability of their data and metadata. The most common means is *journaling*. A journaled filesystem maintains some sort of a log of the modifications done as part of each transaction in the filesystem. For instance, a transaction might include appending to a file, updating the file's metadata to list the new blocks occupied by the file, and updating the modification and access times of the file. The filesystem writes the log ahead of performing the modification on the actual data and metadata, and the information about the transaction is deleted from the log only when all of the transaction's operations are complete.

Should the power fail in the middle of modification, the filesystem driver logic will finalize or revert the transaction as a whole once power is back on. The last few writes may be lost, but the filesystem as a whole is uncorrupted.

The journal or log of a journaled filesystem may either be kept on the same storage device as the filesystem data or stored in a separate location. Some journaled filesystems log all modifications to the filesystem content, whereas others log only changes to metadata.

Another distinction that can be made between different types of journaled filesystems is the nature of the transaction log they keep. A *physical journal* contains verbatim copies of blocks that are later to be written to a permanent location on the storage device, whereas a *logical journal* contains some information about the changes made to the filesystem in a specialized, usually much more compact form. This distinction is vitally important to builders of embedded devices because a physical journal requires every block of data to be written to the storage device twice (once to the log and once to the permanent location on the storage device). Because the number of writes to flash storage devices is limited, the use of a such a filesystem can severely impact the lifetime of the device. Note that even logical journals engender double writes of information in many cases.

Another way to provide power-down reliability in a filesystem is to use a *log-structured* filesystem. In a log-structured filesystem, all the data and metadata kept in the filesystem are stored in a log structure that spans the entire storage device. Every write to the filesystem is implemented as a transaction in the log that can be either committed or reverted in an atomic fashion by invalidating previous log entries. (Note that reverting need not involve writing to previous log entries, because revision numbers can be used to mark the current log entries.)

A log-structured filesystem is somewhat similar to a journaled filesystem with a physical journal, with the very important exception that because the log contains the filesystem data itself, there is no double-write penalty.

Compression

A filesystem may automatically compress some or all of the data and metadata before it is written to the storage device and decompress it when read from storage. If supported, compression and decompression happen under the filesystem control and do not require any operation from the application layer, although some implementations allow the filesystem's user to tag specific files on the filesystem in order to recommend or discourage their compression. Most common compressing filesystems compress and decompress each block of data separately, instead of a whole file as a unit.

Although compressing and decompressing may have significant impact on both file access and write times and CPU consumption related to file access, whether this will negatively impact system performance depends on many factors, such as the compression algorithm used and the specific target architecture.

In addition, because information read from the filesystem storage is normally cached in the Linux page and buffer caches, the overhead of decompression will affect only the first access to a specific file block. That is true so long as the file block is used sufficiently often or enough system RAM is available for the kernel page and buffer caches to preserve the block's decompressed state.

Characteristics specific to storage device types

Different filesystems may be built for use with different types of storage devices. Some filesystems support only specific device types; some are more flexible but are still more suitable for certain types of storage devices than others.

It is important to note that the storage device type used may determine or influence the characteristics of the filesystem on it. As a trivial example, consider a persistent filesystem that is built to work on top of a persistent block device, such as an IDE disk or CompactFlash. When such a filesystem is used with underlying storage on a RAM disk, which is also a type of a block device but does not maintain its information when powered down, the information stored in the filesystem is obviously volatile, despite the filesystem itself being nominally a persistent filesystem.

One particularly important characteristic specific to device types is whether a filesystem performs *wear leveling*. This feature, which spreads data as evenly as possible across a device, is crucial when the filesystem is stored on an on-board NOR or NAND flash, because each block of this flash device can be written a limited, fixed number of times (including flash updates) before it is no longer usable. Wear leveling can be implemented in firmware (as with CompactFlash devices), in an intermediate software layer between the filesystem and the storage device driver (such as through an FTL or NFTL translation layer, described in Chapter 3), or in the filesystem itself.

 Wear leveling suffers from some serious drawbacks if implemented at any level other than the filesystem itself. The wear leveling algorithm implemented by the firmware of some CompactFlash devices is low quality and not to be trusted. Wear leveling in FTL or NFTL suffers from redundant journaling, which is implemented at both the FTL or NFTL layer and the filesystem layer in order to maintain reliability in case of an abrupt power failure. In addition, because FTL and NFTL do not actually know which filesystem blocks are currently in use, they must keep the information from all filesystem blocks regardless of whether they are used. This requires even more writes when moving around flash blocks due to garbage collection of outdated log entries.

Filesystem Types

Linux supports over 50 different filesystem types, but only a small subset are normally used in embedded Linux systems. The following sections will classify these popular filesystems according to the characteristics described in the previous sections and provide details about each filesystem's creation.

The second extended filesystem (Ext2)

The second extended filesystem is writable and persistent, built for use with block devices. It does not provide any power-down reliability or compression (unlike its follow-on, the Ext3 filesystem, described in the next section). The filesystem is very fast and supports up to 16 or 32 TB of storage.

Ext2 is one of the earliest filesystems to be used with Linux and is still a very suitable choice when used with any of the following:

- RAM disks in read/write mode
- CompactFlash devices in IDE mode
- NAND or NOR flash in read-only (or mostly read-only) mode, implemented either via MTD subsystem raw block device emulation or with an FTL/NFTL translation layer

We don't recommend using Ext2 when you have to write persistent data to the storage device in production, because this filesystem doesn't offer power-down reliability.

Creating an Ext2 filesystem and populating it is quite simple. First, you need to format the storage partition. You can do this using the *mke2fs* command from the `e2fsprogs` package, available at *http://e2fsprogs.sourceforge.net*.

 Because the Ext2 and Ext3 filesystems are commonly used in Linux desktop and server systems as well, this command is very likely already installed on your development machine.

The following example formats a NAND flash using the NFTL translation layer to present a block device to Ext2. Note, however, that any block device would have worked just the same. The example assumes that you are issuing these commands from your project's *${PRJROOT}* directory. It also assumes that the DOC device is accessible on your host as */dev/nftla* and you want to create an Ext2 filesystem on the first partition of that device:

```
# mke2fs /dev/nftla1
mke2fs 1.18, 11-Nov-1999 for EXT2 FS 0.5b, 95/08/09
Filesystem label=
OS type: Linux
Block size=1024 (log=0)
Fragment size=1024 (log=0)
```

```
8160 inodes, 32574 blocks
1628 blocks (5.00%) reserved for the super user
First data block=1
4 block groups
8192 blocks per group, 8192 fragments per group
2040 inodes per group
Superblock backups stored on blocks:
        8193, 24577

Writing inode tables: done
Writing superblocks and filesystem accounting information: done
```

Now, mount the partition and copy the filesystem data to it:

```
# mkdir /mnt/doc
# mount -t ext2 /dev/nftla1 /mnt/doc
# cp -a rootfs/* /mnt/doc
```

If you cannot access the storage device from your host machine (such as over NFS), you have two options:

- Mount an NFS root filesystem on the target, and then copy the contents of the root filesystem onto your storage device. Using an NFS filesystem is described in Chapter 9.

- Generate a binary image file of the filesystem data, and copy it onto the storage device using an external device, such as a JTAG connector or a flash programmer.

Yet a third option is to create an empty file of the required filesystem image size, format it using *mke2fs* with the -F flag, and then loopback mount it using *mount* with the *-o loop* option. However, using *genext2fs* is much better, so we mention this option only for the sake of completeness.

To generate the binary image file containing the filesystem, use the *genext2fs* program. As its name suggests, *genext2fs* generates an image file containing an Ext2 filesystem that you can copy later to the target storage device. An additional advantage of using *genext2fs* over mounting the storage device on the host (as suggested previously) is that you don't require root permissions to create the image. Therefore, it is both safer and easier, and we recommend it.

genext2fs can be downloaded from the project website at *http://genext2fs.source forge.net*; the latest version at the time of this writing is 1.4.1. The build and installation procedure is straightforward:

```
$ tar zxvf genext2fs-1.4.1.tar.gz
$ cd genext2fs-1.4.1
$ ./configure
$ make
$ make check
$ make install
```

Using *genext2fs* is also quite straightforward:

```
$ genext2fs -b 1024 -d src -D device_table.txt -e 0 flashdisk.img
```

This command will create a file called *flashdisk.img* in the current directory, 1024 KB in size, that will contain an image of an Ext2 filesystem with all the files and directories from the *src* directory. The *-e* option zeroes out all the unallocated space on the filesystem.

The file *device_table.txt*, which is passed as a parameter to the *-D* option, contains a list of regular and special files and directories that either need to be added to the filesystem image (in addition to the files and directories present in the *src* directory) or need to have their ownership or permission changed. Each line in this file is of the form:

```
name type mode uid gid
        major minor start inc
        count
```

In each line, *name* is a relative or absolute path to the filename. *type* is one of the following:

f

A regular file

d

A directory

c

A character device file

b

A block device file

p

A FIFO or named pipe

mode is the file permission, and *uid* and *gid* are the user ID and group ID (respectively) that own the file or directory.

The rest of the entries (*major*, *minor*, etc.) apply only to device files. *major* and *minor* are the device file major and minor numbers. *start*, *inc*, and *count* can be used to create multiple device files in a single command, where a serial number is appended to the device file name, starting from *start* and incremented by *inc* for each of the *count* device files created. The minor number can also be incremented in the same fashion.

The following is an example device table file, written by Erik Andersen and taken from the *genext2fs* manpage:

```
# name type mode uid gid major minor start inc count

/dev        d    755  0    0    -     -     -     -    -
/dev/mem    c    640  0    0    1     1     0     0    -
/dev/tty    c    666  0    0    5     0     0     0    -
/dev/tty    c    666  0    0    4     0     0     1    6
```

```
/dev/loop  b  640  0  0  7  0  0  1  2
/dev/hda   b  640  0  0  3  0  0  0  -
/dev/hda   b  640  0  0  3  1  1  1  16
/dev/log   s  666  0  0  -  -  -  -  -
```

This device table creates the */dev* directory and the device nodes */dev/mem* (major 1, minor 1), and also */dev/tty*, */dev/tty[0-5]*, */dev/loop[0-1]*, */dev/hda*, */dev/hda[1-15]*, and */dev/log socket*.

Many other options for *genext2fs* are described in the command's manpage; we recommend reading it.

The third extended filesystem (Ext3)

The third extended filesystem is an extension of the second extended filesystem that adds reliability, via journaling, to Ext2's writability and persistence.

By default, Ext3 will operate in ordered mode, meaning it will journal only filesystem metadata, and only after all data updates have been written directly to storage. This behavior is usually a good compromise that protects the filesystem metadata but does not slow down writes by having any file data updates go through the filesystem journal. You can change the behavior, at the cost of significantly slowing down writes, with the *data=journal* mount option.

Another recommended mount option is *noatime*, which will disable the default behavior of updating the last access time on files stored in the filesystem. This breaks the filesystem's POSIX compatibility, but can greatly improve the lifetime of flash devices, as well as often providing better I/O throughout the system.

Here is an example showing both options used to mount an Ext3 filesystem from the first partition of a CompactFlash in IDE mode (once again, the command would be similar for any block device):

```
# mount -t ext3 /dev/hda1 /media/cf -o noatime,data=journal
```

Ext3 is recommended for use with CompactFlash devices in IDE mode, provided that their hardware provides wear level control (most do). It is also recommended for NAND or NOR flashes via FTL/NFTL translation layers.

An Ext3 filesystem can be created using exactly the same methods described in the previous section for Ext2, as they both share a common storage device format. The first time an Ext2 filesystem is mounted as an Ext3 filesystem, the filesystem driver will automatically create a journal entry and start using it. You can, however, create the journal entry in advance when using the *mke2fs* program, by supplying it with the *-f* option.

Cramfs

Linus Torvalds wrote Cramfs as a filesystem with a bare-minimum feature set. It is a very simple, and sometimes simplistic, compressed and read-only filesystem aimed at embedded systems.

Cramfs can be used with any block device and is recommended for use in the following situations:

- As a read-only filesystem on NOR and NAND flash via the "raw" MTD block device emulation, in the common situation where updates of the filesystem image are rare
- With NAND or NOR flash via FTL or NFTL translation layers
- On CompactFlash in IDE mode
- As a RAM disk image

Apart from being read-only, Cramfs has the following limitations:

- The maximum size of a file is 16 MB.
- There are no current (.) or parent (..) directory entries.
- The user-ID field for files is 16 bits wide, and the group-ID field is 8 bits wide. Normal filesystems usually support either 16- or 32-bit uids and gids. On Cramfs, gids are truncated to the lower 8 bits. In other words, you can have at most 255 groups on a root filesystem built on Cramfs.[*]
- All file timestamps are set to the Epoch (00:00:00 GMT, January 1, 1970). The timestamps may be updated at runtime, but the updated values will last only as long as the inode is cached in memory. Once the file is reloaded, its timestamp will revert to the Epoch.
- Only kernels using 4096-byte page sizes (the value of `PAGE_CACHE_SIZE` must be 4096) can read Cramfs images.
- All files, whether they are linked or not, have a link count[†] of 1. Even when multiple filesystem entries point to the same file, that file has a link count of only 1. This is fine for most operations, however, because no files can actually be deleted from Cramfs.

The limited number of gids is not a problem as long as your target's root filesystem contains no group with a gid above 255. For instance, if your target is a single-user system, you don't need to worry about this limitation. If your system must support a multiuser environment, make sure the gids of all files and directories are below 255.

---

[*] See Chapter 5 in *Running Linux* by Matthias Dalheimer and Matt Welsh (O'Reilly) for a discussion of uids and gids.

[†] Typically, filesystems maintain a count of the number of links made toward a file, and when this count reaches 0, the file is deleted.

Otherwise, any gid above 255 will wrap around to a number below 255 and, possibly, create a security risk.

In addition to Cramfs's limitations, the tools provided for creating Cramfs filesystem images used to be subject to the host's byte ordering. Hence, you needed to use a host that had the same byte ordering as your target to create a Cramfs image. At the time of this writing, this limitation still applies to version 1.1 of this package, which is the latest official Cramfs creation tools package found in the package website at *http://source forge.net/projects/cramfs/*. But patches exists that enable filesystem creation independently of the host's byte ordering. You can find these patches in the "Patches" section of the website.

This same website offers several additional patches, enabling such things as using a device table file in the same format *genext2fs* supports and using Execution In Place for certain files in a Cramfs filesystem.

If your system can function with Cramfs's limitations, it should probably be a serious candidate for your project. If you are interested in Cramfs but chafe at its limitations, look into Squashfs, described in the next section.

To create a Cramfs image of your root filesystem, you first need to create and install the Cramfs tools, *cramfsck* and *mkcramfs*. Both of these utilities are part of the package `Cramfs tools` package, which can be downloaded from the project website at *http://sourceforge.net/projects/cramfs*.

To build the utilities, download the package, un-tar the archive, and issue the *make* command:

```
$ tar zxvf cramfs-1.1.tar.gz
$ cd cramfs-1.1
$ make
```

Unfortunately, the package Makefile does not provide an install target. Therefore, copy the tools to an appropriate directory:

```
$ cp cramfsck mkcramfs ${PREFIX}/bin/
```

You can now create a Cramfs image of your target's root filesystem:

```
$ cd ${PRJROOT}
$ mkcramfs rootfs/ images/cramfs.img
  bin
  boot
  dev
  etc
  lib
  linuxrc
  proc
  sbin
  tmp
  usr
'bin':
  addgroup
```

```
...
'boot':
  boot.b
...
'sbin':
  chroot
Directory data: 6484 bytes
166.67% (+15 bytes)      addgroup
-31.46% (-2196 bytes)    allinone
-40.27% (-240 bytes)     arch
185.71% (+13 bytes)      ash
...
-49.60% (-3700 bytes)    wall
-49.54% (-695 bytes)     include
Everything: 3560 kilobytes
Super block: 76 bytes
CRC: f18594b6
warning: gids truncated to 8 bits.  (This may be a security concern).
```

In this case, *rootfs* contains 7840 KB, while the Cramfs image's size is 3560 KB, a compression ratio of approximately 50 percent. This ratio is consistent with Cramfs's typical yields.

With the filesystem image ready, you can now write it to your storage device (note that the following command requires root privileges):

```
# dd if=rootfs/cramfs.img of=/dev/mtd4 bs=1024
```

This command assumes that the storage device is accessible on the host. The same image file also can be copied to the storage device using alternative methods, such as using a flash programmer via a JTAG port to copy the filesystem image unto the flash, via a bootloader debug shell (the bootloader will be discussed further in the next chapter), or by running from an NFS-mounted root filesystem on the target. To verify the content of a Cramfs filesystem, use the *cramfsck* utility built earlier.

Squashfs

The Cramfs filesystem described in the previous section is quite useful for many embedded system setups. However, it suffers from some serious limitations. Squashfs is a compressed, read-only filesystem that enjoys many of Cramfs's advantages without its limitations. It is intended for general read-only filesystem use, for archival use (i.e., in cases where a *.tar.gz* file may be used), and in systems with constrained disk sizes and memory (which includes most embedded systems) where low overhead is needed. The filesystem is currently stable, and has been tested on PowerPC, i586, Sparc, and ARM architectures.

The following are some of Squashfs's features:

- Data, inodes, and directories are compressed.
- Squashfs stores full uid/gids (32 bits) and file creation time.
- Files up to 2^{64} bytes in size are supported. Filesystems can be up to 2^{64} bytes.

- Inode and directory data are highly compacted, and packed on byte boundaries. Each compressed inode is, on average, 8 bytes in length. (The exact length varies by file type; that is, regular files, directories, symbolic links, and block or char device inodes have different sizes.)

- Squashfs can use block sizes up to 64 KB (which is the default size). Using 64 KB blocks achieves greater compression ratios than the normal 4 KB block size.

- File duplicates are detected and removed.

- Both big- and little-endian architectures are supported. The *mksquashfs* program can generate filesystems for situations where the host byte ordering is different from the target.

Despite all its advantages, Squashfs does suffer from one drawback: it is not part of the Linux kernel tree. Using Squashfs requires applying a patch to the kernel, available together with other tools from the project website at *http://squashfs.sourceforge.net*.

By itself, Squashfs supports only GZIP compression. However, external patches available at *http://www.squashfs-lzma.org* enable the use of the LZMA compression. There are plans to integrate LZMA compression into the upcoming 2.6.24 Linux kernel version.

After downloading the Squashfs tar archive of the latest version (3.2-r2 at the time of this writing), unpack the archive:

```
$ tar zxvf squashfs3.2-r2.tar.gz
$ cd squashfs3.2-r2/
```

Next, locate the kernel patch for your kernel version from the *kernel-patches* directory:

```
$ cp kernel-patches/linux-2.6.20/ ${PRJROOT}/kernel
```

Now, apply the patch to your kernel source tree:

```
$ cd ${PRJROOT}/kernel/
$ patch -p1 < squashfs3.2-patch
```

 If the patch you are using does not exactly fit the kernel version you are using, or if earlier patches applied by you or a vendor made some changes in related code, you might need to manually inspect the *patch* command output and manually integrate the code where *patch* failed to find a match.

Next, build the kernel as usual, but make sure to turn on the new "Squashed filesystem" option in the "Miscellaneous filesystems" section of the "Filesystems" menu. If you do not plan on using Squashfs on an initial RAM disk (described soon), you can opt to build Squashfs as a kernel module instead of building it statically into the kernel image.

In addition to patching and rebuilding the target's kernel, you need to build and install the Squashfs tools package for the host:

```
$ cd squashfs3.2-r2/squashfs-tools/
$ make
$ cp mksquashfs /usr/sbin
```

At last, you can use the *mksqushfs* tool you have just built to build a Squashfs filesystem:

```
mksqushfs source1 source2 ... destination [options]
```

where *source1*, *source2*, etc. are the pathnames of files or directories to be added to the resulting filesystem image, and *destination* is the path of the Squashfs filesystem image file to create.

Many additional options exist; we recommend that you consult the extensive Squashfs how-to document available at *http://www.artemio.net/projects/linuxdoc/squashfs*.

JFFS2

JFFS2 is a writable, persistent, compressed, power-down-reliable filesystem that is well suited for use on NOR or NAND on-board flashes or DoC devices. The filesystem uses a log structure and provides wear leveling. We already described JFFS2's features in Chapter 3.

Because JFFS2 is an important component of the embedded Linux system builder's tool set, a few words regarding its design are in order. The following information is an extremely high-level and not completely accurate description of JFFS2's inner workings, but it will hopefully serve to provide sufficient background for you to understand the remainder of the section. Additional in-depth information regarding JFFS2's design and implementation can be found on its documentation page, *http://www.linux-mtd.in fradead.org/doc/jffs2.html*.

Despite its name, JFFS2 is not in fact a journaling filesystem. Instead, JFFS2 keeps all the filesystem information in a log structure that spans the entire flash storage space. This log is comprised of nodes, each describing a single block of data or metadata. The nodes are grouped together in chunks the size of erase blocks. Each node that carries filesystem data has information identifying which part of which file it is describing, as well as a serial number.

When the contents of part of a file need to be updated, JFFS2 simply writes a new node with the changed information, giving the node a higher serial number than all previously written nodes describing the same file part. All these older log entries are subsequently ignored.

When the free space in the flash storage device drops down below a certain threshold, or when additional storage space is needed, a background garbage-collection process begins. It walks all the erase blocks, creates new copies of nodes that reside in erase blocks with a significant number of stale nodes, and recycles each erase block it replaces by erasing it. The process also writes clean blocks to insert special nodes called "clean marker" nodes. This kind of node designates the block as a fresh erase block that is ready to receive new nodes, thus allowing the filesystem code to quickly identify clean blocks when the filesystem is mounted. When the last erase block at the end of the flash device is full, the JFFS2 code simply wraps around and starts populating clean blocks from the beginning of the flash device.

When a JFFS2 filesystem is mounted, the JFFS2 code scans the entire flash device and builds a representation of the filesystem data by going over the log node by node and identifying the most current node for each file part. One optimization recent versions of JFFS2 has introduced is the use of erase block summary nodes, which are written to the end of the erase block and contain a summary of the nodes present in the block. If such an erase block summary is found, the JFFS2 code will use the summary information instead of reading the entire erase block, which provides faster mount times.

One caveat that may be apparent now is JFFS2's behavior when full. As described previously, JFFS2 makes use of a garbage-collection technique on the MTD blocks that contain stale information. This garbage collection takes place either in a background task that is triggered whenever the free space in the filesystem drops below a preconfigured threshold, or whenever a pending filesystem update requires more free space then is currently available. This scheme works fine in most cases.

Under extreme conditions, however, such as when the filesystem is nearly full and a large number of filesystem updates are required, the additional CPU consumption required to decompress and compress data as it is being moved from garbage-collected MTD blocks to new ones, and the consequent delay in filesystem operations, may have negative effects on time-sensitive parts of your device software that were not designed to take this into consideration.

In addition, attempting to update or truncate a file's content in a full JFFS2 filesystem might fail with an error indicating that the filesystem is full, even though it might seem that the action does not require additional storage blocks. Once again, this is expected behavior for a log-structured filesystem, as every action in such a filesystem results in an append to the log, but it may come as an unpleasant surprise to those who do not understand how JFFS2 works.

Don't interpret these side effects as indications that JFFS2 is not production-worthy. Just take the constraints as well as the advantages of this filesystem design into account when considering and coding around it in an embedded device. Make sure that sufficient storage space is allocated to the JFFS2 filesystem in order to efficiently make use of the storage device resources. Use the filesystem with applications that can tolerate delays, as well as the previously mentioned error condition when the filesystem gets close to being full.

JFFS2 Evolution

JFFS2 is a the second incarnation of the original JFFS filesystem. But JFFS2 itself is beginning to show its age, especially with ever-bigger flash device sizes becoming common. It is not designed to handle the newest size of flash devices all that well.

An effort is underway to redesign and rewrite the next generation of the JFFS2 filesystem and its logical flash volume manager, under the names UBI (Latin for "Where?") and UBIFS. At the time of this writing, this project is not ready for use in a production system, but it may very well be by the time you read this book. So, have a look at the project's websites, *http://www.linux-mtd.infradead.org/doc/ubi.html* and *http://www.linux-mtd.infradead.org/doc/ubifs.html*.

A second and very serious contender to the title of the "next JFFS2" is Logfs, whose website can be found at *http://logfs.org/logfs*.

Leaving the characteristics of JFFS2 now and moving to practical details, let us now concentrate on the creation and installation of a JFFS2 filesystem image. We will focus on the *mkfs.jffs2* utility installed in the previous chapter as part of the MTD utilities installation.

Creating a JFFS2 image is fairly simple:

```
$ cd ${PRJROOT}
$ mkfs.jffs2 -r rootfs/ -o images/rootfs-jffs2.img -e 128KiB
```

Use the *-r* option to specify the location of the directory containing the root filesystem, and the *-o* option to specify the name of the output file where the filesystem image should be stored. The *-e* option provides the size of the erase block of the flash device to which the filesystem will be written.

Importance of Using Correct Erase Block Size

JFFS2 is specifically designed to be used with NOR or NAND flashes, and its design is tightly coupled to the concept of a flash erase block. It is therefore very important to provide a correct erase block size when creating a JFFS2 filesystem image using *mkfs.jffs2*.

JFFS2 treats each flash erase block as a separate storage block. The nodes that make up the JFFS2 log structure will never cross an erase block boundary. Nodes that seem to do so will be ignored as invalid by the JFFS2 code, with the result that all data stored in it will be lost and the filesystem will be corrupted. This last scenario is exactly what will happen if you specify a bigger erase block than the device's actual erase block size when creating an JFFS2 image.

Creating an image with a smaller erase block size than the true one is less catastrophic, but still has some undesirable results.

If a node cannot be written in its entirety to free space in the current erase block, the remainder of the current erase block will stay empty and the node will be written starting from the beginning of the next erase block instead.

In addition, JFFS2 expects all nodes in an erase block to be consecutive. There should never be empty, unused space between nodes in the same erase block. Should such a condition be detected at runtime, the JFFS2 code will log a message similar to the following in the kernel log buffer:

```
jffs2_scan_empty(): Empty block at 0x0012fffc ends at
        0x00130000 (with 0xe0021985)! Marking dirty
```

Other than that, and aside from the waste of unused space between the end of the logical erase block with which the filesystem was created and the true erase block in the flash device, the situation is harmless in the sense that no data will be lost. It is still recommended, however, that you recreate the filesystem image with the correct erase block size.

In addition to the options just listed, you can use -l or -b to create little- or big-endian images, respectively. Without such an option, the command uses the byte ordering of the system on which it runs.

JFFS2 can achieve somewhat better compression than Cramfs: a little more than 50 percent. For a root filesystem containing 8484 KB, for example, the resulting JFFS2 image is 3844 KB in size. The LZMA compression algorithm mentioned earlier may improve this ratio even more.

Before we proceed to write the JFFS2 image to flash itself, let's look at one additional procedure that is optional but highly recommended: adding erase block summary nodes to the JFFS2 image *mkfs.jffs2* created. This functionality is not yet implemented in the *mkfs.jffs2* command and is done using the separate *sumtool* command:

```
# sumtool -i rootfs-jffs2.img -o rootfs-jffs2-summed.img -e 128KiB
```

Once you create the JFFS2 image, you can write it to its designated MTD device in one of the following ways:

- If the device is accessible on the host, you can carry out the appropriate commands directly on the host.
- You can follow the instructions in the upcoming section "Writing a Filesystem Image to Flash Using an NFS-Mounted Root Filesystem: boot your target with an NFS-mounted root filesystem, place the JFFS2 image on that filesystem, and issue the commands on the target to write the image to the designated MTD device.
- Use an external flash programmer or the bootloader debug shell to write the JFFS2 image to flash.

Regardless of your setup, you first need to erase the MTD device where the image will be placed:

```
# flash_eraseall -j /dev/mtd5
Erased 8192 Kibyte @ 0 -- 100% complete.
```

The -j option in the *flash_eraseall* command instructs it to place clean marker log nodes in the erased blocks, indicating that they are truly erased. This may reduce mount time dramatically when the partition is later mounted. The marker nodes go at the beginning of the block for NOR flashes, and in the spare area of the first page for NAND.

Obviously, the space available on the MTD storage device must be equal to or larger than the JFFS2 image you are placing on it. With the MTD device erased, copy the JFFS2 image to the MTD partition. For NOR flashes, you can use the *dd* command:

```
# dd if=images/rootfs-jffs2-summed.img of=/dev/mtd5 bs=1024
```

For NAND flashes, you must use the *nandwrite* command, which takes into consideration bad blocks that are part of a NAND flash:

```
# nandwrite -j /dev/mtd5 rootfs-jffs2-summed.img
```

Now, mount the copied filesystem to take a look at it:

```
# mount -t jffs2 /dev/mtdblock5 /mnt
# mount
...
/dev/mtdblock5 on /mnt type jffs2 (rw)
# ls mnt
bin      etc      linuxrc  sbin     usr
dev      lib      proc     tmp      var
# umount mnt
```

The previous example shows the mtdblock device corresponding to the MTD partition that is used as the mount device, /dev/mtdblock5, in this case. Using the device name is not strictly needed, or even recommended. Instead, you can use the MTD minor number (e.g., mtd2) or even the MTD partition name (e.g., mtd:my_root_fs) instead of the mtdblock device file name.

Unfortunately, the version of the *mount* command that ships with Busy-Box does not work with these more straightforward formats, and because the BusyBox version of this command is used in almost all embedded Linux systems, we chose to provide the example as-is.

Also, note that you cannot use the minor number or the MTD partition-type-based naming format for specifying an MTD partition as a root filesystem on the kernel command line.

Unlike disk filesystems, JFFS2 cannot be mounted on loopback using the *mount -o loop* for you to view its content. Instead, it must be mounted from a real MTD device, as done previously. If you have no real MTD device on your host, such as CFI flash, you could use the virtual memory MTD device presented in Chapter 3. You could also use the *jffs2reader* command, introduced in the previous chapter, to view the image's content.

If your target had previously been using an NFS-mounted root filesystem, you are now ready to boot it using the JFFS2 filesystem as its root filesystem.

YAFFS2

Yet Another Flash Filing System, version 2 (YAFFS2) is a writable, persistent, power-down-reliable filesystem for NAND and NOR flash devices. It is widely used with Linux and RTOSes in consumer devices. It provides wear leveling and is optimized for use with NAND flash devices. YAFFS2 is dual-licensed under the GPL, but a separate license with different terms is available for a fee. The YAFFS2 website can be found at *http://www.yaffs.net.*

YAFFS2 is not part of the mainline Linux kernel tree and therefore requires you to obtain the sources from the project CVS repository and patch the target kernel source. The latest kernel version supported at the time of this writing is 2.6.25, according to the YAFFS2 website. Here is the procedure to patch your kernel source with YAFFS2 support:

```
$ export CVSROOT=:pserver:anonymous@cvs.aleph1.co.uk:/home/aleph1/cvs cvs logon
(Just press the Return key if you are asked for a password)
$ cvs checkout yaffs2
$ cd yaffs2
$ ./patch-ker.sh c ${PRJROOT}/kernel
```

Now rebuild the target kernel image. Do not forget to configure the kernel, turning on CONFIG_YAFFS_FS and related options!

After the target kernel is ready, build and install the YAFFS2 tools used to create filesystem images:

```
$ cd yaffs2/utils
$ make
$ cp mkyaffsimage mkyaffs2image /usr/bin/
```

Creating a YAFFS2 filesystem image file is quite straightforward:

```
$ mkyaffs2image ${PROJROOT}/rootfs yaffs2.img
```

This creates the filesystem image file *yaffs2.img* with the content of the *${PROJROOT}/rootfs* directory. The *convert* option may also be specified on the command line in order to create cross-endian filesystem images.

You can use the same methods described in the previous section on JFFS2 to install the filesystem image on the target device flash.

Tmpfs

Tmpfs is a filesystem stored in virtual memory. As such, it is writable but not persistent: its content is not saved across reboots. Because it can grow and shrink according to its content, it is quite useful for storing temporary files. One common use for it is to mount directories that do not require permanent storage, such as */tmp.*

Tmpfs is unique in that it uses the Linux page and dentry caches for storing the file data and metadata. The Linux page cache is the kernel's internal data structure where the kernel copies and caches pages of the data that is read, written, or executed from filesystems on physical storage devices so that code running on the CPU can interact with the pages. The Linux dentry cache is a similar construct that caches information about directory entries in mounted filesystems. Please do not get confused by the use of the term "cache" here, as there is no backing store involved when Tmpfs uses these caches. Instead, the objects in the caches are the only copies of the data in the system.

 A similar and related filesystem, called Ramfs, is also available. Just like Tmpfs, it is writable but not persistent, and uses the Linux page and dentry caches for storage.

In fact, Ramfs is an earlier and simpler version of the same code from which Tmpfs was derived. The two biggest differences between them, as far as functionality goes, is that data stored on a Tmpfs filesystem can be swapped to disk, whereas data in Ramfs cannot. Because swap is hardly ever used in embedded systems, this difference is of no importance. The second difference is that you can't limit a Ramfs filesystem's size, and therefore you can't limit its memory use, but you can with Tmpfs.

In Linux kernel version 1.6.19, another functional difference has cropped up between Tmpfs and Ramfs: files on a Tmpfs filesystem can now be exported via the internal Linux NFS server, whereas no such support is available to Ramfs filesystems.

Tmpfs should always be preferred to Ramfs, except for very special circumstances.

To use Tmpfs, enable the "Virtual memory filesystem support (former shm fs)" item in the "Filesystems" submenu of the kernel configuration menu.

With kernel support for Tmpfs enabled, you can mount a Tmpfs filesystem on */tmp*, which will use up to 4 MB of RAM; for example:

```
# mount -t tmpfs none /tmp -o size=4m
```

Alternatively, you can add a line in your */etc/fstab* file and modify your */etc/init.d/rcS* file to mount Tmpfs at boot time. If you do not provide a size limit, the filesystem will grow in accordance with its content up to half of the available RAM. If maximum filesystem size is exceeded, file operations requiring more storage space will fail with an appropriate error.

In contrast with most other *mount* commands, Tmpfs does not require a device or file to be mounted. Hence the use of none as the device in the previous example. *mount* ignores the name of the device for Tmpfs, and replacing none with any other name would have no effect on the command.

Writing a Filesystem Image to Flash Using an NFS-Mounted Root Filesystem

Although Chapter 9 will discuss the setup and configuration of the NFS server on the host for providing a root filesystem to a target, let's take a look at how this configuration can be useful at this stage.

Exporting a root filesystem from the host to the target over NFS during early development stages simplifies the development process by allowing quick modification of the files the target used. Later, the target needs to have a filesystem stored in its flash in order to be self-hosting. Although some bootloaders can be used to copy images to flash, you can also use the MTD utilities running on the target to copy files available on the NFS-mounted root filesystem. To do so, copy the designated filesystem image to the directory on the host containing the NFS-mounted target root filesystem, boot the target, and use MTD commands on the target to copy the filesystem image to flash.

To copy an initial RAM disk image to your target's flash, for example:

1. Configure your target to mount its root filesystem from a directory exported by your host using NFS.

2. On your host, copy the filesystem image to the directory exported to your target. Though the filesystem image is not physically on your target, it will be visible on its root filesystem once the kernel mounts it using NFS at startup.

3. Boot your target and use the MTD utilities on your target to copy the filesystem image from the NFS-mounted root filesystem to the appropriate flash device entry in your target's /dev directory.

Placing a Disk Filesystem on a RAM Disk

RAM disks, as their name indicates, live in RAM and act like block devices. The kernel can support many active RAM disks simultaneously. Because they act like block devices, any disk filesystem can be used with them. But because their content lasts only until the system is rebooted, RAM disks are usually reserved for compressed images of disk filesystems, such as Ext2 filesystems. These images are known as compressed RAM disk images.

One instance where the use of such compressed RAM disk images is particularly attractive for embedded Linux systems is during system initialization. Specifically, the kernel can extract an *initial RAM disk* (initrd) image from a storage device for use as its root filesystem.

At startup, the kernel verifies whether its boot options indicate the presence of an initrd. If so, it extracts the filesystem image, whether or not it is compressed, from the designated storage media into a RAM disk, and mounts it as its root filesystem. Up to kernel version 2.6, the initrd mechanism was, in fact, the simplest method to provide a kernel with a root filesystem in RAM. It is still in widely used today, which is why we cover it here.

For new systems, however, we strongly recommend using the Initramfs mechanism described in the next section. In this section, we discuss the creation of a compressed RAM disk image for use as an initrd. We will explain how this image can actually be used as an initrd in Chapter 9.

For our purposes, we will create an Ext2-based RAM disk image for use in our target. Although Ext2 is the filesystem most commonly used with RAM disks, other disk filesystems can also be used. Some developers, for instance, prefer Cramfs.

In this section, we'll create and compress an initial RAM disk from an Ext2 filesystem. If you use the Cramfs filesystem for the initial RAM disk, there is no point to compressing the image file, because the filesystem format itself is compressed.

First, create a new filesystem image file using the *genext2fs* utility and the procedure described earlier in "The second extended filesystem (Ext2):

```
$cd ${PRJROOT}
$ genext2fs -b 1024 -d rootfs -D device_table.txt -e 0 initrd.img
```

The -*e* option will zero out the unallocated space in the image. Initializing the filesystem in this way achieves a maximum compression ratio for the unused portions of the filesystem later when you use *gzip* to compress the entire image.

The *images/initrd.img* file now contains the filesystem. The final step is to compress this filesystem to obtain a compressed RAM disk:

```
$ gzip -9 < images/initrd.img > images/initrd.bin
$ ls -al images/initrd*
-rw-rw-r--  1 karim   karim   3101646 Aug 16 14:47 images/initrd.bin
-rw-rw-r--  1 karim   karim   8388608 Aug 16 14:46 images/initrd.img
```

It is compressed using the *gzip* command. The -9 option tells the command to use the highest compression algorithm available. In this case, the compression ratio is above 60 percent, which is comparable to JFFS2 and superior to Cramfs. Of course, JFFS2 and Cramfs have the advantage of being persistent, whereas a RAM disk is not.

You can place the RAM disk image created here, *images/initrd.bin*, on the appropriate device on your target and configure your bootloader accordingly. See Chapter 9 for more information on using RAM disks for initrd.

Rootfs and Initramfs

Linux 2.6 stores its startup *init* program in a compressed archive in CPIO (a somewhat arcane Unix backup file compression format still widely used) format. The boot procedure extracts the archive into a special instance of a Tmpfs (or Ramfs, if Tmpfs is not available) filesystem, which is always present in a 2.6 system.

Rootfs cannot be unmounted, for more or less the same reason you can't kill the init process. Rather than having special code to check for and handle an empty list, it's simpler for the kernel to just make sure certain lists can't become empty.

Most systems just mount another filesystem over Rootfs and ignore it. An empty instance of Ramfs takes up a tiny amount of space.

After extraction, the kernel will try to locate an *init* program in the Rootfs filesystem. If present, Rootfs is used as the root filesystem, and the *init* program in it is responsible for setting up the rest of the running system (and perhaps mounting a different root filesystem on top of Rootfs). If no *init* program is in Rootfs, the 2.6 kernels fall back to executing older code that looks for the root filesystem via the kernel command-line root parameter or an initrd mechanism.

Populating such an Initramfs can be done via the `CONFIG_INITRAMFS_SOURCE` kernel configuration option, which can be used to hardcode the location of the Initramfs archive into the kernel binary. The option value can point to an existing gzipped CPIO archive, a directory containing files to be compressed into a new archive, or a text file that contains lines in the following syntax:

```
# a comment
file name location mode uid gid
dir name mode uid gid
nod name mode uid gid dev_type maj min
slink name target mode uid gid
pipe name mode uid gid
sock name mode uid gid
```

where the parameters have the following meanings:

name
    The name of the file, directory, etc. in the archive

location
    The location of the file in the current filesystem

target
    The target of a link

mode
    The permissions of the file in octal notation (e.g., 777 denotes full permission)

uid
    The user ID (0 for *root*)

gid
    The group ID (0 for *root*)

dev_type
    The device type (b for block or c for character)

maj

The major number of the node

min

The minor number of the node

Here is a simple example:

```
dir /dev 755 0 0
nod /dev/console 644 0 0 c 5 1
nod /dev/loop0 644 0 0 b 7 0
dir /bin 755 1000 1000
slink /bin/sh busybox 777 0 0
file /bin/busybox initramfs/busybox 755 0 0
dir /proc 755 0 0
dir /sys 755 0 0
dir /mnt 755 0 0
file /init initramfs/init.sh 755 0 0
```

The Linux kernel build does not rely on any external utility to create or extract the CPIO created; the code to do this is self-contained. However, should you want to create an Initramfs CPIO archive yourself, run the *cpio* utility as follows:

```
$ cd ${PROJDIR}/rootfs
$ find . | cpio -o -H newc | gzip > ${PROJDIR}/initramfs.cpio.gz
```

For completeness, the following commands may be used to extract an already existing GZIP-compressed CPIO archive:

```
$ gunzip initramfs.cpio.gz
$ cpio -i -d -H newc -F initramfs_data.cpio --no-absolute-filenames
```

 The *cpio* manpage contains some bad advice that will break your Initramfs archive if you follow it. It says: "A typical way to generate the list of filenames is with the find command; you should give find the -depth option to minimize problems with permissions on directories that are unwritable or not searchable." This will not work while creating an Initramfs archive, because the Linux kernel CPIO extractor will refuse to create files in a directory that does not exist. Therefore, directory entries must precede the files that go in those directories. The example shown in this section will produce a correct CPIO archive.

If the kernel is compiled with Initial RAM disk support (Initrd), an external compressed CPIO archive can also be used by the Linux kernel in place of a RAM disk. The kernel will detect that the type of the Initrd is an Initramfs archive and not a filesystem image, and will extract the content of the archive into the Rootfs prior to attempting to locate the *init* program (which by default is located in */sbin/init*). The files in this external archive will overwrite any file in the internal built-in archive in the kernel image file.

Because Initramfs uses the Linux dentry and page caches to store the file and metadata content of the filesystem, an Initramfs can make much more efficient use of system memory then a RAM disk. This is why Initramfs should be used in preference to the Initrd mechanism in all new systems.

Choosing a Filesystem's Type and Layout

As must be obvious by now, the number of filesystem types and related options in Linux can be a bit overwhelming at first, and it might not be obvious how to pick the right one.

The touchstone for making a correct choice is to list the types of data stored on the filesystem in question and their intended uses: to cite a couple of examples, executable binary files and libraries that form the software running the device versus XML files holding variable configuration information. Then reduce this list to a set of requirements using the same (or similar) terms as those used earlier in this chapter to define different embedded filesystems, characteristics (e.g., online writable, persistent, power-down reliable, and compressed).

Next, find a combination of filesystem type and hardware storage medium, among those available on your system, that best fits the requirements.

Keep in mind that developers commonly make use of not one but several different filesystems of different types, dedicating different filesystems to different system functions.

 Using multiple filesystems does not require multiple storage devices. Linux supports partitioning with practically any storage medium, and different partitions on the same storage medium can contain different filesystem types.

The upcoming sections will attempt to provide some guidelines to following the process we recommend in this section for various common filesystem roles. These are general rules of thumb that may or may not be suited for your specific design and circumstances. As an example, if you need to carry out online updates of your embedded device's software, that may impose additional considerations to the ones outlined here, as discussed later in "Handling Software Upgrades." However, these rules do provide a good starting point for your own design process.

Applications, Libraries, and Static Data

Embedded systems store the application's executable code, the code libraries, and static data (such as read-only databases, XML files, etc.) in some sort of persistent storage. After all, we would like our system to be able to load its software back in after a reboot.

Having said that, we actually require only a very specific kind of persistence for these elements: we would like to get the device software loaded back in RAM after a reboot in the form that it was stored during the last software update (or factory installation).

However, we do not need to keep any changes made to the software or files in RAM, except those specifically done for the purpose of upgrading the software. In fact, it is actually a useful requirement to *not* keep any changes to the content of this filesystem, except those made specifically to update the software.

One way to achieve this nuanced persistence requirement is to use a read-only filesystem, either one that is does not support writing to the filesystem when the system is online at all, or one that makes the filesystem read-only through mount options. In other words, online writability is not a requirement for us.

The other way to achieve the desired safety is to use a writable but nonpersistent filesystem that is "seeded" from some persistent storage. As we shall see, the Initramfs mechanism described earlier in "Rootfs and Initramfs provides an excellent way to implement such a feature.

One additional requirement you may have, especially if your filesystem content is large and your intended storage medium is small, is to use a compressed filesystem. This is an optional requirement that depends on your specific device system properties.

Keeping the filesystem in RAM

The Tmpfs filesystem discussed earlier in "Tmpfs," especially when used as a Rootfs via the Initramfs mechanism, can fulfill the requirement of nonwritable persistence nicely.

The compressed CPIO archive that is statically linked into the kernel image, or loaded with it during system boot by the bootloader, provides the required persistence. The CPIO is compressed, preserving precious storage space. Because Tmpfs is nonpersistent, any accidental changes to the code and static data done on the filesystem in RAM will be discarded upon system shutdown, and it will take a deliberate act of updating the kernel image in the CPIO archive to affect the software. This update is generally done only as part of a software upgrade.

Furthermore, because Tmpfs uses the Linux page and dentry caches as temporary storage areas, and because the Linux kernel usually keeps data and executable code file blocks in these caches for execution or access, using Tmpfs will save memory in the common case where the embedded device frequently uses system software and static data.

Using read-only persistent storage

If RAM is in short supply, and if system software and static data files are very big but are not normally all used together at the same time, using Tmpfs may not be a viable option. In this case, you could opt for a read-only compressed filesystem.

The two most suitable candidates are Cramfs and Squashfs. As noted in the sections about them earlier in this chapter, we recommend using Cramfs if its limitations are not an obstacle for your system, and otherwise recommend implementing Squashfs.

Because both filesystems are persistent, compressed, read-only filesystems, they meet our requirement.

In this case, system software upgrades will be performed by updating the entire filesystem image on storage, which will be done either:

- When the system is offline. The update could be done from the bootloader, or by replacing a removable storage device, such as a CompactFlash.

- By storing two (or more) such filesystems on different partitions or storage devices. You can then update them in alternation: run the system from one partition or device while updating the other one, and then switch roles in the next update.

The next section presents a slightly more complex variant of this scheme that offers some advanced features and makes full use of Linux's powers and filesystem capabilities.

Using online writable persistent storage

As an alternative—but, we believe, less desirable—option to the previous choices, you can use one of the other persistent filesystems that are appropriate for your chosen storage device. Mount the filesystem in read-only mode (using the *ro* mount option) during normal system usage, and switch to read/write mode on the fly (using the *remount* mount option) to perform a software update. Then switch back to read-only mode at the end of the update.

If your storage device is a CompactFlash or a NAND flash with an NFTL layer, such as DoC, Ext3 is the recommended filesystem because it is both persistent and power-down reliable. If NAND without NFTL is the storage medium, and if storage space is not an issue (as one would expect, because NAND flashes are typically big), YAFFS2 is the recommended filesystem because it offers power-down reliability and wear-leveling support in addition to persistence. Last but not least, use JFFS2 for either NOR or small NAND flashes when NFTL is not in use, because it adds compression to persistence and power-down reliability.

As will be explained in the next section, using this option requires special care and attention due to the nonatomic nature of the update process. Due to this issue, and others discussed in the next section, we do not recommend this option.

Dynamic Configuration Files and Data

Almost every embedded system has some dynamic configuration files or data, such as the device's IP networking information, logfiles, or license information.

The filesystem storing this kind of information must be persistent, writable online, and power-down reliable. Because frequent file information updates are expected, wear leveling must be supported at some level of hardware or software if NAND or NOR flash is used. In many situations, compression may also be a requirement.

Keeping this type of information on a separate partition or storage device from all other information is highly recommended, because you should reserve a specific amount of storage space to these files. Otherwise, you could find yourself blocked from updating your configuration files, perhaps because a software update filled up the device or partition, or even because logfiles grew too much.

As with previous types of filesystem roles, the best filesystem for the job depends on the storage medium. If your storage device is either a Compact Flash or a NAND flash with an NFTL layer, such as DoC, Ext3 is recommended because it is both persistent and power-down reliable. If NAND with NFTL is the storage medium, assuming storage space is not an issue, YAFFS2 is the recommended filesystem because it's persistent and has power-down reliability and wear-leveling support. Last but not least, use JFFS2 for either NOR or small NAND flashes when NFTL is not used, to add compression to persistence and power-down reliability.

Temporary Files

Many embedded systems use various types of temporary files that are meaningful only during the current system uptime and need not be kept when the system is taken offline. One common example is temporary configuration files, which are kept in a volatile storage and whose change affects the system behavior only until the next reboot, unless a specific save command (e.g., *copy running-config startup-config*) is given to retain the configuration changes across reboots.

The best place to store this kind of volatile information is in the Tmpfs filesystem (this time not as an Initramfs). One thing to note is that it is important to limit the maximum size of the Tmpfs filesystem used for this purpose via the *size* mount option, so as not to drain system RAM because of a rogue task that creates many temporary files.

Layout Example

Figure 8-1 shows a simple but typical layout for an embedded system with a Compact-Flash storage device. The root filesystem with the system software is placed in a read-only, compressed Squashfs filesystem. Configuration files are stored in a read/write Ext3 filesystem on a separate partition. Temporary files are stored only in RAM using Tmpfs.

Handling Software Upgrades

One of the most critical tasks you need to take into consideration when designing your filesystem layout, and your embedded devices in general, is how to do software upgrades in the field.

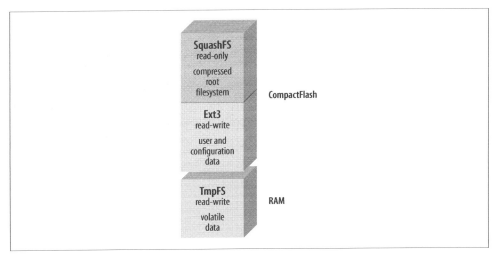

Figure 8-1. Simple filesystem layout example

For some embedded systems, you can plan on having their software updated only by a qualified technician in a controlled lab environment. Perhaps their function is not critical, or the costs of implementing a truly fail-safe software upgrade mechanism are prohibitive. In the next section, we'll present three simple methods for such situations, where you upgrade the software in your development environment.

Many other systems, however, need to support upgrades in the field, over a network connection, with no competent manual intervention available if something goes wrong. The key to achieving this upgradability is to design the system to support a software upgrade in an atomic fashion. This means putting in place a process that moves the device from one working state (the old version) to another (the new version) in a single, uninterruptible operation. You should not allow any intermediate state in which the device will be left nonfunctional if disaster, such as an unplanned power outage, strikes as the upgrade procedure is being run. We will show how to accomplish this using Linux, in the last section of this chapter.

Software Upgrades in Controlled Environments (Non-Fail-Safe)

Here we'll present three simple ways to upgrade your software: replace a filesystem in place in RAM, file-level upgrades use the *rsync* utility for file-level upgrades, and how to use package management tools.

Replacing a filesystem in-place in RAM

This simple and efficient upgrade procedure is common in many consumer electronic devices that are not considered critical systems and whose design tends to be highly influenced by cost considerations.

The method assumes that the device, when running, keeps the kernel and the other critical software that runs the system in temporary memory, as described earlier in "Keeping the filesystem in RAM." During boot, the bootloader copies the system software from the root filesystem to RAM. To install new software, therefore, you can simply rewrite the compressed CPIO archive storing the software with a new version, and then reboot the system.

So long as power is not lost during the critical moments of writing the new software to the storage, and so long as the new software is functional, the system works fine. However, losing power during an upgrade cycle, or loading a corrupt or simply buggy image, can turn a $200 consumer electronic product into a worthless plastic brick. In other words, you need minimally functional software in order to upgrade the system.

rsync

A different upgrade approach involves updating individual files on the root filesystem while it is online. This kind of method works only when the software runs directly from a writable, persistent root filesystem, as described earlier in "Using online writable persistent storage."

rsync is a remote updating utility that allows you to synchronize a local directory tree with a remote server. Its algorithm optimizes the transfer by transferring only the differences between the local and remote files. Run with the appropriate options, *rsync* can preserve file permissions, file ownership, symbolic links, access times, and device entries. It can use either *rsh* or *ssh* to communicate with the remote server. All these features make *rsync* a good candidate for updating network-enabled embedded systems.

rsync is available from its project website at *http://samba.anu.edu.au/rsync*. The site also hosts its documentation and a mailing list. A good introductory tutorial by Michael Holve is available at *http://everythinglinux.org/rsync*.

To use *rsync*, you must have the *rsync* executable running as a daemon on your server, and you must invoke the executable as a client on the embedded system. We will not cover installation of the server or details about the use of the client, because the tutorial and *rsync* documentation mentioned earlier cover them well. We'll just explain how to cross-compile and install *rsync* for use on your target. The examples in this section install *rsync* version 2.6.9.

To begin, download and extract a copy of the *rsync* package to your *${PRJROOT}/sysapps* directory. With the package extracted, move to its directory for the rest of the procedure:

```
$ cd ${PRJROOT}/sysapps/rsync-2.6.9/
```

Now, configure and compile the package:

```
$ CC=arm-linux-gcc ./configure --host=$TARGET --prefix=${TARGET_PREFIX}
$ make
```

With the compilation complete, install the *rsync* binary on your target's root filesystem and strip it:

```
$ cp rsync ${PRJROOT}/rootfs/bin
$ arm-linux-strip ${PRJROOT}/rootfs/bin/rsync
```

The stripped binary is 291 KB in size when dynamically linked with glibc, and 286 KB when dynamically linked with uClibc.

The same binary can be used both on the command line and as a daemon. Run it on the server by including the *--daemon* option. We will be using *rsync* on the command line only.

To use *rsync*, you need to have either *rsh* or *ssh* installed on your target. *rsh* is available as part of the netkit-rsh package at *ftp://ftp.uk.linux.org/pub/linux/Networking/netkit*. *ssh* is available as part of the OpenSSH package, which is discussed in depth in Chapter 10. Although that discussion concentrates on the use of the SSH daemon generated by Dropbear (*sshd*), the SSH client (*ssh*) can also be generated during the compilation of the Dropbear package. The following procedure assumes you are using *ssh*, not *rsh*, because *ssh* provides a secure transfer channel and is therefore considered superior by most administrators.

Once *rsync* is installed on your target, you can use a command such as the following on your target to update its root filesystem:

```
# rsync -e "ssh -l root" -r -l -p -t -D -v --progress \
> 192.168.172.50:/home/karim/control-project/user-interface/rootfs/* /
root@192.168.172.50's password: Enter your password
receiving file list ... done
bin/
dev/
etc/
lib/
sbin/
tmp/
usr/bin/
usr/sbin/
bin/busybox
750756 (100%)
bin/tinylogin
39528 (100%)
etc/inittab
377 (100%)
etc/profile
58 (100%)
lib/ld-2.2.1.so
111160 (100%)
lib/libc-2.2.1.so
1242208 (100%)
...
sbin/nftl_format
8288 (100%)
sbin/nftldump
```

```
7308 (100%)
sbin/unlock
3648 (100%)
bin/
dev/
etc/
lib/
sbin/
wrote 32540 bytes   read 2144597 bytes    150147.38 bytes/sec
total size is 3478029   speedup is 1.60
```

This command copies the contents of your user interface module project from the *rootfs* directory on the host, whose IP address is 192.168.172.50, to the target's root directory. For this command to run successfully, the host must be running both *sshd* and the *rsync* daemon.

The following are the options you need:

-e

Passes to *rsync* the name of the application to use to connect to the remote server. (In this case, we use *ssh -l root* to connect as root to the server. You could replace root with whatever username is appropriate. If no username is provided, *ssh* tries to connect using the same username as the session's owner.)

-r

Recursively copies directories.

-l

Preserves symbolic links.

-p

Preserves file permissions.

-t

Preserves timestamps.

-D

Preserves device nodes.

-v

Provides verbose output.

--progress

Reports progress of the transfer.

While running, *rsync* provides a list of each file or directory copied and maintains a counter displaying the percentage of the transfer already completed. When done, *rsync* will have replicated the remote directory locally, and the target's root filesystem will be synchronized with the up-to-date directory on the server.

If you would like to check which files would be updated without carrying out the actual update, you can use the *-n* option to do a "dry run" of *rsync*:

```
# rsync -e "ssh -l root" -r -l -p -t -D -v --progress -n \
> 192.168.172.50:/home/karim/control-project/user-interface/rootfs/* /
root@192.168.172.50's password:
receiving file list ... done
bin/busybox
bin/tinylogin
etc/inittab
etc/profile
lib/ld-2.2.1.so
lib/libc-2.2.1.so
...
sbin/nftl_format
sbin/nftldump
sbin/unlock
wrote 176 bytes  read 5198 bytes  716.53 bytes/sec
total size is 3478029  speedup is 647.20
```

For more information on the use of *rsync*, as both a client and a server, have a look at the command's manpage and the documentation available from the project's website.

Upgrading files through *rsync* suffers from the same reliability problem as the single-file update described in the previous section. A power outage during the upgrade can render the system unusable, although the the failure mode would be slightly different: a halted update may have one file updated but fail to update other files on which it depends. If, for example, the upgrade process has upgraded an executable in the system to a newer version, but has not managed to update the dynamic shared library required by the executable, the system may not even be able to boot when the power is restored.

An update method that involves multiple files leaves open another, less obvious, source of problems. Support staff and professional services may update particular files to deliver "hot fixes" to users as they deal with daily issues, leaving any number of slightly different software versions in the field.

Only a clearly stated policy and organizational discipline will protect you from being confronted with the maintenance headache of systems you don't fully know. Careful records must be kept of when and how all systems are updated, because it may be hard to tell exactly which files have been replaced after the fact. The technique in the next section can also help you avoid the chaos of multiple versions.

Package management tools

Updating all the software packages that make up a root filesystem simultaneously, as we did in the previous section using *rsync*, is not always possible or desirable. Also, as we have already stated, it is quite difficult to track. Sometimes, the best approach is to upgrade each package separately using a package management system such as those commonly used in workstation and server distributions. If you are using Linux on your workstation, for example, you are probably already familiar with one of the two main package management systems used with Linux, the *RPM Package Manager* (RPM) or *Debian package* (*dpkg*), whichever your distribution is based on. Because of these systems' good track records at helping users and system administrators keep their systems up-to-date and in perfect working condition, it may be tempting to try to cross-compile the tools that power these systems for use in an embedded system. Both systems are, however, demanding in terms of system resources, and are not well adapted for direct use in embedded systems.

Fortunately, there are tools aimed at embedded systems that provide much of the functionality provided by more powerful packaging tools, without requiring as much system resources. Two such tools are BusyBox's *dpkg* command and the *Itsy Package Management System* (iPKG).

The *dpkg* BusyBox command allows us to install packages in the *dpkg* format on an embedded system. Much like other BusyBox commands, it can be optionally configured as part of the *busybox* binary. It is explained in the BusyBox documentation. For instructions on how to build dpkg packages, see *Debian New Maintainers' Guide* and *Dpkg Internals Manual*, both available at *http://www.debian.org/doc/devel-manuals*.

iPKG is the package management system Familiar distribution uses. It is available from its project website at *http://www.handhelds.org/z/wiki/iPKG*, along with usage documentation. iPKG relies on its own package format, but can also handle dpkg packages.

Instructions for building iPKG packages are available at *http://www.handhelds.org/z/wiki/BuildingIpkgs*, and the use of the *ipkg* tool, part of the iPKG package management system, is explained on the project's website.

Note that using a package management tool such as these is still not a fail-safe method to upgrade a device's software. Thus, we will turn to a truly robust solution in the next section.

Fail-Safe Software Upgrades

As mentioned before, a fail-safe software upgrade system must change the system in an atomic fashion from a state where the old software is used to a state where the new software is operational, with no other state possible even if power is lost in the middle of the upgrade. Like a database transaction, you always end up booting either a valid new version (when the upgrade succeeds) or a valid old version (when the upgrade fails).

Because Linux software is comprised of several files containing executable files, shared code libraries, device files, kernel modules, and the kernel image itself—all of them potentially interdependent—we cannot perform the upgrade file by file. We must work on a whole filesystem.

Architecture of a fail-safe solution

In essence, the procedure used in this section is very simple: set aside two (or more) filesystems for system software. At boot time, the bootloader chooses one filesystem by consulting a control data structure, such as a file on a power-down-reliable filesystem, or a structure in battery-backed RAM.

To perform a fail-safe update:

- Download the new filesystem image to the storage location that is not currently in use by the running system.
- Inspect the image (e.g., by checking a CRC or cryptographic signature) to make sure it has been transferred without corruption.
- Atomically change the data structure that tells the bootloader which software storage to use during boot.
- Reboot the system.

The data structure that tells the bootloader which software storage to use is, of course, bootloader-specific, and so does the method that can be used to update it atomically. As an example, assuming the bootloader reads a configuration file from the filesystem, as would be the case with the GRUB and LILO bootloaders, atomically replacing the data structure may be implemented by creating a temporary file with the changed configuration on the same filesystem where the original configuration file resides. Then, use the `rename` system call to rename it over the original configuration, relying on the Linux guaranteed behavior that such a rename is atomic, under certain conditions (see the rename system call manpage for additional details).

Additional fail-safe measures can also be added. As an example only, the bootloader may create a special record in the control data structure before it loads the system and transfers control to it. After the boot process has completed successfully and the device is functioning, the device's software will erase this record—again in an atomic fashion. The bootloader will look for the existence of this special marker in the control data structure at each boot and, if it is found, will deduce that someone tried to update the system software during the previous boot but did not succeed in bringing it to a state that allows the device to boot. By tracking the number of such occurrences (in the same control data structure), the bootloader can be programmed to, for example, boot the system software image in the other storage position instead of the image that the control data structure points to. Thus, a corrupted upgrade just causes the bootloader to fall back on the older, still operational version of the software.

Other operating systems have used the scheme in this section. This section demonstrates how to implement it using the tools and filesystems we have learned thus far. The bootloader on which it relies will be discussed in the next chapter.

The simplest type of root filesystem to support with the upgrade method in this chapter is Initramfs, described earlier in "Rootfs and Initramfs." But instead of placing the kernel and associated compressed CPIO archive directly on a storage partition in the flash, use a writable, persistent, power-down-reliable filesystem to store several such kernel and embedded CPIO archive files. Then have the bootloader pick the right file according to either a file on the same filesystem or a record in the internal bootloader configuration.

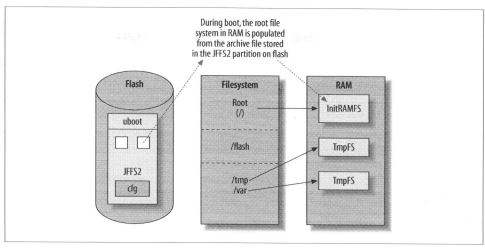

During boot, the root file system in RAM is populated from the archive file stored in the JFFS2 partition on flash

Figure 8-2. Fail-safe upgrade of a RAM-based root filesystem

 The following text shows just one example of how to implement the scheme. Many other methods exist.

As an example of this kind of setup, consider a system containing a JFFS2 filesystem on top of a NOR flash device, and the U-Boot bootloader. For our root filesystem, we will use an compressed CPIO archive, loaded into an Initramfs filesystem and separate from the Linux kernel. We shall load this compressed CPIO archive as part of an initrd image, as described earlier in "Placing a Disk Filesystem on a RAM Disk." The process is shown in Figure 8-2.

Example procedure for a fail-safe solution

This section will guide you step by step through a procedure that works with the sample system layout described in the previous section. First, create a U-Boot image from the kernel and the compressed CPIO archive, by wrapping the files with a U-Boot header using the *mkimage* command supplied with the U-Boot source package:

```
# mkimage -A mips -O Linux -T multi -C gzip \
> -n 'Linux with Initramfs' \
> -d vmlinux.gz:initramfs_data.cpio.gz runtime.img
```

The command creates a file named *runtime.img*, which is a U-Boot image file containing the kernel and the compressed CPIO archive. Next, create a directory (on the host) called *jffs2_image*, and put the image file there:

```
# mkdir jffs2_image
# cp runtime.img jffs2_image/
```

Create a JFFS2 image, which you will later put onto the flash device:

```
# mkfs.jffs2 --big-endian --eraseblock=0x100 --root jffs2_image --output image.jffs2
```

 This command assumes you are building the filesystem for a big-endian host and are going to use a NOR flash device with an erase block size of 0x100 KB (specified in hexadecimal), or 256 KB in decimal. This setting may need to be adjusted according to the target hardware and flash used.

In our next step, we will build the U-Boot bootloader binary. The configuration and build of U-Boot is described in the next chapter.

Make sure you compile U-Boot with JFFS2 support, because the U-Boot configuration considers it an optional feature. In addition, set the default values of the default boot command to boot the version image file in your U-boot config file:

```
#define CONFIG_BOOTCOMMAND "fsload a2000000 runtime.img; bootm a2000000"
#define CONFIG_BOOTDELAY 3
```

Now write to the NOR flash (using a JTAG, a flash programmer, or an NFS root filesystem, as explained previously in this chapter) both the U-Boot binary and the *image.jffs2* file created earlier.

When the board boots up, U-Boot will wait three seconds (the number is specified via the *CONFIG_BOOTDELAY* option), and it will then load the kernel image from the JFFS2 partition on the flash and boot it. After the boot has completed and the Linux system is up and running, the files on the JFFS2 partition on the flash can be accessed by mounting the JFFS2 flash partition using the *mount* command:

```
# mount -t jffs2 /dev/mtdblock0 /flash
```

To upgrade the device's software, create an updated image of the *runtime.img* file using the same procedure you did before. Download the image to the JFFS2 flash partition as *runtiem2.img*, either from U-Boot (using the *tftpboot* command) or from Linux (using, for example, the *wget* command to retrieve the file from an FTP server).

After verifying that the new image is correctly saved to the JFFS2 partition on the flash, change the `bootcmd` U-Boot environment variable to boot the newer image. This can be done either from the U-Boot shell using the *setenv* command, or from the running Linux system using the *fw_setenv* command supplied with U-Boot:

```
# fw_setenv bootcmd "fsload a2000000 runtime2.img; bootm a2000000"
```

Using the *fw_setenv* command requires a valid */etc/fwenv.config* file with the correct offsets in the flash partition where the U-Boot environment is stored. Read the next chapter for details on U-Boot, and consult its documentation for information on how to set up this file.

Finally, note that the update of the `bootcmd` environment variable on the flash is not atomic in itself. However, a higher-level integrity check ensures that the whole upgrade is fail-safe. A CRC checksum is computed and written as part of the new environment. U-Boot will ignore an environment with a bad CRC, and instead use the default command that you have set up to boot the original version. Thus, the worst that can happen in case of a power failure during the upgrade is that the system ends up booting into the older version of the software, assuming it is still available in storage, of course.

## CHAPTER 9

Setting Up the Bootloader

Although a bootloader runs for a very short time during the system's startup and is mainly responsible for loading the kernel, it is nevertheless a very important system component. Almost any system running a Linux kernel needs a bootloader, but embedded systems typically have further constraints that make the process somewhat different from that used by a typical desktop Linux development system. In this chapter, we will examine some of these differences in detail, and explain how to set up and configure some examples, including a server providing dynamic host configuration protocol (DHCP) and NFS services for network booting. By the end of this chapter, you will have installed all of the components discussed earlier, configured your target with an appropriate bootloader, and will be finally ready to boot your embedded Linux system.

A bootloader is responsible for loading an operating system kernel and its supporting infrastructure into memory, and beginning the kernel's execution. Typical tasks performed by bootloaders include kernel selection (your desktop Linux system likely offers an optional list of kernels to choose from if you press a key early during boot) and loading an initial RAM-based filesystem (whether initrd, initramfs, or something different). The RAM-based filesystem contains enough of an environment to mount the root filesystem and begin the normal bootup process (starting system daemons and the like).

Most regular desktop and server systems have extensive system firmware (a BIOS, UEFI, OpenFirmware, etc.) that provides information such as the configuration of hardware devices, interrupt routing details, and other information Linux will need to make use of later. Embedded Linux systems, however, usually don't have such extensive firmware. Instead, they perform these tasks through the bootloader, which contains the functionality of the firmwares used in larger systems.

Embedded Linux systems, therefore, have somewhat unique bootloader requirements. Not only must the firmware load the kernel image into system memory, but it must also program the system memory controllers, initialize processor caches, enable various hardware devices, directly implement support for network booting infrastructure, and do a myriad of other activities. If you've never heard of most of the software discussed in this chapter, even if you are an avid convert to Linux, don't be at all surprised (or disheartened)!

There are a slew of bootloaders available for Linux, thousands upon thousands of embedded boards, and many possible boot configurations for a single board. It is, therefore, inconceivable to cover all the possible combinations within a single chapter. Nor is it possible to give an in-depth description of the use of each of the bootloaders covered. Many existing bootloaders for Linux already have an entire book describing their use. Also, the number and quality of bootloaders vary greatly between architectures. Some architectures have well-known, established bootloaders providing support for a range of hardware. Others have few or no standard bootloaders and mainly use bootloaders provided by the hardware manufacturer (with highly varying quality).

A Word on Vendor Support

If you are using a bootloader provided by the manufacturer of your embedded target board, make sure that you have all the binaries and documentation that you need. If possible, obtain the source code as well so that you can build, modify, and reprogram your target board freely without the assistance of the board vendor. This extra step may not seem all that important initially, but hardware design changes will occasionally necessitate small tweaks to underlying bootloader and kernel code. Besides, your embedded project may live a *lot* longer than the interest of any given vendor in providing technical assistance and support.

This chapter will concentrate on the bootloader/boot setup combinations most commonly used in embedded systems to load Linux. We will concentrate on one bootloader in particular: U-Boot. Unless you have worked with embedded Linux systems, you probably haven't heard of U-Boot, the "Universal" bootloader, but it is widely used in embedded systems that need a combination of bootloader, system firmware, and other features not provided by a more desktop/server-oriented bootloader such as GRUB. Don't worry, the differences will soon become apparent.

Embedded Bootloaders

As we said before, most typical IA32/X86_64 (x86) desktop or server Linux systems use a bootloader such as LILO or GRUB. The system contains a firmware (also known as a BIOS) whose job it is to program various core system components (initialize the RAM controllers, ensure the CPU is in a particular state, etc.) and to provide various information for use by the OS (legacy BIOS calls, ACPI tables, and so forth). Since the firmware supplied by the manufacturer already does most of the heavy lifting, a regular Linux bootloader need only concentrate on loading a kernel image (and perhaps an initrd/initramfs image) from some kind of storage and starting its exection. GRUB doesn't need to worry about interrupt-routing arrangements on a particular system board, since the "PC BIOS" provided by the system manufacturer has already taken care of initial configuration and published this information via ACPI tables that the operating system (Linux) can normally understand.

Embedded systems typically don't come with handy, prewritten system vendor firmware. After all, you're likely building the embedded system yourself, and you probably are looking to use Linux precisely because you want to cut down the number of operating system components you write. Because your system won't have preexisting firmware, it will need some of the heavy lifting to be done in the bootloader itself. The embedded bootloader will therefore need to initialize the RAM timings in the memory controller circuitry, flush the processor caches, and program up the CPU registers with sane default values. It will also need to determine precisely what hardware is installed within the system and supply this to the Linux kernel in the form of architectural-dependent software tables. On the x86, these might be similar to those provided by a BIOS, whereas on a PowerPC, they might be in FDT form (flattened device tree—refer to the U-Boot documentation for more examples).

Because many embedded systems don't come with prewritten firmware, those firmware implementations that are available often require additional features. After all, your embedded project's first task is likely to be porting U-Boot, or a similar bootloader, to your board. You will require debugging support, various built-in diagnostic routines, and a whole host of configurable options to tailor your configuration to the specific hardware at hand. With any luck, getting the bootloader up and running will be the hardest task, as your embedded device is likely to be based upon a standard reference design that otherwise can already run a Linux kernel. Recent developments, such as the flattened device tree support on PowerPC, allow the Linux kernel to automatically receive information about the system it is running on from the embedded bootloader, without that data having to be precompiled into the kernel. So, even though data such as the physical addresses of nondiscoverable bus devices (so-called platform device components) can vary from one board to the next, the same kernel image might be usable on both boards, even without recompilation.

LILO

Werner Almesberger introduced the *LInux LOader* (LILO) very early in Linux's history, and some x86 systems still use it to boot the kernel. Whereas LILO historically required a special command to be run whenever the filesystem was updated with a new kernel image, this is no longer true. LILO is maintained by John Coffman, and the latest releases are available at *http://lilo.go.dyndns.org*.

LILO is very well documented. The LILO package, for instance, includes a user manual and an internals manual. The LILO mini-HOWTO, available from the Linux Documentation Project (LDP), answers some of the most common questions about LILO's use. In addition, *Running Linux* by Matthias Dalheimer and Matt Welsh (O'Reilly) contains a "Using LILO" section in Chapter 5.

We will not cover LILO in detail, because it is already well documented, is no longer the de facto bootloader of choice, and is intended only for x86 PC-type systems with a PC BIOS.

GRUB

The *GRand Unified Bootloader* (GRUB) is the main bootloader for the GNU project, and it is also the most popular Linux bootloader on x86 systems these days. It is used by all the major "Enterprise Linux" distributions on the server and is fairly common on embedded x86 "PC" based boards, too. If you are developing an embedded Linux system that is based substantially upon standard PC hardware (and is perhaps, therefore, also already running a major distribution), GRUB is your friend, not U-Boot.

Erich Boleyn originally wrote GRUB in the course of finding an appropriate bootloader for what would later be known as GNU Mach. Erich's work was later picked up by Gordon Matzigkeit and Okuji Yoshinori, who continue to maintain and develop GRUB. The project's website is located at *http://www.gnu.org/software/grub*. There you will find the GRUB manual, which discusses the package's use extensively. Though GRUB's code can be retrieved using CVS, the latest stable releases are also tar-gzipped and made available for download through the project's website.

One aspect of GRUB's capabilities you may find helpful during development is its ability to boot over the network using TFTP and BOOTP or DHCP. You will also find that its ability to recognize several standard filesystems (including tab completion of filename paths) simplifies testing without making persistent configuration changes.

You can find out more about GRUB by visiting the website and by experimenting with any x86 desktop or server Linux system.

loadlin

loadlin, maintained by Hans Lermen, is a Microsoft MS-DOS-compatible utility that can load Linux from an already running MSDOS, Windows 3.x, Windows 95, 98, or ME system (but not from NT, XP, Windows 2000, Windows 2003, VISTA, or others based upon the Microsoft NT kernel). We mention it for completeness, but strongly discourage using loadlin in any new designs, because it has not been updated in many years and is not compatible with newer Microsoft operating systems. However, you may find loadlin useful in very limited circumstances.

Coreboot (Formerly the LinuxBIOS)

Coreboot is a complete PC BIOS replacement, also available on PowerPC systems. Coreboot boots Linux from ROM, which requires that Linux then perform the initial system bringup, interrupt-routing assignments, device initialization, and so forth. When Linux takes over these roles, the software used is called LinuxBIOS.

Coreboot was originally created to provide speed and efficiency, because booting large clusters of machines necessitates high reliability and the speed benefits gained through running Linux directly from ROM. A typical LinuxBIOS-based system might boot entirely within a mere couple of seconds, whereas a traditional desktop or server Linux distribution typically can take several minutes from power-on to system login prompt.

LinuxBIOS was developed as part of clustering research conducted at the Los Alamos National Laboratory and has gathered support from many hardware manufacturers. It may be particularly useful if you are building an x86 system and need to provide your own BIOS replacement, require very fast boot times on "standard" PC hardware, or for some other uses. The Coreboot package and documentation are available at *http://www.coreboot.org*.

U-Boot

Although there are many bootloaders, as we have just seen, "Das U-Boot" is arguably the richest, most flexible, and most actively developed open source embedded bootloader available. Wolfgang Denk of DENX Software Engineering (based just outside Munich, Germany) wrote and currently maintains U-Boot, and a wide range of developers contribute to it.

U-Boot is based on the earlier PPCBoot project (written for PowerPC systems) and the ARMBoot projects. PPCBoot was itself based on 8xxrom sources, and ARMBoot was an ARM port of PPCBoot created by Sysgo GmbH. At the time of this writing, U-Boot supports many standard development boards based upon ARM, AVR32, Blackfin, x86, Motorola 68K, Xilinx Microblaze, MIPS, Alterra NIOS, NIOS2, PowerPC, Super-H, and other processors. If you have a standard reference board for which there is already "Linux support," the odds are extremely high that it's utilizing U-Boot. This is certainly true of the GTA01 hardware reference platform and software for an OpenMoko open source cell phone, which we use as an example in this chapter.

Among other things, U-Boot is capable of booting a kernel through TFTP over a network connection, from an IDE or SCSI disk, from USB, and from a wide variety of flash devices. It supports a range of filesystems, including Cramfs (Linux), ext2 (Linux), FAT (Microsoft), and JFFS2 (Linux). Besides having an extremely extensive, configurable command set and quite a few capabilities, it is also fairly well documented. The *Manual* file included with the package provides an in-depth discussion of how to use U-Boot. There is extensive documentation, information about the project mailing lists, discussion archives, and much, much more on the DENX wiki (including links to the latest project source code, maintained in a Linux-kernel-style "git" repository) at *http://www.denx.de/wiki/UBoot*.

We will concentrate on U-Boot in this chapter because it supports a wide variety of systems and is designed from the ground up for embedded use. Additionally, you are very likely to encounter U-Boot as you begin to work with Linux on your own designs.

RedBoot

RedBoot is a bootloader based upon the Embedded Configurable Operating System (eCos), originally written by Cygnus Solutions and later acquired by Red Hat. eCos itself remains quite popular on some embedded devices that are too small to run a full Linux kernel, but RedBoot has been extended to boot other operating systems, such as Linux. RedBoot is extremely flexible and still preferred by some developers, although we strongly recommend that you investigate U-Boot for your new embedded designs.

You can find out more about RedBoot by visiting *http://sourceware.org/redboot.*

Server Setup for Network Boot

As we saw in Chapter 2, setting up a target for network boot is ideal during the early stages of development, because you can gradually modify the kernel and the root filesystem without having to update the target's storage devices every time you make a modification. Although not all bootloaders can use this setup to boot (especially when no network hardware is present in the hardware design to begin with!), we recommend that you use such a setup whenever possible, at least initially. Once you successfully have a working base system, you should then customize it to be fully self-hosting, but retain an optional network filesystem for ease of additional development and testing as your embedded project progresses. Some systems make use of a special "flag" file, environment variable, or other indicator that instructs the system whether to boot via the network or the local filesystem. For example, one of the authors once designed a system whose startup scripts would check for a file called */nfsboot* and then attempt to mount an NFS filesystem during bootup if this file was present.

As we said earlier, the simplest way to boot your target device from a network is to use BOOTP/DHCP (DHCP replaces BOOTP, but most DHCP servers also contain support for the legacy BOOTP protocol), TFTP (Trivial FTP), and NFS.

DHCP is the standard way to provide a network host with basic boot information, including the location of other servers such as TFTP and NFS. But DHCP does not actually transfer the kernel image to the target. This is the job of TFTP, the simplest network protocol for downloading remote files. In the case of an embedded Linux system, the target uses TFTP to obtain a kernel image from a TFTP server.

As for NFS, it's the simplest protocol, and the standard on Unix-style systems, for sharing entire directory trees between a client and a server. An embedded Linux target can use NFS to mount its root filesystem from an NFS server. NFS cannot be used for any earlier activity, because it requires a booted Linux kernel to operate.

Together, these three protocols provide a very efficient host/target development setup, one that has not changed substantially in almost a decade of building embedded Linux systems.

To enable network booting of the target, you must set up the development host's network services so that the target can access the components it needs. In particular, you need to set up a host to respond to BOOTP/DHCP requests, provide a kernel using a TFTP server, and enable NFS mounts. The following subsections will discuss each issue separately.

Setting Up the DHCP Daemon

Unlike other network services, DHCP cannot be invoked from the Internet super-server, *inetd* or *xinetd*. Instead, the DHCP daemon is a service of its own, and you need to start it manually. First, make sure that the DHCP server is installed on your host system. Download it if necessary from *http://www.isc.org*.

If you are using an RPM-based distribution—such as Fedora, OpenSuSE, or something similar—use the following command to check for the presence of the DHCP daemon:

```
$ rpm -q dhcp
dhcp-3.0.6-12.fc8
```

In this case, DHCP 3.0.6 is already installed. If it is not already installed on your system (typically, DHCP is no longer installed by default with many of the more popular Linux distributions), use the appropriate tools for your distribution to install the DHCP server. On a Debian GNU/Linux or Ubuntu Linux system, use *apt*, *aptitude*, or a similar package management utility to select the DHCP server for installation, and then perform the installation. Note that most distributions include two DHCP packages, a client and a server. The package containing the client is sometimes called *dhcpc-version* (or *dhclient*, or a variety of other names). In this case, the additional "c" after "dhcp" identifies the package as the client. Your mileage may vary, depending upon the distribution.

Don't Break Your Network!

Many modern networks (including almost all corporate IT networks, most academic networks, and even the average home at this point) are already highly reliant on DHCP service for their operation. If you are installing your own DHCP server for development use within your organization, be sure to check with your IT department (if one exists) beforehand. Many companies restrict installation of services such as DHCP, may require that they run it centrally (something to be avoided, especially if "central" means Microsoft's DHCP services), etc. In order to avoid confrontation, it may be easier to run your own network segment inside a lab environment, complete with a Linux development host attached to its own miniature network that includes your target systems. Consult your company's IT department for advice before installing any services that may violate its policies.

Finally, note that this is one area where company IT departments can be forgiven for having aggressive, even counterproductive, network policies. One of the authors recalls horror stories of badly configured DHCP servers appearing on networks (especially in academia) and handing out addresses to other regular users of the network, resulting in a denial of service and general upset. This is also another reason to make sure you

---

confine your DHCP configuration to the minimal IP addresses necessary for your
project. Even if your DHCP server is on a private network segment, don't tell it to hand
out addresses to every machine on your company network, or your coworkers will be
extremely unhappy with you, very quickly.

To operate properly, the kernel on which the DHCP server runs has to be configured
with the *CONFIG_PACKET* and *CONFIG_FILTER* options. The kernels shipped by
default in most distributions almost always have these enabled. If you are in the habit
of building your own kernels for your workstation, as we often do, watch out for those
options when configuring the kernel. If the kernel wasn't built properly, the DHCP
daemon will output a message similar to the following when it tries to start:

```
socket: Protocol not available - make sure CONFIG_PACKET and CONFIG_FILTER are
defined in your kernel configuration!
exiting.
```

With the package installed and the kernel properly configured, create or edit the */etc/
dhcpd.conf* file and add an entry for your target. Here's an example based on a home
development network:

```
subnet 192.168.1.0 netmask 255.255.255.0 {
        option routers 192.168.1.254;
        option subnet-mask 255.255.255.0;

        host virtex4 {
                hardware ethernet 00:C0:FF:EE:01:02;
                fixed-address 192.168.1.201;
                option host-name "virtex4";
                next-server 192.168.1.3;
                filename "/data/kernel/virtex4-vmlinuz-2.6.24.img";
                option root-path "/data/root/virtex4";
        }
}
```

Essentially, this entry states that the host and target are on the 192.168.1.0 network,
the TFTP server is located at 192.168.1.254, and the address allocated to the target
when it issues its DHCP or BOOTP request is 192.168.1.201. In the host entry, the
fields have the following meanings:

hardware ethernet
    Uniquely identifies the target through its MAC address, which in this case is the
    fictitious (yet valid) example 00:C0:FF:EE:01:02.

fixed-address
    Tells the DHCP server which IP address should be allocated to the target device
    with the designated MAC address.

option host-name
    Specifies the hostname to the target so that it can use it internally.

next-sever
    Tells the target where the TFTP server is located.

`filename`
>The filename of the image that has to be loaded by the target. According to RFC 2131, which specifies DHCP, the filename length is limited to 128 bytes.

`option root-path`
>Provides the path to the target's root filesystem on the NFS server. If your target does not need to load its root filesystem from an NFS server, you can omit this last field. Because the host is the only network link to the target in this case, `option routers` points to the host's address. If the target was linked to an entire network with a real router, `option routers` should point to that network's default router.

This example configuration should be easy to adapt to your own target. If you need more information about the configuration of the DHCP server, have a look at the manpage for *dhcpd.conf* and the sample configuration file your distribution installed, if one is present.

With the DHCP server configured to serve the target, you are almost ready to start the server. Before you do so, however, you need to make sure the */var/state/dhcp/ dhcpd.leases* file exists. (All recent Linux distributions will take care of this step for you when you first install the DHCP server package(s), so this is mainly a word of warning to those building the ISC DHCP daemon from source.) If that file does not exist, create it using the *touch* command. If the file doesn't exist, the DHCP daemon will refuse to start.

Finally, start the DHCP server. On RPM-based distributions, such as those from Red Hat and Novell, enter:

```
# /etc/init.d/dhcpd start
```

On Debian GNU/Linux and Ubuntu Linux systems, you can use a similar command, or the *service* command to start the DHCP service.

Setting Up the TFTP Daemon

The first step in setting up the TFTP daemon is to make sure the TFTP package is installed. If you are using an RPM-based distribution, use the following command to check for the presence of the TFTP daemon:

```
$ rpm -q tftp
tftp-0.42-5.fc8
```

In this case, TFTP 0.42 is already installed. If it is not available on your system, install the TFTP package using the appropriate tool for your distribution. Alternatively, if your system doesn't rely on a package manager or if some components have been installed without a package manager, you can also check for the presence of the actual TFTP daemon binary using the *whereis* command, just in case.

If you need to install TFTP and don't have a package available for your distribution, the latest version of the daemon is available for download as part of the NetKit package at *ftp://ftp.uk.linux.org/pub/linux/Networking/netkit*.

With the package installed, enable the TFTP service by modifying the appropriate Internet super-server configuration file. In brief, the super-server listens on designated ports on behalf of the various network services. When a request for a certain service is received, the super-server spawns the appropriate daemon and hands it the request. Hence, only the minimal number of daemons run at any time. TFTP is one of the daemons normally handled by the super-server.

To enable the TFTP service in a system based on the *inetd* super-server, edit */etc/inetd.conf*, uncomment the line for the TFTP service by removing the # character at the beginning, and send a SIGHUP signal to the *inetd* process so that it rereads its configuration file.

To enable the TFTP service in a system based on the *xinetd* super-server, edit */etc/xinetd.d/tftp* and comment out the line containing disable = yes by adding a # character at the beginning. As with *inetd*, you must send a SIGHUP to *xinetd*.

Finally, you must provide the TFTP server with a list of directories containing files that should be made available to TFTP clients. In a system based on the *inetd* super-server, append the list of directories to the TFTP line in */etc/inetd.conf*. In a system based on the *xinetd* super-server, edit the */etc/xinetd.d/tftp* file and append the list of directories to the server_args = line. The default directory for TFTP is */tftpboot*. You may choose to modify this to match your setup. Whichever directory you choose, make sure its access permissions include read and execute permissions for "other."

For example, here is a TFTP line in */etc/inetd.conf* for a host using the *inetd* super-server:

```
tftp   dgram udp    wait   root  /usr/sbin/tcpd  in.tftpd /data/kernel/
```

In this case, kernel images are placed in the */data/kernel* directory, which has the following permissions:

```
$ ls -ld /data/kernel/
drwxr-xr-x 2 jcm jcm 4096 2008-02-24 03:52 /data/kernel/
```

Here is a modified */etc/xinetd.d/tftp* file from a Fedora-based installation providing the same functionality for a host using the *xinetd* super-server:

```
service tftp
{
        socket_type          = dgram
        protocol             = udp
        wait                 = yes
        user                 = root
        server               = /usr/sbin/in.tftpd
        server_args          = /data/kernel
#       disable              = yes
        per_source           = 11
```

```
          cps                  = 100 2
    }
```

Regardless of the super-server in use on a host, the TFTP service is usually disabled by default. Hence, even if you use the default */tftpboot* directory, you need to modify the super-server's configuration files to enable TFTP.

Mounting a Root Filesystem on an NFS Server

As we explained in Chapter 2, although the bootloader and Linux kernel must be stored locally or retrieved to local storage through one of the methods shown earlier, the target's kernel can subsequently mount its root *filesystem* from a remote NFS server. To this end, the NFS server must be properly installed and configured. Chapter 6 showed how to build your target's root filesystem. If this filesystem is retrieved from an NFS server, the filesystem does not need any of the preparations described in Chapter 8.

The NFS server daemon is available in two flavors: as a standalone user application or as a part of the kernel. Besides being faster, the latter is also the standard configuration in most distributions. In addition to the NFS server itself, you need to have the NFS utilities installed. Usually, an nfs-utils package is part of your distribution. On an RPM-based distribution, use the following command to identify whether nfs-utils is installed:

```
$ rpm -q nfs-utils
nfs-utils-1.1.0-6.fc8
```

With the nfs-utils package installed, you need to make sure that the appropriate configuration files are present and the corresponding services are started.

The main file we need to configure for the NFS server is */etc/exports*. Entries in this file describe the directories that each host or set of hosts can access. Here's an example:

```
/data/root/virtex4 192.168.1.201(rw,no_root_squash)
```

This entry states that the machine with address 192.168.1.201 has read and write (`rw`) access to the */data/root/virtex4* directory, which is the path to a root filesystem similar to that which we built for the target in Chapter 6. In addition, the `no_root_squash` argument indicates that the server should allow the remote system to access the directory with its root privileges.

These are very powerful rights that we are granting to the target. If we have total control over access to the device, as is the case in most development setups, there is obviously no security risk. If, however, the target's location is less secure or if it is directly connected to the Internet (a configuration you really want to avoid with any NSF server), for example, you may prefer to use the default `root_squash` instead. Otherwise, it is trivial for others to forge access from the 192.168.1.201 address and trash, or otherwise compromise, your exported data. With `root_squash` in effect, the target will not be able to write to most of its own root filesystem, though it will still be able to read and write to all directories and files that are readable and writable by anybody. In practical terms, however, the target's operation will be very limited.

Because offering the NFS service also involves the risk of network abuse, it is often pertinent to use some minimal protection mechanisms to avoid intrusions. One simple way to do this is to customize the */etc/hosts.deny* and */etc/hosts.allow* files to restrict access to network services. The following is an example */etc/hosts.deny* file:

```
#
# hosts.deny
#

portmap: ALL
lockd: ALL
mountd: ALL
rquotad: ALL
statd: ALL
```

And an example */etc/hosts.allow* file is:

```
#
# hosts.allow
#

portmap: 192.168.1.201
lockd: 192.168.1.201
mountd: 192.168.1.201
rquotad: 192.168.1.201
statd: 192.168.1.201
```

The rules specified in these files restrict the access that users on remote systems have to the various file-sharing services. Together, these files indicate that only the machine with address 192.168.1.201 can use the NFS services. This is fine in the case of our sample setup, since we don't want to share the development workstation in these examples with anyone else just now. Even if you do not customize */etc/hosts.deny* and */etc/hosts.allow*, we still encourage you to take security issues to heart and use reasonable measures, such as backups, to protect your work.

Once the configuration files are created, you can start the portmapper service, which the NFS server requires:

 # /etc/init.d/portmap start

Finally, you can start the NFS server itself:

 # /etc/init.d/nfs start

If you would like more information on the configuration of remote boot using NFS, see the two Diskless root NFS HOWTOs on the issue at the LDP. Additionally, you may be interested in the NFS HOWTO, also at the LDP.

Using the U-Boot Bootloader

A growing majority of embedded Linux devices is now using Das U-Boot (also informally known as "U-boot," "u-boot," and "uboot") to handle system bringup, initial development, and debugging, as well as the bootloader needs of the finished system. U-Boot is a richly documented bootloader. Not only does it come with extensive documentation detailing its use and development on a wide variety of systems, but the website also houses an extensive wiki (*http://www.denx.de/wiki/UBoot*) that is maintained by many contributors to the project. In addition to the official versions, documentation, mailing lists, and so forth, the website has pointers to "custodian" source code development trees that contributors have made to specific parts of U-Boot. These are often where support for new boards is first added, before appearing in the official releases.

The *README* file included with U-Boot covers the use of U-Boot extensively. Among other things, it discusses the package's source code layout, the available build options, U-Boot's command set, and the typical environment variables used in U-Boot. The following discussion will cover the essential aspects of U-Boot and provide practical examples of its use. An in-depth discussion of U-Boot would, however, require a book of its own. For this reason, we encourage you to print a copy of the *documentation* file provided with U-Boot and spend some time reading through the wiki at your leisure.

Compiling and Installing

Start by downloading and extracting the latest version of U-Boot from the project website, either a snapshot release or (if you will be performing development of your own) the project's GIT source code repository. As of this writing, the latest U-Boot version is 1.3.3. Here's how to retrieve the latest GIT development repository sources using the *git* command (you may need to install the *git* utility on your host system):

```
$ git clone git://git.denx.de/u-boot.git
```

OpenMoko (GTA01) Hardware

The following sections are based on the OpenMoko revision 1 hardware (GTA01 "neo1973") platform, as was mentioned at the end of Chapter 2. The board runs on a Samsung S3C442 B54 ARM-based SoC at 400Mhz, has 256 MB of NAND flash (for the bootloader, kernel, and root filesystem), and 128 MB of RAM. The U-Boot configuration file specifies the Physical Memory Map, where the RAM is mapped from the physical address 0x30000000 to address 0x38000000 (128 MB), and the NAND flash is accessed via commands issued to the interface at physical address 0x4e000000. The documentation provided with U-Boot explains how it uses the physical memory on targets.

In this book, we have occasionally used the OpenMoko hardware as a reference, in part because a fully functional emulator (based on the QEMU sources) exists that is also capable of running U-Boot. Therefore, you can experiment with the information contained within this chapter even if you don't own one of these devices. On this book's website (*http://www.embeddedlinuxbook.org/*), you will find a snapshot of the emulator and U-Boot sources used for this book, and some scripts that will assist you in experimenting with U-Boot "upgrades" on emulated hardware. You will also find some additional documentation. Please do visit the book's website for further information.

You can find further information about running U-Boot on the GTA01 at the Open-Moko website (the wiki is at *http://openmoko.org/wiki/Bootloader*). There you will find detailed instructions as well as references to the available Toolchains needed to build U-Boot and other applications software for the OpenMoko reference hardware. These will save you much time and effort.

Before you can build U-Boot, you need to configure it for your target. The package includes a number of preset configurations for quite a few boards, so a configuration may very well exist for your target already. Check the *README* file to see whether your board is supported. For each supported board, U-Boot's *Makefile* typically includes a *boardname*_config target, which is used to configure U-Boot's build for the designated board. (If you don't see one for your board, refer to the wiki and to the custodian trees to see whether there is a work in progress that you can help test on your development system.) The configuration target for the GTA01 board we use in this chapter, for example, is gta01_config. Once you have determined the proper *Makefile* target to use, configure U-Boot's build process:

```
$ make gta01_config
```

Now build U-Boot by following the build process covered in the U-Boot documentation:

```
$ make ARCH=arm CROSS_COMPILE=arm-angstrom-linux-gnueabi- u-boot.udfu
```

As you can see, in this case, the OpenMoko development board is ARM-based and requires the use of a cross-compiler. The arm-angstrom-linux-gnueabi- reference refers to the ARM cross-compiler released by the OpenMoko project, while the .udfu extension on the U-Boot binary target instructs the build process to produce a binary in a special format known as "USB Device Firmware Update." This binary format can also be used for field upgrades to the version of U-Boot running on an OpenMoko device, using the existing U-Boot as a bootstrap. Further information about the precise mechanics of using U-Boot on the OpenMoko reference hardware is provided at the project website referenced previously.

In addition to generating bootloader images, the build process will compile a few tools to be used on the host for conditioning binary images before downloading them off to the target to a running U-Boot. Table 9-1 lists the files generated during an example of U-Boot's compilation. (These can vary depending upon the target in question and the image formats supported.)

Table 9-1. Files generated during U-Boot's compilation

Filename	Description
u-boot.map	The symbol map
u-boot	U-Boot executable in ELF binary format
u-boot.bin	U-Boot raw binary image, which can be written to the boot storage device
u-boot.udfu	U-Boot image in the special U-Boot Device Firmware Upgrade (DFU) file format used by the OpenMoko devices

You can now download the U-Boot image onto your target's boot storage device using the appropriate procedure. If you already have U-Boot or one of its ancestors (PPCBoot or ARMBoot) installed on your target, you can use the installed copy to update U-Boot to a new version, as we shall see later in "Updating U-Boot." If you have another bootloader installed, follow the procedures described in its documentation. If you have the OpenMoko reference hardware, used in this example, follow the wiki documentation. Finally, if you have no bootloader whatsoever installed on your target, you need to use a hardware programming device, such as a flash programmer or a BDM/JTAG debugger, to copy U-Boot to your target at the configured flash address. This may require extra steps if your new project board is booting from NAND flash, as is the case in this example, because the flash cannot be accessed directly, unlike a NOR flash.

Booting with U-Boot

Once U-Boot is properly installed on your target, you can boot it while being connected to the target through a serial line and using a terminal emulator to interface with the target. You will need to ensure that you have set your terminal emulator to use the serial port at the correct baud rate and with the correct flow control settings, which will be documented for your development board. As we said in Chapter 4, not all terminal emulators interact cleanly with all bootloaders. HyperTerminal on Microsoft Windows actually works surprisingly well (most of the time), as do most of the Linux terminal emulators (such as Minicom), although you might want to look for problem reports concerning your terminal emulator of choice if it is not one of the major ones used by other developers.

Here is a sample boot output from the OpenMoko GTA01 reference hardware:

```
U-Boot 1.3.2-rc2-dirty-moko12 (Mar 30 2008 - 23:40:43)

I2C:   ready
DRAM:  128 MB
NAND:  64 MiB
Found Environment offset in OOB..
Video: 640x480x8 31kHz 59Hz

NAND read: device 0 offset 0x25c000, size 0x5000

Reading data from 0x260e00 -- 100% complete.
 20480 bytes read: OK
```

```
USB:   S3C2410 USB Deviced
In:    serial
Out:   serial
Err:   serial
```

As you can see, U-Boot prints version information and then provides some detail regarding the hardware it is running on. As soon as it boots, a configurable timer starts ticking at the last output line. If you do not press a key during those seconds, U-Boot boots its default configuration. After pressing a key, you get a prompt:

```
GTA01Bv4 #
```

One of the first things you probably want to try is to obtain help from U-Boot:

```
GTA01Bv4 # help
?        - alias for 'help'
askenv   - get environment variables from stdin
autoscr  - run script from memory
base     - print or set address offset
bdinfo   - print Board Info structure
bmp      - manipulate BMP image data
boot     - boot default, i.e., run 'bootcmd'
...
```

As the output will show you, U-Boot has a lot of commands. These will vary based upon the architecture, platform, development board, configuration, and release of U-Boot. Fortunately, U-Boot also provides per-command help:

```
GTA01Bv4 # help cp
cp [.b, .w, .l] source target count
    - copy memory
```

When U-Boot appends the [.b, .w, .l] expression to a command, this means that you need to append one of the indicated strings to the command to invoke the desired version of the command. In the case of *cp*, for example, there are three versions: *cp.b*, *cp.w*, and *cp.l*, for copying bytes, words, and longs, respectively.

U-Boot is strict in its argument parsing. It expects most values to be provided in hexadecimal form. In the case of the *cp* command, for example, this means that the source address, the target address, and the byte count must be provided as hexadecimal values. You don't need to prepend or append those values with any sort of special characters, such as "0x" or "h." If your source address is 0x40000000, for example, simply type 40000000.

U-Boot accepts any unique subset of characters that starts a command name. If you want to use the *base* command, for example, you can type just the first two letters, *ba*, because *ba* is the only command to start with those two letters in this particular configuration. On the other hand, you can't type *lo* and expect U-Boot to understand it, because there are four commands that start with those letters: *loadb*, *loads*, *loady*, and *loop*.

Using U-Boot's Environment Variables

Once U-Boot is up and running, you can configure it by setting the appropriate environment variables. The use of U-Boot environment variables is very similar to the use of environment variables in Unix shells such as *bash*. To view the current values of the environment variables on your target, use the *printenv* command. Here is a subset of the environment variables found on the OpenMoko GTA01 development hardware:

```
GTA01Bv4 # printenv
bootargs=
bootdelay=3
baudrate=115200
usbtty=cdc_acm
bootargs_base=rootfstype=jffs2 root=/dev/mtdblock4 console=ttySAC0,115200 console=tty0
    loglevel=8
stdin=serial
stdout=serial
stderr=serial
dontask=y
bootcmd=setenv bootargs ${bootargs_base} ${mtdparts}; bootm 0x30100000
menu_1=Set console to USB: setenv stdin usbtty; setenv stdout usbtty; se
menu_2=Set console to serial: setenv stdin serial; setenv stdout serial; \
    setenv stderr serial
menu_3=Power off: neo1973 power-off
splashimage=nand read.e 0x36000000 splash 0x5000; unzip 0x36000000 0x33d00000 0x96000
mtdids=nand0=neo1973-nand
mtdparts=mtdparts=neo1973-nand:0x00050000(u-boot),0x00004000(u-boot_env),
    0x00208000(kernel),0x00010000(splash),0x039a4000(rootfs)
partition=nand0,0
mtddevnum=0
mtddevname=u-boot

Environment size: 766/16380 bytes
```

You can see, for example, that the bootargs_base environment variable, when passed to the kernel on boot, will instruct it that a JFFS2 root filesystem is present on the MTD device (refer to Chapter 7) named */dev/mtdblock4*, and that a serial console should be established, running at a baud rate of 115200 bps. See the *README* file for a complete discussion of U-Boot's environment variables and their meanings.

As with Unix shells, you can add environment variables in U-Boot. To do so, you must use the *setenv* command. Here is an example session where we add a few environment variables to the GTA01 configuration (the commands must always be entered as a single line and are wrapped here only for printing purposes):

```
setenv bootcmd 'setenv bootargs \${bootargs_base} \${mtdparts}; bootm $kernel_addr'
setenv menu_1 'Set console to USB: setenv stdin usbtty; setenv stdout usbtty; \
    setenv stderr usbtty'
setenv menu_2 'Set console to serial: setenv stdin serial; setenv stdout serial; \
    setenv stderr serial'
setenv menu_3 'Power off: neo1973 power-off'
setenv splashimage 'nand read.e $splash_addr splash $splash_size; \
    unzip $splash_addr 0x33d00000 0x96000'
```

```
setenv mtdids nand0=neo1973-nand
setenv mtdparts mtdparts=neo1973-nand:0x00050000(u-boot),0x00004000(u-boot_env),
  0x00208000(kernel),0x00010000(splash),0x039a4000(rootfs)nand
  write.e $kernel_addr u-boot $uboot_size
```

In this case, we set U-Boot to boot from the kernel found at the address `$kernel_addr` (which was hardwired into the build of U-Boot for the GTA01) and to mount its root filesystem from flash memory. The remaining commands configure menu choices displayed to the user on the GTA01's screen (not shown on the serial console), as well as a fancy splash image that will be used as a background graphical image on the screen shown to the user of the device during the bootloader process.

The *setenv* command adds the environment variables to the current session only. Hence, if you reset the system (either through software, or with the *reset* command), any environment variable you set only with *setenv* will be lost. For the environment variables to survive reboots in a persistent fashion, they must be saved to flash, which is done using the *saveenv* command:

```
=> saveenv
Saving Environment to NAND...
Erasing Nand...Writing to Nand... done
```

Be careful when using *saveenv*, because it will save all the environment variables currently defined, even those that you have intended to use temporarily. Before using *saveenv*, use *printenv* to take a look at the currently defined environment variables and delete any that you don't need to save. Deleting a variable can be done simply by issuing *setenv* on the variable without providing any values. Here's an example that defines and deletes an arbitrarily chosen variable name called `RAMDisk_addr`:

```
=> setenv RAMDisk_addr 40500000
=> printenv RAMDisk_addr
RAMDisk_addr=40500000
=> setenv RAMDisk_addr
=> printenv RAMDisk_addr
## Error: "RAMDisk_addr" not defined
```

Note that the *setenv* does not require an equals sign between the variable and its value. Thus, equals signs can be entered as part of the string making up the environment variable, as we saw earlier in this section. The following command, for example, has poor syntax (notice the extra = displayed by *printenv* compared to the same *printenv* shown in the previous capture):

```
=> setenv RAMDisk_addr = 40500000
=> printenv RAMDisk_addr
RAMDisk_addr=  = 40500000
```

Creating Boot Scripts

U-Boot environment variables can be used to create boot scripts. Such "scripts" are actually just U-Boot environment variables containing a set of U-Boot command sequences. Using a combination of the *run* command and the ; (semicolon) operator allows you to make U-Boot run boot scripts. (The semicolons must be escaped because they have meaning to the shell and you want the shell to ignore them, so they are entered as part of the string in the environment variable.)

The environment variables we set in the previous section, for instance, are actually part of a boot script, bootcmd. It sets the special variable bootargs using other environment variables before calling the *bootm* command to "boot from memory" the kernel at the predefined flash memory address configured for the GTA01 hardware.

Rather than setting bootcmd directly (which limits you to only one boot command at a time), you can set it to "run" another boot script. This is useful, for example, if you will need to switch between network booting and direct flash booting on your embedded device. Here is an example:

```
=> setenv bootcmd run other_boot_script
```

Or you can run boot scripts directly from the command line without changing the value of the bootcmd environment variable:

```
=> run other_boot_script
```

Scripts are a very useful feature of U-Boot, and you should use them whenever you need to automate a certain task. You can find much more information about their use and several examples on the U-Boot wiki pages, as well as on this book's website.

Preparing Binary Images

Since the raw flash within your embedded device (the partitions on your flash not already devoted to a filesystem such as JFFS2) is not structured like a filesystem and does not contain any sort of file headers, binary images downloaded to the target must carry headers for U-Boot to recognize their content and understand how to load them. The *mkimage* utility we installed earlier was packaged with U-Boot for this purpose. It adds the information U-Boot needs to recognize binary images while also attaching a checksum for verification purposes.

 Although the use of image headers is not a technical requirement for a bootloader, such headers are very convenient both during development and in the field. Hence U-Boot's use of them.

To see the typical use of *mkimage*, type the command without any parameters:

```
$ mkimage
Usage: mkimage -l image
          -l = => list image header information
        mkimage -A arch -O os -T type -C comp -a addr -e ep -n name -d
            data_file[:data_file...] image
          -A = => set architecture to 'arch'
          -O = => set operating system to 'os'
          -T = => set image type to 'type'
```

```
-C =   => set compression type 'comp'
-a =   => set load address to 'addr' (hex)
-e =   => set entry point to 'ep' (hex)
-n =   => set image name to 'name'
-d =   => use image data from 'datafile'
-x =   => set XIP (execute in place)
```

For example, here is how we create a U-Boot image of the 2.6.24 kernel for the GTA01 reference hardware (normally entered as a single line, but printed here on two lines using shell's input continuation backslash in order to fit on the page):

```
$ mkimage -A arm -O linux -T kernel -C gzip -a 30008000 -e 30008000
\ -n "Kernel Image QT2410" -d
linux.bin.gz uImage-2.6.24+svnr4301-r4251-r5-om-gta01.bin
```

The command takes quite a few options, but their meanings are easily understood by looking at the usage message provided by *mkimage*. Note that the name of the image, provided in the *-n* option, cannot be more than 32 characters. *mkimage* will ignore any excess characters. The rest of the command line tells *mkimage* that the input file is a gzip-compressed ARM Linux kernel image that should be loaded at address 0x30008000, and started from that same address. The image being provided as input is *linux.bin.gz* (which is in fact a compressed kernel image that is produced by the OpenMoko build scripts), and the U-Boot-formatted image will be output to *uImage-2.6.24+svnr4301-r4251-r5-om-gta01.bin*.

RAM disk images can be processed in a similar fashion:

```
$ mkimage -n 'RAM disk' \
> -A arm -O linux -T ramdisk -C gzip \
> -d initrd.bin initrd.boot
Image Name:    RAM disk
Created:       Sun Mar 30 14:20:35 2008
Image Type:    ARM Linux RAMDisk Image (gzip compressed)
Data Size:     4000000 Bytes = 3906.25 kB = 3.81 MB
Load Address: 0x00000000
Entry Point:  0x00000000
```

In this case, the number of parameters is shorter because a RAM disk is not executable code and therefore you don't specify start and load addresses. Note that the image type has changed to `ramdisk`.

Once you have prepared an image with *mkimage*, it is ready to be used by U-Boot and can be downloaded to the target. As we'll see later in "Downloading Binary Images to Flash," U-Boot can receive binary images in a number of different ways. One way is to use images formatted in Motorola's S-Record format. If you intend to use this format, you need to further process the images *mkimage* generated by converting them to the S-Record format. Here is an example conversion of the `multi`-type image generated previously, using the *objcopy* command from the binutils package:

```
$ arm-angstrom-linux-gnueabi-objcopy -I binary -O srec \
> uImage-2.6.24+svnr4301-r4251-r5-om-gta01.bin \
> uImage-2.6.25+svrn4301-r4251-r5-om-gta01.srec
```

Booting Using BOOTP/DHCP, TFTP, and NFS

If you have properly configured a server to provide the target with DHCP, TFTP, and NFS services, as we explained earlier, you can boot your target remotely. This allows you to quickly make changes to the root filesystem without lengthy reflashing cycles to the device. It also allows you to share the root filesystem between the device itself (usually not an ideal development environment) and a fully featured development host that can mount the same filesystem (on a different mountpoint) at the same time.

A Note About Networking and the GTA01

The OpenMoko GT01 reference hardware used in this chapter doesn't have a real Ethernet adapter, so it cannot boot directly over a network from within U-Boot iself. This means that U-Boot on the GTA01 does not contain built-in support for commands such as *bootp*. Instead, GTA01 developers have created a special fake network interface built upon support already present within Linux kernels for USB "gadgets." This allows OpenMoko developers to instruct the Linux kernel to mount its root filesystem over the special emulated network running over USB, but only once the kernel itself has booted. As a consequence of this, the network boot examples in this section are actually based upon another reference hardware platform from Xilinx, the ML403. Further information about configuring this board and examples of its use are also included on this book's website.

U-Boot contains a variety of commands (depending upon its build-time configuration) that are useful for booting over a network. One of these is the *bootp* command. It no longer actually uses the original BOOTP protocol but instead supports the modern DHCP alternative. The following output was taken from a development board that does have a built-in network interface, performing a *bootp* command:

```
=> bootp
BOOTP broadcast 1
DHCP client bound to address 192.168.1.202
TFTP from server 192.168.1.3; our IP address is 192.168.1.202
Filename '/tftpboot/uImage-2.6.24.img'.
Load address: 0x100000
Loading: #########################################
        #########################################
        #########################################
        #########################################
done
```

The *bootp* command issues a request that is answered by the DHCP server. Using the DHCP server's answer, U-Boot contacts the TFTP server and obtains the Linux kernel image file, which it places at the configured load address in the target RAM.

After an image has been loaded (either over the network, serial console, or via any other means), you can verify the image's header information using the *iminfo* command. For example, on our GTA01 reference hardware:

```
=> GTA01Bv4 # imi 30100000
## Checking Image at 30100000 ...
   Image Name:   Openmoko/2.6.24+svnr4301-r4251/o
   Created:      2008-04-03   0:26:48 UTC
   Image Type:   ARM Linux Kernel Image (uncompressed)
   Data Size:    1763108 Bytes =  1.7 MB
   Load Address: 30008000
   Entry Point:  30008000
   Verifying Checksum ... OK
```

As you can see, the information printed by *iminfo* on the target is very similar to that printed out on the host by *mkinfo*. The OK string reported for the checksum means that the image has been downloaded properly and we can boot it:

```
=> bootm 30100000
## Booting image at 30100000 ...
   Image Name:   Openmoko/2.6.24+svnr4301-r4251/o
   Created:      2008-04-03   0:26:48 UTC
   Image Type:   ARM Linux Kernel Image (uncompressed)
   Data Size:    1763108 Bytes =  1.7 MB
   Load Address: 30008000
   Entry Point:  30008000
   Verifying Checksum ... OK
OK

Starting kernel ...

Uncompressing Linux................................................................
done,
booting the kernel.
Linux version 2.6.24 (oe@buildhost.openmoko.org) (gcc version 4.1.2)
#1 PREEMPT Thu Apr 3 00:20:41 UTC 2008
CPU: ARM920T [41129200] revision 0 (ARMv4T), cr=c0007177
Machine: GTA01
Memory policy: ECC disabled, Data cache writeback
On node 0 totalpages: 32768
  DMA zone: 256 pages used for memmap
  DMA zone: 0 pages reserved
  DMA zone: 32512 pages, LIFO batch:7
  Normal zone: 0 pages used for memmap
  Movable zone: 0 pages used for memmap
CPU S3C2410A (id 0x32410002)
S3C2410: core 266.000 MHz, memory 133.000 MHz, peripheral 66.500 MHz
S3C24XX Clocks, (c) 2004 Simtec Electronics
CLOCK: Slow mode (1.500 MHz), fast, MPLL on, UPLL on
CPU0: D VIVT write-back cache
CPU0: I cache: 16384 bytes, associativity 64, 32 byte lines, 8 sets
CPU0: D cache: 16384 bytes, associativity 64, 32 byte lines, 8 sets
Built 1 zonelists in Zone order, mobility grouping on.  Total pages: 32512
Kernel command line: console=ttySAC0,115200 console=tty0 loglevel=8
mtdparts=neo1973-nand:0x00050000(u-boot),
0x00004000(u-boot_env),0x00208000(kernel),0x00010000(splash),0x039a4000(rootfs)
Calibrating delay loop... 255.59 BogoMIPS (lpj=638976)
...
```

```
Root-NFS: No NFS server available, giving up.
VFS: Unable to mount root fs via NFS, trying floppy.
VFS: Cannot open root device "<NULL>" or unknown-block(2,0)
Please append a correct "root=" boot option; here are the available partitions:
1f00        320 mtdblock0 (driver?)
1f01         16 mtdblock1 (driver?)
1f02       2080 mtdblock2 (driver?)
1f03         64 mtdblock3 (driver?)
1f04      59024 mtdblock4 (driver?)
Kernel panic - not syncing: VFS: Unable to mount root fs on unknown-block(2,0)
```

In this case, the kernel eventually panics because it is unable to find any root filesystem. To solve this problem, we must use U-Boot environment variables to create a boot script for passing appropriate boot options to the kernel. The following commands create a new boot script in an environment variable named bootnfs and modify the special bootcmd script (as we did earlier in "Using U-Boot's Environment Variables) in order for the system to boot and mount its root filesystem over NFS (several of the lines in this example are wrapped but should be entered on the same command line):

```
GTA01Bv4 # setenv bootargs_nfs root=/dev/nfs nfsroot=192.168.1.3:/data/root/openmoko
ip=192.168.1.201:192.168.1.3:192.168.1.3:255.255.255.0:ezx:usb0:off
rootdelay=5 console=ttySAC0,115200 console=tty0 loglevel=8
GTA01Bv4 # setenv bootnfs setenv bootargs \${bootargs_nfs} \${mtdparts}\;
nand read.e 0x32000000 kernel\; bootm 0x32000000
GTA01Bv4 # printenv bootnfs
bootnfs=setenv bootargs ${bootargs_nfs} ${mtdparts}; nand read.e 0x32000000 kernel;
bootm 0x32000000
GTA01Bv4 # setenv bootcmd run bootnfs
GTA01Bv4 # printenv bootcmd
GTA01Bv4 # bootcmd=run bootnfs
```

In this case, the bootnfs script configures the boot arguments for the Linux kernel so that it will attempt to boot using the remote NFS server 192.168.1.3 and the local IP address 192.168.1.201. It will also mount the remote exported directory /data/root/openmoko as the root filesystem. We are not using the bootp command in this case because the GTA01 device does not support this operation from within U-Boot. The kernel will be loaded from flash instead. If you have a regular Ethernet device on your hardware and instead want to perform a boot entirely over the network (that is, load the kernel as well as use an NFS root device), you need to prepend the bootnfs command with a call to the U-Boot bootp command. For example, on a non-GTA01 hardware platform, you might enter:

```
=> setenv bootnfs setenv bootargs \${bootargs_nfs} \${mtdparts}\; nand bootp\;
bootm 0x32000000
```

If you use the boot command now, U-Boot will boot entirely from the network. It will download the kernel through TFTP and mount its root filesystem on NFS. If you would like to save the environment variables you just set, use the saveenv command before rebooting the system. Otherwise, you will have set the same variables again at the next reboot.

Downloading Binary Images to Flash

Booting from the network is fine for early development and testing. For production use, the target must have its kernel stored in flash. As we will see shortly, there are a few ways to copy a kernel from the host to the target and store it to flash. Before you can copy any kernel image, however, you must first choose a flash region to store it and erase that region for the incoming kernel. Depending upon your development board, the flash might be partitioned (simply a logical concept—no physical separation exists) into several regions, as in the case of the GTA01 development board. The flash memory might also be one of two types, as explained in Chapter 7. For NOR flash, it is pretty trivial to erase and program regions of the flash, because it is directly mapped into memory. For example, to erase a NOR flash region, you might enter:

```
=> erase 40100000 401FFFFF
Erase Flash from 0x40100000 to 0x401fffff
........ done
Erased 8 sectors
```

Erasing NAND flash requires use of the special U-Boot *nand* command, which can erase NAND memory regions. The NAND *read* and *write* commands actually include a form with a postfixed *.e* that also performs an erase cycle. Here is an example session writing a new release of U-Boot to NAND flash memory on the GTA01 reference hardware:

```
GTA01Bv4 # nand write.e 0x30100000 u-boot 0x35724

NAND write: device 0 offset 0x0, size 0x35724

Writing data at 0x35600 -- 100% complete.
 218916 bytes written: OK
```

The simplest way to install a kernel in the target's flash is to download it first into RAM and then copy it to the flash. On a network-attached device, such as the Xilinx ML403 development board, you can use the *tftpboot* command to download a kernel from the host to RAM:

```
=> tftpboot 00100000 /data/kernel/virtex4-vmlinux-2.6.24.img
ARP broadcast 1
TFTP from server 192.168.1.3; our IP address is 192.168.1.202
Filename '/data/kernel/virtex4-vmlinux-2.6.24.img'.
Load address: 0x100000
Loading: ################################################# ...
done
```

When *tftpboot* runs, it adds the `filesize` environment variable to the existing environment variables and sets it to the size of the file downloaded. For example:

```
=> printenv filesize
filesize=819a6
```

You can use this environment variable in subsequent commands to avoid typing in the file size by hand. Don't forget to erase this environment variable before saving the other ones, or it, too, will be saved.

In addition to *tftpboot*, you can use the *loadb* command to download images to the target:

```
=> loadb 00100000
## Ready for binary (kermit) download ...
```

At this point, U-Boot suspends and you must use the terminal emulator on the host to send the image file to the target. In this case, U-Boot expects to download the data according to the Kermit binary protocol, and you must therefore use Kermit (or another terminal emulator program that supports the protocol) to download a binary image to U-Boot. Once the transfer is done, U-Boot will acknowledge the transfer with output similar to the following:

```
## Total Size      = 0x000819a6 = 530854 Bytes
## Start Addr      = 0x00100000
```

Here, too, U-Boot will set the `filesize` environment variable to the size of the file downloaded. As we did earlier, you may want to use the *iminfo* command to verify that the image has been properly downloaded.

Once the image is in RAM, you can copy it to flash. In the case of NAND flash, you might use this command:

```
=> cp.b 00100000 40100000 $(filesize)
Copy to Flash... done
=> imi 30100000

## Checking Image at 30100000 ...
    Image Name:    Openmoko/2.6.24+svnr4301-r4251/o
    Created:       2008-04-03   0:26:48 UTC
    Image Type:    ARM Linux Kernel Image (uncompressed)
    Data Size:     1763108 Bytes =  1.7 MB
    Load Address: 30008000
    Entry Point:  30008000
    Verifying Checksum ... OK
```

Alternatively, instead of downloading the image to RAM first using *tfptboot* or *loadb* and then writing it to flash, you can download the image directly to flash using *loads*. In this case, the host sends the image to the target in S-Record format. In comparison to the two previous methods, however, downloading an S-Record file is extremely slow. In most cases, it is preferable to use *tftpboot* or *loadb*.

The *loadb* command and, by default, the *tftpboot* command can't be used to download directly to flash. U-Boot can be configured at compile time, however, to allow direct flash download using *tftpboot*. Direct flash download using *loadb* is not supported at all.

Updating U-Boot

U-Boot is like any other open source project: it continues to evolve over time as contributions are made and bug fixes are integrated into the codebase. And although we generally caution against updating U-Boot on production systems without strong justification, there will be times during design or testing, and even perhaps after eventual deployment, when such updates may be necessary. Fortunately, because U-Boot loads into and runs itself from RAM and not from flash memory, it can be used to update itself (updating the copy stored in persistent flash storage). Essentially, we have to download a new version to the target, erase the old firmware version, and copy the new version over it.

 There are obvious dangers to this operation, because a mistake or a power failure will render the target unbootable. Hence, utmost caution must be used when carrying out the steps below. Make sure you have a copy of the original U-Boot (or other bootloader) you are about to replace so that you can at least fall back to a known working version. Also, seriously consider avoiding the replacement of your firmware if you have no hardware method to reprogram the target's flash in case the upgrade fails. If you do not have access to a BDM/JTAG hardware debugger or a flash programmer, for example, there is a great risk that you will be left with a broken system if one of the steps below fails. Dealing with a buggy release of a software program is one thing; ending up with unusable hardware is another. You might prefer to experiment with a hardware emulator for the following section—for example, the GTA01 emulator, as referenced on this book's website.

Once you have taken the necessary precautions, download the U-Boot image into RAM using TFTP:

```
=> tftp 00100000 /data/u-boot/u-boot.bin-1.3.2
TFTP from server 192.168.1.3; our IP address is 192.168.1.202
Filename '/data/u-boot/u-boot.bin-1.3.2'.
Load address: 0x100000
Loading: #################################
done
```

If you do not have a TFTP server set up, you can also use the terminal emulator to send the image:

```
=> loadb 00100000
## Ready for binary (kermit) download ...

## Start Addr     = 0x00100000
```

Unlike other images we have downloaded to the target, you cannot use the *imi* command to check the image, because the U-Boot image downloaded was not packaged on the host using the *mkimage* command. You can, however, use *crc32* before and after copying the image to flash to verify that it was copied accurately.

The next step will vary depending upon whether your board uses NOR or NAND flash for U-Boot. As we have previously mentioned, NOR flash is the widely used standard for boot firmware because it is directly executable, but U-Boot now supports modern devices that are capable of booting indirectly from NAND flash alone. This is the case, for instance, with the GTA01 reference hardware used by the OpenMoko project. If you have such a board, you will need to replace the following commands with appropriate calls to the *nand* commands, as documented in U-Boot's help and documentation and in the OpenMoko online wiki documentation. Here we will document the more common situation in which you are likely to use a board based on NOR flash, at least for the bootloader itself.

To actually write the updated U-Boot image to flash, you will first need to unprotect the region of flash that it is occupying. This will vary depending upon the specific board in use. The following example assumes a board storing U-Boot in flash within the area covered by a physical address space of 40000000–4003FFFF:

```
=> protect off 40000000 4003FFFF
Un-Protected 5 sectors
```

Next, you'll need to actually erase the previous bootloader image:

```
=> erase 40000000 4003FFFF
Erase Flash from 0x40000000 to 0x4003ffff
... done
Erased 5 sectors
```

Copy the new bootloader to its final destination:

```
=> cp.b 00100000 40000000 $(filesize)
Copy to Flash... done
```

And now you can erase the `filesize` environment variable set during the download (so that the following step will not store it persistently to the U-Boot environment data):

```
=> setenv filesize
```

Since you've just replaced U-Boot, you'll need to resave its environment variables:

```
=> saveenv
Saving Enviroment to Flash...
Un-Protected 1 sectors
Erasing Flash...
. done
Erased 1 sectors
Writing to Flash... done
Protected 1 sectors
```

At this stage, the new bootloader image has been installed and is ready to be used. Until you issue the *reset* command, however, you can still use the old U-Boot currently running to fix any problems that may have occurred during the update. Once you are satisfied that every step of the update has gone through cleanly, you can go ahead and restart the system:

```
=> reset
```

If you can see the U-Boot boot message again, U-Boot has been successfully updated. Otherwise, there is a problem with the replacement of the firmware and you need to reprogram the flash device using the appropriate hardware tools.

## CHAPTER 10

Setting Up Networking Services

Increasingly, embedded systems are called upon to include networking capabilities. An embedded system may, for example, provide a web server to enable web-based configuration. It may also enable remote login for maintenance and upgrading purposes. Because the Linux kernel and the networking software that runs on it are often the preferred software for running networking services that require high reliability and high availability, you will find Linux particularly well suited for networking applications.

In this chapter, we will discuss the setup and configuration of the networking services most commonly found in embedded Linux systems. This discussion includes instructions on how to cross-compile each networking package and how to modify the target's root filesystem to run the services each package provides. In particular, we will cover:

- Use of the Internet super-server (*inetd*)
- Remote administration with SNMP
- Network login through Telnet
- Secure communications with SSH
- Serving web content through HTTP
- Dynamic configuration through dynamic host configuration protocol (DHCP)

There are, of course, many other networking services that can run on top of Linux. Though we couldn't realistically cover all of them in a single chapter, the explanations included here should provide you with some hints as to how to install and use other networking packages. Also, we won't cover the setup, configuration, and use of actual networking hardware, nor many of the Linux advanced networking options—such as IPv6, source-based routing, firewalling and network address translation support—as most are not specific to embedded systems. If you need information regarding these issues, have a look at *Running Linux* by Matthias Dalheimer and Matt Welsh and *Linux Network Administrator's Guide* by Tony Bautts et al. (both from O'Reilly). We also will not provide in-depth coverage of the configuration and use of the various networking packages, since many already have entire books dedicated to them. For more information regarding Linux networking in general, look at books such as the ones previously mentioned that discuss the issue from the perspective of a server or a workstation.

This chapter builds on the material presented in Chapter 6. The operations presented here are supplemental to the procedure for building the target's root filesystem, and are discussed in this chapter because they are essential if network services are used, but otherwise not always required.

Throughout this chapter, we will use an ARM-based system as our system management (SYSM) module[*] to present the operations you need to carry out.

Network Settings

The first order of business in enabling most network services (the DHCP client being the major exception) is the correct configuration of network settings. At minimum, this includes the target IP address and routing table; if the target will use DNS, a domain name server IP address needs to be configured.

A full and detailed configuration of Linux's extensive networking stack is beyond the scope of this book. The following script sets up the most basic setting required for a machine with a fixed IP address that will allow most network services to work and be accessible over the network. Example values that you need to replace with the values for your site are shown in italics:

```sh
#!/bin/sh


HOSTNAME=shu
DOMAINNAME=codefidence.com
IP=192.168.1.2
NETMASK=255.255.255.0
GATEWAY=192.168.1.1
NS1=192.168.1.200

# This sets the hostname and FQDN
echo 127.0.0.1 $HOSTNAME.$DOMAINNAME $HOSTNAME > /etc/hosts
/bin/hostname   $HOSTNAME

# This sets up the loopback interface
/sbin/ifconfig lo 127.0.0.1 up
/sbin/route add -net 127.0.0.0 netmask 255.0.0.0 lo

# This sets up our IP and default gateway
/sbin/ifconfig eth0 $IP up
/sbin/route add -net $GATEWAY netmask $NETMASK eth0

echo nameserver $NS1 > /etc/resolv.conf
```

---

[*] See "Design and Implementation Methodology in Chapter 1 for details about the components in the example system used by the author of this chapter.

Edit the script to modify the first few lines and run it from */etc/inittab* during boot, as explained in Chapter 6. This will set up a basic, static IP configuration that's sufficient for supporting the network services described in this chapter.

For a dynamic configuration using the DHCP protocol, see the upcoming section "Dynamic Configuration Through DHCP."

 The network setup example provided previously is minimalist at best and uses the deprecated, but more commonly encountered, *ifconfig* and *route* commands, as opposed to the current and more powerful *ip* command from the iproute2 package. The sole purpose of this example is to assist you in setting up in the quickest and most hassle-free way possible the most rudimentary network configuration that will allow you to experiment with the network services and packages described ahead. You are encouraged to consult the references at the beginning of the chapter for a more in-depth look at Linux network configuration options.

Busybox

As described in Chapter 6, Busybox is an "all-in-one" application suite for embedded systems. Many network services are now implemented as BusyBox applets, including a DHCP client and server, a minimal web server, and a Telnet server program. In fact, Busybox applets make excellent network services, especially for low-key services that do not require any level of high performance or advanced features.

Refer to Chapter 6 to configure, build, and install Busybox.

Dynamic Configuration Through DHCP

The DHCP allows for the automatic network configuration of hosts. Automatic configuration usually involves assigning IP addresses, but it can include other configuration parameters, as we saw in Chapter 9. A network that uses DHCP hosts two sorts of entities: clients that request a configuration and servers that provide the clients with functional configurations. The configuration information that the server gives to the client is called a *lease*, a term that reflects its temporary assignment. If a client is dormant for a certain amount of time (which can be configured on the server), the IP address and other information might become invalid and be given to another client.

An embedded Linux system can easily be used as a DHCP server. In our example system, for instance, the SYSM module can provide dynamic configurations to the UI modules. Conversely, an embedded Linux system may need to obtain its own configuration from a DHCP server. Our UI modules, for example, may obtain their configurations from the SYSM module.

The standard DHCP package used in most Linux distributions is the one distributed by the Internet Software Consortium (ISC). Although the package may seem to be a good candidate for use in embedded Linux systems because of its widespread use and the fact that it includes both the client and the server, it's actually not suitable, because its *Makefiles* and configuration scripts cannot easily be adapted to cross-compilation.

There is, nevertheless, another open source package that provides both a DHCP server and a DHCP client, and it can be used in an embedded Linux system: udhcp. The udhcp project is maintained as part of the BusyBox project, and its website is located at *http://udhcp.busybox.net/*. The package is available on that website and is distributed under the GPL. udhcp depends only on the C library and can be compiled with both *glibc* and *uClibc*.

Begin by downloading and extracting the udhcp package in your *${PRJROOT}/sysapps* directory. For our SYSM module, for example, we used *udhcp 0.9.8*. Move to the package's directory for the rest of the operations:

```
$ cd ${PRJROOT}/sysapps/udhcp-0.9.8
```

The package needs no configuration. The only important option is *CROSS_COMPILE*, which should contain the prefix to the cross toolchain, for example, `arm-uclibc-` (you need the trailing hyphen) if using *uClibc* on ARM, or `arm-linux-` if *glibc* is preferred.

Compile and link the package:

```
$ make CROSS_COMPILE=arm-uclibc-
```

Compilation time is short. When linked against *glibc* and stripped,[†] the server and the client are around 16 KB in size. When linked against *uClibc* and stripped, the server and the client are around 15 KB in size.

 The file sizes provided throughout this chapter correspond to one author's setup, and you are likely to obtain slightly different sizes. Use the numbers provided here as an indication only. ARM code, for instance, and RISC code in general, is usually larger than x86 code.

If you are using the server in your system, copy it to your target's */usr/sbin* directory:

```
$ cp udhcpd ${PRJROOT}/rootfs/usr/sbin
```

If you are using the client, copy it to your target's */sbin* directory:

```
$ cp udhcpc ${PRJROOT}/rootfs/sbin
```

Both server and client need configuration files and runtime files to store information regarding lease status. As you can see in the commands in this section, the server (daemon) is named *udhcpd* and the client is named *udhcpc*.

---

† The udhcp *Makefile* automatically strips the binaries once they are built.

For the server, create a */var/lib/misc* directory and a lease file, and copy the sample configuration file to your target's root filesystem:

```
$ mkdir -p ${PRJROOT}/rootfs/var/lib/misc
$ touch ${PRJROOT}/rootfs/var/lib/misc/udhcpd.leases
$ cp samples/udhcpd.conf ${PRJROOT}/rootfs/etc
```

If you forget to create the lease file, the server will refuse to start.

For the client, create a */etc/udhcpc* directory and a */usr/share/udhcpc* directory, and copy one of the sample configuration files to */usr/share/udhcpc/default.script*:

```
$ mkdir -p ${PRJROOT}/rootfs/etc/udhcpc
$ mkdir -p ${PRJROOT}/rootfs/usr/share/udhcpc
$ cp samples/sample.renew \
> ${PRJROOT}/rootfs/usr/share/udhcpc/default.script
```

Also, edit your target's */etc/inittab* file to start the daemon you need. For instance, here is the line for the DHCP server used in our SYSM module:

```
::respawn:/usr/sbin/udhcpd
```

For a complete discussion of the configuration and use of *udhcpd* and *udhcpc*, read the manpages included with the package and look at the project's website.

The Internet Super-Server

As in most Unix systems, networking services are implemented as daemons in Linux. Each networking daemon responds to requests on a particular port. The Telnet service, for example, operates on port 23, whereas the more secure SSH service uses port 22. For networking services to function properly, some process must be alive and listening on each corresponding port. Instead of starting all the networking daemons so that each listens to its own port, however, some systems make use of an Internet "super-server." This super-server is a special daemon that listens to the ports of all the enabled networking services. When a request comes in from a particular port, the corresponding networking daemon is started, and the request is passed on to it for service.

There are two main benefits to this scheme. First, only the minimal set of needed daemons is active at all times, and therefore no system resources are wasted. Second, there is a centralized mechanism for managing and monitoring network services.

Although many networking services can be managed by the Internet super-server, some services—such as an HTTP server or an SNMP agent—are almost always set up to have direct control of their ports for reasons of scalability and reliability.

There are two main Internet super-servers available for Linux, *inetd* and *xinetd*. Though *inetd* used to be the standard super-server for most Linux distributions, it is gradually being replaced by *xinetd*, which contains more features. But because *inetd* contains fewer features than *xinetd*, it is also smaller and may be better for an embedded Linux system.

inetd

inetd is part of one of the netkit packages available at *ftp://ftp.uk.linux.org/pub/linux/Networking/netkit*. Netkit is a set of packages that provide various networking capabilities. *inetd* is part of the netkit-base package (which also contains other useful network programs, such as *ping*). Like other netkit packages, netkit-base is distributed under a BSD license.

First, download netkit-base and extract it into your *${PRJROOT}/sysapps* directory. For our SYSM module, we used netkit-base version 0.17. Now, move to the directory from which netkit-base was extracted:

```
$ cd ${PRJROOT}/sysapps/netkit-base-0.17
```

Before you begin configuring netkit-base, you need to modify the *configure* script to prevent it from trying to run test programs on your host. Because you are instructing it to use the compiler you built for the target, the test programs it compiles will be fit only for your target. Hence, these test programs will fail to run on the host, and the *configure* script fails to complete if it is not modified. To avoid these problems, edit the *configure* script and comment out all the lines that attempt to execute the compiled binary (adding a # symbol at the beginning of each line). The actual test programs that *configure* tries to run are all called *__conftest*. Here is an example commented line:

```
# ./__conftest || exit 1;
```

Under most circumstances, editing the *configure* script of a package to overcome a build problem or to skip a test in the manner described is ill-advised. The *configure* script is normally autogenerated using the GNU autoconf tools, and thus editing it in such a fashion is a futile and error-prone endeavor. The right thing to do is either find the correct options to the *configure* script to make it behave properly, or in lieu of appropriate options, edit the *configure.in* from which the *configure* file is automatically built and regenerate the *configure* script using the autoconf tools.

In this specific case, however, the configure script was not created using the GNU autoconf tools and, after close examination, one of the authors has established that editing the script in this manner is the only valid option here.

inetd can be built with either *glibc* or *uClibc*. To link it against *uClibc*, however, you need to make sure that RPC support was enabled in *uClibc*. If *uClibc* was built with RPC disabled, which is the default, you must reinstall *uClibc*.

Once the *configure* script has been properly edited, configure and compile netkit-base:

```
$ CC=arm-linux-gcc ./configure --prefix=${TARGET_PREFIX}
$ make
```

Netkit-base builds quite rapidly. The binary generated is 24 KB in size when built with *glibc* and stripped. With *uClibc*, the stripped binary is 23 KB. Regardless of the actual link method you choose, the resulting *inetd* binary is much smaller than the *xinetd* binary, as we shall see in the next section.

In contrast with other packages we've built in other chapters, don't use *make install* to install *inetd*, because the *Makefiles* were not properly built for cross-platform development. Among other things, they attempt to use the host's *strip* command to strip the binaries of their symbol tables.

Instead, copy the *inetd* binary and the sample configuration file manually to your target's root filesystem:

```
$ cp inetd/inetd ${PRJROOT}/rootfs/usr/sbin
$ cp etc.sample/inetd.conf ${PRJROOT}/rootfs/etc
```

Edit the *inetd.conf* file according to your own setup. In addition to *inetd.conf*, the *etc.sample* directory contains other file samples that may be used in your target's */etc* directory, such as *resolv.conf* and *services*. For our SYSM module, here's the *inetd.conf* entry for the Telnet daemon discussed later in "Network Login Through Telnet:

```
telnet  stream  tcp     nowait  root    /usr/sbin/telnetd
```

Once *inetd* is copied and configured, edit your target's */etc/inittab* file to add a line for *inetd*. Here is an example line for our SYSM module that uses BusyBox's *init*:

```
::respawn:/usr/sbin/inetd -i
```

The *-i* option instructs *inetd* not to start as a daemon. Hence, *init* can respawn *inetd* if it dies for some unexpected reason.[‡]

Because netkit-base also includes *ping*, you will find a *ping* binary in the *ping* directory. You don't need to use this binary if you are already using BusyBox, however, because BusyBox includes a *ping* command.

For more information regarding the use of *inetd*, have a look at the manpages included in the netkit-base package under the *inetd* directory.

xinetd

xinetd is preferable to *inetd* on some systems because it allows some secure authorization, provides extensive logging abilities, and can prevent denial-of-access attacks, among other things. Although the FAQ on the *xinetd* project website contains a complete list of advantages it has over *inetd*, suffice it to say that you should use the *xinetd* super-server only if your embedded system is designed to provide extensive networking services or live in a hostile networking environment, such as the Internet.

[‡] The super-server doesn't crash often. The reliance on *init* is therefore just an extra precaution.

xinetd is distributed at *http://www.xinetd.org/* under a BSD-like license. For our SYSM module, we used *xinetd* version 2.3.14. Download and extract the *xinetd* package into your *${PRJROOT}/sysapps* directory, and move into the package's directory for the rest of the procedure:

```
$ cd ${PRJROOT}/sysapps/xinetd-2.3.14
```

As with *inetd*, *xinetd* can't be compiled with *uClibc* if it lacks certain features. In particular, *xinetd* will fail to build with *uClibc* if it doesn't support RPC and C99. In addition to the C library, *xinetd* depends on the math library (*libm*) and the cryptography library (*libcrypt*).

Configure, compile, and install *xinetd*:

```
$ CC=arm-linux-gcc ./configure --host=$TARGET --prefix=${TARGET_PREFIX}
$ make
$ make install
```

xinetd builds quite rapidly. The dynamically linked, stripped binary itself is quite large at 126 KB in size with either *uClibc* or *glibc*. When statically linked and stripped, the binary's size is 650 KB with *glibc* and 210 KB with *uClibc*. The *xinetd* package installs its components in the *${TARGET_PREFIX}* directory. The build also installs manpages. The *xinetd* binary itself is installed in *${TARGET_PREFIX}*. Copy it from that directory to your target's root filesystem and strip it:

```
$ cp ${TARGET_PREFIX}/sbin/xinetd ${PRJROOT}/rootfs/usr/sbin
$ arm-linux-strip ${PRJROOT}/rootfs/usr/sbin/xinetd
```

A sample configuration file is provided with *xinetd*, named *xinetd/sample.conf*. Use this sample as the basis for configuring your target. Copy it to your target's root filesystem and edit it according to your needs:

```
$ cp xinetd/sample.conf ${PRJROOT}/rootfs/etc/xinetd.conf
```

Here is the entry in our SYSM module's *xinetd.conf* for the Telnet daemon discussed later in "Network Login Through Telnet:

```
service telnet
{
        socket_type             = stream
        wait                    = no
        user                    = root
        server                  = /usr/sbin/telnetd
        bind                    = 127.0.0.1
        log_on_failure          += USERID
}
```

Note that the example here instructs *xinetd* to bind the Telnet service to the loopback address 127.0.0.1, making the service accessible only from the target board itself. This was done to assure readers wouldn't accidentally copy and paste themselves into a security breach. If you wish to allow Telnet access from outside the target board, you can replace the bind field with one of the machine IP addresses, or simply 0.0.0.0 to request binding to all available IP addresses.

Before doing so, however, please make sure to read and understand the Telnet service security considerations, as discussed in "Network Login Through Telnet," later in this chapter.

Finally, edit your target's */etc/inittab* file to add a line for *xinetd*. As for *inetd*, I had to add a line for *xinetd* in our SYSM module's *inittab*:

```
::once:/usr/sbin/xinetd
```

Unlike *inetd*, *xinetd* can be started only as a daemon. Therefore, it cannot be respawned by *init* if it dies.

For more information regarding the use and configuration of *xinetd*, look at the man-pages included in the *xinetd* directory of the *xinetd* package. The project's website also includes an FAQ and a mailing list.

Remote Administration with SNMP

The Simple Network Management Protocol (SNMP) allows the remote management of devices on TCP/IP networks. Though networking equipment such as routers and switches are the most likely to be SNMP-enabled, almost any device that connects to a TCP/IP network can be managed through SNMP.

Your embedded device will most likely be an SNMP *agent*, which is the SNMP software component that runs in the networked device to enable remote management. In contrast, an SNMP *manager* is the SNMP software component that runs on a normal workstation or server and that is responsible for monitoring remote systems running SNMP agents.

Thus, an SNMP agent allows you to monitor the target remotely and automatically. In other words, you don't need to have an operator stand by the system to make sure it's still alive and watch over its current performance. The agent running in your target can also be configured to send SNMP *traps* to the SNMP manager to inform it of software or hardware failure. If your target is part of a complex network or if you need to be able to constantly monitor its status remotely, you should think about including an SNMP agent in it.

A negative factor, however, is the large size of the agent: the SNMP MIB information weighs in at around 1.3 MB. Added to the stripped binary, this brings the minimum cost of the total SNMP package to a little over 2 MB in storage. This is a fairly large package for most embedded Linux systems.

There are quite a few SNMP agents and packages that enable interaction with SNMP-enabled devices, many of them quite expensive. In the open source world, Net-SNMP is the standard package for building and managing SNMP-enabled systems. It is distributed at *http://net-snmp.sourceforge.net/* under a composite license similar to the BSD license.§

The Net-SNMP package is relatively large and contains many software components. For most targets, however, we will be interested only in the SNMP agent, since this is the software component that will allow our device to be remotely managed. Start by downloading and extracting the Net-SNMP package to your *${PRJROOT}/sysapps* directory. For our SYSM module, for example, we used Net-SNMP version 5.4. Now move to the package's directory for the rest of the manipulations:

```
$ cd ${PRJROOT}/sysapps/net-snmp-5.3.1
```

The Net-SNMP package can be compiled with either *uClibc* or *glibc*. There are a few requirements when using *uClibc*, however, as we'll see. In addition to the C library, Net-SNMP depends on the shared object dynamic loading library (*libdl*) and the math library (*libm*).

To configure Net-SNMP for building with *glibc*, enter:

```
$ ./configure --host=$TARGET --with-endianness=little --with-cc=arm-linux-gcc
    --with-install-prefix=${TARGET_PREFIX}
```

If used with *uClibc*, Net-SNMP expects *uClibc* to be configured with IPv6 support. If it isn't, you can add the *--disable-ipv6* option to Net-SNMP's configuration command line to disable IPv6 support within Net-SNMP. Then, issue the *configure* command using *arm-uclibc-gcc* instead of *arm-linux-gcc*.

Note that we avoid using the *--prefix* option when configuring Net-SNMP. If we used it, the resulting SNMP agent would always look for its files in the directory provided in the option. Instead, we want the SNMP agent to take its configuration from the default */usr/local/share/snmp* directory. Luckily, the Net-SNMP configure script supports the *--with-install-prefix* option, which sets the place where the install make target will copy the binaries and files but does not affect the runtime paths.

During its execution, the configuration script will prompt you for certain information about the functionality of the SNMP agent, including the SNMP version to use, the contact information for the device, and the system's location. The instructions provided by the configuration script are usually sufficient to understand the purpose of the information requested. If you need more information regarding the configuration process of the Net-SNMP agent, see *Essential SNMP* by Douglas Mauro and Kevin Schmidt (O'Reilly).

§ See the *COPYING* file in the Net-SNMP package for complete details about the license.

Once the configuration script has completed, build and install the Net-SNMP components:

```
$ make
$ make install
```

The SNMP agent executable built by default by Net-SNMP seems like a rather small binary. If you compile it against *glibc* and strip it, it will measure a measly 24 KB when linked dynamically. However, much of the code resides in dynamic libraries that are built together with the executable and are needed for its proper operation at runtime. Together with these libraries, the total space taken by the SNMP agent is a whopping 1276 KB. If you compile it against *uClibc* and strip it, it will measure 625 KB. Because the figures for the unstripped binaries all exceed 1.7 MB, we strongly encourage you to strip the agent binary.

The complete build and installation will take around 10 minutes, depending on your hardware, because Net-SNMP is quite a large package. In addition to copying binaries, the installation copies manpages and headers into the *${TARGET_PREFIX}* directory. The SNMP daemon (*snmpd*), which is the actual SNMP agent, is installed in *${TARGET_PREFIX}/sbin*. The dynamic libraries built during the build and required by the binary reside in *${TARGET_PREFIX}/libs*. The other SNMP utilities, such as *snmpget*, are installed in *${TARGET_PREFIX}/bin*. The SNMP trap daemon is also installed in *${TARGET_PREFIX}/sbin* (this daemon is used to monitor incoming traps). The MIB information required by the SNMP daemon is installed in *${TARGET_PREFIX}/share/snmp*.

With all the Net-SNMP components installed in your development workspace on the host, copy the SNMP daemon, and dynamic libraries to your target's root filesystem:

```
$ cp ${TARGET_PREFIX}/sbin/snmpd ${PRJROOT}/rootfs/usr/sbin
$ cp -a ${TARGET_PREFIX}/libs/libnetsnmp*.so* ${PRJROOT}/rootfs/usr/lib
```

Copy the relevant components found in *${TARGET_PREFIX}/share/snmp* to the */usr/local/share/snmp* directory of your target's root filesystem:

```
$ mkdir -p ${PRJROOT}/rootfs/usr/local/share
$ cp -r ${TARGET_PREFIX}/share/snmp ${PRJROOT}/rootfs/usr/local/share
```

To run properly, the SNMP agent requires a configuration file. An example configuration (*EXAMPLE.conf*) was created during the build of the Net-SNMP package in the package's root directory. Customize that file and copy it to your *${PRJROOT}/rootfs/usr/local/share/snmp* directory:

```
$ cp EXAMPLE.conf ${PRJROOT}/rootfs/usr/local/share/snmp/snmpd.conf
```

Finally, edit your target's */etc/inittab* file to add a line for *snmpd*. Here is the line we added for *snmpd* in our SYSM module's *inittab*:

```
::respawn:/usr/sbin/snmpd -f
```

The *-f* option instructs *snmpd* not to fork from the calling shell. In other words, *snmpd* will not become a daemon and *init* will respawn it if it dies.

For more information regarding SNMP, including the configuration and use of Net-SNMP, look at *Essential SNMP*, mentioned earlier. The Net-SNMP project's website contains quite a few resources, including an FAQ, various documents, and a mailing list. The manpages installed by Net-SNMP are also informative.

Network Login Through Telnet

The Telnet protocol is one of the simplest ways to log into a remote network host. Consequently, it's the easiest way to access your target system once it is connected to a network. To enable remote login, your target must run a Telnet daemon. There are two main Telnet daemons available for use in embedded Linux systems: *telnetd*, which is part of the netkit packages mentioned earlier, and *utelnetd*, which is maintained by Robert Schwebel of Pengutronix.

In terms of size, the binary generated by the *utelnetd* package is clearly smaller than the one generated by the netkit Telnet package. In addition, *utelnetd* does not require an Internet super-server, while *telnetd* does. If your system has very limited resources and does not include other network services managed by an Internet super-server, use *utelnetd*.

Though Telnet is a convenient, lightweight communications mechanism for managing your device on a dedicated network, it's not a secure protocol and therefore not fit for use on the Internet. If you need to remotely log into a device that resides on the Internet, use SSH instead. We will discuss SSH in detail later in "Secure Communication with SSH."

netkit-telnetd

As with other netkit packages, the netkit-telnet package that contains *telnetd* is distributed at *ftp://ftp.uk.linux.org/pub/linux/Networking/netkit* under a BSD license. For our SYSM module, we used netkit-telnet version 0.17.

Download and extract the netkit-telnet package into your *${PRJROOT}/sysapps* directory and move to the package's directory for the rest of the procedure:

```
$ cd ${PRJROOT}/sysapps/netkit-telnet-0.17
```

As with the netkit-base package described earlier, the *configure* script included in the netkit-telnet package attempts to run some test programs. Because these test programs are compiled using the target's compiler, they will fail. To avoid this, edit the *configure* script and comment out all the lines that attempt to execute test binaries. As earlier, here is an example commented line:

```
# ./__conftest || exit 1;
```

After modifying the script, you are ready to configure and compile the Telnet daemon. To link with *glibc*, type:

```
$ CC=arm-linux-gcc ./configure --prefix=${TARGET_PREFIX}
$ touch ${TARGET_PREFIX}/include/termcap.h
$ make -C telnetd
```

To build with *uClibc*, type:

```
$ CC=arm-uclibc-gcc ./configure --prefix=${TARGET_PREFIX}
$ touch ${PREFIX}/uclibc/include/termcap.h
$ make -C telnetd
```

As you can see, we compile only *telnetd*. The package also includes the *telnet* client, but the *Makefile* for that client doesn't allow cross-compilation. Even if it did, you'll find it better to use the miniature *telnet* client included in BusyBox. We used *touch* to create a *termcap.h* file in the appropriate header directory because *telnetd*'s source files include this header file. We don't need the termcap library, however. The build process requires only the termcap header file to be present, and the file can be empty.

The complete build process for *telnetd* is fairly short, and the resulting binary is quite small. When built with *uClibc* and stripped, the binary is 30 KB if linked dynamically and 65 KB if linked statically. When built with *glibc* and stripped, the binary is 30 KB if linked dynamically and 430 KB if linked statically.

Don't use *make install*, because the *Makefile* was not properly built for cross-platform development and attempts to use the host's *strip* command instead of the version we built earlier for the target. Instead, copy the *telnetd* binary by hand to your target's root filesystem:

```
$ cp telnetd/telnetd ${PRJROOT}/rootfs/usr/sbin
```

You need to have a properly configured copy of either *inetd* or *xinetd*, the Internet super-server that allows Telnet connections to your target. Alternatively, you could edit your target's */etc/inittab* to start the Telnet daemon using the *-debug* option so that it doesn't need to rely on any super-server. However, *telnetd* wasn't meant to be used this way.

Common Pitfalls

The Telnet daemon uses pseudoterminal devices, called pty for short, to provide a terminal for the shell and other programs to run in, when invoked from the network via this daemon.

One of the most common pitfalls for novice embedded Linux system builders regarding the Telnet service is to neglect some configuration detail related to ptys that prevents users from logging in to the system via Telnet.

If the Telnet daemon is running and networking is otherwise working (you can, for example, ping other hosts), make sure of the following:

- The */dev/ptmx* exists and that it is a character device file with a major number of 5 and a minor of 2; if not, create it using the command:

```
$ mknod /dev/ptmx c 5 2
```

- Support for the *devpts* pseudofilesystem is enabled in the kernel by looking for the *devpts* entry in the */proc/filesystems* file, or add the support by turning on the `CONFIG_UNIX98_PTYS` Linux kernel build option.

- The */dev/pts* directory exists and that the *devpts* pseudofilesystem is mounted on it correctly, either by issuing the *mount* command and looking for the *devpts* entry or mounting it using the command:

```
$ mkdir /dev/pts && mount -t devpts none /dev/pts
```

In addition to the C library, *telnetd* depends on the login routines library (*libutil*). Hence, do not forget to copy this library to your target's */lib* directory if you link *telnetd* dynamically.

For further information regarding the use of *telnetd*, have a look at the manpage included in the *telnetd* directory of the netkit-telnet package, or look at the manpage installed on your host for your workstation's native *telnetd*.

Secure Communication with SSH

Although you can easily communicate with your target using Telnet, it is a very insecure protocol and its vulnerabilities are widely documented. The user password, for instance, is transmitted in clear text from the client to the server. It would therefore be rather unprudent, and in most cases downright dangerous, to include a Telnet daemon in your product in the hopes of being able to remotely fix problems once the product is at the client's site. Instead, it would be preferable to use a protocol that relies on strong encryption and other mechanisms to ensure the communication's confidentiality. Currently the best way to do this is to use the SSH protocol and related tool suite. SSH uses public-key cryptography to guarantee end-to-end communication encryption, and it is fairly easy to use and deploy.

Because SSH is an IETF standard, there are a few competing implementations, some of which are proprietary commercial products. The canonical open source implementation is OpenSSH. However, it is not for the faint of heart to try and cross compile this program. It is dependent on the separate OpenSSL library, and the resulting binary is over 1MB in size. Luckily, an open source SSH server (and client) for embedded systems called Dropbear, written by Matt Johnston, has proved in recent years to be a good fit for embedded systems. It is this implementation that we will cover here.

The security of any network service depends not only on the cryptographic properties of the algorithms used to implement the protocol, but also—and some would say mainly—on the details of the specific implementation used.

Choosing an SSH service implementation is therefore a delicate balance between achieving secure communication with the target at the least possible cost and lulling ourselves into a false sense of security.

OpenSSH and the OpenSSL library it relies on comprise a much more tested and mature implementation of the SSH protocol and are therefore more secure. Having said that, the author of this chapter considers choosing Dropbear over OpenSSH as an acceptable risk in this regard, but you should be aware of the choice that is being made here.

If you are seriously considering using an SSH package in your target, we suggest you take a look at *SSH, The Secure Shell: The Definitive Guide* by Daniel Barrett and Richard Silverman (O'Reilly). It provides the in-depth coverage we cannot undertake here.

Dropbear can be downloaded from the author's website at *http://matt.ucc.asn.au/drop bear/dropbear.html*. The version used in the examples is 0.49, the current version at the time of this writing. We recommend you use the most recent version available, due to the security implications of this package.

Download and extract the Dropbear package into your *${PRJROOT}/sysapps* directory, and move to the package's directory for the rest of the procedure:

```
$ cd ${PRJROOT}/sysapps/dropbear-0.49
```

Proceed to configure the package using the following command:

```
$ STRIP=arm-linux-strip CC=arm-linux-gcc ./configure --host=${TARGET}
```

If you're compiling for a 386-class CPU, you will probably need to add CFLAGS=-DLTC_NO_BSWAP so that libtomcrypt doesn't use 486+ instructions.

To link against *uClibc*, simply use the *uClibc* compiler:

```
$ STRIP=arm-linux-strip CC=arm-linux-gcc ./configure --host=${TARGET}
```

Note that we are providing the location of the cross-toolchain *strip* executable as well as the compiler. This is not strictly needed, but it will allow us to easily strip the result binary later using the convenience build target supplied by the Dropbear *Makefile*.

The configure script offers several addtional options, which can be used to customize the program further to your needs. As an example, you can remove support for the zlib compression library using the switch --disable-zlib.

In addition to using the options offered by the configure script, you can also edit the *options.h* include file directly, removing some uneeded ciphers and check codes (such as MD5) as a way to produce a smaller runtime binary.

 If you disable zlib support, you must explicitly disable compression support in the client side. Certain versions of the commonly used OpenSSH client are possibly buggy in this regard, so disable compressions support globally (not just for the particular host) in *~/.ssh/config* by adding the 'Compression off' keyword.

In addition, you may want to disable *lastlog* recording when using *uClibc* if *uClibc* was not built with *lastlog* support. This can be done by providing the `--disable-lastlog` switch to the configure script.

Last but not least, note that the tips regarding the pseudoterminal interface presented in the section about the netkit-telnetd daemon apply also to the SSH service and Dropbear.

Next, we'll build the package, which combines the SSH server itself, the *scp* utility (which performs secure file transfer on top of the SSH secure channel), and the *dropbearkey* utility, (which allows you to compute a unique key for your target during its first boot). (The DESTDIR build variable denotes the location to which the install target will copy the generated binary.) We will use a nice feature that the Dropbear package offers that lets us build a single binary executable for all three programs, which will produce a smaller footprint for the SSH server. In addition, we will strip the binary.

```
$ make PROGRAMS="dropbear dropbearkey scp" --prefix=/usr/
    MULTI=1 DESTDIR=${TARGET_PREFIX} strip install
```

The generated multiprogram binary, called *dropbearmulti* (241 KB in size) needs to be copied to its location on the root filesystem. We will need to create symbolic links that link the names of the three different programs we have created to the actual binary:

```
$ cp ${TARGET_PREFIX}/usr/bin/dropbearmulti \
    ${PRJROOT}/rootfs/usr/sbin/dropbear
$ ln -s ../sbin/dropbear ${PRJROOT}/rootfs/usr/bin/dropbearkey
$ ln -s ../sbin/dropbear ${PRJROOT}/rootfs/usr/bin/scp
```

Now, edit your target's */etc/inittab* file to add a line for starting the dropbear daemon at boot. Here is the line we added for Dropbear in our SYSM module's *inittab*. As you might recall, the respawn directive tells init to run the specified program (*dropbear*, in our case) and restart it if it ever terminates:

```
::respawn:/usr/sbin/dropbear -F -d /etc/dropbear_dsa_host_key
    -r /etc/dropbear_rsa_hos_key
```

We are not done yet, however. When the *dropbear* daemon starts, it will look for two files: one containing an RSA cryptographic key, the other a DSA key. The keys are used to identify the target to SSH clients connecting to it and are part of the SSH protocol defense against what is known as "Man in the Middle" attacks. We will need to create these keys, by running the *dropbearkey* program twice, once for each key type.

In theory, we could compile the *dropbearkey* utility as a native executable on our development host, create the files containing the keys there, and copy them to our target filesystem just like any other file. That, however, would not be a good idea as it will mean the keys will not be unique to each system.

One of the most practical ways to create different keys for each unit is to generate them on the first boot. For this purpose, we will create a small shell script that will create these key files on the target machine, but only if they do not exist already (as would be the case when starting from the second run of the script, at least in most circumstances):

```
#!/bin/sh

RSA_KEY=/etc/dropbear_rsa_host_key
DSA_KEY=/etc/dropbear_dsa_host_key

if ! test -f $RSA_KEY; then
    /usr/bin/dropbearkey -t rsa -f $RSA_KEY;

fi;

if ! test -f $DSA_KEY; then
    /usr/bin/dropbearkey -t dsa -f $DSA_KEY;

fi;
```

 We are relying on the root filesystem not being read-only or volatile, as would be the case with a *cramfs* image, an *initrd* RAM disk, or an initramfs filesystem. If this is not the case with your system, you can simply create the files at a different path and point the *dropbear* daemon program to this alternate location.

Name the file *create_dropbear_keys.sh*, and copy it to the target filesystem:

```
$ cp create_dropbear_keys.sh ${PRJROOT}/rootfs/usr/sbin/
```

Finally, all we have to do is get the script to run at target system startup. Add the following line to the target's */etc/inittab* to accomplish this:

```
::sysinit:/usr/sbin/create_dropbear_keys.sh
```

Serving Web Content Through HTTP

One of the biggest trends in network-enabled embedded systems is the inclusion of a web (HTTP) server. The added HTTP server can then be used for enabling remote administration or remote data viewing. In the case of our SYSM module, for example, the HTTP server lets users configure and monitor various aspects of the control system.

Although the open source Apache HTTP server is the most widely used HTTP server in the world, it is not necessarily fit for embedded systems. The main reasons are that it is very difficult to cross-compile, and it tends to demand a rather large amount of storage. There are other open source HTTP servers that are much better adapted to embedded systems. In particular, Boa and *thttpd* are small, lightweight, fast, and a perfect fit for embedded Linux systems.

There does not seem to be a clear set of characteristics to help you choose between Boa and *thttpd*. The only really notable difference is that Boa is distributed under the GPL, whereas *thttpd* is distributed under a BSD-like license. The sizes of the resulting binaries are, however, comparable. Both packages also support CGI scripting. Therefore, we suggest you have a look at both to decide which one you prefer.

Boa

Boa is available at *http://www.boa.org/* and is distributed under the GPL. Boa requires only a C library and can be compiled against both *glibc* and *uClibc*. For our SYSM module, we used Boa 0.94.13.

Download and extract Boa in your *${PRJROOT}/sysapps* directory. With the package extracted, move to the appropriate directory:

```
$ cd ${PRJROOT}/sysapps/boa-0.94.13/src
```

Configure and compile Boa:

```
$ ac_cv_func_setvbuf_reversed=no CC=arm-linux-gcc ./configure \
> --host=$TARGET
$ make
```

The compilation time is short. When linked against either *uClibc* or *glibc* and stripped, the resulting binary is 60 KB in size, at least for the toolchain version used by one of the authors.

Once the binary is ready, copy it to your target's root filesystem and strip it:

```
$ cp boa ${PRJROOT}/rootfs/usr/sbin
$ arm-linux-strip ${PRJROOT}/rootfs/usr/sbin/boa
```

For Boa to run, it needs a *boa* subdirectory in the target's */etc* directory and a configuration file in the new */etc/boa* directory. Create Boa's directory and copy the sample configuration file to it:

```
$ mkdir -p ${PRJROOT}/rootfs/etc/boa
$ cp ../boa.conf ${PRJROOT}/rootfs/etc/boa
```

At runtime, Boa will need a user account to run. This user account is specified in the *boa.conf* file. Edit this file, as well as your target's */etc/passwd* and */etc/groups* files, to add a user for Boa. Boa also needs a */var/log/boa* directory on your target's root filesystem to log accesses and errors:

```
$ mkdir -p ${PRJROOT}/rootfs/var/log/boa
```

Remember that logfiles can be a problem in an embedded system if their growth is not restricted. Having a script that runs periodically to clean out such files is a simple way to ensure they don't use up the available storage space.

When running, Boa finds its web content from the target's */var/www* directory. This is where you should put any HTML files, including *index.html*. Create the directory and copy your content to it:

```
$ mkdir -p ${PRJROOT}/rootfs/var/www
$ cp ... ${PRJROOT}/rootfs/var/www
```

Finally, add a line in your target's */etc/inittab* for Boa. On our SYSM module, for example, here is the line we added:

```
::respawn:/usr/sbin/boa
```

For more information on how to use Boa, see the documentation included in the Boa package and on the project's website.

thttpd

thttpd is available at *http://www.acme.com/software/thttpd/* and is distributed under a BSD-like license. In addition to the C library, *thttpd* also depends on the cryptography library (*libcrypt*). Download and extract *thttpd* in your *${PRJROOT}/sysapps* directory. The current version is 2.25b. Move to the package's directory for the rest of the instructions:

```
$ cd ${PRJROOT}/sysapps/thttpd-2.25b
```

Now, configure and compile *thttpd*:

```
$ CC=arm-linux-gcc ./configure --host=$TARGET
$ make
```

The compilation ends quickly. When linked against *uClibc* and stripped, the resulting binary is 72 KB in size. When linked against *glibc* and stripped, the resulting binary is 73 KB.

Copy the resulting binary to the target's root filesystem and strip it:

```
$ cp thttpd ${PRJROOT}/rootfs/usr/sbin
$ arm-linux-strip ${PRJROOT}/rootfs/usr/sbin/thttpd
```

Unlike Boa, you can configure *thttpd* either using a configuration file or by passing the appropriate command-line options. Use the -C option to provide a configuration file to *thttpd*. A sample configuration file is provided in *contrib/redhat-rpm/thttpd.conf*. If you wish to use a configuration file, edit this sample file to fit your target's configuration after copying it to your target's root filesystem:

```
$ cp contrib/redhat-rpm/thttpd.conf ${PRJROOT}/rootfs/etc
```

Like Boa, *thttpd* operates with a special user account, the nobody account, by default. Create this account using the procedures outlined earlier, or set *thttpd* to use an account of your choice. The configuration file copied earlier specifies the use of the httpd user. It also identifies the target's */home/httpd/html* directory as the location for source HTML files:

```
$ mkdir -p ${PRJROOT}/rootfs/home/httpd/html
```

Finally, edit your target's */etc/inittab* file. Here is the line we added for *thttpd* in our SYSM module's *inittab*:

```
::respawn:/usr/sbin/thttpd -C /etc/thttpd.conf
```

For more information on how to install and run *thttpd*, see the manpage included in the package and the project's website.

A Word on Apache

Apache is available from *http://www.apache.org/* and is distributed under the Apache license.[||] As we said earlier, Apache does not lend itself well to cross-compiling. If you are not deterred by this warning and are still interested in attempting to cross-compile Apache, have a look at the procedure outlined by David McCreedy in his posting to the Apache development mailing list: *http://hypermail.linklord.com/new-httpd/2000/May/0175.html*. If you succeed, you'll probably want to take peek at *Apache: The Definitive Guide* by Ben Laurie and Peter Laurie (O'Reilly) for more information regarding the configuration and use of Apache.

Dynamically Generated Web Content

Since the most common use for an HTTP server on an embedded system is providing a graphical management interface, your embedded system would most likely make use of dynamically generated web pages.

With the exception of Apache, none of the web servers mentioned earlier provides any internal scripting engine or plugin interface that would allow creation of dynamic web content, at least by themselves. Not all is lost, however, because all of them definitely do support the standard CGI interface that is used to delegate this task to some external program.

The idea behind CGI is a very simple and a very powerful one: when the client web browser requests a certain URL from the web server, the server, according to some internal logic, will locate a program in the target filesystem and run it, providing some needed information (such as request headers) in environment variables. The CGI program will then compute whatever dynamic page content its programmer had in mind,

---

[||] This license is similar to the BSD license. See the *LICENSE* file included with the package for the complete licensing details.

complete with HTTP headers, and write this to its standard output, which the web server in turn will send happily to the user.

Through the CGI interface, therefore, creating dynamic web content boils down to writing the dynamic web page-generating program itself and configuring the web server to run that program in response to certain URL requests.

Using PHP As a CGI Engine

While somewhat unorthodox, one of the authors has had very good results supporting the generation of dynamic web pages for embedded systems using the interpreter of the PHP scripting language, which supports a mode in which it is run as a CGI program by a web server.

For more information about doing this, see *http://www.php.net/manual/en/install.unix.commandline.php*.

While the science and art of writing CGI programs is a general topic which lies outside the scope of this book, the configuration of web servers to run CGI programs is a less general matter.

For Boa, add the `ScriptAlias` directive to map a URL path to the directory containing CGI programs:

```
ScriptAlias /cgi-bin/ /usr/local/boa/cgi-bin/
```

For *thttpd*, you can specify a pattern that when matched by *thttpd* in a URL request will cause it to run the specified file rather than send its content to the client. You can use either the *-c* command-line option, the `cgipat` keyword in the thttpd configuration file, or the `CGI_PATTERN` build-time define option in the *thttpd* source code's *config.h* file:

```
thttpd ... -c /cgi-bin/*
```

The pattern is a simple shell-style filename pattern. You can use * to match any string not including a slash, or ** to match any string including slashes, or ? to match any single character. You can also use multiple patterns separated by |. The patterns get checked against the filename part of the incoming URL. Don't forget to quote any wildcard characters so that the shell doesn't mess with them.

With both *thttpd* and Boa, and indeed with any web server, you also need to make sure that your CGI program file permissions allow the user running the web server to execute it.

Provisioning

One of the most important aspects of building embedded systems is provisioning adequate resources to each of the system services and prioritizing the access to these resources. This is not different with Linux and network services, such as those described earlier.

Indeed, choosing packages whose resource consumption and footprint match those of the typical embedded device was one of the major considerations behind describing certain implementations and not others in this chapter.

Unfortunately, describing the resources required for each of these services in anything but the most general terms (other than the executable sizes), without specific details about networking hardware, service usage, and other important factors, is an extremely difficult and risky endeavor.

Keep in mind that none of the packages described is a heavy memory consumer, even in embedded systems terms. Using the early allocation and locking the memory of other real-time-critical tasks using the mlockall() system call would guarantee that even an occasional non typical burst will not harm the system as a whole—even if a network service will be temporarily rendered unresponsive due to memory constraints—so long as it will keep running and return to normal operation once this abnormal peak usage has ended. Using a software watchdog, such as the *init* program's respawn directive, is a good safety measure in this regard.

Regarding CPU consumption, network services such as those described in this chapter tend to be I/O rather then CPU-bound. Thus, their CPU consumption tends to be characterized by periods of inactivity followed by bursts of activity as incoming network traffic requires processing, parsing of protocols, and work performed as a result of the former.

The Linux kernel scheduler implementation ,up until Linux version 2.6.22.1, allots extra "priority points" to tasks which are I/O bound, thus allowing them to run past their fair share of CPU time in order to complete a pending I/O transaction, as these are typically short.

 In Linux version 2.6.23, a new scheduler was introduced, dubbed completely Fair Scheduler, which only takes into account the latency of the task, regardless of whether it is I/O bound.

However, the generic network packages presented in this chapter have not been written with real-time requirements in mind, and so running them under any scheduling domain other than SCHED_NORMAL (called SCHED_OTHER in POSIX) is ill-advised. Bursts of CPU activity during peak usage may very well starve any lower-priority task for a long time if the scheduling domain allows it to. Therefore, using the "nice" command to set a priority under the SCHED_NORMAL scheduling command for these applications is recommended instead.

Real-time tasks should be scheduled using either the SCHED_FIFO or SCHED_RR scheduling domain. Since such tasks always have higher priority with regard to scheduling than any SCHED_NORMAL task, the worst-case scenario would then be that our network services would be starved during peak workloads by the real-time tasks, but not the other way around.

This may render our network-embedded device nonresponsive to management functions, such as a command-line interface accessed via SSH or a web interface. However, at least a web GUI user repeatedly clicking the browser Reload button will not cause our system to lose important real-time deadlines due to CPU bursts of the CGI program that generates the management interface web pages.

The most problematic application is the NET-SNMP agent. The SNMP MIB wire protocol parsing and assembling, as well as the context switches, copying, and lock operations involved in acquiring SNMP MIB information from the Linux kernel may amount to a significant overhead if many repeated queries for many MIBs are performed in short succession.

As an example, repeatedly reading the network interface usage counter and routing tables of a busy router in short period of time may require significant CPU resources, despite the mitigation factors in both the Linux kernel and the SNMP daemon itself.

On the other hand, we would not like our SNMP agent to linger at the end of the scheduler run queue while it is needed to report a critical condition of the system via the SNMP protocol trap mechanism. Finding the correct priority can be a delicate balancing act.

Except for logfiles, which should be taken care of by log rotating programs and dedicated RAM backed filesystems, the network services described in this chapter do not normally raise any significant concerns regarding filesystem and storage usage.

 The BusyBox suite comes with a nifty little applet called `logrotate`, which can be used to trim old logfiles.

CHAPTER 11
Debugging Tools

Michael Boerner

In this chapter, we will discuss the installation and use of software debugging tools in the development of embedded Linux systems. We will discuss several applications—including the classic GDB and the spiffier Eclipse with its graphical interface—along with tracing applications, system behavior monitors, performance analysis, and memory debugging. We will finish with a brief review of some of the hardware tools often used in developing embedded Linux systems. Because the operating system on the target makes little difference in the way the hardware debugging tools are used, we won't discuss how to use them. However, we will discuss ways that you can use hardware tools to facilitate debugging software running in your embedded Linux system.

> Most of the packages discussed in this chapter were not developed for cross-platform work. Many of them have *Makefiles* and sample code designed to test the tools to make sure they are working. These are likely to generate a severe problem, such as a segmentation fault on a target system, except in the unlikely situations where you are developing on your target board or have a binary-compatible host. It's hard to tell whether the binary is actually broken for the tool you are using, or whether the tests simply don't understand that there is a difference between the host and target. The solution is to allow the build process to generate the test suite, if there is one, but then remember to copy it to your target and run it there.

To best use the tools discussed in this chapter, the authors strongly recommend using an NFS-mounted root filesystem for your target. In essence, an NFS-mounted root filesystem simplifies the updating and debugging process and therefore reduces development time. Its primary advantage is that you can rapidly update your software once you've identified and corrected a bug. In turn, this speeds up debugging because you can continue debugging the updated software much sooner than if you had to transfer the updated binary manually to your target first. In addition, NFS allows performance data generated on the target to be available immediately on the host.

This chapter will cover the most important free and open source debugging tools for Linux, but it certainly is not exhaustive. A great diversity and variety exists among these tools, many of which are simply modifications or tools built on top of the ones we discuss. Consequently, the material covered in this chapter should help you make the best use of any additional Linux debugging tools you may find on the Web or in your distribution. Among the debugging tools we do not discuss are all the tools used for kernel debugging. If you need to debug a kernel, have a look at Chapter 4 of *Linux Device Drivers* by Jonathan Corbet et al. (O'Reilly).

 Several significant changes have occurred in the embedded Linux world since the first edition of this book was published. Principally among these has been the proliferation of target processors, along with the decline of some processors, as well as the emergence of powerful software development tools. For example, the author of the first edition relied on a PPC-based target board, whereas the authors of the second edition used a Gumstix (*http://www.gumstix.com*) board based on the Intel XScale processor family. Although PPC is still available, the XScale boards are more widely available and generally cheaper for the average hobbyist and developer.

The implication of the dynamism is that any over-reliance on one particular processor or software package would call the longevity of this chapter into question. Therefore, the author has chosen to discuss techniques and approaches that should apply to all processors, and to more fully explore foundational tools, such as GDB, upon which higher-level tools are often built.

Eclipse

One of the most fundamental changes in embedded Linux has been the advent of the award-winning development platform, Eclipse (*http://www.eclipse.com*). IBM originally developed the foundations of the open source Eclipse as a follow-on to another successful but proprietary IDE called Visual Age, but Eclipse has now been spun off and is run by an independent foundation.

In truth, Eclipse is more of a platform than a monolithic IDE. The advantage of a modular system like Eclipse is that any number of problems can be addressed by simply developing or acquiring the appropriate plug-ins. Although Eclipse is most often associated with Java, a set of plug-ins gives much of the benefits of Java Development Tools (JDT) to the C/C++ developer, namely the C/C++ Development Tools (CDT). Although not as mature as the JDT, the CDT is very capable and is closing the gap quickly. This is due primarily to the efforts of third-party vendors that have taken advantage of the modular nature of Eclipse and have developed plug-ins of their own to support their products.

Eclipse supports many features that improve the embedded system development process for both single-developer and team development efforts, notably the use of revision control and centralized repository support via native support for CVS repositories. Unlike broad audience applications such as word processors, embedded application development is historically done by a single engineer or a small team of developers who divide different aspects of the project among themselves. This isolation all too often makes it easy to bypass the use of revision control and repositories—but don't. As many other authors can attest, revision control will save you one day, and you will be glad of it.

All these tools are well and good, but without the ability to generate binaries that run on the target, we are essentially just wasting paper and ink discussing Eclipse. Obviously, it is necessary to make Eclipse support different processors and boards with customized toolchains. The process of customization depends on which toolchain is used and how it is packaged. In an admittedly brief survey, the author found that some processor/target board vendors provided Eclipse plug-ins for their toolchains, others relied on GNU toolchains such as GNU/ARM (*http://www.gnuarm.com*), and still others provided customized toolchains for each revision of each design of target board. The type of toolchain and the condition of its development determine how easy it makes embedded systems development. The best case is that you use a plug-in and off you go. In the worst case, you have to manually tell the build tools where to find the required utilities. Either way, it is just a matter of knowing how your toolchain works and how to modify the project preferences as needed.

If a plug-in for your toolchain is not available and you plan to use the same toolchain regularly, or if you are working with a group of developers who need to be doing all the same things, it's worthwhile creating your own plug-in. All you need is a modicum of Java skills. There are tutorials on how to build a plug-in and lots of books on the subject. If you do, be kind and share the plug-in with everyone else.

One major advantage JDT had over CDT was the JUnit project, which facilitated the development of automated unit testing suites. As we all know, regular unit testing is critical for rapid development, because it substantially improves the reliability of software and generally improves its quality by indirectly enforcing the "first do no harm" approach to software development. With the advent of projects such as C++ Unit Testing Easier (CUTE), many of the greatest weaknesses in C and C++ K have been addressed, but there is still room for improvement.

By this time, you should see that Eclipse/CDT is an extremely flexible and valuable tool for embedded systems development. Now for the bad news. Like almost every other Java application, Eclipse is a resource hog, and if you are not careful, you could retire from the field while waiting for it to launch and operate. Among the factors controlling Eclipse's efficiency are the resources on the system; the version and flavor of JVM you are using; and the distance between the source repository, development host, and target host. Although using Eclipse can be very worthwhile, you should take the time to become familiar with your application and do some performance tuning.

Many functions and capabilities that you get with a complete install of Eclipse are not needed and add substantially to the launch and compile times. Other "features" are annoying and cause no end of confusion and frustration.

The bottom line is that if you are unfamiliar with Eclipse, you will have a learning curve. If you are developing a small project completely alone, you can use CVS independently, and there are other ways to approach the unit testing issue, so you might consider skipping Eclipse.

However, given the rapid rise and seeming dominance of Eclipse, if you want a career in embedded system development, you will need learn how to configure and use it sometime. And there's no time like the present. Luckily, there are any number of resources available to you, from the printed page to online sites and tutorials as well as forums. Unfortunately, the very flexibility of Eclipse makes it difficult to discuss any further, and so we'll stop here.

Debugging Applications with gdb

The *GNU debugger* (GDB) is the symbolic debugger (started in 1986 by Richard Stallman) of the GNU project and is arguably the most important debugging tool for any Linux system. GDB has been available for long enough that many non-Linux embedded systems already use it in conjunction with what is known as GDB stubs to debug a target remotely. GDB has evolved in several ways since the publication of the first edition of this book, most notably the ability to handle target core files has been integrated into its functionality.[*] Because the Linux kernel implements the `ptrace()` system call, however, you don't need GDB stubs to debug embedded applications remotely. Instead, a GDB server is provided with the GDB package. This server is a very small application that runs on the target and executes the commands it receives from the GDB debugger running on the host. Hence, any application can be debugged on the target without having the GDB debugger actually running on the target. This is very important because, as we shall see, the actual *gdb* binary is fairly large.

This section will discuss the installation and use of GDB in a host/target configuration, not the actual use of GDB to debug an application. To learn how to set breakpoints, view variables, and view backtraces, for example, read one of the books or manuals that discusses the use of GDB. In particular, have a look at Chapter 21 of Matthias Dalheimer and Matt Welsh's *Running Linux*, Fifth Edition (O'Reilly) and the GDB manual, which is available both within the GDB package and online at *http://www.gnu.org/manual*.

---

[*] GDB stubs are a set of hooks and handlers placed in a target's firmware or operating system kernel to allow interaction with a remote debugger. The GDB manual explains the use of GDB stubs.

Building and Installing gdb Components

The GDB package is available at *ftp://ftp.gnu.org/gnu/gdb* under the terms of the GPL. Download and extract the GDB package in your *${PRJROOT}/debug* directory. For our test module, for example, we used GDB version 6.6. As with the other GNU toolset components described in previous chapters, it is preferable not to use the package's directory to build the actual debugger. Instead, create a build directory, move to it, and build GDB as follows:

```
$ mkdir ${PRJROOT}/debug/build-gdb
$ cd ${PRJROOT}/debug/build-gdb
$ ../gdb-6.6.xx/configure --target=$TARGET --prefix=${PREFIX}
$ make
$ make install
```

These commands build the GDB debugger to handle target applications. As with other GNU toolset components, the name of the binary depends on the target. For our test module, for example, the debugger is *architecture-linux-gdb*. This binary and the other debugger files are installed within the *$PREFIX* directory. The build process proper takes only a few minutes on my hardware, and the binary generated is fairly large. For a PPC target, for example, the stripped binary is 4 MB in size when linked dynamically. This is why the *gdb* binary can't be used as-is on the target and the GDB server is used instead.

We didn't build the GDB server until now because it has to be cross-compiled for the target using the appropriate tools. To do so, create a directory to build the GDB server, move to it, and build the GDB server:

```
$ mkdir ${PRJROOT}/debug/build-gdbserver
$ cd ${PRJROOT}/debug/build-gdbserver
$ chmod +x ../gdb-6.6/gdb/gdbserver/configure
$ CC=powerpc-linux-gcc ../gdb-6.6/gdb/gdbserver/configure \
> --host=$TARGET --prefix=${TARGET_PREFIX}
$ make
$ make install
```

The GDB server binary, *gdbserver*, has now been installed in your *${TARGET_PRE FIX}/bin* directory. Compared to *gdb*, the size of *gdbserver* is much more palatable.

Once built, copy *gdbserver* to your target's root filesystem:

```
$ cp ${TARGET_PREFIX}/bin/gdbserver ${PRJROOT}/rootfs/usr/bin
```

There are no additional steps required to configure the use of the GDB server on your target. The next section will cover its use.

Using the gdb Components to Debug Target Applications

Before you can debug an application using GDB, you need to compile your application using the appropriate flags. Mainly, you need to add the *-g* option to the *gcc* command line. This option adds the debugging information to the object files generated by the compiler. To add even more debugging information, use the *-ggdb* option. The final binary's size will grow, sometimes substantially, because the required debugging information will be embedded within the binary. But you can still use a stripped binary on your target, assuming you have the original unstripped version with the debugging information on your host. To do so, build your application on your host with complete debugging information. Copy the resulting binary to your target's root filesystem and use *strip* to reduce the size of the binary you just copied by removing all symbolic information, including debugging information. On the target, use the stripped binary with *gdbserver*. On the host, use the original unstripped binary with *gdb*. Although the two *gdb* components use different binary images, the target *gdb* running on the host is able to find and use the appropriate debugging symbols for your application, because it has access to the unstripped binary.

Here are the relevant portions that are required in a *Makefile*:

```
...
DEBUG      = -g
CFLAGS     = -O2 -Wall $(DEBUG)
...
```

Although *gcc* allows us to use both the *-g* and *-O* options at the same time, it is often preferable not to use the *-O* option when generating a binary for debugging, because the optimized binary may contain some subtle differences from your application's original source code. For instance, some unused variables may not be incorporated into the binary, and the sequence of instructions actually executed in the binary may differ in order from those contained in your original source code.

There are two ways for the GDB server running on the target to communicate with the GDB debugger running on the host: using a crossover serial link or a TCP/IP connection. Although these communication interfaces differ in many respects, the syntax of the commands you need to issue is very similar. Starting a debug session using a GDB server involves two steps: starting the GDB server on the target and connecting to it from the GDB debugger on the host.

Once you are ready to debug your application, start the GDB server on your target with the means of communication and your application name as parameters. If your target has a configured TCP/IP interface available, you can start the GDB server and configure it to run over TCP/IP:

```
# gdbserver
     host_ip_address:2345 application
```

For example:

```
# gdbserver 192.168.172.50:2345 command-daemon
```

In this example, the host's IP address is 192.168.172.50 and the port number used locally to listen to GDB connections is 2345. Note that the protocol used by GDB to communicate between the host and the target doesn't include any form of authentication or security. Therefore, we don't recommend that you debug applications in this way over unsecured channels, such as the public Internet, but if you must, you may want to consider using SSH port forwarding to encrypt the GDB session. *SSH, The Secure Shell: The Definitive Guide* by Daniel Barrett and Richard Silverman (O'Reilly) explains how to implement SSH port forwarding.

As mentioned earlier, the *command-daemon* being passed to *gdbserver* can be a stripped copy of the original *command-daemon* built on the host.

If you are using a serial link to debug your target, use the following command line on that target:

```
# gdbserver /dev/ttyS0 command-daemon
```

In this example, the target's serial link to the host is the first serial port, */dev/ttyS0*.

After the GDB server is started on the target, you can connect to it from the GDB debugger on the host using the *target remote* command. If you are connected to the target using a TCP/IP network, use the following command:

```
$ architecture-linux-gdb command-daemon
(gdb) target remote 192.168.172.10:2345
Remote debugging using 192.168.172.10:2345
0x10000074 in _start (  )
```

In this case, the target is located at IP 192.168.172.10, and the port number specified is the same one we used earlier to start the GDB server on the target. Unlike the GDB server on the target, the *command-daemon* used here has to be the unstripped copy of the binary. Otherwise, you will have no debugging information and GDB will be of little use.

If the program exits on the target or is restarted, you do not need to restart GDB on the host. Just reissue the *target remote* command after *gdbserver* is restarted on the target.

If your host is connected to your target through a serial link, use the following command, specifying the target's serial port in the *target remote*:

```
$ architecture-linux-gdb progname
(gdb) target remote /dev/ttyS0
Remote debugging using /dev/ttyS0
0x10000074 in _start (  )
```

Although this example uses */dev/ttyS0* on both the target and the host, this is only a coincidence. The target and the host can use different serial ports to link to each other. The device to specify in each command is the local serial port where the serial cable is connected.

With the target and the host connected, you can now set breakpoints and do anything you would normally do in a symbolic debugger.

A few GDB commands are likely to be particularly useful when debugging an embedded target. Here are some of them and summaries of their purposes:

file

Sets the filename of the binary being debugged. Debug symbols are loaded from that file.

dir

Adds a directory to the search path for the application's source code files.

target

Sets the parameters for connecting to the remote target, as we did earlier. This is actually not a single command, but rather a complete set of commands. Use *help target* for more details.

set remotebaud

Sets the speed of the serial port when debugging remote applications through a serial cable.

set solib-absolute-prefix

Sets the path for finding the shared libraries used with the binary being debugged.

The last command is likely to be the most useful when your binaries are linked dynamically. Although the binary running on your target finds its shared libraries starting from / (the root directory), the GDB running on the host doesn't know how to locate these shared libraries. You need to use the following command to tell GDB where to find the correct target libraries on the host:

```
(gdb) set solib-absolute-prefix ../../tools/architecture-linux/
```

Unlike the normal shell, the *gdb* command line doesn't recognize environment variables such as ${TARGET_PREFIX}. Hence, the complete path must be provided. In this case, the path is provided relative to the directory where GDB is running, but we could use an absolute path, too.

If you want to have GDB execute a number of commands each time it starts, you may want to use a *.gdbinit* file. For an explanation of the file, have a look at the "Command files" subsection in the "Canned Sequences of Commands" section of the GDB manual.

To get information regarding the use of the various debugger commands, you can use the *help* command within the GDB environment or look in the GDB manual.

Interfacing with a Graphical Frontend

In the years since the first edition of this book, the growth of excellent IDEs and other GUI interfaces has in many ways made using the command line passé. They are so pervasive that many young developers, and even a large portion of seasoned ones, have never done any significant development outside the warm confines of a GUI. Fortunately, there are quite a few graphical interfaces that hide much of GDB's complexity by providing user-friendly mechanisms for setting breakpoints, viewing variables, and tending to other common debugging tasks. The most common interface used today is Eclipse, but other seasoned examples include DDD (*http://www.gnu.org/software/*

ddd) and KDevelop. Much like your host's debugger, your favorite debugging interface can very likely use the cross-platform GDB we built earlier for your target to do the actual grunt work.

The widespread support among GUIs for GDB should not be taken as a justification for ignoring the command line, especially in embedded development. The wise developer learns how the command line works, because many GUIs cannot handle all of the available capabilities.

Each frontend has its own way for letting you specify the name of the debugger binary. Have a look at your frontend's documentation for this information. Using the example of our test module, we would need to configure the frontend to use the *architecture-linux-gdb* debugger.

Tracing

Symbolic debugging is fine for finding and correcting program errors. However, it offers little help in finding any sort of problem that involves an application's interaction with other applications or with the kernel. These sorts of behavioral problems necessitate tracing the interactions between your application and other software components.

The simplest form of tracing is monitoring the interactions between a single application and the Linux kernel. This allows you to easily observe any problems that result from the passing of parameters or the wrong sequence of system calls.

Observing a single process in isolation is, however, not always sufficient. If you are attempting to debug interprocess synchronization problems or time-sensitive issues, for example, you will need a system-wide tracing mechanism that provides you with the exact sequence and timing of events that occur throughout the system. For instance, when trying to understand why the Mars Pathfinder constantly rebooted while on Mars, the Jet Propulsion Laboratory engineers resorted to a system tracing tool for the VxWorks operating system.[†]

Both single-process tracing and system tracing are available in Linux. The following sections will discuss each one.

Single-Process Tracing

The main tool for tracing a single process is *strace*. *strace* uses the `ptrace()` system call to intercept all system calls made by an application. Hence, it can extract all the system call information and display it in a human-readable format for you to analyze. Because *strace* is a widely used Linux tool, we will not explain how to use it, just how to install

---

[†] For a very informative and entertaining account of what happened to the Mars Pathfinder on Mars, read Glenn Reeves's account at *http://research.microsoft.com/~mbj/Mars_Pathfinder/Authoritative_Account.html*. Mr. Reeves was the lead developer for the Mars Pathfinder software.

it for your target. The use of *strace* on the target is identical to its use on a normal Linux workstation. For details on using *strace*, see Chapter 21 of *Running Linux, Fifth Edition*.

strace is available at *http://www.sourceforge.net/projects/strace* under a BSD license. For our target application, we used *strace* version 4.5. Download the package and extract it in your *${PRJROOT}/debug* directory. Move to the package's directory, and then configure and build *strace*:

```
$ cd ${PRJROOT}/debug/strace-4.5
$ architecture-linux-gcc ./configure --host=$TARGET
$ make
```

If you wish to statically link against uClibc, add `LDFLAGS="-static"` to the *make* command line. Because *strace* uses NSS, you need to use a special command line if you wish to link it statically to glibc, as we did previously for other packages:

```
$ make \
> LDLIBS="-static -Wl --start-group -lc -lnss_files -lnss_dns \
> -lresolv -Wl --end-group"
```

When linked against glibc and stripped, *strace* is 145 KB in size if linked dynamically and 605 KB if linked statically. When linked against uClibc and stripped, *strace* is 140 KB in size if linked dynamically and 170 KB if linked statically.

After compiling the binary, copy it to your target's root filesystem:

```
$ cp strace ${PRJROOT}/rootfs/usr/sbin
```

No additional steps are required to configure *strace* for use on the target.

System Tracing

One of the main system tracing utilities available for Linux is the next generation Linux Trace Toolkit (LTTng) created and maintained by Mathieu Desnoyers (also author of the kernel markers infrastructure), inspired by Karim Yaghmour's original LTT tool. LTTng is available under the GPL, along with various other tools and utilities such as the LTTV viewer. You can download LTTng and sign up to the user or developer mailing lists for these tools at the LTTng website: *http://ltt.polymtl.ca*.

In contrast to other tracing utilities, such as *strace*, LTTng does not use the `ptrace()` mechanism to intercept applications' behaviors. Instead, it includes a kernel patch that instruments key kernel subsystems. The data generated by this instrumentation is then collected by the trace subsystem and forwarded to a trace daemon to be written to disk. The entire process has very little impact on the system's behavior and performance. Extensive tests have shown that the tracing infrastructure has marginal impact when not in use, and an impact lower than 2.5 percent under some of the most stressful conditions.

In addition to reconstructing the system's behavior using the data generated during a trace run, the user utilities provided with LTTng allow you to extract performance data regarding the system's behavior during the trace interval. Here's a list of some of the tasks for which LTTng can be used:

- Debugging interprocess synchronization problems
- Understanding the interaction between your application, the other applications in the system, and the kernel
- Measuring the time it takes for the kernel to service your application's requests
- Measuring the time your application spends waiting because other processes have a higher priority
- Measuring the time it takes for effects of interrupts to propagate throughout the system
- Understanding the exact reaction the system has to outside input

To achieve this, LTTng's operation is subdivided into four components:

- The kernel instrumentation that generates the events being traced (runs on target)
- The tracing subsystem that collects the data generated by the kernel instrumentation into a single buffer (runs on target)
- The trace daemon that writes the tracing subsystem's buffers to disk (runs on target)
- The visualization tool that post-processes the system trace and displays it in a human-readable form (runs on target and host)

With the advent of LTTng, the version numbering has become somewhat confusing. So, be diligent when reviewing the version comparison chart on the LTTng website, which compares the compatibility of the various components, support modules, kernel revisions, and processors that make up an entire system.

Historically, the first two software components are implemented as a kernel patch, and the last two are separate user space tools. Although the first three software components must run on the target, the last one—the visualization tool—can run on the host.

In early versions of LTT, the tracing subsystem was accessed from user space as a device through the appropriate /dev entries. But later versions have dropped this abstraction, following the recommendations of the kernel developers. The next generation of LTT, called LTTng, has implemented several improvements, along with support for many more target processors and capabilities.

A very helpful feature of LTTng is it detects and handles traces that have different byte ordering. This allows you to generate and read traces on systems with incompatible byte orderings. The traces generated for a PPC-based test module, for example, can be read transparently on an x86 host.

In addition to tracing a predefined set of events, LTTng enables you to create and log your own custom events from both user space and kernel space. Have a look at the *Examples* directory in the package for practical examples of such custom events.

The change in complexity and nuance of the LTTng over the LTT tool was so profound that a discussion of its installation and use is simply beyond the scope of a single chapter. We recommend that you join the mailing list and contact the maintainers of the code to fully utilize this powerful and versatile tool. Further, there are several white papers available that will provide substantially more detail than we could include in this chapter.

Performance Analysis

In order to make optimal use of the resources of your target board and maximize the performance of your application on that board, it is crucial to obtain an in-depth understanding of the capabilities of your target board, the operating system you are using, and detailed data about the performance of your application and operating system on your target board. For example, some boards have lots of registers and others have relatively few. This has a performance impact on the operating system, which has to deal with registers during context switches and function calls. If your application has lots of functions that put heavy demands on the registers, you might find your compiler changing your programs and operations without your knowledge, affecting performance and behavior. It is beyond the scope of this book to fully explore performance analysis, but in the following sections we will touch on some of the highlights, including process profiling, code coverage, system profiling, kernel profiling, and measuring interrupt latency.

Process Profiling

The essence of profiling is gathering and analyzing the actual behavior of the machine code created by the compiler. The machine code generated from source code will differ depending on the compiler suite used, the options chosen for the compiler and linker, and the architecture of the target. The information process profiling gathers includes the time spent in a given function, the time spent entering and leaving a function, how much time a called function spends on behalf of the calling function, and how much time is spent in each of its children, if any.

In Linux, a single process is usually profiled using a combination of special compiler options and the *gprof* utility. Basically, source files are compiled with a compiler option (*-pg* in the case of *gcc* and most other traditional Unix compilers) that results in profiling data being written to file upon the application's exit. You can then run the generated data through *gprof*, which displays a call graph showing profiling data. The use of *gprof* and the interpretation of its output are standard Unix and Linux lore and are thoroughly covered in the GNU *gprof* manual. We will cover cross-platform aspects here.

First, you must ensure that your applications' Makefiles include appropriate compiler and linker options, either manually or through the build process in an IDE such as

Eclipse. Here are the portions of the *Makefile* provided earlier that must be changed to build a program that will generate profiling data:

```
CFLAGS        = -Wall -pg
...
LDFLAGS       = -pg
```

The *-pg* option appears for the compiler and the linker. As a compiler option, *-pg* tells the compiler to include the code for generating the performance data into the object code. As a linker option, it tells the linker to link the special version of the object file for profiling.

Also note we aren't using the -O2 compiler optimization option. Omitting the option ensures that the application generated executes exactly the same way as we specified in the source file. We can then measure the performance of our own algorithms instead of measuring those optimized by the compiler.

Once your application has been recompiled, copy it to your target and run it. The program must run for quite a while to generate meaningful results. Provide your application with as wide a range of input as you can to exercise as much of its code as possible. Upon the application's exit, a *gmon.out* output file is generated with the profiling data. This file is cross-platform readable, and you can therefore use your host's *gprof* to analyze it. After having copied the *gmon.out* file back to your application's source directory, use *gprof* to retrieve the call graph profile data:

```
$ gprof command-daemon
```

This command prints the call graph profile data to the standard output. Redirect this output using the > operator to a file if you like. You don't need to specify the *gmon.out* file specifically; it is automatically loaded. For more information regarding the use of *gprof*, see the GNU *gprof* manual.

Code Coverage

In addition to identifying the time spent in the different parts of your application, it is interesting to count how many times each statement in your application is being executed. This sort of coverage analysis can bring to light code that is never called or code that is called so often that it merits special attention.

The most common way to perform coverage analysis is to use a combination of compiler options and the *gcov* utility. This functionality relies on the *gcc* library, *libgcc*, which is compiled along with the *gcc* compiler.

Versions of *gcc* earlier than 3.0 don't allow the coverage functions to be compiled into *libgcc* when they detect that a cross-compiler is being built. In a compiler of that vintage, *libgcc* doesn't include the appropriate code to generate data about code coverage. It is therefore impossible to analyze the coverage of a program built against unmodified *gcc* sources.

To circumvent the same problem in *gcc* versions earlier than 3.0, edit the *gcc-2.95.3/ gcc/libgcc2.c* file (or the equivalent file for your compiler version) and disable the following definition:

```
/* In a cross-compilation situation, default to inhibiting compilation
   of routines that use libc.  */

#if defined(CROSS_COMPILE) && !defined(inhibit_libc)
#define inhibit_libc
#endif
```

To disable the definition, add #if 0 and #endif around the code so that it looks like this:

```
/* gcc makes the assumption that we don't have glibc for the target,
   which is wrong in the case of embedded Linux. */
#if 0

/* In a cross-compilation situation, default to inhibiting compilation
   of routines that use libc.  */

#if defined(CROSS_COMPILE) && !defined(inhibit_libc)
#define inhibit_libc
#endif

#endif /* #if 0 */
```

Now recompile and reinstall *gcc*. You don't need to rebuild the bootstrap compiler, because you've already built and installed *glibc*. Build only the final compiler.

To build the code needed for coverage analysis in versions of *gcc* later than 3.0, just configure them with the - -*with-headers*= option.

Next, modify your applications' Makefiles to use the appropriate compiler options. Here are the portions of the *Makefile* that must be changed to build a program that will generate code coverage data:

```
CFLAGS      = -Wall -fprofile-arcs -ftest-coverage
```

As we did before, omit the -O optimization options when compiling the application to generate profiling data to obtain the code coverage data that corresponds exactly to your source code.

For each source file compiled, you should now have a *.bb* and *.bbg* file in the source directory. Copy the program to your target and run it as you would normally. When you run the program, a *.da* file will be generated for each source file. Unfortunately, however, the *.da* files are generated using the absolute path to the original source files. Hence, you must create a copy of this path on your target's root filesystem. Though you may not run the binary from that directory, this is where the *.da* files for your application will be placed. Our command daemon, for example, is located in */home/ karim/control-project/control-module/project/command-daemon* on our host. We had to create that complete path on our target's root filesystem so that the daemon's *.da* files would be properly created. The -*p* option of *mkdir* was quite useful in this case.

Once the program is done executing, copy the *.da* files back to your host and run *gcov*:

```
$ gcov daemon.c
 71.08% of 837 source lines executed in file daemon.c
Creating daemon.c.gcov.
```

The *.gcov* file generated contains the coverage information in a human-readable form. The *.da* files are architecture-independent, so there's no problem using the host's *gcov* to process them. For more information regarding the use of *gcov* or the output it generates, look at the *gcov* section of the *gcc* manual.

System Profiling

Linux systems always have multiple processes competing for system resources. Being able to quantify the impact each process has on the system's load is important in trying to build a balanced and responsive system. This is particularly important for embedded systems because of their limited resources and frequently critical response requirements. Such quantification is often interchangeably called performance, kernel, or system tuning. We will focus on just two of these kinds of tuning: extracting information from */proc* and using LTTng.

Basic /proc figures

The */proc* filesystem contains virtual entries, whereas the kernel provides information regarding its own internal data structures and the system in general. Some of this information, such as process times, is based on samples collected by the kernel at each clock tick. The traditional package for extracting information from the */proc* directory is procps, which includes utilities such as *ps* and *top*. The first edition of this book discussed what was then a forked development of procps; now there is essentially one version, available at *http://procps.sourceforge.com*. Further, the author felt that neither flavor lends itself well to embedded systems. Currently, in direct response to inquiries by one of this book's authors, the maintainer of the *http://procps.sourceforge.com* version states that, if these issues indeed existed, they have been resolved, as long as one uses the proper libraries and compilers and follows the instructions with the distribution. Be that as it may, for consistency, we will continue to focus on the *ps* replacement found in BusyBox, because BusyBox is so commonly available. Although it doesn't output process statistics, as the *ps* in procps does, the BusyBox version does provide you with basic information regarding the software running on your target:

```
# ps
  PID  Uid     VmSize Stat Command
    1 0          820 S    init
    2 0              S    [keventd]
    3 0              S    [kswapd]
    4 0              S    [kreclaimd]
    5 0              S    [bdflush]
    6 0              S    [kupdated]
    7 0              S    [mtdblockd]
```

```
    8  0                   S    [rpciod]
   16  0           816 S    -sh
   17  0           816 R    ps aux
```

If you find this information insufficient, you are encouraged to explore the aforementioned procps package or browse /proc manually to retrieve the information you need regarding each process.

Complete profile using LTTng

Because LTTng records crucial system information, it can extract very detailed information regarding the system's behavior. Unlike the information found in /proc, the statistics LTTng generates are not sampled. Rather, they are based on an exact accounting of the time spent by processes inside the kernel. LTTng provides two types of statistics: per-process and system. This allows a developer a level of fidelity that is either not available or much less direct than any other method.

Kernel Profiling

Sometimes the applications are not the root of performance degradation, but are rather suffering from the kernel's own performance problems. In that case, it is necessary to use the right tools to identify the reasons for the kernel's behavior.

There are quite a few tools for measuring the kernel's performance. However, most are designed for conventional computing and are not suitable for embedded applications. There remains the sample-based profiling functionality built into the kernel. This profiling system works by sampling the instruction pointer on every timer interrupt. It then increments a counter according to the instruction pointer. Over a long period of time, it is expected that the functions where the kernel spends the greatest amount of time will have a higher number of hits than other functions. Though this is a crude kernel profiling method, it is the one of the best free tools at this time for most embedded Linux systems. There are several commercial products available for embedded systems profiling, but they are outside our focus.

To activate kernel profiling, you must use the profile= boot parameter. The number you provide as a parameter sets the number of bits by which the instruction pointer is shifted to the right before being used as an index into the sample table. The smaller the number, the higher the precision of the samples, but this also necessitates more memory for the sample table. The value most often used is 2.

The sampling activity itself doesn't slow the kernel down, because it occurs only at each clock tick and because the counter to be incremented is easily obtained from the value of the instruction pointer at the time of the timer interrupt.

Once you've booted a kernel to which you passed the profile= parameter, you will find a new entry in your target's /proc directory, /proc/profile. The kernel's sample table is exported to this /proc entry.

To read the profile samples available from */proc/profile*, you must use the *readprofile* command. Version 2.0 is usually included in most Linux distributions, but for our purposes we need the source code. Therefore, we can use either version 3.0, which is available as an independent package at *http://sourceforge.net/projects/minilop*, or version 2.0, which is part of the util-linux package at *http://www.kernel.org/pub/linux/utils/util-linux*. In the following explanations, we will cover only the independent package, because util-linux includes a lot more utilities than just *readprofile*.

Download the *readprofile* package and extract it in your *${PRJROOT}/debug* directory. Move to the package's directory and compile the utility:

```
$ cd ${PRJROOT}/debug/readprofile-3.0
$ make CC=architecture-uclibc-gcc
```

To compile the utility statically, add LDFLAGS="-static" to the *make* command line. The binary generated is fairly small. When statically linked with uClibc and stripped, for example, it is 30 KB in size.

Once *readprofile* is built, copy it to your target's */usr/bin* directory:

```
$ cp readprofile ${PRJROOT}/rootfs/usr/bin
```

For *readprofile* to operate adequately, you must also copy the appropriate *System.map* kernel map file to your target's root filesystem:

```
$ cp ${PRJROOT}/images/System.map-2.6.18 ${PRJROOT}/rootfs/etc
```

Now your target root filesystem is ready. Change the kernel boot parameters and add the profile=2 boot parameter. After the system boots, you can run *readprofile*:

```
# readprofile -m /etc/System.map-2.6.18 > profile.out
```

The resulting *profile.out* file contains the profiling information in text form. At any time, you can erase the sample table collected on your target by writing to your target's */proc/profile*:[‡]

```
# echo > /proc/profile
```

When done profiling, copy the *profile.out* file back to your host and have a look at its contents:

```
$ cat profile.out
    ...
   30 _ _save_flags_ptr_end      0.3000
   10 _ _sti                     0.1250
    8 _ _flush_page_to_ram       0.1053
    7 clear_page                 0.1750
    3 copy_page                  0.0500
    1 m8xx_mask_and_ack          0.0179
    2 iopa                       0.0263
    1 map_page                   0.0089
    ...
```

[‡] It doesn't matter what you write; a blank *echo* is fine. Just the action of writing erases the profiling information.

```
     1 do_xprt_transmit              0.0010
     1 rpc_add_wait_queue            0.0035
     1 __rpc_sleep_on                 0.0016
     1 rpc_wake_up_next              0.0068
     1 __rpc_execute                  0.0013
     2 rpciod_down                   0.0043
    15 exit_devpts_fs                0.2885
 73678 total                         0.0618 0.04%
```

The left column indicates the number of samples taken at that location, followed by the name of the function where the sample was taken. The third column indicates a number that provides an approximation of the function's load, which is calculated as a ratio between the number of ticks that occurred in the function and the function's length. See the *readprofile* manpage included with the package for in-depth details about the utility's output.

Measuring Interrupt Latency

Arguably the most important metric for real-time embedded systems is the time it takes for them to respond to outside events. Failure to handle such events efficiently can cause catastrophic results.

There are ad hoc techniques for measuring a system's response time to interrupts (more commonly known as *interrupt latency* and explained in Chapter 12). These measurement techniques can be roughly divided into two categories:

Self-contained
> The system itself triggers the interrupts. To use this technique, you must connect one of your system's output pins to an interrupt-generating input pin. On a PC-based system, this is easily achieved by connecting the appropriate parallel port pins together, as is detailed in *Linux Device Drivers*. For other types of systems, this may require more elaborate setups.

Induced
> The interrupts are triggered by an outside source, such as a frequency generator, by connecting it to an interrupt-generating input pin on the target.

In the case of the self-contained method, you must write a small software driver that initiates and handles the interrupt. To initiate the interrupt, the driver does two things:

- Records the current time. This is often done using the do_gettimeofday() kernel function, which provides microsecond resolution. Alternatively, to obtain greater accuracy, you can read the machine's hardware cycles using the get_cycles() function. On Pentium-class x86 systems, for example, this function will return the content of the TSC register.

- Toggles the output bit to trigger the interrupt. On a PC-based system, just write the appropriate byte to the parallel port's data register.

The driver's interrupt handler, on the other hand, must do the following:

- Record the current time.
- Toggle the output pin.

Subtracting the time at which the interrupt was triggered from the time at which the interrupt handler is invoked gives you a figure that is very close to the actual interrupt latency. The reason this figure is not the actual interrupt latency is that you are partly measuring the time it takes for do_gettimeofday() and other software to run. Have your driver repeat the operation a number of times to quantify the variations in interrupt latency.

To get a better measure of the interrupt latency using the self-contained method, plug an oscilloscope on the output pin toggled by your driver and observe the time it takes for it to be toggled. This number should be slightly smaller than that obtained using do_gettimeofday(), because the execution of the first call to this function is not included in the oscilloscope output. To get an even better measure of the interrupt latency, remove the calls to do_gettimeofday() completely and use only the oscilloscope to measure the time between bit toggles. This is particularly easy with high-speed digital oscilloscopes that have trace recall. However, as we will discuss later, this solution costs a great deal.

Although the self-contained method is fine for simple measurements on systems that can actually trigger and handle interrupts simultaneously, the induced method is usually the most trusted way to measure interrupt latency, and is closest to the way in which interrupts are actually delivered to the system. If you have a driver that has high latency and contains code that changes the interrupt mask, for example, the interrupt driver for the self-contained method may have to wait until the high-latency driver finishes before it can even trigger interrupts. Because the delay for triggering interrupts isn't measured, the self-contained method may fail to measure the worst-case impact of the high-latency driver. The induced method, however, does not suffer from this shortcoming, because the interrupts' trigger source does not depend on the system being measured.

It's much simpler to write a software driver for the induced method than for the self-contained method. Basically, your driver has to implement an interrupt handler to toggle the state of one of the system's output pins. By plotting the system's response along with the square wave generated by the frequency generator, you can measure the exact time it takes for the system to respond to interrupts. Instead of an oscilloscope, you can use a simple counter circuit that counts the difference between the interrupt trigger and the target's response. The circuit would be reset by the interrupt trigger and would stop counting when receiving the target's response. You could also use another system whose only task is to measure the time difference between the interrupt trigger and the target's response.

However efficient the self-contained and the induced methods and their variants may be, Linux is not a real-time operating system out-of-the-box, although, as described in Chapter 12, the 2.6 kernel brings it closer to this than ever before. In Linux's standard configuration, even in version 2.6, you may observe steady interrupt latencies when the system is idle, but the response time will vary greatly whenever its processing load increases. A useful exercise is to type ls -R / on your target while conducting interrupt latency tests to increase your target's processing load and look at the flickering oscilloscope output to observe this effect on latency.

To decide whether you need more consistency and faster response times, carefully analyze your applications' requirements. If you find that interrupt latency is a critical issue, you have two options. First, measure the latency of your target under load as described earlier. If that is not adequate for your needs, try rebuilding the kernel with support for kernel interrupts and remeasure. If that is not good enough either, you will have to look through the kernel documentation for more narrowly defined optimizations or consider purchasing third-party commercial real-time Linux distributions.

Memory Debugging

Unlike desktop Linux systems, embedded Linux systems cannot afford to let applications eat up memory as they go or generate dumps because of illegal memory references. Among other things, there is no user to stop the offending applications and restart them. In developing applications for your embedded Linux system, you can employ special debugging libraries to ensure their correct behavior in terms of memory use. The following sections will discuss two such libraries: Electric Fence/DUMA and MEMWATCH.

Production systems should not include these libraries. First, both libraries substitute the C library's memory allocation functions with their own versions of these functions, which are designed for debugging, not performance. Second, both libraries are distributed under the terms of the GPL. Hence, though you can use MEMWATCH and Electric Fence/DUMA internally to test your applications, you cannot distribute them as part of your applications outside your organization unless you distribute your applications under the terms of the GPL.

Electric Fence and DUMA

Electric Fence is a library that replaces the C library's memory allocation functions, such as malloc() and free(), with equivalent functions that implement limit testing. It is, therefore, very effective at detecting out-of-bounds memory references. In essence, linking with the Electric Fence library will cause your applications to fault and dump core upon any out-of-bounds reference. By running your application within GDB, you can identify the faulty instruction immediately.

Electric Fence is still available in most distributions at the time of this writing. But its development has essentially ceased in favor of DUMA, which has all the capabilities of Electric Fence and adds several enhancements:

- It detects read violations as well as writes.

- It pinpoints the exact instruction that causes an error.

- It overloads all standard memory allocation functions, such as `malloc()`, `calloc()`, `memalign()`, `strdup()`, and the C++ `new` and `new[]` operators, along with their deallocation counterparts functions, such as `free()`, and the `delete` and `delete[]` operators.

- Utilizing the memory management unit of the CPU, it allocates and protects an extra memory page to detect any illegal access beyond the top of the buffer (or bottom, at the user's option).

- It stops the program at the exact instruction that requested an erroneous access to the protected memory page, allowing you to locate the defective source code in a debugger.

- It detects erroneous writes at the nonprotected end of the memory block during deallocation of the memory block.

- It detects mismatched allocation and deallocation functions; for instance, allocation with `malloc()` matched with deallocation by `delete`.

- It detects leaks: memory blocks that are not deallocated until the program exits.

- It preloads its library on Linux (and some Unix) systems, allowing tests without the necessity of changing the source code or recompilation.

Electric Fence

As we mentioned, Electric Fence is still widely available, so we will include the discussion from the first edition for version 2.1, which the author found easier to use although the source code was a bit of a challenge. At the time of this writing, the author's Fedora 7 distribution was 2.2.2-23, and the author found that it required significant modifications before it could be compiled. This is left as an exercise for the reader.

Download the package and extract it into your *${PRJROOT}/debug* directory. Move to the package's directory for the rest of the installation:

```
$ cd ${PRJROOT}/debug/ElectricFence-2.1
```

Before you can compile Electric Fence for your target, you must edit the *page.c* source file and comment out the following code segment by adding `#if 0` and `#endif` around it:

```
#if ( !defined(sgi) && !defined(_AIX) )
extern int        sys_nerr;
extern char *     sys_errlist[ ];
#endif
```

If you do not modify the code in this way, Electric Fence fails to compile. With the code changed, compile and install Electric Fence for your target:

```
$ make CC=architecture-linux-gcc AR=architecture-linux-ar
$ make LIB_INSTALL_DIR=${TARGET_PREFIX}/lib \
> MAN_INSTALL_DIR=${TARGET_PREFIX}/man install
```

The Electric Fence library, *libefence.a*, which contains the memory allocation replacement functions, has now been installed in *${TARGET_PREFIX}/lib*. To link your applications with Electric Fence, you must add the *-lefence* option to your linker's command line. Here are the modifications we made to our command module's *Makefile*:

```
CFLAGS      = -g -Wall
...
LDFLAGS     = -lefence
```

The *-g* option is necessary if you want GDB to be able to print the line causing the problem. The Electric Fence library adds about 30 KB to your binary when compiled and stripped. After building it, copy the binary to your target for execution as you would usually.

If the program runs without core dumping—congratulations! You have managed to write a program without faulty memory accesses. But almost always, when you run the program on the target, you will get something similar to:

```
# command-daemon

Electric Fence 2.0.5 Copyright (C) 1987-1998 Bruce Perens.
Segmentation fault (core dumped)
```

You can't copy the *core* file back to the host for analysis, because it was generated on a system of a different architecture. Therefore, start the GDB server on the target and connect to it from the host using the target GDB. As an example, here's how we start our command daemon on the target for Electric Fence debugging:

```
# gdbserver
      host_ip_address:2345 command-daemon
```

And on the host we enter:

```
$ architecture-linux-gcc command-daemon
(gdb) target remote 192.168.172.10:2345
Remote debugging using 192.168.172.10:2345
0x10000074 in _start (  )
(gdb) continue
Continuing.

Program received signal SIGSEGV, Segmentation fault.
0x10000384 in main (argc=2, argv=0x7ffff794) at daemon.c:126
126              input_buf[input_index] = value_read;
```

In this case, the illegal reference was caused by an out-of-bounds write to an array at line 126 of file *daemon.c*. For more information on the use of Electric Fence, look at the ample manpage included in the package.

DUMA

The DUMA package lives at *http://duma.sourceforge.com*. It is clearly more powerful than Electric Fence, but with that power comes complexity. The author found, after experimenting with the build procedure, that it was easier and simpler to move the package to the build partition shared with the target board. Then, use the native *gcc*, *g++*, and *ar* to build the package on the target board. If you export an NFS partition to the target, DUMA is not difficult to build and does not take long. Always keep in mind that it is often a better solution to "go native" than spend hours trying to figure out why a *Makefile* or some other peculiarity of cross-compilation does not produce a binary you can port from the host to the target.

DUMA can be operated similar to Electric Fence and has its own documentation.

MEMWATCH

Like Electric Fence and DUMA, MEMWATCH replaces the usual memory allocation functions, such as `malloc()` and `free()`, with versions that keep track of allocations and deallocations. MEMWATCH is very effective at detecting memory leaks and violations, such as when you forget to free a memory region or try to free a memory region more than once. MEMWATCH isn't as efficient as Electric Fence, however, at detecting pointers that go astray. It was unable, for example, to detect the faulty array write presented in the previous section.

MEMWATCH is available on its project site at *http://www.linkdata.se/source code.html*. Download the package and extract it in your *${PRJROOT}/debug* directory.

MEMWATCH consists of a header file and a C file, both of which must be compiled with your application. To use MEMWATCH, start by copying the files to your application's source directory:

```
$ cd ${PRJROOT}/debug/memwatch-2.71
$ cp memwatch.c memwatch.h ${PRJROOT}/project/command-daemon
```

Modify the *Makefile* to add the new C file as part of the objects to compile and link. For my command daemon, for example, I used the following *Makefile* modifications:

```
CFLAGS        = -O2 -Wall -DMEMWATCH -DMW_STDIO
...
OBJS          = daemon.o memwatch.o
```

You must also add the MEMWATCH header to your source files:

```
#ifdef MEMWATCH
#include "memwatch.h"
#endif /* #ifdef MEMWATCH */
```

You can now cross-compile the binary as you normally would; there are no special installation instructions for MEMWATCH. The *memwatch.c* and *memwatch.h* files add about 30 KB to your binary, once built and stripped.

When the program runs, it generates a report on the behavior of the program, which it puts in the *memwatch.log* file in the directory where the binary runs. Here's an excerpt of the *memwatch.log* generated by the test program on the target machine:

```
============= MEMWATCH 2.71 Copyright (C) 1992-1999 Johan Lindh =============

Started at Sun Jan 11 12:55:04 1970

Modes: __STDC__ 32-bit mwDWORD==(unsigned long)
mwROUNDALLOC==4 sizeof(mwData)==32 mwDataSize==32

statistics: now collecting on a line basis
Hello world!
underflow: <5> test.c(62), 200 bytes alloc'd at <4> test.c(60)
relink: <7> test.c(66) attempting to repair MW-0x1b2c8...
relink: MW-0x1b2c8 is the head (first) allocation
relink: successful, no allocations lost
assert trap: <8> test.c(69), 1==2
breakout: MEMWATCH: assert trap: test.c(69), 1==2


Stopped at Sun Jan 11 12:58:22 1970

unfreed: <3> test.c(59), 20 bytes at 0x1b194    {FE FE FE FE FE FE FE FE FE FE F

- memwatch.log 1/89 1%
```

The unfreed line tells you which line in your source code allocated memory that was never freed later. In this case, 20 bytes are allocated at line 59 of *test.c* and are never freed.

Look at the *FAQ*, *README*, and *USING* files included in the package for more information on using MEMWATCH and the output it provides.

A Word on Hardware Tools

The first edition of this book touched on the use of hardware in debugging and noted the wealth of tools. This is no less true today. A cursory Google search on the subject produces over 36,000 hits, and by the time you read this book, it will be more. Hardware and software tools are available at costs that range from nothing to several thousands of dollars.

Board developers have realized that ease of debugging is a real asset and have made great strides to provide access to hardware and support for hardware debugging. Many boards, particularly JTAG ones, have connectors or schematics showing how to connect to the board for debugging purposes. The best place to start is your hardware vendor's website and tech support. More than likely, they have a low-cost option for supporting hardware debugging tools.

A discussion of the tools here would be hampered by the speed at which things change in embedded systems, which particularly affects debugging. For example, many of the projects and links from the first edition of this book are dead now. The first edition discussed the use of a 100 MHz oscilloscope that the author quoted as costing over a thousand dollars. As of this writing, you can buy that same scope for under $100 on eBay.

The reason for the shift in the market is that embedded applications, which used to be the poor stepchildren of desktop processors, are now are on a par with them in performance and capability. Therefore, a simple 100 MHz analog oscope will be of little use, and this obsolescence is reflected in their prices. Currently, a 1 GHz or higher-speed digital scope is required. They cost thousands of dollars today, with good-quality used equipment easily exceeding $10,000 at the time of this writing.

This does not diminish the desirability of oscilloscopes—far from it. But given the tremendous cost of truly effective diagnostic hardware, such as digital oscopes and high-performance logic analyzers, we will not discuss them further.

The first edition recommends the following books for further research: Arnold Berger's *Embedded Systems Design* (CMP Books) and Jack Ganssle's *The Art of Designing Embedded Systems* (Newnes). If you are actively involved in designing or changing your target's hardware, you are likely to also be interested in John Catsoulis's *Designing Embedded Hardware* (O'Reilly). There are numerous other excellent titles on the subject, so spend liberally. We also recommend *Programming Embedded Systems* by Michael Barr and Anthony Massa (O'Reilly).

## CHAPTER 12

Introduction to Real-Time Linux

Many developers, sometimes in open competition, have been trying to add real-time support to Linux and thereby fill the major gap in its capabilities as an embedded system. But although real-time is critical to some applications, most embedded systems can get by without it. Some programmers who assume they need real-time (for streaming media, for instance) may not need it, whereas real-time may prove valuable in industries where one wouldn't expect it, such as finance.

In this chapter, we will explain the kinds of situations where you will want real-time, define real-time requirements, and summarize how Linux can be enhanced to support those requirements. Chapters 13 and 14 will describe two particular real-time solutions.

What Is Real-Time Processing?

The canonical definition of a real-time system is as follows: "A real-time system is one in which the correctness of the computations not only depends upon the logical correctness of the computation but also upon the time at which the result is produced. If the timing constraints are not met, system failure is said to have occurred," (see *http://www.faqs.org/faqs/realtime-computing/faq*). In other words, whatever task the real-time application carries out, it must do it not only properly but on time.

Real-time doesn't mean fast. Some programmers who assume they need a real-time system can actually get the performance they need just by choosing a suitably fast hardware platform (processor, memory subsystem, and so on). In contrast, a true real-time application may get by with slower and cheaper hardware and an operating system that controls processing so that critical operations get done by guaranteed times. Real-time deals with *guarantees*, not with *raw speed*.

Basically, real-time systems are characterized by their ability to process events in a timely manner. In other words, real-time applications do not impose their own schedules on the environment they run in; rather, it is the environment—the physical world —that imposes its schedule on the real-time application by sending it events through device interrupts. The application has to process these events within a specified time.

Therefore, real-time processing requires some form of predictability from the system software that supports it. The point of all real-time systems is to guarantee timely behavior when interacting with the physical world (provided there is no hardware failure). In practice, real-time may even involve sacrificing throughput, because the salient issue is not how many jobs may be carried on in a given period of time, but rather the timely manner in which each job is finished.

To illustrate the point of real time, let's imagine you own a factory that makes donuts. The donuts in their initial shape don't have a hole, so your factory has a machine with a conveyor belt, a sensor, and a hole puncher to make donuts that look like donuts.

The embedded software detects the donut moving on the conveyor belt and triggers the hole puncher to punch the hole in the donut. Knowing the speed of the conveyor belt and the distance of the sensor to the hole puncher, the software has been given a precise time to trigger that hole puncher. Because more donuts means more money, you want to run this conveyor belt as fast as possible. In effect, you end up having a very short interval from the time the sensor detects the donut to the time that the software triggers the hole puncher.

If the computer were doing nothing but punching holes, you'd have little to worry about. But on the same machine that runs the hole puncher, you also have other tasks to carry out, such as reading data from optical sensors measuring donuts for quality control purposes. If any of those tasks takes too much time, and your hole puncher is triggered late, you end up with missed donut holes or lopsided donuts.

Obviously, missing deadlines in a real-time application is going to be even more worrisome if the software is aimed at controlling the fly-by-wire system of an aircraft rather than a bakery. Therefore, when choosing Linux to support an application, you need to determine whether the application has real-time requirements.

Linux does not come natively with any real-time guarantee. Fortunately, it is possible to enhance the standard Linux implementation to address this limitation.

Should Your Linux Be Real-Time?

Should you bother to enhance the Linux kernel for real-time capabilities in the context of your application? Adding real-time requirements to the software specifications without the need for it would make the overall system needlessly complex, and its performance might even be suboptimal. On the other hand, if your application does have real-time requirements, the inability of a vanilla Linux kernel to meet the requirements reliably could be an inescapable showstopper.

Answer a few basic questions to determine the need for predictability and accuracy that is typical of a real-time system:

- Do my requirements include deadlines? Would my application still produce valuable results if it is late completing its work? As a corollary, would such misses be harmful to anyone's safety or unacceptable with respect to the quality of the provided service?

  Predictability need not be absolute for a system to be considered real-time. For instance, an absolute requirement might be, "the function must finish within 3 ms," whereas a more relaxed real-time system might specify, "there should be an 80 percent probability that the function finishes within 3 ms and a 99.9 percent probability that it finishes within 5 ms." The absolute requirement is called *hard real-time*, while the more relaxed requirement is called *soft real-time*.

  A system that normally has hard requirements but still tolerates a low probability of error falls into the intermediate category called *firm real-time*. A measure of this probability gives us the Quality of Service (QoS) one may expect from such a system. For instance, a system that misses only 1 percent of its deadlines over a given period of time may still provide an acceptable quality of service if that degradation does not make it unsafe or unusable.

- Does any external device that interacts with my application software place any time-bound requirement on the handling of its messages?

- Could some of my application tasks have higher priority in my design than, say, Linux's own networking code or filesystem services?

  Remember that Linux runs many background daemons and threads along with user applications, and that any of these things can interfere with the operation of your application.

- Is fine-time granularity needed to express delays and timeouts?

  For instance, your application might express delays coarsely, as hundreds of milliseconds and beyond, or use fine-grained microsecond ranges. This said, having only coarse timings does not preclude also having strict real-time requirements, but honoring fine-grained timings accurately certainly requires a real-time capable Linux.

If any of the previous questions matches your requirements, you should consider using a real-time-capable Linux kernel.

Why Does the Kernel Need to Be Real-Time Aware?

Is real-time still a relevant consideration? Aren't the processors fast enough these days, and other hardware, such as timers, precise enough to provide the system with the required level of responsiveness and accuracy? The answer is no, because real-time behavior is also a software issue. As this is being written, the standard Linux kernel * does not provide the required *guarantees* that all the deadlines you set for your application will be effectively met. To understand where real-time comes in, let's first define the notion of latency, then illustrate some of the current Linux kernel limitations regarding the basic requirements listed earlier.

What Is Latency?

Because real-time systems are about timeliness, we want to measure the delay that might take place between the triggering of an event and the time the application actually processes it. Such delay is commonly called "latency." For instance, the amount of time that elapses between an interrupt and the execution of the associated interrupt handler is called the *interrupt latency*.

Many things could delay interrupt handling, including system bus contention, DMA operations, cache misses, or simply interrupt masking. The latter is requested by the kernel software during periods when it is processing critical pieces of code, so no interrupt handler can change a particular data structure while the kernel is working on it.

Similarly, the interrupt handler may place a task on a queue to run later and process any pending data received from the device in a less time-critical context. After the interrupt handler has returned, it may take some time for the kernel to complete its current duties before yielding the CPU to the task. This delay is called the *dispatch latency* or *scheduling latency*. The bad thing is that the Linux kernel might resume from the interrupt on behalf of a task that has a lower priority than the one just awakened. The kernel will realize that it has moved from a high-priority task to a lower-priority one but cannot just immediately stop and switch its attention to the high-priority task. That task has to wait for the kernel to reach a safe *rescheduling point* where it can switch context, after all of the nonpreemptible code has exited. In that case, we have a common problem called *priority inversion*, which is one of the hardest technical issues to solve because it has a deep impact on the internal design.

Let's illustrate the previous issue with an analogy about a road junction suffering from sporadic traffic jams. Suppose your car arrives at the junction (a low-priority task entering a critical section). You think that you can cross it immediately, but you find out at just the last second that you're wrong: all the traffic in front of you suddenly stops

---

* By "standard" kernel, we mean the mainline Linux 2.6 development tree, as well as any previous branch leading to it. There is development going on to produce preemption technology called PREEMPT_RT (see Chapter 14), which definitely has real-time characteristics, but it is not mainline yet.

(some unexpected resource contention happens), and you remain blocked in the middle of the crossroads.

Then you hear a dreaded siren and see a huge, red, shiny firetruck (a high-priority task) roaring down the side road in your direction to cross the junction. Your vehicle is stuck in the traffic jam and simply cannot move in any direction, so the firetruck has to stop too, possibly causing a house to burn to ashes.

Unlike real life's transport infrastructure, a kernel can be implemented so that it creates new roads on-the-fly for high-priority tasks to bypass the less urgent traffic; the scheduler is in charge of creating such roads. Those bypasses are provided by the previously mentioned rescheduling points, which obey the rules of priority when electing the next task to run. What makes real-time kernels different from others is the existence of enough rescheduling points along all of their execution paths to guarantee a bounded dispatch latency. To this end, the scheduler may temporarily adjust task priorities in order to avoid the kinds of issues we just illustrated with the road junction analogy. Later, we will discuss a common OS technique used to solve such matters, called "priority inheritance."

When talking about latency, real-time researchers are usually talking about *worst-case latency*. This means the longest time that could elapse before the desired event can occur. It's useful because it measures the ability of the system to perform in a timely and predictable manner.

The worst-case latency can be calculated by listing all the activities that could potentially intervene between the request for an event and the event itself, and adding together the longest time each of those activities could take.

This said, the notion of "deadline" should always be defined in the context of the application. For instance, which operations are subject to real-time response? A task that opens some I/O channels before running a real-time acquisition loop over them might not care how long it takes to establish the connection.

Sometimes, one even has to mitigate the definition of how "hard" real-time should be. For instance, how resilient must the system be to hardware failures that cause latencies? Would one consider defective hardware causing interrupt storms, which in turn slow the system down to a crawl, part of the equation? For this reason, as Paul McKenney puts it, "[hard] real time is the start of a conversation rather than a complete requirement" (see *http://www.linuxjournal.com/article/9361*).

Figure 12-1 illustrates the two kinds of latency, from the moment an interrupt is marked pending—waiting to be handled by the interrupt service routine (the ISR or IRQ handler)—to the moment the task in charge of processing the corresponding event actually resumes.

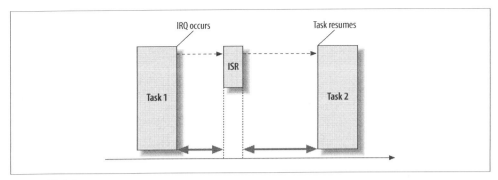

Figure 12-1. Latency

Common Real-Time Kernel Requirements

By now you understand what real-time means and what role it plays in processing external events. Now we can look at more detailed requirements a software system must meet in order to qualify as real-time. There are many types of real-time, as we have seen, and therefore many types of systems that qualify in different ways as real-time systems. But certain concepts run through all of them.

A Fine-Grained Preemptible Kernel

Because real-time behavior is a matter of reacting early enough and properly to internal and external events, a real-time kernel has to be able to switch as soon as possible from a low-priority context to a high-priority task that needs attention. The time this takes is called the *preemption granularity*, and the longest time that could be spent waiting for a pending rescheduling to take place defines the worst-case dispatch latency of a kernel.

This issue has already been addressed by different patches to the Linux 2.4 series, which introduce opportunities for task scheduling in the kernel code. Previously, a new task could be scheduled only upon exit from the kernel context—that is, as long as the kernel was handling activities required by a system call or another user space request, the kernel wouldn't stop in order to allow a new task to run.

Probably the best-known approach to a preemptible kernel, called the *preemptible kernel* support, was instituted by Robert Love while he was at Montavista. This was merged into the mainline kernel during the 2.5 development phase and is now available as a standard feature of Linux 2.6. It offers significantly better preemptability on average. On the other hand, the concurrency between tasks is still suboptimal, because kernel preemption remains globally disabled as long as any task on the system holds any exclusive resource, even if no other task could compete for the same resource. As a consequence of this, only the average latency shows some improvement, but unfortunately, the worst-case latency still remains incompatible with hard real-time requirements.

A simple way to illustrate the limitation this approach raises is with another traffic analogy. Imagine a rather absurd situation in which a single traffic light (the preemption disabling lock) for an entire city (the Linux kernel) blocks all cars (the tasks) each time one crosses an intersection anywhere in town (the exclusive resource). A way to get rid of this restriction is to make the acquisition and release of each exclusive resource truly independent from the others. Not surprisingly, this is a fundamental aspect of the PREEMPT_RT effort, which we will discuss later.

Strictly Enforced Task Priorities

Even with a fine-grained preemptible kernel, a preempted low-priority task could hold an exclusive resource long enough for a high-priority task requesting the same resource to be delayed catastrophically; after all, it is just a matter of something unexpectedly delaying the low-priority task while it holds the resource. This is an example of priority inversion, discussed earlier. Because exclusive resources are spread all over the Linux kernel, the odds of encountering this priority inversion are pretty high. This issue must be addressed by specific operating system techniques, such as priority inheritance or priority ceiling (*http://lwn.net/Articles/178253/*), which guarantee that such an inversion would remain short and time-bounded, or would not even happen.

Handling External Events in a Bounded Time Frame

A real-time application frequently reacts to device interrupts in order to handle normal processing input or receive out-of-band information about the state of the physical world. The latter may be quite important, such as sensors sending critical alerts about hardware overheating or warning the controller for an automated chainsaw about some unexpected obstacle on its course. The longest time needed for the kernel to dispatch a pending interrupt to the appropriate software handler is the worst-case interrupt latency. We definitely want our target platform to have a known, predictable value for this latency before designing any real-time software to run over it.

Unfortunately, the standard Linux kernel may mask external interrupts when entering critical sections, sometimes for an unbounded amount of time. The kernel does this not only to prevent concurrent tasks on the same processor from wrongly accessing some nonshareable resource at the same moment, but also to reduce the opportunity for unrelated activities to disturb the current task. Yet another advantage of cutting down on interrupts is that the kernel does not have to flush and reload its cache as often. On this issue, the standard kernel favors throughput over responsiveness.

In particular, regular subsystems such as the virtual memory management code, the virtual filesystem layer, and the networking stack enforce long critical sections of this sort. The time that elapses without being able to handle any external interrupt usually depends on the pressure imposed onto those subsystems, so the odds for delaying some critical event processing is often a function of the overall system load. This situation is likely the best deal available for a throughput-oriented, general-purpose operating system. But because a real-time system must be predictable regardless of the current load, the potential interrupt latency in the standard Linux kernel is not acceptable.

As a corollary, we should also stress the issue introduced by delayed timer interrupts. Naturally, timing—and specifically the accurate delivery of timed events—is a fundamental resource upon which real-time systems depend. For instance, real-time applications often acquire data at a fixed frequency from some dedicated hardware on behalf of a periodically scheduled task. Because the timing services, which support periodic scheduling, depend on the accurate delivery of interrupts sent by the timer hardware, interrupt latency in general must be kept within acceptable bounds for the application to work properly.

It should be pointed out that data acquisition, as just described, is quite different from typical computer I/O, where one can assume that a dropped network packet (for instance) will eventually be resent and the application on the other end can wait. In the case of a real-time system performing I/O operations for data acquisition purposes, timeliness and reliability are most often fundamental.

Similar requirements for bounded latencies apply all along the line to any activity that could hold up a critical task. It's little help to a critical task if interrupt latencies are kept low but it takes the kernel a long time to start up the critical task.

Some Typical Users of Real-Time Computing Technology

Real-time computing technology has become pervasive over the years, and a number of applications are now based on the critical assumption that timeliness may be provided by the kernel software. It would be too long a list to enumerate all of them, if even possible, but still, let's discuss a few industries that heavily depend on real-time systems.

The measurement and control industry

People in this industry who implement real-time applications want their systems to interact with the physical world. The donut hole example cited near the beginning of this chapter illustrated the concept. Another example is software used to control a robot, such as those that operate conveyor belts in industrial plants.

As a typical example for applications that perform cyclic data acquisition, the time required to process each sample must be less than the time in between samples. The reason to rely on a real-time operating system here is to make sure incoming samples will be processed on-the-fly at the right pace, keeping the input and output processes perfectly synchronized.

Other applications may need to react to external events; for instance, they may send requests to some of their devices in response to information they have received from others. An illustration is the overheat detection sensor mentioned earlier: the application really needs to get the alarm notification from the heat sensor on time and react within the appropriate time frame to shut down the malfunctioning device, or the latter is likely going to be toast.

The aerospace industry

This industry is a large consumer of real-time technology at various levels of its product development process, from the early design stage to its exploitation. For instance, Integrated Modular Avionics (IMA) is a blanket term used to describe a distributed real-time computer network aboard an aircraft. This network consists of a number of computing modules capable of supporting numerous applications involving various safety criticality levels.

Another typical use of real-time capabilities in this industry involves simulation systems with real hardware attached to it, an approach called *hardware-in-the-loop* (HIL) simulation. Real-time is needed here because portions of this software have to interact with the physical world. By making it possible to test new, actual devices in a virtual environment, this solution allows the designers to predict whether the overall airborne system will meet initial performance specifications, without actually having to build it for real in its entirety.

The financial services industry

It is particularly interesting that even high-level online financial services could depend on basic real-time technology issues. As a matter of fact, some of the complex distributed applications that are critical to this business may have requirements for exchanging messages reliably and in a timely fashion.

For instance, when it comes to connecting trading systems to stock exchanges around the world, with hundreds of financial transactions taking place every minute, too much delay in processing trading opportunities within a handful of seconds could mean significant losses.

For this reason, trading systems are increasingly dependent on real-time response. The fact that such applications operate on a millisecond timescale, instead of the microsecond one used by measurement and control systems, does not change their basic requirement for always being on time (i.e., for being real-time).

The multimedia business

Generally speaking, multimedia systems have to process visual and auditive information in a time frame short enough for the audience not to perceive visible or audible artifacts. Such applications can allow some deadlines to be missed once in a while, but this should remain a rare case so that they maintain an overall good quality of service.

The Linux Paths to Real-Time

In contrast to traditional real-time operating systems (RTOSes) that have been designed from the ground up to provide for predictable response time, Linux is a general-purpose operating system (GPOS) that was initially designed around fairness (sharing resources fairly among its users) and good average performance under sustained load conditions. This history changes our perspective on real-time a lot. The Linux solution boils down to adding real-time hooks or special cases to a general-purpose multitasking core.

As the hardware available to real-time applications—including those in the embedded space—follows Moore's law, people implementing the applications that interact with the hardware want to make the applications richer and more featureful, which in turn requires a sophisticated operating system such as Linux.

The days are almost gone when real-time applications single-mindedly processed real-time events. Nowadays, real-time software is often interacting with other non-real-time components within the same system. For this reason, designers do not choose an operating system solely because it has predictable response time, but also because it has, for instance, good networking capabilities, a wealth of device drivers for off-the-shelf hardware, and sometimes rich graphic support. Additionally, the pressure for producing cost-effective computing platforms dictates a set of requirements, which may be summarized as: "you shall follow the standards." This is because standards means interoperability, off-the-shelf hardware, and common skill sets shared by more engineers who may enter into product development.

It is interesting to notice how Linux fits well into this current trend. It outperforms proprietary operating systems in the number of device drivers supporting all kinds of off-the-shelf hardware; it provides a reliable and efficient networking stack that actually runs a significant part of the Internet nowadays; and it provides various graphical environments with characteristics ranging from embedded-compatible footprints to rich desktop systems.

Generally speaking, Linux benefits from the richness of a successful GPOS in terms of software and hardware support. Conversely, traditional RTOSes most often had to build ad hoc and proprietary solutions to meet those general-purpose requirements as best they could, suffering from the tininess and rigidity of their initial real-time cores that were specifically aimed at fitting in low-end embedded systems.

On the other hand, as a GPOS, Linux was not designed to provide real-time capabilities to its applications, therefore, a cornerstone was missing in the edifice for anyone with such a requirement.

With this point in mind, we can now explain the two major real-time approaches Linux supports and the reasons behind their respective designs.

The Co-Kernel Approach

The earliest solution found for adding real-time capabilities to Linux was to place a small real-time kernel running side-by-side with Linux on the same hardware, instead of turning the standard kernel into an RTOS. Clearly, nothing was new in this technical path. Similar implementations already existed, for instance, in the Windows world, based on proprietary software such as Intel's iRMX back in 1992 and its INTime derivatives or RTX from Venturcom (now Ardence).

Put bluntly, the basic argument leading to a co-kernel design is that one should not trust the standard Linux kernel to honor real-time duties under any circumstances, because a GPOS kernel is inherently complex, and real-time people usually don't trust what they cannot specify in detail with clear bounds. As a matter of fact, more code usually leads to more uncertainty, which in turn barely fits with the need for predictability. Add in the extremely fast development cycle of the Linux kernel, which brings in a lot of changes in a short time frame.

Therefore, in order to get the best of both the GPOS and RTOS worlds, the real-time processes are handed over to the small co-kernel, which schedules them appropriately, and the usual GPOS business continues to be carried over to the standard Linux kernel. Practically speaking, a co-kernel is usually available as a set of dynamically loadable modules, or may be directly compiled inside the Linux source tree just like any regular subsystem. Some co-kernel implementations (notably RTAI and Xenomai) support the running of real-time programs in user space with MMU protection just like any regular Linux application. Others (notably RTLinux/GPL) require real-time applications to be embodied in kernel modules.

For this approach to work, all device interrupts must go through the co-kernel before they are processed by the standard kernel so that Linux may never defer them, thus ensuring predictable response time on the real-time side. A co-kernel should operate as transparently as possible; for this reason, the Linux kernel is barely aware of its presence and does not actually know that interrupts may be dispatched to the co-kernel before it has a chance to handle them.

Several methods have been developed over time to share interrupts between the two kernels. They basically all boil down to interposing a software-based interrupt masking mechanism between the Linux kernel and the programmable interrupt controller (PIC) hardware. Because this software mechanism mimics the basic interrupt control operations the real hardware performs, it is often described as a *virtual PIC*. It ultimately allows the RTOS to maintain a separate interrupt-masking state from the one controlled by the Linux kernel.

The net effect is that interrupts are barely masked at the hardware level and get delivered almost immediately to the co-kernel—which has the highest priority in terms of interrupt delivery—regardless of whether the Linux kernel would accept them or not. If the interrupts are actually associated with Linux processes, the virtual PIC has the effect of simply deferring the invocation of the interrupt handlers until Linux eventually takes control of a processor and accepts the interrupts.

To sum up, a virtual PIC scheme almost always works as follows: it accepts hardware interrupts, records them into an internal log, and checks a per-OS software flag in a prioritized manner to see whether the logged interrupts may be delivered to the OS for processing.

Such a design brings a great advantage: regardless of the ongoing Linux activity, the real-time processes always benefit from extremely low interrupt and dispatch latencies, because they're never adversely affected by any regular Linux code. Meanwhile, the isolation between the two kernels simplifies maintenance of the RTOS itself. The RTOS developer usually has to worry only about adapting the interrupt virtualization layer to new Linux kernel releases, regardless of how many significant changes went into them.

However, this design also holds a significant drawback: because the Linux kernel still has no real-time capabilities, one must stick exclusively to co-kernel services in order to keep predictable latencies for the real-time processes, regardless of whether the application may run in user space or not. In other words, the whole set of regular Linux drivers and libraries that rely on the standard kernel do not benefit from any real-time guarantee. For instance, device drivers that are standard and immediately available in the regular Linux kernel still need to be forked and ported to work over a co-kernel predictably. For the same reason, services from the standard C library (glibc) may cause unexpected latencies whenever they call into the Linux kernel. This fact affects the programming model, and unfortunately may add complexity to the development and maintenance tasks, at least for applications that do not exhibit a straightforward design, functionally split between real-time and non-real-time activities.

The Fully Preemptible Kernel Approach

The other approach deals with converting Linux itself into a full RTOS. This implies that changes are made to the Linux kernel that allow for real-time processes to run without experiencing interference from unpredictable or unbounded activities by non-real-time processes. The main criticism of combining a GPOS and an RTOS boils down to this: it is very difficult to be 100 percent sure that the GPOS code will never hinder the real-time behavior of the RTOS, in any circumstance. Development of the RT patch (see Chapter 14) focuses on the parts of the Linux kernel that allow non-real-time tasks to affect real-time tasks.

The Linux kernel is indeed very large. It contains several million lines of code, but most of that lies in drivers, as well as all the different architectures that it supports. No one has a machine that contains all the devices that the Linux kernel supports. When choosing to use the RT patch for an embedded real-time platform, one only needs to audit the drivers that are used for that platform. Drivers must be inspected by a trained RT kernel programmer to search for areas that might disable preemption or interrupts for long periods of time.

The core part of the Linux kernel is only a fraction of the entire kernel. The core contains the code that controls the scheduling of processes, interrupt handling, internal locking, creation, and destruction of new threads, memory management, filesystems, and timers. Parts of the core are also modular, supporting different filesystems and memory management. The core kernel code implements the same things that a microkernel would need to implement. Thus, the conversion of the Linux kernel into a RTOS can be isolated to changing these core parts of the kernel. This greatly simplifies the effort to convert Linux into a full RTOS.

The main areas in the Linux kernel that cause problems for real-time tasks are even smaller than the ones listed in the previous paragraph: they essentially concern locking and interrupts. The mainline Linux kernel (as of 2.6.23) contains large areas where preemption is disabled, as well as mutexes that can cause priority inversion within the kernel. The mainline Linux kernel also has interrupt service routines that can preempt any process (real-time included) to do work for the lowest-priority process. The RT patch addresses these issues and converts the Linux kernel into an RTOS.

By converting Linux itself into a full RTOS, the user gets the benefits of the wide range of devices that Linux supports, as well as all the different architectures. Applications for embedded devices can be tested on a PC desktop without any changes. All the utilities to control the real-time processes, as well as the OS in general, come with every major distribution.

Although all the drivers Linux provides are available to the real-time applications, they still need to be verified as real-time safe. Some companies are willing to provide this service. A developer will be needed to look at the source code of the device driver and verify that it does not disable preemption or interrupts for large amounts of time. This is uncommon for a driver to do. In fact, it is considered a bug even in a GPOS if a driver disables preemption or interrupts for a substantial amount of time. But few users of the mainline kernel would report a 10-millisecond delay caused by a device driver, so this bug may go unreported.

As more multimedia users (both audio and video) start using the RT-patched Linux kernel, more device drivers will be verified, because these are the types of users who can notice and report long latency delays caused by these devices.

The RT patch strives to covert the Linux kernel into a full RTOS system, but it is still a GPOS as well. This means that it is harder to verify a lack of bugs. For most applications that need real-time determinism, the RT-patched Linux kernel provides adequate service. But for those real-time applications that need more than low latencies and actually have a system that can be vigorously audited against bugs, the Linux kernel, with or without the RT patch, is not sufficient. These applications are those that would put people's lives at stake; for example, an aircraft engine control system. But the RT-patched Linux kernel is sufficient for most other real-time embedded activities (such as robotics).

To sum up, there is no "one-size-fits-it-all" approach to real-time, but rather there are varying degrees of real-time requirements that have an impact on the overall system design.

## CHAPTER 13

The Xenomai
Real-Time System

Xenomai is a real-time subsystem that can be tightly integrated with the Linux kernel to guarantee predictable response times to applications. Its current incarnation is based on a dual kernel approach, with a small co-kernel running side-by-side with Linux on the same hardware. Xenomai supports the running of real-time programs in user space with memory management unit (MMU) protection when it is available from the host kernel, just like any regular Linux application. Real-time tasks are exclusively controlled by the co-kernel during the course of their time-critical operations so that very low latencies are achieved for their code running inside a standard Linux kernel.

Xenomai was created in 2001 to facilitate the migration of industrial applications coming from the proprietary world to a GNU/Linux-based environment, while keeping stringent real-time guarantees. To allow porting traditional RTOS APIs to Linux-based real-time frameworks, the Xenomai core provides generic building blocks for implementing real-time APIs, also known as *skins*. This way, a skin can mimic proprietary/in-house APIs efficiently, based on reusable objects supplied by the real-time framework.

The Xenomai core running in kernel space is offered under the GPL 2. User space interface libraries are released under the LGPL 2.1.

Today, it runs over several architectures (PowerPC32 and PowerPC64, Blackfin, ARM, x86, x86_64, and ia64) in a variety of embedded and server platforms, and it can be coupled to two major Linux kernel versions (2.4 and 2.6), for MMU-enabled and MMU-less systems. Supported real-time APIs include VxWorks, pSOS+, VRTX, uITRON, and POSIX 1003.1b.

The official Xenomai project website, offering source code, documentation, technical articles, and other resources, is *http://www.xenomai.org*.

Porting Traditional RTOS Applications to Linux

A growing number of industrial applications are being ported to Linux, which translates into large amounts of legacy source code that projects need to accommodate. As of early 2007, most applications that relied on an operating system were based on traditional real-time operating systems controlled by software vendors or some home-brewed solution (*http://www.embedded.com/columns/showArti cle.jhtml?articleID=187203732*). A number of those RTOSes came with their own non-POSIX, proprietary API.

Because real-time applications are most often embedded ones, a significant debugging and tuning effort usually takes place before they are fully stable in the field. Such efforts likely require very specific knowledge from experienced people who may not always be involved in the porting process. For this reason, embedded product teams are not keen on changing the pillars of their software, such as the real-time API being used. As a matter of fact, a real-time API carries particular semantics and exhibits well-defined behaviors that the entire application can depend upon to work.

Let's look at a few examples of features that make porting to Linux a daunting task:

- Most traditional embedded RTOS APIs provide a service to forcibly suspend a particular task; for instance, VxWorks calls this feature taskSuspend(), whereas pSOS+ exports t_suspend() for the same purpose. A number of existing embedded applications still rely on such system calls, although they are a bit dangerous because they could stop execution in the middle of a critical section if used improperly.

  It would superficially seem that the way to mimic this behavior through POSIX-compatible calls would be to issue pthread_kill() to send a SIGSTOP signal to the task to be suspended. Unfortunately, doing so would also suspend all the POSIX threads belonging to the same process, because the POSIX specification requires pthread_kill() to affect the process as a whole, even if the signal is directed at a particular thread.

  In other words, in a system following the POSIX specification, there is no way for a thread to forcibly suspend another thread without disturbing others.

- Traditional RTOS APIs export a wealth of task synchronization services, and often allow the developer to specify whether waiting tasks should be restarted by priority or in FIFO order. For instance, on a uITRON-compliant RTOS, a FIFO/PRIO parameter may be passed to the system call creating an IPC semaphore by calling cre_sem(). The equivalent on VRTX is sc_screate(). Many RTOSes offer similar fine-grained control over synchronization for such IPC mechanisms as message queues and mailboxes.

Once again, unfortunately, the POSIX specification states that implementations supporting the *priority scheduling* option may always use a priority-based queuing order. Otherwise, the order remains unspecified, leaving the POSIX implementation to do whatever it sees fit with no recourse by the application programmer. The POSIX specification even goes on to say: "Synchronization primitives that attempt to interfere with scheduling policy by specifying an ordering rule are considered undesirable." And as a matter of fact, the POSIX interface does not allow it.

Because it has a direct impact on the scheduling order, this disparity between POSIX and other popular RTOSes can raise subtle bugs whenever the application strictly depends on the behavior depicted in another vendor's specification. In modern Linux kernels, most POSIX IPC services are based on the Fast Userspace Mutex (*futex*) support, which always uses a priority-based queueing order for all tasks belonging to the real-time scheduling class. Therefore, no FIFO queuing order could be available for those IPCs anyway.

- Traditional RTOSes allow an application to lock the scheduler, effectively preventing the current task from being preempted by any other, regardless of their respective priorities. Even if the rationale for using such a feature is questionable, since this basically boils down to asking a real-time system to ignore task priorities, a number of legacy applications still use it. We think it fortunate that, in this case, POSIX does not define any such option, but the drawback is that legacy code is left with a missing feature. The scheduler lock may often be replaced by recursive mutexes, properly set to protect the same section of code from preemption. However, in some cases, the original code is so entangled that removing the giant lock could have unexpected and unfortunate side effects. It all depends on how much of the original implementation has to change, and how much time is available to fix the potential regression errors.

To sum up, two real-time APIs may be similar, but still have subtle differences that could change the way applications actually behave if the original system calls were simply mapped to their closest equivalents in the target environment. Therefore, moving from a non-POSIX interface to Linux's POSIX-based one may introduce unexpected issues, particularly in stable applications that one wants to change only in small steps, and very carefully.

At the same time, the similarities among the traditional RTOSes are obvious, so building a common software framework for developing these emulators makes sense.

For instance, what are the actual differences among VxWorks, pSOS+, Virtuoso, VRTX, and Chorus O/S semaphores? VxWorks may support mutexes as part of its semaphore API, whereas other RTOSes may implement mutexes separately or not at all, but the basic semaphore model they all use must behave identically in all implementations.

In the same vein, all traditional RTOSes offer, at the very least, a preemptive, fixed-priority task scheduler, and most support round-robin scheduling, too. They all offer

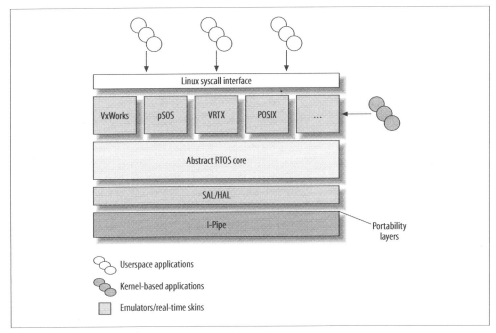

Figure 13-1. Xenomai architecture

familiar IPC mechanisms, such as event flag groups, mailboxes, and message queues. Memory management features, such as fixed-size or dynamic block allocators, can be found with little core differences among a variety of embedded real-time systems, regardless of whether one calls them partitions, regions, or heaps.

In other words, a significant number of commonalities among traditional RTOSes may be abstracted into a framework so that only the proper window-dressing has to be provided on top in order to mimic each RTOS's interface properly.

The Xenomai Architecture

Xenomai eases the porting process from traditional embedded environments to Linux by providing real-time API emulators that mimic the system calls exactly as described by RTOS vendor specifications. Thus, Xenomai preserves the real-time guarantees that applications rely on. Because all Xenomai emulators are built from a common set of building blocks, leveraging the commonalities found among RTOSes, each of those emulators benefits, at no cost, from improvements made to the Xenomai core.

Figure 13-1 shows the overall architecture of Xenomai.

The Interrupt Pipeline

In order to keep latency predictable for real-time tasks, we must ensure that the regular Linux kernel never defers external interrupts. The interrupts should be blocked or masked for minimal times at the hardware level and be delivered as quickly as possible to Xenomai, regardless of whether the Linux kernel would accept them. At the same time, interrupts directed at the Linux kernel should never trigger a handler when the kernel is in a section where it blocks interrupts.

Therefore, we need an additional piece of software between the hardware, Linux, and Xenomai, to act as a virtual programmable interrupt controller. This allows Linux and Xenomai to maintain separate masks for interrupts and policies for handling interrupts. The software layer Xenomai uses for that purpose is called the *interrupt pipeline*, or I-pipe. It is based on a technical proposal for a system called Adeos,[*] by the author of this book's first edition, Karim Yaghmour. The I-pipe is a simplified implementation of his proposal that relies on a modification of the Linux kernel sources for virtualizing the interrupt mask, instead of depending on features of the x86 chip.

The I-pipe organizes the system as a set of domains connected through a software pipeline. In the I-pipe implementation, these domains share a single address space, which proves useful when a thread needs to invoke services at one point from Linux and at another point from Xenomai.

At the Linux kernel level, a domain is usually a kernel module that calls some I-pipe service to register itself. The I-pipe implementation is available as patches against a number of Linux 2.4 and 2.6 versions, because it has to be specifically adapted to each version of the core kernel code.

Within an I-pipe-enabled kernel, Xenomai is the highest priority domain, ahead of the Linux kernel itself. The I-pipe dispatches events such as interrupts, system calls, processor faults, and other exceptions to domains according to each domain's static priority.

Xenomai registers a set of handlers for various I-pipe events. These handlers notify Xenomai of any noteworthy event before Linux can handle it. This way, Xenomai can preprocess the event in order to have both the real-time system and the regular Linux kernel share it properly.

For instance, when a processor exception is caught on behalf of a real-time task controlled by the Xenomai co-kernel, the co-kernel usually lets the regular kernel handle the fault, because there's no point in duplicating the exception-handling code that Linux already provides. However, the faulting task has to re-enter a normal Linux context before doing so. The exception handler allows Xenomai to intervene during processor faults and exceptions so that it can switch faulting tasks back to a normal Linux context when required.

---

[*] *http://www.opersys.com/adeos*

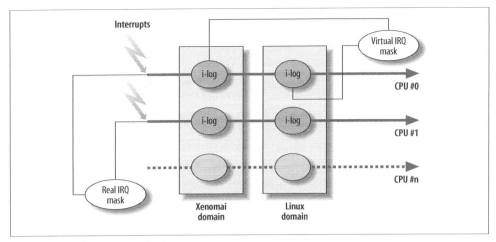

Figure 13-2. The interrupt pipeline

One of the most important aspects of the I-pipe is that it exposes an architecture-neutral API, which has been ported to a variety of CPUs. This way, client domains such as Xenomai require changes to only a small amount of architecture-dependent code when developers port the domains to other CPUs, and they may rely on a normalized interface to hook onto the host hardware platform.

Figure 13-2 shows the main characteristics of an I-pipe-enabled Linux kernel, with a number of domains receiving external events in sequence, and a per-domain virtual interrupt mask that preserves the ability to lock out interrupts when the domain code requires it. In essence, the I-pipe replaces the hardware interrupt mask provided by the CPU with multiple virtual masks so that domains may run unaffected by another domain's action on their own interrupt state.

The way Xenomai puts the interrupt pipeline into action is described in detail at *http://www.xenomai.org/documentation/branches/v2.3.x/Life-with-Adeos-rev_B.pdf*.

The Hardware and System Abstraction Layers

The Xenomai hardware abstraction layer (HAL) gathers all the CPU and platform-dependent code needed to implement a particular Xenomai port so that every layer starting from the nucleus and higher is free from machine-dependent code.

The Xenomai HAL is combined with a system abstraction layer (SAL), which makes the bulk of the nucleus and skins more portable as well. Xenomai uses HAL and SAL to place its core services on top of an event-driver simulator. This tool is heavily used in testing and debugging new RTOS skins so that developers can run them in a fully sandboxed environment in the context of a regular Linux process.

The Xenomai Core and Nucleus

The Xenomai core is in charge of supplying all the operating system resources that skins may require to properly mimic traditional RTOS APIs. This requirement is a direct consequence of the underlying co-kernel design: because Xenomai runs on non-real-time Linux kernels, real-time processes must stick exclusively to calling Xenomai services in order to keep predictable latencies. Therefore, the Xenomai core has to provide all of the basic RTOS resources; skins cannot rely on regular Linux services.

The Xenomai core is best described as an abstract RTOS because it defines generic building blocks. These can be specialized to implement any kind of real-time API that fits the generic model. The building blocks are gathered into a single loadable module called the Xenomai *nucleus* (which is in no way related to the component of ATI called the nucleus). The following are the main components that the Xenomai nucleus provides:

- A real-time thread object controlled by the Xenomai scheduler. The scheduler is a preemptive and fixed-priority, supporting a number of thread priority levels. FIFO ordering applies within a priority level. This scheduler also enables round-robin scheduling on a per-thread basis.

  Each RTOS emulator bases its task or thread implementation on the Xenomai thread abstraction so that basic scheduling operations—such as priority management, preemption control, and eager suspension/resumption requests—are already available through the nucleus interface.

- A generic interrupt object that connects the RTOS skin to any number of IRQ lines provided by the underlying hardware. Because interrupt handling is one of the least well-defined areas in RTOS design, the nucleus focuses on providing a simple mechanism with sufficient hooks for each skin to emulate the specific behavior of its RTOS. Xenomai's support for interrupts includes nested and shared interrupts.

- A memory allocator with predictable latencies that RTOS skins can specialize to support the dynamic allocation of variable-size memory blocks.

- An extendable synchronization object. This is one of the most important features of the Xenomai core. This object implements thread blocking on any kind of resource for all RTOS services. Xenomai supports timeouts, priority inheritance, and priority-based or FIFO queuing order when multiple threads have to block on a single resource. For instance, all kinds of semaphores, mutexes, condition variables, message queues, and mailboxes defined by the RTOSes are based on this core abstraction.

- Timer management, allowing any time-related service to create any number of software timers. Xenomai also implements the notion of a *time base*, by which software timers that belong to different RTOS skins can be clocked separately and concurrently, according to distinct frequencies, or even in a tickless fashion. A lot of traditional RTOSes are tick-based, expressing delays and timeouts as counts of ticks (what the Linux kernel calls *jiffies*). However, Linux and Xenomai also support tickless timing so that RTOS emulators may ask for nanosecond-level clock resolutions that are too fine-grained to depend on periodic operating system ticks.

To illustrate a typical use of Xenomai building blocks, let's look at the actual implementation of the t_suspend() call from the pSOS+ emulator module, which forcibly puts a given task on hold:

```
u_long t_suspend(u_long tid)
{
    u_long ret = SUCCESS;
    psostask_t *task;
    spl_t s;

    if (tid == 0) { /* Is this a self-suspension call? */
        if (xnpod_unblockable_p())
            /* E.g. we can't block on behalf on an ISR. */
            return -EPERM;

        /* Ok, ask the nucleus to schedule us out. */
        xnpod_suspend_self();

        /*
         * We woke up due to a Linux signal. We need to tell
         * the caller about this, so that regular signal
         * handling is carried out properly on the Linux side.
         */
        if (xnthread_test_info(&psos_current_task()->threadbase, XNBREAK))
            return -EINTR;

        /*
         * Someone must have fired t_resume() upon us. Let's
         * go back to our caller to resume running.
         */
        return SUCCESS;
    }

    /* Protect from preemption in the Xenomai domain. */
    xnlock_get_irqsave(&nklock, s);

    /* Let's check first whether the task identifier is valid. */
    task = psos_h2obj_active(tid, PSOS_TASK_MAGIC, psostask_t);

    if (!task) {
        ret = psos_handle_error(tid, PSOS_TASK_MAGIC, psostask_t);
        goto unlock_and_exit;
    }

    /* Is the target task already suspended? Ask the nucleus about this. */
    if (xnthread_test_state(&ask->threadbase, XNSUSP)) {
        ret = ERR_SUSP;     /* Task already suspended. */
        goto unlock_and_exit;
    }

    /* Ok, let's ask the nucleus to hold on execution for that task. */
```

```
    xnpod_suspend_thread(&task->threadbase, XNSUSP, XN_INFINITE, XN_RELATIVE, NULL);

    if (task == psos_current_task() &&
        xnthread_test_info(&task->threadbase, XNBREAK))
        ret = -EINTR;

unlock_and_exit:

    xnlock_put_irqrestore(&nklock, s);

    return ret;
}
```

As the code sample shows, the Xenomai nucleus handles the most complex part of the system call by carrying out the actual suspension and maintaining task state information so that the pSOS emulator can decide what has to be done next. The rest of the code is just window-dressing around the threadbase anchor object, which is the thread-specific data structure exported by the nucleus to model real-time tasks.

The example that follows was taken from the VRTX emulator. It implements the sc_pend() call from the *mailbox* IPC, which makes the caller wait on a memory cell until some nonzero data has been written to it (this is a timed service, so the caller may specify a timeout value):

```
char *sc_pend(char **mboxp, long timeout, int *errp)
{
    char *msg = NULL;
    vrtxtask_t *task;
    vrtxmb_t *mb;
    spl_t s;

    /* Protect from preemption in the Xenomai domain. */
    xnlock_get_irqsave(&nklock, s);

    /* Find out our control block for this mailbox. */
    mb = mb_map(mboxp);

    if (!mb) {
        *errp = ER_NOCB;
        goto unlock_and_exit;
    }

    if (mb->msg != NULL)
        /*
         * Something has been written in there already, return
         * that value without blocking the caller.
         */
        goto done;

    /* May we block the calling context? */
    if (xnpod_unblockable_p()) {
        *errp = -EPERM;
        goto unlock_and_exit;
    }
```

```
    task = vrtx_current_task();
    /*
     * Set up a few status bits the VRTX way, so that inquiries
     * about the task state will return proper information.
     */
    task->vrtxtcb.TCBSTAT = TBSMBOX;

    if (timeout)
        task->vrtxtcb.TCBSTAT |= TBSDELAY;

    /* We have to wait for a message now. */
    xnsynch_sleep_on(&mb->synchbase, timeout, XN_RELATIVE);

    /* Are we waking up due to a Linux signal, or some unblocking call? */
    if (xnthread_test_info(&task->threadbase, XNBREAK)) {
        *errp = -EINTR;
        goto unlock_and_exit;
    }

    /* Did we reach the timeout limit? */
    if (xnthread_test_info(&task->threadbase, XNTIMEO)) {
        *errp = ER_TMO;
        goto unlock_and_exit;
    }

  done:

    /*
     * Ok, we got a message, let's reset the mailbox before passing
     * it on to the caller.
     */
    msg = mb->msg;
    mb->msg = NULL;
    *errp = RET_OK;

  unlock_and_exit:

    xnlock_put_irqrestore(&nklock, s);

    return msg;
}
```

Once again, the nucleus did most of the job of implementing the core activities. The main anchor object used here is the **synch** building block, which the Xenomai core exports to model a variety of IPC features.

The Xenomai Skins

When looking at the Xenomai system, one is most struck by the lack of any central or master API for application development, not even a preferred API based on one of the popular RTOSes. In fact, the Xenomai core considers all RTOS APIs equal. Developers can pick any skin that fits the extremely flexible Xenomai model, or even develop a new skin in order to port applications from an RTOS that isn't yet supported.

RTOS emulators, and more generally any kind of real-time API, are built on the Xenomai nucleus using the set of common building blocks described earlier. In practical terms, the skin representing an API is embodied in a loadable kernel module, just like the nucleus, and simply appears as a specialized Linux driver that the programmer may enable statically or as a module when building the target kernel image.

Xenomai comes with several canned real-time APIs:

- A POSIX interface maintained by Gilles Chanteperdrix, aiming at 1003.1b standard conformance. It acts as a drop-in replacement for the glibc services it reimplements over the Xenomai co-kernel. The POSIX interface works on top of both the LinuxThreads and NPTL-enabled Glibc.

- A VxWorks emulator, which mimics the WIND kernel 5.x API.

- A pSOS+ emulator based on the pSOS 2.x core API definition.

- A VRTX emulator, supporting both the VRTX32 and VRTX/sa system call interfaces.

- An uITRON-compliant skin, based on specification rev. 3.02 (E-level).

- A RTAI 3.x emulator for porting legacy applications embodied into kernel modules over Xenomai.

- A so-called native API, in the sense that it has been designed as part of the Xenomai development effort. This API is reminiscent of traditional RTOS APIs. Even if it has no particular preeminence over any other skin, it allows people with a non-POSIX RTOS culture to easily develop applications, based on a feature-full but still reasonably compact API.

- Last but not least, the Real-Time Driver Model (RTDM), which provides a unified interface to both users and developers of real-time device drivers. Specifically, it addresses the constraints of dual kernel–based systems like Xenomai, where applications exhibit both real-time and non-real-time runtime phases, depending on which kernel is controlling their tasks at any point in time. RTDM conforms to POSIX semantics (IEEE Std 1003.1) where available and applicable.

How Xenomai Works

The fundamental difference between Xenomai and other dual kernel systems available for Linux (e.g., RTAI or RTLinux) is a higher level of integration with the native Linux environment. For the Xenomai project, keeping the regular Linux programming model available for real-time applications has always been considered just as important as guaranteeing the lowest latency figures achievable on any given hardware.

This said, using a co-kernel technology raises several significant usability issues when programmers try to benefit from Linux's rich POSIX environment. Sometimes real-time

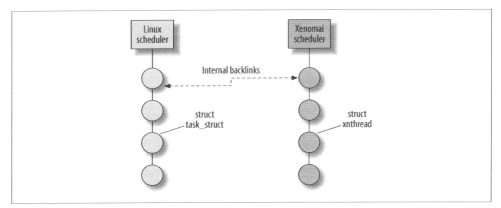

Figure 13-3. Xenomai real-time shadow

applications may need to call Linux services with unpredictable latencies, such as accessing disk files to log data or establishing communication over the network.

More fundamentally, you may ask how one could call into regular Linux services from a real-time program if both kernels are operating in full independence, with Linux barely knowing about the co-kernel. For instance, how could the real-time tasks controlled by the co-kernel properly receive and process POSIX signals, which the Linux kernel relies on heavily to provide debugger support via the `ptrace()` system call? Without `ptrace()` access to the Xenomai thread, a real-time program could not be traced by GDB.

This section will explain how Xenomai makes cross-platform access possible in a dual kernel environment.

The Real-Time Shadow

Xenomai derives its own real-time threads from regular Linux tasks created through the standard POSIX API. Therefore, Xenomai threads inherit Linux tasks' ability to invoke regular Linux services when operating in non-time-critical mode.

When promoted to the real-time application domain, a Linux task is attached to a Xenomai-specific extension called the *real-time shadow*. A real-time shadow allows the mated Linux task to be scheduled by the Xenomai co-kernel when running in real-time mode. Figure 13-3 illustrates how the Linux and Xenomai schedulers share a Linux task context. Each scheduler uses its own data structures to denote tasks, but has access to particular fields in the other scheduler's data structure.

New Sets of System Calls

Xenomai expands the target's operating system by adding several sets of new system calls, which the skins implement. Each time a skin module is loaded, it exports the set

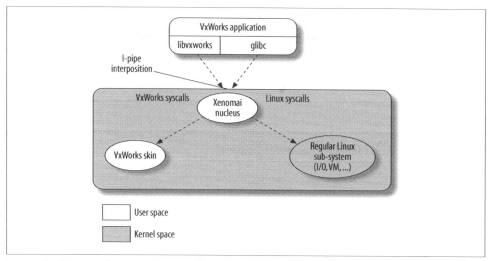

Figure 13-4. Dispatching a real-time call to a Xenomai skin

of services it brings to the Xenomai nucleus, which will in turn dispatch application requests to the proper skin.

To this end, Xenomai uses the I-pipe capability to intercept the regular Linux system call dispatcher and direct the extra system calls to the skin module that implements them.

In user space, system call wrappers are embodied into libraries as a set of C functions. Real-time applications must be linked against those libraries. Those Xenomai libraries are the equivalent of glibc, but they call into the Xenomai system instead of the Linux kernel.

Figure 13-4 depicts how a system call flows from a VxWorks-based application to the proper Xenomai emulator.

Sharing Kernel Features and Domain Migration

Looking at the previous example again, you may notice that a real-time thread can invoke both the standard glibc services and the set of additional system calls brought in by Xenomai. As a matter of fact, application threads may be satisfied with best-effort latencies the Linux kernel can bring when it comes to setup and cleanup tasks, such as accessing the filesystem or setting up communications with some device driver. In between setup and cleanup, however, during the course of their main processing work, the same threads might require stringent real-time guarantees, with low and bounded latencies.

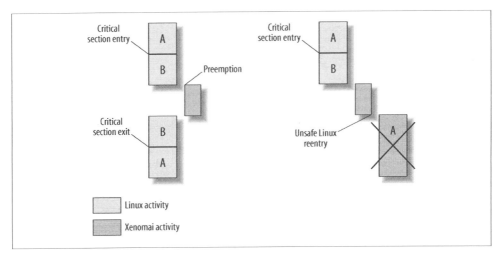

Figure 13-5. The dual kernel issue

Therefore, it's desirable to reuse the rich POSIX environment Linux provides with the glibc when predictability and responsiveness are not critical. However, this requires the dual kernel system to specifically allow for it.

In a co-kernel environment, two kernels run concurrently without synchronizing their activities. In the Xenomai case, one of these kernels even has absolute priority over the other one, and as such may preempt it with no delay to serve a real-time event. Therefore, extreme care must be taken to prevent real-time threads from calling into the regular Linux kernel code when they are controlled by the Xenomai core. Otherwise, we would allow unsafe reentrance that would terminally harm the entire system.

Figure 13-5 illustrates a typical case of bad reentrance, caused by a real-time thread calling into a Linux kernel service from an unsafe context. A regular Linux task enters a critical section and then gets preempted by a real-time thread in the middle of that section. Remember that domains connected through the interrupt pipeline (e.g., Xenomai and Linux) are totally independent, so the high-priority Xenomai domain can never be delayed by the activity of a lower-priority domain. Therefore, regular Linux spinlocks and local interrupt disabling won't protect the Linux kernel from preemption by the Xenomai core. If the real-time task then changes or reads data that the critical section is in the middle of changing, application and operating system errors can result.

The solution to such conflicts is two-fold:

- A Xenomai thread may be exclusively controlled either by the Xenomai co-kernel or the Linux kernel at any given time. When the co-kernel is managing the real-time thread, it may use Xenomai's deterministic system calls. When the Linux kernel is in control, the thread may enter regular Linux system calls—but with no real-time guarantees. Xenomai calls these contexts the *primary* (i.e., Xenomai-controlled) and *secondary* (i.e., Linux-controlled) modes.

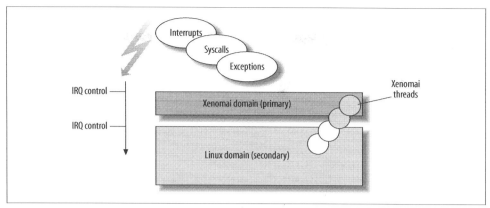

Figure 13-6. Dual kernel support for real-time tasks

- Xenomai automatically put its threads in the right mode as needed when system calls are issued, so that the mechanism remains transparent from the application's point of view. Switching modes boils down to moving a Xenomai thread from one kernel's scheduler to the other. This mechanism is called *domain migration*.

Figure 13-6 sums up the relationships between the interrupt pipeline (I-pipe), the Xenomai and Linux domains, and the real-time applications that move between them as various interrupts, system calls, and other events require their services.

The Real-Time Driver Model

Developing real-time device drivers for a dual kernel architecture has certainly been one of the most painful tasks in real-time programming, at least when the driver has to do more than sending a few bytes polled from a wire over a FIFO to a user space process. The issues one had to face often led to reinventing the Linux driver framework wheel on a driver-by-driver basis.

The key requirement is that we must stick exclusively to calling co-kernel services within real-time drivers in order to keep predictable latencies, as well as reliability. But it is impossible for the standard character device interface in glibc, such as open(), read(), write(), and ioctl(), to provide predictable latencies. In other words, the kernel split between Linux and the real-time extension implies a driver interface split as well.

This situation has led too often to the following issues:

- Device driver developers had to devise an ad hoc solution for their application to call into the driver in order to submit their requests and get results back. One example of such kluges provides a real-time safe FIFO. Another is a piece of system memory coupled to some common IPC, shared between a real-time helper that did the job in kernel space and the user space process.

In all these cases, an entirely nonstandard protocol had to be designed just to implement a driver. Obviously, such an interface had little chance for reuse when porting the driver to another real-time extension.

- Because the regular Linux kernel API was unsuited to implementing the driver, one had to base it on a specific API provided by the underlying real-time extension. For instance, a co-kernel-based device driver may not use a plain Linux mutex or wait in the queue to perform its duty; it ought to obtain the equivalent resources from the real-time kernel instead. Therefore, changing to another Linux real-time extension could require porting the driver code to a new API as well.

To sum up, developers of real-time device drivers have been confronted by the lack of a common framework that would define a normalized interface between the real-time kernel and the device driver, as well as between the user space process and the device driver.

The nightmare is now over, because a common framework is now available in the form of the Real-Time Driver Model (RTDM) by Jan Kiszka and Jörg Langenberg.[†] RTDM has been supported by Xenomai since its early stages.

Major contributions based on RTDM include the following:

- The well-known Comedi framework (*http://www.comedi.org*), used to develop drivers and various tools for data acquisition, is currently being ported to Xenomai over the RTDM layer by Alexis Berlemont.

- A real-time protocol stack for Controller Area Network (CAN) devices, implemented by Sebastian Smolorz and Wolfgang Grandegger and named RT-Socket-CAN, is based on the BSD-like socket interface supplied by RTDM. It is available from the standard Xenomai distribution.

In addition to Xenomai, RTDM has been ported to the native preemption technology (PREEMPT_RT) and RTAI as well, therefore delivering on its promise to unify the interfaces for developing device drivers and their applications under real-time Linux.

RTDM Mediation

RTDM acts as a mediation layer connecting a real-time application process to the services exported by a device driver. Each device driver may belong to one of two classes:

Protocol drivers
These expose a socket interface, and are therefore well suited to managing message-oriented communication with real-time devices. A userland library wraps the standard socket calls (e.g., `socket()`, `send()`/`sendto()`, `recv()`/`recvfrom()`, etc.) around Xenomai system calls that invoke callbacks in the device driver that operates the requested protocol family.

[†] *http://www.xenomai.org/documentation/branches/v2.4.x/pdf/RTDM-and-Applications.pdf*

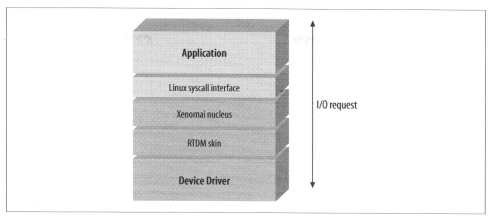

Figure 13-7. RTDM mediation

Named devices

These are comparable to character devices in the Linux device driver model. They are named with an arbitrary text label defined by the driver. The named device has no counterpart whatsoever within the standard Linux device hierarchy; it exists only within the RTDM layer, in parallel with the regular Linux device namespace. Here again, the userland library wraps the standard POSIX 1003.1 routines for I/O communication (e.g., open(), read()/write(), ioctl(), etc.) into Xenomai system calls that invoke the device driver that matches the name originally passed to open().

Figure 13-7 shows the role RTDM plays in relation to Xenomai and the two device classes.

The following code illustrates an RTDM-based named device driver. It implements a simple hardware polling loop performed by a real-time task in kernel space, which periodically wakes up a userland process waiting for some event to be signaled.

Because we want low and strictly bounded latencies, we cannot rely on the regular kernel_thread() function to run the polling task; similarly, we need the userland process to resume execution within a short and bounded delay once the event flag it waits for has been signaled. Therefore, we will use the RTDM driver API to provide both the task and the event flag, which are based exclusively on the Xenomai core, not on the host kernel services.

However, the implementation of real-time device drivers should be based on a driver framework that remains as close as possible to the Linux one:

```
struct rtdev_context {
    rtdm_task_t task;
    rtdm_event_t event;
};

static void task_body(void *arg)
```

```
{
    struct rtdev_context *ctx = (struct rtdev_context *)arg;

    /*
     * Tell RTDM that we want to be scheduled periodically, with a
     * 100 microsecond base period.
     */
    rtdm_task_set_period(&ctx->task, 100000);

    while (1) {
        /* Wait for the next release point in the timeline. */
        rtdm_task_wait_period();
        poll_hardware();
        /* Signal the event userland waits for. */
        rtdm_event_pulse(&ctx->event);
    }
}

int rtdev_open(struct rtdm_dev_context *context,
          rtdm_user_info_t *user_info, int oflags)
{
    struct rtdev_context *ctx = context->dev_private;

    /*
     * Userland just called open("/dev/rtdev", ...); so set up a
     * driver context for the new channel. We first initialize the
     * event flag, then tell RTDM to start the polling task, with
     * priority 72.
     */

    rtdm_event_init(&ctx->event, 0);

    return rtdm_task_init(&ctx->task, "rtdev", &task_body, ctx, 72, 0);
}

int rtdev_close(struct rtdm_dev_context *context,
          rtdm_user_info_t *user_info)
{
    struct rtdev_context *ctx = context->dev_private;

    /* Userland just closed the file; do some housekeeping here. */
    rtdm_event_destroy(&ctx->event);
    rtdm_task_destroy(&ctx->task);

    return 0;
}

int rtdev_ioctl_rt(struct rtdm_dev_context *context,
          rtdm_user_info_t * user_info, unsigned int request, void *arg)
{
    struct rtdev_context *ctx = context->dev_private;
    int ret;

    /*
     * The only request this driver honors is to wait for the next
```

```
     * pulse sent by the polling task, then copy back some data
     * received from the hardware. We won't specify what this data
     * may be here.
     */

    switch (request) {

    case DEMO_RTIOC_RTDEV_WAIT:
        /* Wait for task_body() to wake us up. */
        ret = rtdm_event_wait(&ctx->event);
        if (!ret)
            ret = rtdm_safe_copy_to_user(user_info, arg,
                             &hwdata, sizeof(hwdata));
        break;

    default:
        ret = -EINVAL;
    }

    return ret;
}

static struct rtdm_device device = {
    struct_version:RTDM_DEVICE_STRUCT_VER,

    .device_flags = RTDM_NAMED_DEVICE,
    .context_size = sizeof(struct rtdev_context),
    .device_name = "rtdev",

    .open_rt = NULL,
    .open_nrt = rtdev_open,

    .ops = {
    .close_rt = NULL,
    .close_nrt = rtdev_close,
    .ioctl_rt = rtdev_ioctl_rt,
    .ioctl_nrt = NULL,
    },

    .device_class = RTDM_CLASS_DEMO,
    .device_sub_class = RTDM_SUBCLASS_RTDEV,
    .driver_name = "rtdev",
    .driver_version = RTDM_DRIVER_VER(0, 0, 0),
    .peripheral_name = "RTDM-compliant demo device driver",
    .proc_name: device.device_name,
};

int __init __rtdev_init(void)
{
    /* Make this driver known to RTDM. */
    return rtdm_dev_register(&device);
}

void __rtdev_exit(void)
{
```

```
        rtdm_dev_unregister(&device, 1000);
    }
```

In the `rtdm_device` structure, you can see an entry for each of the interface routines the driver implements, such as `open_rt()` and `open_nrt()`. As their suffixes tells us, those routines are invoked by RTDM depending on the calling context. It calls `open_rt()` for a real-time operation controlled by the Xenomai scheduler and `open_nrt()` for a standard operation controlled by the Linux scheduler.

For instance, if opening the device should be a time-bounded real-time operation, RTDM must call the real-time entry point, which in turn may only use co-kernel services. On the other hand, if the operation is not time-critical or needs services from the Linux kernel API, then RTDM should call the non-real-time entry point. It is up to the developer to provide only one entry point, or both of them, depending on the desired behavior.

RTDM over Xenomai will pick the best context matching routine depending on the calling context and available entry points. For instance, our previous example does not define any real-time entry point for the `open()` operation. Therefore, real-time callers will be downgraded to a plain Linux mode before the *open_nrt* callback is invoked. Conversely, a Xenomai thread currently controlled by the Linux scheduler will be switched back to its primary mode—i.e., real-time—before the *open_rt* callback is fired.

A typical application process using the driver we previously sketched out may be as follows. This code would have to link against a Xenomai library that wraps RTDM calls. Xenomai's POSIX interface provides such a wrapping, and can be used to create a real-time thread (running the `test_thread()` function in the following example) that communicates with the driver through the RTDM-wrapped `open()` and `ioctl()` calls:

```
    void *test_thread(void *arg)
    {
        int ret;

        for (;;) {
            ret = ioctl(fd, DEMO_RTIOC_RTDEV_WAIT, &hwdata);

            if (ret) {
                perror("ioctl failed");
                pthread_exit(EXIT_FAILURE);
            }
        }
    }

    int main(int argc, char *const argv[])
    {
        struct sched_param param = { .sched_priority = 70 };
        pthread_attr_t attr;
        pthread_t tid;
        int fd;

        mlockall(MCL_CURRENT | MCL_FUTURE);
```

```
        fd = open("/dev/rtdev", O_RDWR);

        if (fd < 0)
            error(1, errno, "open failed");

        pthread_attr_init(&attr);
        pthread_attr_setdetachstate(&attr, PTHREAD_CREATE_JOINABLE);
        pthread_attr_setinheritsched(&attr, PTHREAD_EXPLICIT_SCHED);
        pthread_attr_setschedpolicy(&attr, SCHED_FIFO);
        pthread_attr_setschedparam(&attr, &param);
        pthread_create(&tid, &attr, &test_thread, NULL);

        pthread_join(&tid, NULL);

        return 0;
    }
```

This code snippet also illustrates an interesting aspect of Xenomai's POSIX skin, which comes as close as possible to the regular Linux programming model. The POSIX skin is a drop-in replacement for a number of services normally available from the Linux kernel through glibc. Xenomai implements real-time counterparts that ensure short and predictable response times. In the previous example, we actually used the Xenomai implementation of `pthread_create()`, `pthread_join()`, `open()`, and `ioctl()`. All other POSIX services invoked from this code are still obtained from the standard glibc.

Thus, calls from Xenomai's POSIX implementation can be mixed with a standard RTOS POSIX implementation such as Linux in a single application. Xenomai threads are allowed to invoke both kinds, although only the Xenomai-provided ones guarantee real-time behavior. The Xenomai interface library will automatically relay the requests it cannot handle to the regular glibc, such as when opening a non-RTDM device.

Xenomai, Chameleon by Design

Xenomai currently exhibits a dual kernel architecture based on the lightweight and mature Adeos/I-pipe virtualization layer. It is available for various platforms at low engineering and maintenance costs. This approach has the following key advantages:

- It decouples Xenomai from the development cycle of mainline Linux, which gives the developer more freedom in selecting the kernel base and reduces the impact that potential regression failures in the standard kernel may have on the real-time subsystem.

- It protects Xenomai applications from regular applications that behave badly, because Xenomai applications are not controlled by the same kernel when they run in real-time mode.

- Xenomai developers and embedded developers alike can track real-time problems, such as unexpected latencies, by looking for causes in the co-kernel domain. This involves auditing much less code than the regular kernel.

- Co-kernels are inherently lightweight, because they rely on the host kernel to provide non-time-critical services, which represent most of the feature set. Consequently, the price of implementing real-time guarantees in the system is paid only by the applications that require them. In other words, the Linux host kernel does not have to deal with real-time issues at all, aside from virtualizing the interrupt mask, which is a cheap operation.

However, this design excludes all the regular Linux drivers and libraries that rely on the standard kernel from the real-time domain, because they are not served by the co-kernel. In a number of application cases, this requirement may be a significant drawback, particularly when the implementation entangles non-real-time and time-critical activities, or simply because having regular drivers with bounded response times would fit the system's need at a lower engineering cost.

Additionally, Xenomai is primarily about supporting traditional RTOS APIs over a Linux-based real-time framework so that projects can migrate legacy applications to Linux at a lower cost. In some cases, the dual kernel approach is the right one; in other cases, a fully native real-time Linux framework would deliver a better port. In any case, getting the best possible trade-off between Linux integration and real-time predictability should be the decisive factor in picking the right base technology.

As a matter of fact, the PREEMPT_RT effort[‡] opens up a promising path to getting short, bounded latencies within a single kernel system for a variety of real-time application profiles and platforms.

Because the goal of the Xenomai project is to ease the porting of applications from traditional RTOSes to Linux, PREEMPT_RT creates opportunities to extend its relevance as a migration tool, provided the emulation technology is fully ported to a single-image real-time kernel.

At the time of this writing, as of Linux kernel 2.6.24, the Xenomai emulators are being ported to PREEMPT_RT-enabled kernels. This effort, codenamed Xenomai/SOLO, is taking place in parallel with the normal development of the dual kernel version. It is cosponsored by the Open Source Automation Development Lab (*http://www.osadl.org*), DENX Software Engineering (*http://www.denx.de*), and the Xenomai project. This purely native implementation, coupled with the already existing native version of the RTDM layer, will complete the jigsaw puzzle.[§] Traditional real-time applications will be ported more easily to Linux, keeping all options open for selecting the underlying kernel technology used to support them, and taking advantage of a growing base of drivers for industrial devices.

[‡] *http://people.redhat.com/mingo/realtime-preempt*

[§] *http://www.osadl.org/RTDM-native.howto-rtdm-native.0.html#introduction*

## CHAPTER 14

The RT Patch

Steven Rostedt

Over the past few years, there has been a large effort in the Linux community to convert the Linux kernel into a true real-time operating system (RTOS), without the help of a microkernel. In order to achieve this, several changes to the kernel were necessary. For Linux to behave properly in a real-time environment, interrupt service routines must not be able to unconditionally preempt any process running on the CPU, protection for critical sections needs to be narrowed to block only those processes that might access them, and unbounded priority inversion must not be allowed. The pros and cons of native Linux real-time versus an accompanying microkernel were covered in Chapter 12.

In the past, several people have tried to implement a full real-time Linux kernel. Some have even built their businesses around it. In the 2.2 and 2.4 Linux time frame, TimeSys, a small real-time Linux company, branched off from the mainline kernel (the kernel provided by *kernel.org*), to create and support its own kernel that implemented the changes just mentioned. But maintaining a kernel outside the mainline Linux tree has proven to be very difficult.

Ingo Molnar, a major contributor to the Linux kernel, showed up on the real-time scene after watching others work on their efforts to turn the Linux kernel into an RTOS. Seeing some of the benefits of having real-time capabilities in Linux, Molnar started his own patch against the mainline kernel to add real-time features.

Molnar's approach was slightly different from others because his viewpoint was not that of real-time developers trying to convert Linux to their environment, but rather that of a long-term Linux kernel hacker giving the system some real-time features that would improve the user's experience. Soon after Molnar started his RT patch, several other kernel developers joined him on his quest, and it evolved from Molnar's experiment to a robust real-time alternative. Many of the features that were developed in the RT patch have already made it into the mainline kernel. Some of these features include high-resolution timers, kernel lock validation, generic interrupts for all architectures, robust futexes, and even priority inheritance. We'll explain some of these features, and others that are being developed, in the following sections.

Interrupts As Threads

The current Linux kernel* has several methods of handling the work of devices. When a device performs an asynchronous event that requires action by the CPU and interrupts are enabled, the device sends an interrupt signal that preempts the CPU from whatever it was doing to perform the interrupt service routine (ISR) for the device that issued the interrupt. The ISR is executed at a higher priority than any user task, and with interrupts disabled on the CPU or, at the bare minimum, with the current interrupt line masked off. So, the only thing that can preempt an ISR is another interrupt, and only if the ISR is nice enough to turn interrupts back on.

A well-written device driver puts as little work as possible into the ISR and pushes other work to a kernel thread, a tasklet, or a softirq. These are the other methods that Linux provides for devices to finish the work needed by asynchronous events, such as device activity.

A *softirq* is a service routine that is performed after the return of an ISR and before resuming the process that was interrupted. If too many softirqs are queued, the kernel wakes up a high-priority kernel thread (*ksoftirqd*) to finish them. There's been debate in the kernel development as to what qualifies as "too many softirqs." The *ksoftirqd* thread is started whenever a softirq is started with interrupts disabled, or if a softirq routine is processed more than once before returning back to the process that was preempted.

A *tasklet* is similar to a softirq in that it also occurs after an ISR and before resuming the interrupted process. The difference between a softirq and a tasklet is that the same softirq can run simultaneously on two separate CPUs, whereas a tasklet cannot. A softirq therefore has to use locks to protect against concurrent accesses to any nonlocal data or other resources, whereas a tasklet does not; in other words, a tasklet need not be reentrant.

Another difference between tasklets and softirqs is that a tasklet function may run on a different CPU from the one that raised (triggered) the tasklet. Tasklets are in fact implemented by a softirq. The softirq function that implements tasklets just makes sure that two tasklet functions are not running at the same time. This also means that tasklets can be executed by the *ksoftirqd* thread.

A kernel thread is a thread that runs only within the kernel, and can be awakened by an ISR to handle any work left to be completed by an interrupt service routine, so that the ISR can return quickly and allow whatever process or kernel activity was preempted to resume. A kernel thread acts much like other threads in Linux. It can be scheduled, have its priority changed, run on given CPUs, and be manipulated by the system administrator like any other thread in the system.

---

* 2.6.22 as of this writing.

In this case, the ISR would usually utilize a *work queue*. A work queue is a kernel utility that, like its name suggests, queues up work to be run in a worker kernel thread. There is a generic worker kernel thread called *keventd* that will execute work functions by the kernel if the kernel did not allocate a specific work queue. Any work queued to the generic *keventd* thread needs to wait for all the previous work functions that were queued ahead of it, because a queue handles work in a FIFO order.

A kernel thread entails a bit more overhead than a softirq or tasklet but is much more flexible. A softirq and tasklet under the non-RT Linux kernel cannot be preempted by any process at any priority. Conversely, a softirq and tasklet can preempt any process. So, even though the overhead of a kernel thread is slightly more than a softirq and tasklet, it allows the kernel scheduler to be more flexible and gives more control to the system administrator. (However, kernel threads may ignore signals.) This flexibility is especially important to running a real-time environment.

When a routine is performed by an ISR, softirq, or tasklet, any process that is running on the CPU will be preempted by it. They will even preempt kernel threads that are doing work for other devices. This Linux behavior effectively creates a policy that makes ISRs, softirqs, and tasklets the highest-priority events in the system. In order to lower latencies that these routines impose on the system, the RT patch transforms them all into kernel threads.

Hard IRQs As Threads

A hard interrupt request (IRQ) is a sort of envelope around an ISR, lasting from the time the interrupt preempts the CPU to the time the ISR returns the CPU back to normal processing. This can lead to *interrupt inversion*, where an interrupt service routine takes time away from a high-priority process in order to perform work that is of lower priority. Figure 14-1 illustrates the latency caused by an ISR that takes away processing time from a high-priority process. The latency consists of both arrows labeled "context switch," in addition to the ISR running time.

Obviously, we cannot keep the hardware interrupt from preempting the CPU. But the RT patch shortens the time of interrupt inversion to a bare minimum. It does this by converting the interrupt handlers into threads. When an interrupt is triggered, the ISR just wakes up a kernel thread that will run the function registered by the device driver, instead of the ISR running the interrupt handler itself. Figure 14-2 illustrates the RT patch's handling of interrupts.

When an interrupt is triggered, whatever is currently executing on the CPU will still be preempted. But this time, the only activity performed before returning to the previous process or thread is the masking of the interrupt line and the waking of the interrupt service thread. If the interrupt service thread is of a higher priority than the currently running thread, it will be immediately scheduled and preempt the process that the interrupt preempted. If the original thread was of a higher priority than the interrupt service thread, processing continues with the original thread, and the interrupt service

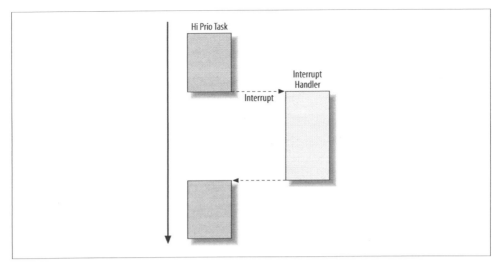

Figure 14-1. Interrupt inversion

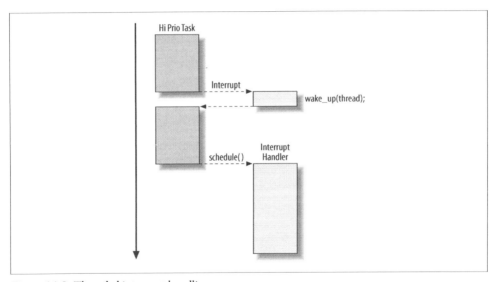

Figure 14-2. Threaded interrupt handling

thread is either scheduled on another CPU or has to wait for the higher-priority thread to voluntarily give up the CPU.

 A few interrupt handlers still run as normal interrupt service routines instead of waiting to run in another thread; the most notable example is the timer interrupt. The RT patch tries to make the timer interrupt return as fast as possible to limit latencies that it can cause.

The threads that are created to service the interrupts are named IRQ_*n*, where *n* is the number of the interrupt vector. One can see these threads in the *ps* command:

```
$ ps -e -o pid,rtprio,comm | grep IRQ
   41       50 IRQ-9
  769       50 IRQ-14
  771       50 IRQ-15
  784       50 IRQ-12
  785       50 IRQ-1
 1714       50 IRQ-8
 1722       50 IRQ-20
 1730       50 IRQ-21
 1751       50 IRQ-19
 1762       50 IRQ-22
 1772       50 IRQ-16
 1774       50 IRQ-7
 1839       50 IRQ-17
 1918       50 IRQ-18
$ cat /proc/interrupts
           CPU0
  0:         91    IO-APIC-edge      timer
  1:      31336    IO-APIC-edge      i8042
  7:          0    IO-APIC-edge      parport0
  8:          0    IO-APIC-edge      rtc
  9:     517591    IO-APIC-fasteoi   acpi
 12:        368    IO-APIC-edge      i8042
 14:     257832    IO-APIC-edge      ide0
 15:     950323    IO-APIC-edge      ide1
 16:          1    IO-APIC-fasteoi   yenta
 17:          1    IO-APIC-fasteoi   yenta
 18:         27    IO-APIC-fasteoi   Intel 82801DB-ICH4 Modem, Intel 82801DB-ICH4
 19:    1288060    IO-APIC-fasteoi   uhci_hcd:usb3, wifi0
 20:     163173    IO-APIC-fasteoi   uhci_hcd:usb1, eth0
 21:          0    IO-APIC-fasteoi   uhci_hcd:usb2
 22:          2    IO-APIC-fasteoi   ehci_hcd:usb4
NMI:          0
LOC:   32797885
ERR:          0
MIS:          0
```

The previous listing shows how all the interrupts besides the timer interrupt have their service routines handled by threads. The default priority of all IRQ threads is 50, but it is easy to change them. In the following example, run as the *root* user, we modify the priority of the interrupt service thread for the Ethernet NIC to a priority of 80. The *chrt* utility is supplied with most distributions in an auxiliary package:

```
# chrt -p -f 80 1722
# ps -e -o pid,rtprio,comm | grep IRQ
   41       50 IRQ-9
  769       50 IRQ-14
  771       50 IRQ-15
  784       50 IRQ-12
  785       50 IRQ-1
 1714       50 IRQ-8
 1722       80 IRQ-20
```

```
1730      50 IRQ-21
1751      50 IRQ-19
1762      50 IRQ-22
1772      50 IRQ-16
1774      50 IRQ-7
1839      50 IRQ-17
1918      50 IRQ-18
```

On this system, the interrupt vector number for *eth0* is 20. (This can be determined by
examining */proc/interrupts*.) The *ps* command after the change of priority shows that
that IRQ-20 (pid 1722) now has a priority of 80. Now this interrupt service thread will
have a higher priority than any of the other interrupt service threads. Thus, having
interrupts handled via threads gives the system administrator the ability to prioritize
interrupts even when the hardware does not support prioritized interrupts.

The system administrator must understand how threaded interrupts affect the system.
The RT patch allows for user processes to run at a higher priority than interrupt handlers. This can have dire results if a process goes into an infinite loop waiting to be
preempted by an event that is running at a lower priority than the process doing the
loop.

We'll use the following code for an example (but you don't need to understand the
code to follow the explanation of the problem):

```
int signal_me;

int do_listen(in_port_t port) {
    int sockfd;
    struct sockaddr_in sin;

    if ((sockfd = socket(PF_INET, SOCK_STREAM, 0)) < 0)
        return -1;

    memset(&sin, 0, sizeof(sin));
    sin.sin_family = AF_INET;
    sin.sin_port = htons(port);
    sin.sin_addr.s_addr = htonl(INADDR_ANY);

    if (bind(sockfd, (struct sockaddr*)&sin, sizeof(sin)) < 0)
        goto out_err;

    if (listen(sockfd, 5) < 0)
        goto out_err;

    return sockfd;

out_err:
    close(sockfd);
    return -1;
}

void *run_listener(void *unused)
{
    int fd;
```

```
        fd = do_listen(4321);
        if (fd < 0) {
            perror("bad listen");
            exit(-1);
        }

        while (1) {
            int cfd;
            struct sockaddr_in in;
            socklen_t len;

            cfd = accept(fd, (struct sockaddr*)&in, &len);
            if (cfd < 0) {
                perror("can't accept");
                exit(-1);
            }
            signal_me = cfd + 1;
        }
        close (fd);
        return NULL;
    }

    void *run_worker(void *unused)
    {
        while (1) {
            /*
             * [...]
             *   doing some work
             * [...]
             */
            if (signal_me) {
                signal_me = 0;
                printf("handle the single!\n");
                sleep(100);
            }
        }
        return NULL;
    }
```

Two threads are created to run the functions: run_listener and run_worker. The worker thread is off doing some algorithm and is expecting to receive a packet from some other machine. When the packet is received, the listener thread will accept it and signal the worker thread to stop its loop and handle the packet. The signaling is achieved by a global shared variable, signal_me, that both threads have access to.

Now, let's assume that the listener thread is of higher priority than the worker thread, since it needs to preempt the worker thread to signal it. If the system administrator did not have a good understanding of the system and set both these threads at a higher priority than the network interrupt thread or the softirq thread, then he will have a little surprise when none of this actually works. For an external network packet to make it to the listener thread, both the interrupt thread that services the network interface card and the network softirqs will need to be of higher priority than the worker thread.

Otherwise, the worker thread will not be preempted by the packet being received, and the work done by the worker thread will continue to run and prevent anything of lower priority from running on that CPU. The end result would appear to be a system hang. If all other threads are of lower priority than the worker thread, no other threads will be able to capture control of the CPU.

Interrupts and CPU Affinities

An operating system scheduler on a multiprocessor system tries to keep each thread on the CPU where it started in order to prevent expensive cache flushes. This tendency is called *CPU affinity*. It is very important to note that the CPU affinity of an IRQ thread is determined by the CPU affinity of the interrupt itself. Every time the interrupt handler executes, it compares the thread CPU affinity to that of the interrupt affinity. If they are different, the interrupt service thread affinity is updated to that of the interrupt affinity. So, if you want to set the affinity of the interrupt service thread, simply set the affinity of the interrupt. We'll show the impact of this rule with an example that plays with the affinity of the interrupt service thread, as well as the interrupt itself:

```
# cat /proc/interrupts | grep ide0
 14:     13602       1720    IO-APIC-edge      ide0
# ps ax | grep IRQ-14
 790 ?        S<     0:00 [IRQ-14]
```

The system used two CPUs, as can be seen in the first output. The IDE0 controller with interrupt 14 went off 13,602 times on CPU 0 and 1,720 times on CPU 1. The *ps* command helped the pid (790) of the interrupt service thread for IRQ 14.

In the commands that follow, a simple check of the */proc* filesystem reveals the affinity of the interrupt: it's bound to CPU 0 (which is represented by the affinity mask of 1). We then try to manipulate the affinity:

```
# cat /proc/irq/14/smp_affinity
 1
# taskset -p 790
 pid 790's current affinity mask: 1
# taskset -p 2 790
 pid 790's current affinity mask: 1
 pid 790's new affinity mask: 2
# taskset -p 790
 pid 790's current affinity mask: 2
# cat /proc/irq/14/smp_affinity
 1
```

The first *taskset* command just shows the affinity of the IRQ 14 interrupt service thread (pid 790). It also has the affinity of CPU 0. Next, we try an *incorrect* way of changing the interrupt service thread's CPU affinity mask by using *taskset* to set the thread's affinity to CPU 1 (the CPU affinity bitmask of 2 corresponds to CPU 1). A recheck of the */proc/irq/14/smp_affinity* file shows that changing the CPU affinity of the interrupt service thread had no effect on the affinity of the IRQ. Furthermore, the scheduler will reset the affinity of the interrupt service thread when it runs so that it matches the IRQ, so our *taskset* command was wasted.

Now for the correct approach:

```
# echo 2 > /proc/irq/14/smp_affinity
# cat /proc/irq/14/smp_affinity
2
```

We echo the new bitmask of 2 (corresponding to CPU 1) into the *proc* file to set the affinity of the IRQ to CPU 1. Let's change it back to CPU 0 and see the effect on the interrupt service thread:

```
# taskset -p 790
    pid 790's current affinity mask: 2
# echo 1 > /proc/irq/14/smp_affinity
# taskset -p 790
    pid 790's current affinity mask: 2
# ls -lR / > /dev/null
# taskset -p 790
    pid 790's current affinity mask: 1
```

We had previously set the affinity of the interrupt service thread to CPU 1, shown by the first *taskset* command in the previous output. Changing the CPU affinity of the IRQ back to CPU 0 in the *echo* command seems at first not to change the affinity of the interrupt service thread. But the thread's affinity doesn't update to the interrupt's affinity until an interrupt is triggered. So, we enter *ls -lR /* to trigger some IDE interrupts. After that, we can see the interrupt service thread's affinity went back to CPU 0.

With the latest RT patch the interrupt service thread's affinity (this may change in the future) follows that of the IRQ affinity. Changes don't take place on the thread's affinity until after the first interrupt has occurred since the change was made to the IRQ affinity.

Softirqs As Threads

Softirqs can also create priority inversion. A softirq runs with interrupts enabled so that other interrupts may come in, but they still preempt all threads, including kernel threads. Softirqs can actually cause more harm than kernel threads, because they usually run the routines for the device that take longer to handle. This means that a softirq will cause a longer latency than an interrupt.

Originally, the RT patch simply made all softirqs run under the *ksoftirqd* thread. This gives the system administrator the ability to place high-priority threads at a higher priority than softirqs. The problem with this approach is that all softirqs are grouped as one priority and handled by a single thread per CPU. If the system administrator wanted to give a process that was accessing the network a higher priority than a process that was accessing the disk drive, the end result would not be the desired one, as the disk drive softirq routines would run at the same priority as the network softirq routines. Any work done by a process doing disk I/O could cause long latencies for the high-priority process accessing the network.

Currently, the RT patch separates each softirq routine to run as a separate thread. A softirq thread is created for each CPU, and that thread is bound to the CPU to which it was assigned. This is to maintain consistency with the semantics of the mainline kernel, which always runs a softirq routine on the CPU where it was initiated, and allows the softirq routine to run on multiple CPUs at the same time.[†] These softirq threads are visible by the user the same way the interrupt service threads are, through *ps*:

```
$ ps -e -o pid,rtprio,comm | grep sirq
    5    50 sirq-high/0
    6    50 sirq-timer/0
    7    50 sirq-net-tx/
    8    50 sirq-net-rx/
    9    50 sirq-block/0
   10    50 sirq-tasklet
   11    50 sirq-sched/0
   12    50 sirq-hrtimer
   13    50 sirq-rcu/0
   17    50 sirq-high/1
   18    50 sirq-timer/1
   19    50 sirq-net-tx/
   20    50 sirq-net-rx/
   21    50 sirq-block/1
   22    50 sirq-tasklet
   23    50 sirq-sched/1
   24    50 sirq-hrtimer
   25    50 sirq-rcu/1
```

The names of the softirq threads are defined as softirq-*name*/*n*, where *name* is the name assigned to the softirq and *n* is the number of the CPU. Since the name field is only 16 characters long, and 1 character is needed to hold the end-of-string character, the names shown are truncated at 15 characters. The CPU affinity of these threads can be viewed using the *taskset* command:

```
$ taskset -p -c 10
pid 10's current affinity list: 0
$ taskset -p -c 22
pid 22's current affinity list: 1
```

Even though the CPU number part of the softirq thread for tasklets has been truncated, you can still see the CPU that it was bound to using *taskset*. These kernel threads for softirqs must remain on the CPU to which they were assigned. Forcing them onto other CPUs will have undefined results, and may lock up the system. These threads stay in a sleep state until something on that CPU triggers them, so if you do not have processes that will wake them up on a given CPU, they will never interfere with the processes on that CPU.

[†] Remember that the same softirq routine may run on separate CPUs at the same time, but tasklet routines cannot.

Softirq Optimization During Interrupt Handling

Like interrupt service threads, the priorities of the softirqs are also set at 50 by default. Since scheduling of interrupt service threads and softirq threads requires a context switch, the RT patch performs a slight optimization. The interrupt service threads are the most common threads to trigger a softirq. As mentioned earlier, in the mainline kernel, softirqs are performed upon return from an interrupt. The RT patch has a check in the interrupt service routine loop, after the call to the driver's handler, to see whether there are any pending softirqs on the current CPU that have the same priority as the interrupt service thread. If so, the interrupt service thread runs the softirq functions and eliminates the need to context switch to the softirq thread.

This optimization makes it slightly advantageous to keep the interrupt service threads at the same priority as the corresponding softirq threads. The main users of this optimization are probably the NIC interrupt service thread matching the softirq-net-rx and softirq-net-tx threads, and the disk drive interrupt service threads matching the softirq-block threads.

But there also comes a risk with letting the interrupt service thread run the function of a softirq. A softirq function must always stay on the CPU it was assigned. So, while the interrupt executes the softirq function, it too must be bounded to the CPU. If a higher-priority process on that CPU preempts the interrupt service thread while it is bound to a single CPU, that interrupt line will no longer run the interrupts handlers until the higher-priority process releases the CPU back to the interrupt service thread. Due to this problem, this feature may either go away, or will most likely be redesigned in the future.

Softirq Timer Threads

The timer softirq threads are generally the most important for an RT system administrator to understand. These are the threads that control timing events. The softirq-timer thread handles most timeouts in the system, including the networking layer timeouts. Usually, it is not crucial for these to be executed on time, even for RT systems.

The softirq-hrtimer thread is a bit more important. It thread handles the POSIX timer implementations. If your RT application is using POSIX timer calls, such as timer_create, you must be aware of the impact of the softirq-hrtimer thread's priority.

Timing events that happen through the timer_create POSIX system call register a function to be called by the hrtimer subsystem, which uses the softirq-hrtimer thread to handle the functions that are registered to it. A high-priority process that expects an interrupt from POSIX timers must be of lower priority than the softirq-hrtimer thread. Otherwise, when the timer goes off, the function to signal the high-priority process may be starved by the high-priority process itself. If this signal is used to inform the high-priority process to stop some sort of loop, the system may hang, because the high-priority process may never give up the CPU.

There is development going on that will allow the hrtimer thread to take on a *dynamic* priority. What this means is that the hrtimer-softirq thread will take on the priority of the timer that it will execute, which in turn is derived from the priority of the the task that requested the timer. This feature has been included on various versions of the RT patch, but because of the way Linux is currently designed, it has caused some technical difficulties. A future version of the RT patch will eventually include this feature again, and at that point there will be no need to worry about the priority of the hrtimer-softirq thread because it will automatically change its priority to that of the process that requested the timer.

An RT application must be aware of its use of POSIX timers. If all parts of the application, from low-priority to high-priority processes, use POSIX timers, the lower-priority processes may cause latencies within the higher-priority process when their timers are triggered. These latencies are not particularly critical as long as they are accounted for. A lower-priority process still cannot cause much harm to a higher-priority process by using POSIX timers, even when the higher-priority process is lower in priority than the softirq-hrtimer thread. The only thing that preempts the higher-priority process through the softirq-hrtimer thread is the processing of the timer to send a signal to the lower-priority process.

At the time of this writing, the RT patch's handling of POSIX timers forces each timer intervals to be at least one jiffie, promoting it to a jiffie if a shorter time is requested.[‡] This is to keep the softirq-hrtimer thread from starving if the signal process ignores the signal it is supposed to receive from the timer. Ignored signals cause a re-triggering of the softirq-hrtimer thread. This also prevents lower-priority processes from doing more than one timer event per jiffy that would preempt a higher-priority process, and thus would allow the latency caused by lower-priority processes to overrun the system.

The nanosleep system call is *not* affected by the softirq-hrtimer. As mentioned earlier, timer interrupts are not handled by threads but are performed at the time the ISR runs. Processes that are sleeping with nanosleep will be woken up directly from the interrupt. So, processes that are of higher priority than the sofitrq-hrtimer interrupt will still work fine using nanosleep, and even sleep for that matter.

Priority Inheritance

In Linux kernel version 2.6.18, priority inheritance was, for the first time, part of the mainline Linux kernel. Although this priority inheritance applied only to userland fast mutexes (futex), the infrastructure was in the kernel. This code was developed in the

---

‡ Jiffies are an arbitrary measurement of time in Linux and are defined as a HZ value in the kernel configuration. Distributions usually default this value to 100, 250, or 1,000.

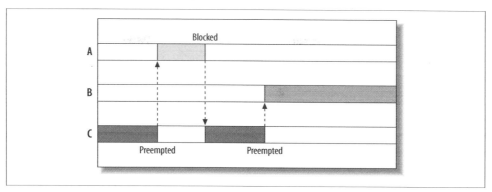

Figure 14-3. Unbounded priority inversion

RT patch, and the algorithm used to implement the futex priority inheritance is the same algorithm that the RT patch uses for internal locks. To take advantage of the priority inheritance futex in 2.6.18, you must have the right glibc version. Version 2.5 and up have support for the priority inheritance mutexes.

Before going further and explaining how to take advantage of priority inheritance futexes, we'll quickly go over what priority inheritance offers and why the kernel has it. It helps to address the classic problem of priority inversion, described in Chapter 12.

Priority inversion itself is not a problem and is sometimes unavoidable. Priority inversion becomes a problem when it is unbounded: when there's no predictable way to calculate the time the higher-priority process must wait for the resource.

The classic example of unbounded priority inversion involves three separate processes, A, B, and C, where A is the highest priority and C is the lowest. C starts out and grabs a lock and then is preempted by A. A tries to take the same lock that C has but must block and wait for C to release it. A gives the CPU back to C so that C can finish the thing it was doing that needed the lock. But B comes along, preempting C, and runs for some undetermined amount of time. The problem is that B is not only preempting the lower-priority process C but also the higher-priority process A, since A was waiting on C. This is unbounded priority inversion, and it is illustrated in Figure 14-3.

As mentioned in Chapter 12, there are various methods to address priority inversion. The RT patch takes the priority inheritance approach. Locks from within the kernel can also suffer from unbounded priority inversion. The RT patch brings priority inheritance to locks within the kernel to prevent unbounded priority inversions from happening there. The code that does this is the same code that works with the light-weight user mutex, also known as a futex.

The futex was initially introduced into the Linux kernel by Rusty Russell as a way to perform locking in user space without having to enter the kernel, except for cases of contention. The idea is to use shared memory addresses between two threads along with atomic operations provided by the hardware to create, lock, and unlock a mutex.

Most of the time a mutex is taken and released with no contention, so any need to enter the kernel would cause unneeded overhead. Using shared memory and hardware atomic operations, the futex is able to grab and release mutex locks without the overhead of a system call. The only time a system call is needed is when contention takes place, because the blocking thread needs to sleep. When the thread that holds the mutex goes to release it, it will notice that there are waiting threads on that mutex. The thread will then make a system call to wake up the waiters.

One problem with this original approach is what to do if the thread that holds the mutex comes to an unexpected end. That is, what happens when the holder of the mutex hits a bug or crashes? The thread will never release the mutex. Now, when other threads come to take the mutex, they will block, and since the owner is no longer running, the waiters will never be awakened. This can cause a system lockup if this happens to a critical application.

The solution to handling an orphaned futex is called *robust futex*. A robust futex (designed by Thomas Gleixner, Ingo Molnar, and others) has a given layout in the user space that the kernel can use to read what futexes a thread may have on exit. The kernel checks the thread of futexes that it holds very carefully.[§] Any futex that was held by the terminated thread is unlocked, and any waiters are woken up. This way, an application does not need to worry about a thread dying while holding a futex and thus locking up the rest of the application.

As of this writing, the only user of the futex functionality in Linux is the pthread mutex. Futexes themselves are not required to be used between threads, but have only the requirement of shared memory.[‖] POSIX mutexes implement futexes with all the latest distributions. Currently, as of this writing, the major embedded libc libraries (uClibc and newlib) do not include the futex features.[#]

If futexes and priority inheritance are implemented by the pthread library, a thread can turn on priority inheritance for a mutex by specifing PTHREAD_PRIO_INHERIT as a mutex attribute. The following sample code snippet implements a pthread mutex that uses priority inheritance:

```
extern pthread_mutex_t mutex;
pthread_mutexattr_t attr;

if (pthread_mutexattr_init(&attr))
    perr("pthread_mutexattr_init");

if (pthread_mutexattr_setprotocol(&attr, PTHREAD_PRIO_INHERIT))
    perr("pthread_mutexattr_setprotocol");
```

[§] The kernel cannot trust anything that comes from user space.

[‖] Rusty Russell implemented a futex library that does not need to be used between threads but can be used between processes. See *http://www.kernel.org/pub/linux/kernel/people/rusty/futex-2.2.tar.gz*.

[#] uClibc and newlib developers would always appreciate new patches. So expect them to be using futexes them in the near future.

```
        if (pthread_mutex_init(&mutex, &attr))
            perr("ptherad_mutex_init");
```

The code initializes a pthread mutex attribute name `attr` and then sets its `PTHREAD_PRIO_INHERIT` flag. Finally, the mutex is initialized with the priority inheritance attribute.

Since the futex priority inheritance code uses the same code as the RT patch in kernel priority inheritance, the two work well together. That means priority inheritance works the same way whether a high-priority process is blocked by either a kernel mutex or a lower-priority process that is blocked on a user futex. The boosting of priority inheritance will still go up the chain of blocked processes.

Configuring the Kernel with the RT Patch

Download the RT patch at *http://people.redhat.com/mingo/realtime-preempt/*. If you are unfamiliar with applying kernel patches, read *http://www.linuxheadquarters.com/how to/tuning/kernelpatch.shtml. Running Linux* by Matthias Dalheimer and Matt Welsh and *Linux Kernel in a Nutshell* by Greg Kroah-Hartman (both O'Reilly) also contain sections on applying kernel patches and rebuilding a kernel.

Another method for patching is to use the tool *ketchup*, written by Matt Mackall. It is available as a package in most distributions, but can also be downloaded from *http://www.selenic.com/ketchup/*, and it is described in *Linux Kernel in a Nutshell. ketchup* is a very handy tool that allows you to update a directory to the latest kernels, including Andrew Morton's -mm development branch and the latest stable kernels. But most importantly, at least for this discussion, it also works for the RT patch. Here's how you can get the RT patch just by being connected to the Internet, and having the *ketchup* tool (*ketchup* expects *wget* and *patch* to already be installed on your system):

```
~$ mkdir tmp
~$ cd tmp
~/tmp$ ketchup -G 2.6.22
None -> 2.6.22
Downloading linux-2.6.22.tar.bz2
--22:13:47--  http://www.kernel.org/pub/linux/kernel/v2.6/linux-2.6.22.tar.bz2
           => `/home/rostedt/.ketchup/linux-2.6.22.tar.bz2.partial'
Resolving www.kernel.org... 204.152.191.5, 204.152.191.37
Connecting to www.kernel.org|204.152.191.5|:80... connected.
HTTP request sent, awaiting response... 200 OK
Length: 45,119,878 (43M) [application/x-bzip2]

100%[====================================>] 45,119,878    596.37K/s    ETA 00:00

22:15:01 (591.74 KB/s) - `/home/rostedt/.ketchup/linux-2.6.22.tar.bz2.partial' saved
[45119878/45119878]

Unpacking linux-2.6.22.tar.bz2
~/tmp$ ketchup -r -G 2.6.22.1-rt9
```

```
2.6.22 -> 2.6.22.1-rt9
Downloading patch-2.6.22.1.bz2
--22:16:39--  http://www.kernel.org/pub/linux/kernel/v2.6/patch-2.6.22.1.bz2
           => `/home/rostedt/.ketchup/patch-2.6.22.1.bz2.partial'
Resolving www.kernel.org... 204.152.191.37, 204.152.191.5
Connecting to www.kernel.org|204.152.191.37|:80... connected.
HTTP request sent, awaiting response... 200 OK
Length: 538 [application/x-bzip2]

100%[====================================>] 538            --.--K/s

22:16:39 (38.95 MB/s) - `/home/rostedt/.ketchup/patch-2.6.22.1.bz2.partial' saved
[538/538]

Applying patch-2.6.22.1.bz2
Downloading patch-2.6.22.1-rt9
--22:16:39--  http://people.redhat.com/mingo/realtime-preempt/patch-2.6.22.1-rt9
           => `/home/rostedt/.ketchup/patch-2.6.22.1-rt9.partial'
Resolving people.redhat.com... 66.187.233.237
Connecting to people.redhat.com|66.187.233.237|:80... connected.
HTTP request sent, awaiting response... 200 OK
Length: 1,779,906 (1.7M) [text/plain]

100%[====================================>] 1,779,906    382.30K/s    ETA 00:00

22:16:44 (381.23 KB/s) - `/home/rostedt/.ketchup/patch-2.6.22.1-rt9.partial' saved
[1779906/1779906]

Applying patch-2.6.22.1-rt9
Current directory renamed to /home/rostedt/linux-2.6.22.1-rt9
~/tmp$ cd .
~/linux-2.6.22.1-rt9$
```

The first two commands made an empty directory and changed into it. Then, we ran
ketchup -G 2.6.22. The *-G* option caused the command to ignore GPG checksums, and
was used because we did not download any checksums. This command automatically
downloaded the Linux kernel tarball from the *kernel.org* site and installed the Linux
tree in the current directory.

The next command was *ketchup -r -G 2.6.22.1-rt9.* The *-r* has *ketchup* rename the
current directory to the Linux version that is installed at completion. You can see from
the output that the command first downloaded and installed the .1 stable patch, then
the *-rt9* version of the RT patch.[*] Finally, we entered *cd .* to display the current directory
and show that ketchup renamed it to *linux-2.6.22.1-rt9.* We could have skipped the
ketchup -G 2.6.22 command and simply entered **ketchup -r -G 2.6.22.1-rt9**, but that
would have downloaded the 2.6.22.1 stable tarball, and we wanted to show how
ketchup can do multiple patches in a single step.

---

[*] All the patches and tarballs that *ketchup* downloads are stored in a *~/.ketchup* directory and will be used for
subsequent *ketchup* executions.

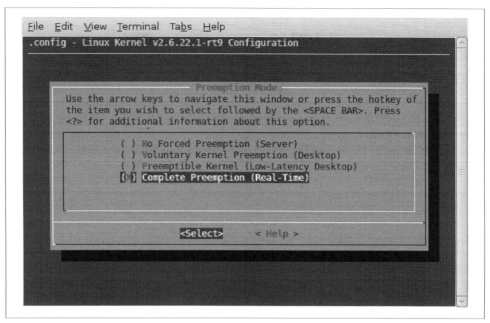

Figure 14-4. Menuconfig preemption mode selection

Now that you have the kernel downloaded and patched with the RT patch, it is time to configure it. The `make menuconfig` build environment is particularly flexible, but you may use the other configuration methods that come with the Linux kernel.

The RT patch adds several options, of which the biggest and most influential is the addition of CONFIG_PREEMPT_RT. It can be found under Processor type and features → Preemption Mode in the configuration menu. Figure 14-4 illustrates the different preemption modes offered by the Linux kernel. The RT patch adds just the mode selected in the figure, Complete Preemption (Real-Time), which specifies CONFIG_PREEMPT_RT. Before explaining this mode, it's a good idea to understand the evolution of preemption. We'll explain the various modes, which increase in sophistication, in the following sections.

No Forced Preemption

When the *No Forced Preemption* option is set, the Linux kernel runs as it did back in the 2.4 kernel series and earlier. No preemption takes place while the CPU is in kernel mode. This means that when a high-priority process is woken up, it must wait until the current process makes the switch back to user mode or needs to wait on some I/O, before the kernel scheduler runs and the high-priority process can get a hold of the CPU.

The advantage of this option is that it has the lowest amount of context switches, and thus leads to the least overhead. The less scheduling that takes place, the more each process gets to run on the CPU, and the more that process will use the full cache as well as the same translation lookaside buffers (TLBs).†

The disadvantage of this option is that it has lower reaction times. This option is best for servers that are doing large batch jobs: applications that just need throughput and are run serially, without the need for fast process switching. Any application that requires low latencies and interaction between applications or users would not be well suited to this option. It is known to give a poor "desktop experience" because it can cause jitter during mouse movements and poor audio playback and recording.

Voluntary Kernel Preemption

This preemption mode is more flexible than no preemption. It relies upon the insertion of points of voluntary preemption into the kernel where such preemption is known to be safe. A slight historical digression can explain how these preemption points are chosen.

The Linux kernel code is not allowed to call for a rescheduling of processes (done by calling the schedule() function) while interrupts are disabled. This is because the kernel code disables interrupts when some atomic operation is taking place on a CPU-specific variable or some lock is being taken that might also be used by an interrupt. With the Linux kernel being so complex, there are several areas of code that can cause a reschedule, because they might allocate memory pages, access user space, or do a number of other things.

It is also a bug to reschedule while a spin lock is held,‡ because it can cause a large latency if a process is scheduled on a CPU that is currently waiting on a spin lock. Under the right conditions, a deadlock could even occur.

These bugs are hard to find because rescheduling can happen at so many places. Any access to user space may cause a reschedule if the user memory was previously swapped out. Some areas of the kernel that allocate memory may cause a reschedule if memory is tight and pages need to be swapped out to accommodate the newly allocated memory. Just simply testing code was not enough to detect areas that have a spin lock held or interrupts disabled at the time of rescheduling, since the code that actually does the schedule may not be hit during testing. For example, if the user-space memory that is accessed happens to still be in memory or there is plenty of memory available when an allocation takes place, no scheduling will occur. Thus, during code testing, kernel developers may never see the scenario where interrupts are disabled and a reschedule takes place. As soon as this code is out in the public and used by thousands of others, they encounter the bug. The Linux scheduler checks for this scenario and prints out nasty messages when it is detected.

---

† TLBs cache page tables and are associated with individual processes by the kernel's paging system.

‡ See the upcoming section "Preemptible Kernel."

In order to help debug these cases, functions containing any code that can cause a reschedule had a function call to `might_sleep`. The `might_sleep` function performs checks and prints out error messages if it detects that interrupts are disabled or a spin lock is held.§

This talk about the `might_sleep` function may seem off-topic, but in fact it is the core of the *Voluntary Kernel Preemption* option. The kernel developers realized that this check to catch areas that should not cause a reschedule also identifies areas that *can* cause one. When the *Voluntary Kernel Preemption* option is set, instead of having a high-priority process wait until the current process switches to user mode or goes to sleep, when a `might_sleep` function is hit, a check is made to see whether a schedule should take place, and if so, causes a reschedule. If a high-priority process that is woken up while the lower-priority current process is in kernel mode performing some system call, the higher-priority process gets the CPU when the current process comes across a call to `might_sleep`.

With the *Voluntary Kernel Preemption* option set, all the places that call `might_sleep` now become preemption points. This greatly improves the feel and interaction of the kernel, and it is considered very safe, because all the places that are preemption points are the same places that must not prevent preemption.

Preemptible Kernel

During the Linux kernel version 2.4 era, Robert Love developed an external patch called preempt-kernel. This patch was maintained very much like the RT patch is today, as a separate patch that needed to be applied against the stable Linux 2.4 kernel. In the 2.5 development, the preempt-kernel patch was incorporated into mainline Linux, giving Linux the ability to be a preemptible kernel. This means that a high-priority process no longer needed to wait for the current process to enter user space or schedule itself (either to simply go to sleep or because of a `might_sleep` call). Instead, the current process may be scheduled out almost anywhere in the kernel.

The trick behind the preempt-kernel patch was the conversion of Linux to work on a symmetric multiprocessor (SMP) system. In an SMP environment, critical sections must be protected from concurrent access of processes running on separate CPUs. To add this protection, a spin lock is usually held. A spin lock is a busy lock, which means that on contention, one CPU will spin in a busy loop waiting for another CPU to release the lock.

Spin locks protect areas of the kernel that must not be accessed concurrently. These areas are also the same places that must be protected from reentrancy. In other words, protecting the kernel in an SMP system (where data access must be atomic in respect to two threads running on two different CPUs) also allows full preemption of processes

---

§ The actual checks involve disabled are on interrupts and a preempt count that is nonzero when spin locks are held. See the later section "Preemptible Kernel."

(where data access must be atomic in respect to a thread running on a single CPU and being preempted, after which the CPU runs a second thread that accesses the same data). Love realized that the areas that must be protected from concurrent access in an SMP system must also be protected from reentrancy in a preemptible kernel.

Love's patch introduced a kernel thread variable called a preempt count. Normally a thread's preempt count is set to zero. Every time a thread acquires a spin lock, its preempt count increments, and every time it releases a spin lock, its preempt count decrements. The kernel does not preempt the current task when its preempt count is nonzero. If a high-priority process is awakened and the current task is in the kernel but its preempt count is zero, a reschedule takes place and the high-priority process takes over the CPU. If the current task's preempt count is nonzero, the high-priority process would have to wait until the preempt count reached zero for the current task, where-upon a check would be done to see whether a reschedule is needed, and the high-priority process is given the CPU.

The addition of the *Preemptible Kernel* option significantly reduced the latency of the Linux kernel. This made for an even better desktop user experience, with better reaction times to user events and smoother mouse movements and audio.

Complete Preemption

Love's patch was a great improvement to the Linux desktop experience, but it was far from attaining the requirements of a real-time system. The places to preempt in the kernel were still very limited, as spin locks are attained often. Grabbing a spin lock was like taking a global lock with respect to preemption. Anytime a spin lock was held, no process could preempt the current task, even if the new process was not going to access the critical section the spin lock was protecting.

The preempt-kernel patch departed here from the protection given by spin locks to an SMP system. An SMP lock protects only a certain critical section of the kernel. Each critical section of the kernel is protected by its own spin lock. But the preempt-kernel patch disabled preemption for all tasks, regardless of whether a task would access the critical section the spin lock was protecting.

The RT patch adds the *Complete Preemption* option to address this issue. The *Complete Preemption* converts spin locks from busy loops into mutexes. Instead of spinning in a busy loop on a CPU, a process that tries to get a spin lock just goes to sleep and lets the kernel schedule other processes on the CPU. When the spin lock is released, the blocked process is awakened. If it is currently the highest-priority running process, it will preempt the current thread and take over the CPU. By eliminating the disabling of preemption at the acquisition of a spin lock, the Linux kernel becomes tremendously more responsive and latencies are reduced to a few microseconds.

Unfortunately, there's a cost to this new feature. Spin locks were introduced to protect small areas from concurrent access on SMP systems. Since a spin lock has the potential of keeping another CPU busy spinning, it was intended to be held for small amounts of code that would execute in a short amount of time. In practice, some of these critical sections that were protected by spin locks were not that small and could indeed keep other CPUs spinning for a good amount of time. But a large number of these spin locks did serve their purpose and kept the spin lock held for a short amount of time. These correctly used spin locks may suffer a larger overhead in scheduling out than they would if they just spun. But, as with most systems, one must weigh the importance of consistency (deterministic latency) with that of high general throughput. Locks that protect small amounts of code in a critical section in one place may also protect a large amount of code (which could be longer to execute) in another.

The purpose of converting spin locks to mutexes was to lower the reaction time of a high-priority process. Even though the cost of contention goes up with the conversion of a spin lock from a busy lock to a mutex, the latency that this conversion retrieves goes down by magnitudes. Luckily, if the critical section is very small, the chances of having contention on that location is also small.

Since interrupts and softirqs must not schedule out unless they are converted into threads, the selection of *Complete Preemption* automatically selects the kernel feature that converts interrupts and softirqs into threads. Interrupt handlers and softirqs use spin locks quite often, so converting spin locks into mutexes (which can schedule) requires interrupt handlers and softirqs to be converted to threads. But the reverse is not true. As Figure 14-5 illustrates, you can select interrupt handlers and softirqs as threads (the *Thread Softirqs* and *Thread Hardirqs* options) under any of the preemption modes; you don't have to select *Complete Preemption*.

One can experiment with these various options. Having interrupts as threads with just the *Preemptible Kernel* option might be enough to satisfy some requirements. It gives the kernel the ability to prioritize interrupts and softirqs, as well as letting user processes have greater priority than interrupts and softirqs. The RT patch is designed to add the control over the operating system that is needed to satisfy most real-time environments

High-Resolution Timers

One thing that is crucial to a real-time system is the ability to trigger an event at a specific time (otherwise there's no sense in calling the system real-time). In the early 2.6 versions of Linux and earlier, the smallest unit of time was called a *jiffy*. A jiffy started out as one 100th of a second. A global variable called HZ represented the hertz of jiffies, and with the one 100th frequency, the HZ was defined as 100. This was all very simple and suited the needs of Linux at the time, but as machines became faster and people ran more applications on Linux, the 100 HZ setting started to show its age. Under a heavy load, applications were not smooth with the low HZ frequency. To get better reaction times, the HZ value became 1,000.

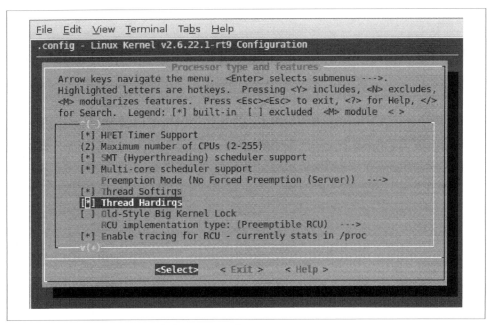

Figure 14-5. Menuconfig Threaded Interrupt Selection

With the 1,000 HZ value for jiffies, the best reaction time that could be set was 1 millisecond. This is still very poor for any serious application that needs the slightest bit of real-time. But for every jiffy, a timer interrupt was needed to update the jiffy variable. So a balance was needed where one could choose to suffer increased overhead (more timer interrupts) in order to gain a finer timer resolution.

To make things more difficult, the design of the timer had a large latency built-in. The timer accounting was designed under what is known as a *timer wheel*. When a user application wanted to be notified when a time was reached (an alarm), the event would be recorded into the timer wheel. The timer wheel was split up into a number of "buckets." The first set of buckets (256 buckets) represented the next 256 jiffies into the future. So if one needed to be notified 20 jiffies into the future, that event would be recorded into the 20th bucket of the timer wheel. If the event was further into the future, it wou,ld need to go into the next level of buckets, where each bucket represented 256 jiffies. If the time was greater than 65,536 (256×256), it would be placed in the next layer. This was a neat idea and worked well.

But for a deterministic system, the design was flawed. Eventually the time will reach the 256, jiffy into the future, and all the events in the second layer need to be rehashed into the lower layer. All the events scheduled from 256 jiffies to 511 jiffies into the future would have been placed in the same bucket in the second level. When it was time to move these events into the single jiffy buckets, each one needed to be hashed. This event was done with interrupts disabled and took O(*n*) time (where *n* is the number of items in the bucket to rehash).

After the release of the 2.6 kernel, Thomas Gleixner started working on a way to solve this issue with a new design timer called *hrtimers*.‖ This work was developed in the RT patch. The base infrastructure made it into mainline Linux in 2.6.16, and the high-resolution timers were incorporated into i386 architecture in 2.6.20.

What Gleixner realized was that two kinds of timers are placed into the timer wheel: *action timers* and *timeout timers*. Action timers are timers that are expected to expire. User applications add action timers frequently to be notified of events. So, when an action timer is added into the timer wheel, it will go through the rehashing every time it's added far enough in the future. The timing wheel is very fast at adding and removing a timer (O(1) for addition and deletion), and each rehash takes O(*n*) time. So, for an action timer, the timer wheel is very inefficient. It will hit the O(*n*) rehash more often than the O(1) deletion.

Timeout timers, on the other hand, are perfect for the timer wheel. A timeout timer goes off only if an event does *not* happen. The networking code, in particular, is loaded with timeout timers. For packets that do not arrive in time, the timeout timer will go off and tell the kernel that it is time to send another acknowledgment. These timers are added and removed constantly, and it is very important that the addition and removal of these timers have as low overhead as possible. In this case, the timer wheel is a good match.

The problem is that previous kernels didn't differentiate between the two types of timers and could experience unpredictable latencies when a large amount of timers needed to be rehashed. This is where hrtimers came into play. They are specifically designed for action timers. The hrtimer complements the timer wheel by handling the action timers and letting the timeout timers stay on the timer wheel. Instead of using hashes, the hrtimer infrastructure uses a red/black tree, which is a binary tree that one can learn about in almost any first-year college data structures course book. It takes O(log *n*) time to add and remove nodes. The algorithm also has hooks into the tree to find the first node in O(1) time. But the major advantage is that the nodes in the tree are sorted, so there is no cost of a rehash, as happens with the timer wheel. In Linux 2.6.18, this infrastructure was put into the mainline Linux kernel.

But timer resolution was still only at the value of jiffies. The next step was to get a clock source infrastructure in place where the timers were no longer bound to the resolution of jiffies. With the clock event/source infrastructure, a specified hardware clock may be used if present. The hrtimer value for an event takes the value of nanoseconds. This is converted into the clock source resolution (and rounded up to avoid early expiration), and the clock is set to trigger at the next timer event that is scheduled. So, the actual resolution of the timer is dependent on the underlying hardware and no longer on a

---

‖ Originally called ktimers.

software variable like HZ. When the timer expires and the clock source sends an interrupt to the CPU, the hrtimer interrupts handles the event. The next event is queried in the red/black tree, and the clock source is set to go off at the next required event. Jiffies no longer need to be counted, which prepares us for the next enhancement.

Once hrtimers removed the requirement for a timer interrupt to go off just for the sake of updating the jiffy variable, kernel developers could eliminate the overhead of unneeded interrupts going off when the system is idle. This is extremely important in the embedded world because removing interrupts from an idle system lets the CPU go into a better power-saving state. This translates to longer battery life for the device on which the operating system is loaded. *Dynamic ticks*, when enabled, trigger the timer interrupt only when it is requested.

With dynamic ticks, the timer interrupt need only fire on demand. However, a caveat to this is that the underlying clock source counter must not be allowed to wrap around in between. To address this, the timer interrupt must be set to fire at least as often as half the time taken for the underlying counter to wrap around. A separate monotonic variable is updated by the timer to keep track of the system time.

Several jiffies can go by while the system is idle, but nothing will suffer as a result. (An idle system doesn't do anything.) The dynamic ticks code keeps track of this time that has elapsed, and updates the jiffies accordingly, bringing the jiffies value back up to where it would have been if interrupts had been going off once a jiffy.

When the system is not idle, the timer interrupt is set to go off once a jiffy, because the jiffy variable is used for schedule accounting of non-real-time tasks.

 Not all of the high-resolution timers and dynamic ticks have made it into the mainline kernel. Some architectures have yet to embrace it (as of this writing). But the RT patch is still the development ground of these new features that will soon be incorporated into mainline Linux.

The Latency Tracer

The RT patch comes with a feature, called latency tracer, that helps developers find areas of large latencies in the kernel. When an application misses a deadline (hopefully only during testing), the developers need to determine whether the latency was due to the application itself (a design flaw or bug) or came from inside the Linux kernel. The latency tracer was created to find latencies caused by the kernel. There are several options to the latency tracer:

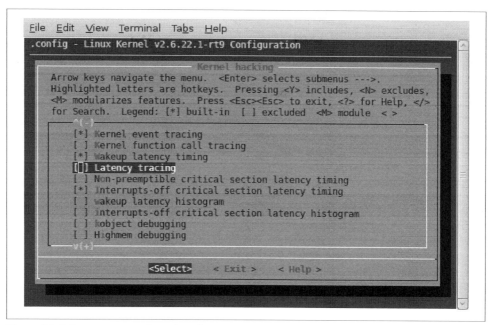

Figure 14-6. Latency tracing kernel config options

- Event tracing
- Kernel function call tracing
- Wakeup latency timing
- Kernel latency tracing
- Non-preemptible critical section latency timing
- Interrupts-off critical section latency timing

 As this book goes to print, a new feature has replaced the latency tracer in the upstream kernel: Ftrace. It is very similar in many respects to the latency tracer, as it was written by the same people, and is documented within the kernel's *Documentation* directory.

Figure 14-6 illustrates the menu options in the Linux kernel configuration under the "Kernel hacking" menu. Some of these options are supersets of others, and when you select them they automatically force those subset options to be enabled. The latency tracer is still under development and may soon be going into the mainline kernel. This section will describe the latency tracer as it operates in the 2.6.22.1-rt9 version of the Linux kernel.

The *interrupts-off critical section latency histogram* option is obsolete, is not being maintained, and will soon be removed, so do not bother using that option unless you want an unstable kernel.

Event Trace

The *Event trace* option is probably the most useful for real-time application developers. It lets you record the latencies of system calls, and other activities as well, if other options are enabled (those activities are explained with the other options). When *Event trace* is enabled, several entries are added to the */proc* filesystem. Here are a few important ones:

```
/proc/sys/kernel/trace_enabled
/proc/sys/kernel/trace_user_triggered
/proc/sys/kernel/trace_freerunning
/proc/sys/kernel/trace_print_on_crash
/proc/sys/kernel/trace_verbose
/proc/sys/kernel/mcount_enabled
/proc/sys/kernel/preempt_max_latency
/proc/sys/kernel/preempt_thresh
proc/sys/kernel/preempt_mark_thresh
```

These settings can be viewed and set by normal shell commands, such as *cat* and *echo*:

```
# cat /proc/sys/kernel/preempt_mark_thresh
100
# echo 200 > /proc/sys/kernel/preempt_mark_thresh
# cat /proc/sys/kernel/preempt_mark_thresh
200
```

You can also use the *sysctl* utility that comes with most distributions:

```
# sysctl kernel.preempt_mark_thresh
kernel.preempt_mark_thresh = 200
# sysctl kernel.preempt_mark_thresh=100
kernel.preempt_mark_thresh = 100
```

Another entry in the */proc* filesystem that is associated with the latency tracer is */proc/latency_trace*. This file contains the output of the longest latency that has exceeded the threshold defined by preempt_thresh.

The *Event trace* option has a very small overhead and is well worth keeping enabled even in production environments. The other, "heavier" latency tracer options (explained later) are also more useful with this option enabled, because it creates the user interface into the kernel's latency tracer variables.

The following is an example use of the event tracer:

```
/* start tracing */
   ret = prctl(0, 1, 0, 0, 0);
   if (ret < 0) {
       perror("prctl");
       exit(-1);
```

```
        }

        /* do some syscalls */
        fd = open("/etc/passwd", O_RDONLY);
        if (fd < 0) {
            perror("open");
            goto out;
        }

        while (read(fd, buf, BUFSIZ) > 0)
            ;

        close(fd);

out:
        /* stop tracing */
        prctl(0, 0, 0, 0, 0);
```

The prctl function is a Linux-specific system call that allows a program to modify its process's internal state. The latency tracer uses this call to allow a running process to enable and disable user tracing. prctl always takes five parameters, but only the first two are important for enabling tracing. The other three are ignored. The first parameter is zero (or PR_SET_TRACING if you include the RT-patched Linux kernel header file *linux/prctl.h*). The second parameter is either 1 to enable tracing or 0 to disable it.

Before you start the tracer, you need to set various */proc* variables. Any of these can be enabled by echoing 1 into them, and disabled by echoing 0 (or using sysctl):

- trace_enabled needs to be enabled to allow tracing.
- trace_user_triggered needs to be enabled to allow the user (not the kernel) to turn tracing on and off.
- preempt_threshold needs to be set to 0. The latency will not be recorded if it is under this threshold. If it is greater than or equal to 0, all latencies above or equal to it will be recorded.
- preempt_max_latency needs to be set to 0. This keeps track of the highest latency that has been recorded. New latencies are recorded only if they are greater than this value latency. The value can also be read to see what the greatest latency of the system was. On bootup, this is set to a high value, so latencies are not recorded unless this is reset back to a reasonable value.

After running the previously shown program on the RT-patched Linux kernel and setting the proper *proc* variables (as explained earlier), you can see the trace output in */proc/latency_tracer*:

```
# cat /proc/latency_trace
preemption latency trace v1.1.5 on 2.6.22.1-rt9-et
--------------------------------------------------------------------
 latency: 48 us, #11/11, CPU#0 | (M:rt VP:0, KP:0, SP:1 HP:1 #P:2)
    ----------------
    | task: eventtrace-7776 (uid:0 nice:0 policy:0 rt_prio:0)
```

```
-----------------
                        ------=> CPU#
                      / _-----=> irqs-off
                     | / _----=> need-resched
                     || / _---=> hardirq/softirq
                     ||| / _--=> preempt-depth
                     |||| /
                     |||||      delay
      cmd     pid  ||||| time  |  caller
        \    /    |||||   \    |   /
   eventtra-7776  0D...    1us < (0)
   eventtra-7776  0....    2us+> sys_open+0x0/0x1e (000000d8 00000000 00000005)
   eventtra-7776  0D...   13us < (3)
   eventtra-7776  0....   14us+> sys_read+0x0/0x64 (000000d8 bfd6e5cc 00000003)
   eventtra-7776  0D...   37us < (1639)
   eventtra-7776  0....   39us > sys_read+0x0/0x64 (000000d8 bfd6e5cc 00000003)
   eventtra-7776  0D...   40us < (0)
   eventtra-7776  0....   41us+> sys_close+0x0/0xb6 (000000d8 bfd6e5cc 00000006)
   eventtra-7776  0D...   46us < (0)
   eventtra-7776  0....   47us > sys_prctl+0x0/0x19f (000000d8 00000000 000000ac)


   vim:ft=help
```

The line beginning with latency in the output shows that the trace took 48 microseconds from the time we called the first prctl to when we called the second one. The trace output 11 of 11 entries (we didn't overrun the buffer) and took place on CPU 0. The preemption mode, shown after the M: string, can be one of the following:

preempt
> Low-latency desktop configuration.

desktop
> Voluntary preemption.

rt
> Full preemption was compiled in (PREEMPT_RT). This is the mode shown in this trace.

server
> No preemption.

The VP and KP fields are always 0. The SP field is 1 if softirqs can be preempted (run as threads), and HP is 1 if interrupts themselves can be preempted (also run as threads).

A typical trace event appears as follows:

```
   eventtra-7776  0D...    1us < (0)
```

The eventtra field is the name of the thread. The actual program name we used was eventrace, but the kernel saves only eight characters of the name. 7776 is the process

ID (pid). The CPU that this trace entry occurred on was 0. The next four characters are flags and counters:

1. Are interrupts disabled?
2. Is a context switch (potential reschedule) needed?
3. Is the system in a hard or soft interrupt context?
4. The depth of disabling of preemption (number of spin locks held by this process).

A dot means off or 0. Sometimes the first dot is replaced with a D. That shows that interrupts were disabled when the trace occurred.

The 1us field shows the time since the trace started. The < field means the process is exiting a system call (remember that the trace started within the prctl system call, so the first event you always see is that the process is leaving a system call). The (0) is the return code for the system call (the value that would end up in errno).

Now let's look at the next event, which has more complex information:

```
eventtra-7776  0....    2us+> sys_open+0x0/0x1e (000000d8 00000000 00000005)
```

The first part is the same as the previous line. A plus sign (+) appears after the trace time if the trace is greater than 1 microsecond from the previous trace. The > shows that the process is entering a system call. The following field shows the system call name from the kernel's perspective (open is implemented by the sys_open function inside the kernel). The numbers in parentheses are the values of the parameters to the system call.

With only the *Event Trace* feature enabled, the latency tracer can produce very useful information. It is easy to track the system calls of an RT application without the overhead of a ptrace tool such as strace. The event trace option has practically no overhead: it does just a single check when entering and exiting a system call, which would be lost in the noise of any benchmarks.

Function Call Trace

The *Function call trace* is much more verbose and is best used for debugging latencies within the kernel. This option is recommended only for debugging the RT system, since it applies a large overhead on the system.

This option asks the gcc compiler to put in a hook to every function call in the kernel. This hook will call a function to trace the function calls when tracing is enabled. With this option on, the same program that we just ran will produce the following output:

```
preemption latency trace v1.1.5 on 2.6.22.1-rt9-fn
--------------------------------------------------------------------
 latency: 432 us, #541/541, CPU#0 | (M:rt VP:0, KP:0, SP:1 HP:1 #P:2)
    ----------------
    | task: eventtrace-4207 (uid:0 nice:0 policy:0 rt_prio:0)
    ----------------
```

```
                 ------=> CPU#
                /  -----=> irqs-off
               | /  ----=> need-resched
               || /  ---=> hardirq/softirq
               ||| /  --=> preempt-depth
               |||| /
               |||||         delay
      cmd    pid |||||  time  |  caller
       \    /    |||||   \    |   /
eventtra-4207  0D...    0us : user_trace_start+0xe6/0x1a9 (sys_prctl+0x21/0x1c4)
eventtra-4207  0....    1us : rt_up+0xc/0x5e (user_trace_start+0x10a/0x1a9)
eventtra-4207  0...1    2us : rt_mutex_unlock+0xb/0x32 (rt_up+0x32/0x5e)
eventtra-4207  0D...    3us < (0)
eventtra-4207  0....    4us > sys_open+0x0/0x2e (08048fea 00000000 000000d8)
eventtra-4207  0....    5us : sys_open+0xb/0x2e (sysenter_past_esp+0x6c/0xad)
eventtra-4207  0....    5us : do_sys_open+0xe/0xfc (sys_open+0x2c/0x2e)
eventtra-4207  0....    6us : getname+0xe/0xc2 (do_sys_open+0xfc)
eventtra-4207  0....    7us : kmem_cache_alloc+0xe/0xa0 (getname+0x23/0xc2)
eventtra-4207  0....    8us : __might_sleep+0xb/0x11f (kmem_cache_alloc+0x87/0xa0)
eventtra-4207  0....    9us : rt_spin_lock+0xd/0x72 (kmem_cache_alloc+0x36/0xa0)
eventtra-4207  0D...    9us : __lock_acquire+0xe/0x6fe (lock_acquire+0x6f/0x87)
eventtra-4207  0....   10us : rt_mutex_trylock+0xb/0x35 (rt_spin_lock+0x49/0x72)
eventtra-4207  0....   11us : lock_acquired+0xe/0x1e4 (rt_spin_lock+0x6b/0x72)

[...]

eventtra-4207  0....  423us : rt_spin_unlock+0xc/0x56 (dput+0xd7/0x125)
eventtra-4207  0....  424us : rt_spin_unlock+0xc/0x56 (dput+0xe1/0x125)
eventtra-4207  0....  425us : mntput_no_expire+0xd/0x8a (__fput+0x185/0x1bb)
eventtra-4207  0....  426us : _atomic_dec_and_spin_lock+0x9/0x56
                              (mntput_no_expire+0x23/0x8a)
eventtra-4207  0D...  427us < (0)
eventtra-4207  0....  428us > sys_prctl+0x0/0x1c4 (00000000 00000000 000000d8)
eventtra-4207  0....  429us : sys_prctl+0xe/0x1c4 (sysenter_past_esp+0x6c/0xad)
eventtra-4207  0....  429us : user_trace_stop+0xe/0x21b (sys_prctl+0x2e/0x1c4)
eventtra-4207  0D...  430us : user_trace_stop+0x45/0x21b (sys_prctl+0x2e/0x1c4)
```

As you can see, the *Function call trace* adds a much larger number of entries. We cut out 517 entries just to avoid filling up the rest of this book with entries. Also, this trace took almost 10 times longer to run than the *Event trace* alone. For tracing code within the kernel itself, this turns out to be a very valuable tool. It gives useful information when a large latency is discovered in the kernel and one must contact the kernel developers to get it solved. Sending the information in this trace can help the kernel developers pinpoint the problem area. We won't try to explain the output here.

Wakeup Latency Timing

The idea behind the wakeup latency is to measure the time it takes for a high-priority process to be scheduled after it has been awakened. This measures *scheduling latency*. Times are measured in microseconds.

This option can be turned on by itself, and will override other options when enabled. The results are placed in */proc/sys/kernel/preempt_max_latency*. To disable wakeup latency timing and let other configured options be available, just set /proc/sys/kernel/ wakeup_timing to zero.

Here is a brief view of what the wakeup latency timer shows:

```
# cat /proc/latency_trace
preemption latency trace v1.1.5 on 2.6.22.1-rt9-lt-w
--------------------------------------------------------------------
 latency: 275 us, #2/2, CPU#1 | (M:rt VP:0, KP:0, SP:1 HP:1 #P:2)
    ----------------
    | task: Xorg-3983 (uid:0 nice:-10 policy:0 rt_prio:0)
    ----------------

                    ------=> CPU#
                 / _----=> irqs-off
                | / ----=> need-resched
                || / ---=> hardirq/softirq
                ||| / --=> preempt-depth
                |||| /
                |||||      delay
    cmd    pid  ||||| time |  caller
      \   /     |||||   \  |   /
    <...>-3983  1D..1  276us :  __sched_text_start+0x2b8/0xc60
                              (__sched_text_start+0x2b8/0xc60)


    vim:ft=help
```

The line starting with task in this output shows that the program *Xorg* with the pid of 3983 is running as root (uid: 0) with a nice value of –10 under no real-time policy or priority. The latency lines shows that the system took 275 microseconds to start the program after it was awakened.

 In order to get accurate readings, it is very important that the */proc* interface is set up properly. To reset the latency timings, just write 0 (using *echo*) into the */proc/sys/kernel/preempt_max_latency* file.

Be warned, though, that until recently the latency tracer has been considered a debug tool only for the RT patch developers. It is now starting to be used more by RT patch users, and will likely change as the focus of the latency tracer changes. New documentation will also be written, so there will be a section that explains the latest features and interfaces.

Conclusion

People will always argue that the Linux kernel will never be a hard real-time operating system. The problem with this statement is that there's no concrete definition of a hard real-time operating system. The argument that comes up most is: "Would you run this on a nuclear power plant?" My answer would be no—not because I don't think that

Linux can be a hard real-time operating system. But because of its size, it will never be bug-free enough to run a nuclear power plant.

I find that those who argue about hard real-time seem to base their ideas on the quality of the code, and not the design of the overall system. But to me, the real-time aspect of Linux is based on the design. If we can prove that the code inside Linux is bug-free, it most certainly can run aircraft engine controls and nuclear power plants. But that is unrealistic.

The main difference between desktop Linux and the RT-patched Linux is that the latter considers it a bug to have long latencies and missed deadlines. The infrastructure of the system with the RT patch is in place to satisfy most hard real-time needs, but the size of the Linux kernel is just too large to use it in life-critical situations.

When using Linux with the RT patch for mission-critical systems, you should remove as many of the unknowns as possible. This means that only the necessary drivers should be loaded, and they must be audited to see that they do not disable interrupts for long periods of time. All kernel configuration options that you set need to be understood. There is no easy way out of thoroughly researching your software when setting up a real-time mission-critical system. The RT patch made Linux much more real-time friendly, but Linux is still itself focused on being a general-purpose operating system. A real-time administrator needs to focus on Linux as a tool for the system and try to understand it as much as possible.

So, it seems that one of the best things going for Linux is also its biggest flaw: the size of the kernel. Most of this bulk is normally drivers, and each system uses only a small fraction of them. The ones you use must be understood and not taken for granted.

The RT patch is still very much under development and will most likely go through more large changes. This is also true for the Linux kernel itself. But rest assured that there are companies out there that are taking the RT patch and creating a stable version. When incorporating the RT patch into a stable environment, it is best not to download it from Ingo Molnar's development repository, because it is always in a state of flux; instead, purchase a service agreement with someone you can trust who will provide service and support and offer a stable release of the RT patch.

For more information about current development on real-time patches, please visit *http://rt.wiki.kernel.org*.

Index

We'd like to hear your suggestions for improving our indexes. Send email to *index@oreilly.com*.

AVR32 architecture, 58

B

Barabanov, Michael, 5
basic hot swapping, 67
.bb files, 338
.bbg files, 338
BBT (Bad Block Table), 224, 226
BDM debugger, 30, 42
"Big and Tall" uClibc submenu, 127
\bin directory, 175, 176, 201
binaries
    downloading to flash, 296–297
    sections for debugging, 329
    strip command, 330
    U-Boot, 291
binary-only modules, allowing with GPL
        licenses, 22
binutils (binary utilities)
    GPL license, 18
    resources, 102
    Unix systems and, 37
    version considerations, 98
binutils package, 95
binutils Ptxdist submenu, 111
BIN_GROUP variable (make command), 203
BIN_OWNER variable (make command), 203
BIOS, 274
    system startup process, 227
block devices, 210, 254
BlueCat (LynuxWorks), 16
Bluetooth
    hardware support, 83
BlueZ stack, 83
Boa, 318–319
Boleyn, Erich, 276
boot configuration, 48–51
\boot directory, 175
boot scripts, 290, 291
booting
    basics of, 48
    BOOTP/DHCP, TFTP, NFS, 293–295
    from DOC, 228
    hard disks and, 233
    network boot, 278–283
    from ROM, 276
    system reboot, 170, 205
    U-Boot and, 287–288
bootloaders

ATA-IDE limitations, 80
    boot configurations, 48–51
    embedded, 274–278
    example, 51, 52
    installing, 227, 228
    minicom constraints, 150
    mounting filesystem, 283–284
    partitions and, 224
    server setup for network boot, 278–283
    setting up, 27, 29, 273–300
    SPL as, 227
    system startup component, 47
BOOTP
    booting with, 293–295
    network boot, 51, 278, 279
bootp command, 293
BSD license
    inetd, 306
    strace, 334
    thttpd, 318
    xinetd, 308
.bss section (ELF binary), 329
buckets, splitting up timer wheels, 408
build process
    compiling kernel image, 166
    configuring kernel, 161–165
    overview, 100
build system (GUI configuration name), 92
Buildroot, 116–121
bus master, 67
buses
    CompactPCI support, 67
    ExpressCard, 65
    GPIB support, 71
    I2C, 72
    I2C support, 71
    PC/104 support, 66
    PCI support, 64, 65
    PCMCIA support, 65
    support overview, 64–72
BusyBox
    compilation, 196
    dpkg command, 267
    features, 194–198
    init program, 204–207
    mdev, 193
    module dependencies, 169
    networking, 303
    ping command, 307

Z

Zakhareivh, Ilya, 132
zImage file, 167
zlib compression library, 218

About the Authors

Karim Yaghmour is the founder and president of Opersys, a company providing expertise and courses on the use of open source and free software in embedded systems, and Kryptiva, a provider of email security services. As an active member of the open source and free software community, Karim has firmly established Opersys's services around the core values of knowledge sharing and technical quality promoted by this community. As part of his community involvement, Karim is the maintainer of the Linux Trace Toolkit and the author of a series of white papers that led to the implementation of the Adeos nanokernel, which allows multiple operating systems to exist side by side. Karim's quest for understanding how things work started at a very young age when he took it upon himself to break open all the radios and cassette players he could lay his hands on in order to "fix" them. Very early, he developed a keen interest in operating system internals and embedded systems. He now holds a B.Eng. and an M.A.Sc. from the École Polytechnique de Montréal. While everyone was hacking away at Linux, Karim even took a detour to write his own distributed microkernel in order to get to the bottom of operating system design and implementation.

When not working on software, Karim indulges in his passion for history, philosophy, sociology, and humanities in general. He's especially addicted to essays and novels by Umberto Eco and Gerald Messadi.

Jonathan Masters is a British Linux kernel engineer working for Red Hat, where he works on the real-time kernel team, and on a variety of other projects. Jon made U.K. history by beginning his first college degree at the tender age of 13. He has been using and has been involved with Linux for most of his life. He has worked on a diverse variety of embedded Linux projects in different capacities—as an independent contractor, an employee of a large scientific research company, and at a well-known embedded Linux vendor. Jon has written several books, many technical articles, and maintains the module-init-tools package used by the Linux kernel.

Jon lives in Cambridge, Massachusetts, and enjoys travel, hacking embedded devices, hiking, U.S. history, obscure legal texts, and any opportunity for random craziness.

Gilad Ben-Yossef is the cofounder and CTO of Codefidence Ltd. and has been assisting OEMs make use of free and open source software in commercial products and services since 1998. He is also cofounder of Hamakor, an NPO devoted to the promotion of FOSS in Israel, and a founding organizer of "August Penguin," an Israeli community FOSS conference.

Gilad is a member of the Israeli chapter of Mensa, the Israeli Information Technology Association, and the Israeli chapter of the Internet Society. He holds a B.A. in computer science from Tel-Aviv Jaffa Academic College.

When not trying to make FOSS software do something the authors never intended, Gilad likes to scuba dive, read science fiction, and spend time with his wife, Limor, and his two adorable girls, Almog and Yael.

Philippe Gerum is the founder and lead maintainer of the Adeos and Xenomai projects.

Colophon

The image on the cover of *Building Embedded Linux Systems*, Second Edition, is a windmill.

The cover image is a 19th-century engraving from the Dover Pictorial Archive. The cover font is Adobe ITC Garamond. The text font is Linotype Birka; the heading font is Adobe Myriad Condensed; and the code font is LucasFont's TheSansMonoCondensed.

18425441R00246

Made in the USA
Lexington, KY
03 November 2012